The Texas Nonprofit Handbook

Everything You Need to Know to Start
and Run Your Texas Nonprofit Organization

Gary M. Grobman

White Hat **Communications**

Harrisburg, Pennsylvania

White Hat Communications
PO Box 5390
Harrisburg, PA 17110-0390
(717) 238-3787 (tel) (717) 803-3008 (fax)
website: *http://shop.whitehatcommunications.com*

Some of the material in Chapter 4 and Chapter 17 of this publication is authored by Michael Sand and is reprinted with permission. The author gratefully acknowledges the contributions Mr. Sand has made to the material that comprises Chapter 16. Some of the material in Chapter 7 is authored by Gerald Kaufman. Some of the material in Chapter 23 is based on the book, *Fundraising Online: Using the Internet to Raise Serious Money for Your Nonprofit Organization* by Gary M. Grobman and Gary B. Grant and is reprinted with permission. Some of the material in Chapter 22 is based on the book, *The Nonprofit Organization's Guide to E-Commerce* by Gary M. Grobman (White Hat Communications, 2001). Some of the material in Chapter 30 is co-authored by Gary M. Grobman, Gerald Gorelick, and Frederick Richmond, and it is used with permission from the authors. The financial statements appearing in Appendix F are reprinted with permission of ARNOVA.

DISCLAIMER: This publication is intended to provide general information and should not be construed as legal advice or legal opinions concerning any specific facts or circumstances. Consult an experienced attorney if advice is required concerning any specific situation or legal matter. Neither the author nor the publisher make any warranties, expressed or implied, with respect to the information in this publication. The author and publisher shall not be liable for any incidental or consequential damages in connection with, or arising out of, the use of this book.

Contact the author in care of White Hat Communications, or by email at: *gary.grobman@gmail.com*

Printed in the United States of America.
ISBN: 978-1-929109-94-4

Table of Contents

Relationship Between Board Members and Staff Members
Parliamentary Procedure
Legal Responsibilities of Board Members

The Mission Statement
The Vision Statement
Examples of Mission and Vision Statements

Purpose of Strategic Planning
Making the Decision To Develop a Strategic Plan
Benefits of Strategic Planning
Costs of Strategic Planning
A Sample Strategic Planning Model

Ethics in the Nonprofit Environment
Accountability
Conflict of Interest
Disclosures
Accumulation of Surplus
Outside Remuneration
Salaries, Benefits, and Perquisites
Personal Relationships
Standards for Excellence
Taxpayer Bill of Rights 2—Intermediate Sanctions
Codes of Ethics
Ethical Dilemmas
Resolving Ethical Dilemmas
Conclusion

Differences Between Private Foundations and Public Charities
How To Apply for 501(c)(3) Status—Form 1023-EZ
How To Apply for 501(c)(3) Status—Traditional Forms
Completing the Application
Fees

Charity Portals
Online Shopping Malls
Charity Auctions
Online Communities
Website Reviews

Advantages of Internet Fundraising
Disadvantages of Internet Fundraising
Direct Marketing
Prospect Research
Major Gifts
Planned Giving
Special Events
Capital Campaigns
Online Fundraising Strategies
"Donate Here" Buttons
Cause-Related Marketing
Tribute Gifts
Personal Fundraising Pages

The Coalition
Structures of Coalitions
Advantages of Forming a Coalition
Disadvantages of Coalitions
To Form a Coalition or Not
How To Form a Coalition

Office Equipment
Staffing Patterns
Stationery/Logo
Filing Systems
Computer
Typical Software for Nonprofits
Open Source Software
Credit Card Sales
Postal Service Issues

Planning for Program Evaluation
Conclusion

Introduction

Americans of all ages, all stations in life, and all types of disposition are forever forming associations. There are not only commercial and industrial associations in which all take part, but others of a thousand different types— religious, moral, serious, futile, very general and very limited, immensely large and very minute. Americans combine to give fetes, found seminaries, build churches, distribute books, and send missionaries to the antipodes. Hospitals, prisons and schools take shape in that way. Finally, if they want to proclaim a truth or propagate some feeling by the encouragement of a great example, they form an association. In every case, at the head of any new undertaking, where in France you would find the government or in England some territorial magnate, in the United States you are sure to find an association.

—Alexis de Tocqueville
Democracy In America
1835

Little has changed about the American propensity to form benevolent associations in the 186 years since de Tocqueville wrote the above words.

In our highly competitive, individualistic society, the nonprofit sector provides a way to express our humanitarian values, to preserve our cultural heritage, to promote various causes, to educate, and to enlighten. It is often through coming together in nonprofit organizations that our citizens exercise their constitutional rights to petition their government, free speech, assembly, and freedom of religion.

Nonprofits play a unique role as an intermediary between the citizens and their government. They maintain and transmit values to a degree that government has been unable to do.

Maybe most important of all, nonprofits formulate much of the moral agenda for society. One only has to think of the response to the COVID-19 pandemic, September 11, 2001 terrorist attacks, the 2005 and 2017 hurricane disasters, the 2010 BP oil spill in the Gulf of Mexico, the environmental movement, rape crisis and domestic violence centers, public subsidies of arts and humanities, public awareness of AIDS and support of AIDS programs, and countless other issues that people coming together in voluntary organizations were able to put on the nation's agenda.

Historically, the primary distinguishing characteristic of the nonprofit sector is that it is mission- and value-driven. Nonprofit organizations exist to accomplish some social good, however that may be defined. A set of values and assumptions underlies this view of the voluntary sector, including altruism, benevolence, cooperation, community, and diversity. The privileges granted to the sector and public expectations are grounded in this belief.

Nonprofits in the United States sometimes take the form of soup kitchens such as Our Daily Bread in Harrisburg, Pennsylvania, which operate on a shoestring budget and charge their clients virtually nothing for their services. They also take the form of enterprises such as hospitals, with budgets in the hundreds of millions of dollars, which often act in ways very much like their for-profit counterparts, seeking to maximize revenue and capture market share.

In January 2000, a Dauphin County (PA) Common Pleas Court judge ruled against the tax exemption eligibility for Hershey Medical Center (HMC), affiliated with Penn State University. One of his objections was that the facility paid salaries to some individuals on staff in excess of a half-million dollars annually. Like almost all hospitals, HMC enters into sophisticated business arrangements. In 1997, the hospital merged with Geisinger, a for-profit health system. The merger collapsed after two years, chiefly as a result of conflicting organizational missions and cultures between the two parent organizations, compounded by financial and operational difficulties. In June 2014, HMC announced a planned merger with a nonprofit hospital system, PinnacleHealth, governed by a new board with equal representation from the two organizations, with the expectation that its new partner would be a much better fit. That merger collapsed, as well. Geisinger Health System eventually agreed to acquire the Catholic-affiliated Holy Spirit Hospital in 2013, and reached agreement to sell it to HMC, now known as "Penn State Health" (PSH), in October 2019.

In contrast to the soup kitchen, the financial aspects of decision-making of nonprofit health-care systems such as PSH are of paramount importance to its decision-making strategy. Yet, as one wag pointed out on the tangible benefits of a nonprofit being selected as a "Point of Light" by the White House, even a "point of light" has to pay the electric bill.

Neither PHS nor Our Daily Bread, about ten miles away from each other, is atypical of the nonprofit sector. Although they may appear to be as different as night and day, they also share many things in common. Both depend on government grants, donations from foundations, businesses, and individuals to keep them operating in the black and to supplement fees for service. Both provide free services to those who are unable to pay for them. Both depend on volunteers. Both are governed by a board of directors whose members do not share in any surplus revenues that may be generated, and that consists of unpaid volunteers from the community.

These are some of the aspects that differentiate nonprofit organizations from their government and private sector counterparts that also provide inpatient health care and food services. Nonprofit organizations, especially those qualified under section 501(c)(3) of the Internal Revenue Code, occupy a special and unique place in American society. Their uniqueness has many attributes.

All such organizations are supported by the nation's taxpayers. They are exempt from federal and state income taxes. Contributors, for the most part, can deduct their contributions from their federal income tax (and from their state income tax in most states). They are eligible to have their postage subsidized by the federal government. Many are exempt from state and local sales and property taxes.

Some people, including those who formulate tax and regulatory policies that apply to charities, have a vision of charitable organizations that resembles those of the 19th century. In that vision, the workers are all volunteers. Recipients of services are too poor to provide for themselves. Funding comes from wherever it can be found. An example of what this looked like is described on the website of Yale University's School of Medicine:

> *A 19th century hospital was predominantly a charity institution, although from the beginning, some patients paid for their stay. It was intended for the worthy poor, for sailors, and for other strangers in town. People of means, such as the donors who were members of the General Hospital Society of Connecticut, would receive medical care in their homes, and not in a hospital. The hospital as yet offered no advantages over home care. Physicians served in the hospital without salary on a rotating basis as attending physicians. They did so as a form of charity and civic duty, but hospital service also provided valuable experience, professional recognition, and the possibility of training students in the wards.*
>
> from *Connecticut and New Haven's First General Hospital: Hospitals in the Nineteenth-Century*
> *https://www.coursehero.com/file/p7h7e96/A-19th-century-hospital-was-predominantly-a-charity-institution-although-from/*

Benjamin Franklin convinced the Pennsylvania Legislature to participate in chartering the nation's first hospital, Pennsylvania Hospital. He received a commitment to match 2,000 pounds donated by private individuals with a like amount appropriated by the state government. Founded in 1751, the institution was created "to care for the sick poor of the Province and for the reception and care of lunaticks" (see: In the Beginning: The Story of the Creation of the Nation's First Hospital; *http://www.uphs.upenn.edu/paharc/features/creation.html; University of Pennsylvania Health System*).

The modern charitable institution, however, may bear little resemblance to the typical charity of the 19th century. Burgeoning demands for services, increased government regulation, keen competition for funds, the advance of technology, demographic changes, and the public's changing perception of our institutions have all worked to increase the complexity of decision-making to those in leadership positions with nonprofit organizations. Pennsylvania Hospital, started with perhaps a handful of employees, has evolved into the University of Pennsylvania Health System.

Virtually every American is touched in some way by the services of this country's nonprofit organizations. Organizations such as institutions of religious worship, civic groups, hospitals, day care centers, libraries, colleges, symphonies, art museums, the Red Cross, Salvation Army, and the American Cancer Society work in partnership with government and the public to improve our lives and those of our neighbors.

The nonprofit sector's participation in the American economy is impressive. According to the Urban Institute, the voluntary sector contributes 5.6% of our national economy ($1.047 trillion in output) (source: *nccs.urban.org/publication/nonprofit-sector-brief-2019*). In 2016, nonprofit organizations reported to the IRS that they collectively controlled property, cash, and investments with a value of about $5.99 trillion (source: *https://nccs.urban.org/publication/nonprofit-sector-brief-2019*). This figure does not include wealth controlled by churches or small nonprofits that are not required to file Form 990 annual tax returns.

According to Independent Sector, Texas is second only to California in the number of federally tax-exempt nonprofits with 97,734, 65,048 of which are 50(c)(3) federally tax-exempt public charities. Texas has a "vibrant and rapidly growing" nonprofit sector, according to a report published by Texas A&M's Bush School of Government and Public Service. Yet data in the same report documents that Texas ranks just 46th among the 50 states and the District of Columbia in per capita nonprofit organizations, with just 38.9 organizations for every 10,000 Texas residents compared to a national average of 50 organizations. And many of these, four out of ten, were established in the century's first decade, compared to the national average of 24%. Thus, there appears to still be room for growth, particularly in Southern Texas, where the per capita organizations per 10,000 residents is just 23. There are also more than 5,000 foundations in Texas, with assets of more than $30 billion. The sector as a whole has assets of more than $300 billion.

As is the case across the nation, the nonprofit sector fuels an impressive segment of Texas's economy. More than 506,000 workers, 5.1% of the total Texas workforce, is employed by the sector, earning almost $17 billion in wages, and contributing approximately $1.6 billion in state and local taxes.

For additional statistics about the scope of the Texas nonprofit sector, see *https://www.nonprofitimpactmatters.org/states/texas/*

Most Americans recognize the value of nonprofit organizations in society. Approximately 30% of taxpayers itemized their deductions before passage of the *Tax Cuts and Jobs Act.* The December 2017 law nearly doubled the value of the standard deduction such that many former itemizers found it more advantageous to take the flat standard deduction rather than itemize and claim credit for charitable contributions. As a result, the amount of charitable contributions claimed on federal income tax returns dropped precipitously, with the number of itemizers in tax year 2018 dropping from 30.6% to 11.4%, according to the IRS (source: Internal Revenue Service. Statistics of Income, Table 1.6 for FY 2017 and FY 2018). In addition to the sums donated to those who continued to itemize, many more billions of dollars were donated by persons who do not itemize, or who do not bother to declare the value of their charity on their tax returns. The business community also donates billions of dollars each year to charitable institutions.

On March 27, 2020, President Trump signed into law the *Coronavirus Aid, Relief, and Economic Security (CARES) Act,* which permits eligible individuals who take the standard deduction to deduct up to $300 of qualified charitable contributions as an adjustment to their adjusted gross income (AGI) for tax years beginning in 2020.

According to the June 2020 annual report of Giving USA, published by the American Association of Fund-Raising Counsel Trust for Philanthropy, total charitable giving by individuals, corporations, and foundations in 2019 increased over the previous year to an estimated $449.64 billion, $309.66 billion of this from private citizens (source: *https://givingusa.org/*). This represented a 2.8% increase in giving over the previous year in current dollars, a reflection of a pre-pandemic improving economy. Additionally, billions of hours annually are volunteered to nonprofits. According to the Corporation for National & Community Service, about 77.3 million Americans, or 30.3 percent of the adult population, averaged 89 hours of volunteer service during 2015 worth an estimated $167 billion (Source: *https://independentsector.org/value-of-volunteer-time-2020/* and *https://www. nationalservice.gov/newsroom/pressreleases/2018/volunteering-us-hits-record-*

high-worth-167-billion). As those who volunteer can attest, the value to society, such as the relief of human suffering, far exceeds the dollar value.

Purpose of the Handbook

As one might expect, a plethora of laws, regulations, court decisions, and other government policies apply to nonprofit corporations.

The purpose of this handbook is to provide answers to questions such as:

- What does one have to do to form a nonprofit corporation in Texas?
- What are the advantages and disadvantages of incorporating?
- How does a nonprofit organization qualify and apply for 501(c)(3) status?
- What kind of paperwork is involved in typical nonprofit operations?
- What should be in a nonprofit corporation's bylaws?
- How does a nonprofit organization qualify for discount bulk mailing privileges?
- How does a nonprofit organization qualify for a state sales tax exemption?
- Can a nonprofit organization engage in unrelated activities that generate income?
- Will the tax exemption of a nonprofit organization be at risk if it engages in lobbying?
- How do nonprofit organizations use the internet to increase revenues?

This handbook cannot purport to answer every conceivable question, but it does attempt to provide sources for answers to many of the questions posed by nonprofit board members and staff. It also provides references to primary source material, much of which is available on the Web, on important state and federal laws and regulations, sources for some of the most useful government forms, and sound advice about many nonprofit management issues.

Who Can Use This Book

This handbook will be a useful reference for—

- those who are considering forming a nonprofit corporation in Texas

- those who need to keep current on laws, regulations, and court decisions that affect nonprofit organizations, including executive staff and board members of existing nonprofit organizations

- those who will benefit from the advice included in this handbook on running a nonprofit organization, such as fundraisers, lobbyists, public affairs consultants, staff and leadership of funding organizations, and government officials, in addition to those who serve as the staff and board members of nonprofit organizations and their associations

- those who are students of nonprofit management at both the graduate and undergraduate levels.

This is the 1st edition of this publication, although it is based on similar handbooks published in other states since 1992. Every effort has been made to make this handbook as useful and free from errors as possible. It is the intent of the author to seek corrections as well as suggestions for improving this publication, and to incorporate these contributions in future editions. A survey/order form has been included as Appendix I to provide feedback to the author and publisher.

Acknowledgments

First, a word of thanks to Norman Dolch of North Texas University, Barry Silverberg of Austin Community College's Center for Nonprofit Studies, and others in Texas who contributed advice and provided answers to questions that were needed to bring this project to completion. Without their support and encouragement, there would not have been a *Texas Nonprofit Handbook.* Barry's review of the final proof of the first edition and suggestions to improve it were most helpful in making this publication the best it could be.

The author gratefully acknowledges the contributions of scores of individuals and organizations to this book. Michael Sand wrote some of the chapter on boards, as well as the chapter on applying for grants. Bob Mills, Esq. was the initial author of the chapter on volunteer and staff liability, which benefited by the efforts of Melanie Herman of the Nonprofit Management Risk Center.

I also appreciate the contributions to this publication made by Gerald Kaufman, whose thoughts and opinions in the chapter on nonprofit ethics deserve to be shared with every board member and staff person who is affiliated with a charity. Joel Cavadel, an attorney from York, PA, made many contributions to the section on mergers and consolidations, for which I am most grateful. Esther Hyatt of Virginia Commonwealth University reviewed the chapter on evaluation. Nearly a score of members of the teaching section of the Association for Research on Nonprofit Organizations and Voluntary Action (ARNOVA) reviewed chapters of *An Introduction to the Nonprofit Sector,* a textbook based on a previous edition of this book. Some of their suggestions have been incorporated into this Handbook. Some of the material in the chapter on change management was adapted from material on outcome-based management jointly written by Frederick Richmond and myself, and from material on large group intervention that Gerald Gorelick and I wrote together. Gary Grant and I wrote the material that comprises Chapter 23, Fundraising on the Internet.

David Williams of Florida deserves a tip of the hat for recognizing the value of these state-specific handbooks, and for encouraging me to expand the number of states with individual publications. He is directly responsible for inspiring me to add both Florida and this second edition of the *Texas Nonprofit Handbook* to the title list of White Hat Communications. .

G.M.G.

Quick Start Guide
to Forming a Nonprofit Organization

The following provides an overview of 21 major steps involved in starting up a nonprofit corporation in Texas. The order in which these appear below is not necessarily the most efficient in every case (and many steps can be accomplished simultaneously), but it should be sufficient for most startups. Changes in laws and regulations will occur that may modify the contents of this list. Because this book does not provide legal advice relating to any specific fact situation, I recommend that you consider consulting a qualified attorney before starting up any corporation.

1. Choose the general purpose and mission of the organization and write a description of it in a single sentence.
2. Conduct research to see—
    - whether there is a sufficient need for a new organization with that purpose
    - whether other organizations are already providing the service you propose to provide
    - who and how many will likely seek to be served by your organization
    - what federal, state, and local laws and regulations will apply to your organization
    - whether you will have enough startup income to finance initial expenses, and whether you can generate enough income (through sales of goods and services, grants, or donations) necessary to sustain your organization
    - whether there is sufficient interest in your community to build a board of directors for this organization.
3. Prepare a business and marketing plan if your startup is likely to require a substantial investment in startup funding.
4. Choose a unique business name, and check on its availability.
5. Choose an internet domain name based on that name.
6. Choose a legal address for your organization.
7. Obtain an EIN number (your taxpayer identification number) from the Internal Revenue Service by filling out a Form SS-4. (This can be obtained online at: *https://www.irs.gov/pub/irs-pdf/fss4.pdf* by using the forms and publications finder using the term "SS-4" or by calling 1-800-829-FORM.)
8. Choose incorporators.
9. Prepare and file your incorporation papers with the Texas Department of State's Corporations Section.
10. Obtain any required local business licenses.

11. Obtain business insurance, and consider obtaining directors' and officers' insurance.

12. Find out about legal requirements relating to employees if you plan on having them, such as federal income tax and Social Security tax withholding, state and local payroll tax procedures, unemployment insurance, and workers' compensation insurance; prepare job descriptions for staff, and develop personnel policies for employees.

13. Prepare draft organization bylaws (See Appendix B).

14. Hold an organizational meeting of the board of directors and approve bylaws, approve organization bank accounts, elect organization officers, and schedule subsequent meetings.

15. Open a bank account for the organization.

16. Set up the organization's accounting/bookkeeping, financial reporting system, and other record-keeping systems.

17. Obtain office space if required, business cards, stationery, office equipment, and supplies.

18. Obtain an internet host, publicize your email address, and build your website.

19. Obtain a Texas sales tax license from the Office of the Comptroller if you will be selling goods and services subject to the tax (see Chapter 27).

20. Apply for mailing permits.

21. If eligible, apply for a federal tax exemption using Form 1023 for 501(c)(3) status and Form 1024 for exemption under other sections of the Internal Revenue Code.

Chapter 1
The Decision To Incorporate

> Synopsis: Among the advantages of incorporating an organization are limits on liability, lower taxes, and increased organizational credibility. Among the disadvantages are loss of centralized control and increased paperwork, time, and expense of running a corporation.

A corporation is a legal entity formed for business activities. Under state and federal laws, a corporation is treated as a separate "person" for purposes of making contracts, paying taxes, and being liable for the consequences of business activity. A nonprofit corporation, also called a "not-for-profit" corporation in some states, generally is not permitted to issue shares of stock, and does not provide shareholders with dividends from the profits that are received from operating the business. While nonprofit corporations can and do make profits, these profits may not inure to the benefit of the "owners" of the corporation—the board of directors or trustees. Rather, these profits must be used to operate and maintain the organization. Some states, including Texas, place limitations on the types of activities that are the primary purpose of the nonprofit corporation.

Texas law (Chapter 22, Section 2.002 of Title 2 of the Business Organizations Code) lists the types of purposes for which incorporation as a nonprofit organization is permitted. These purposes include, but are not limited to—

> Sec. 2.002. PURPOSES OF NONPROFIT ENTITY. The purpose or purposes of a domestic nonprofit entity may include one or more of the following purposes:
>
> (1) serving charitable, benevolent, religious, eleemosynary, patriotic, civic, missionary, educational, scientific, social, fraternal, athletic, aesthetic, agricultural, and horticultural purposes;
> (2) operating or managing a professional, commercial, or trade association or labor union;
> (3) providing animal husbandry; or
> (4) operating on a nonprofit cooperative basis for the benefit of its members.

Generally, there are three classes of nonprofit corporations:

1. Funding agencies (e.g., United Way, Jewish Federation, private foundations)

    The primary purpose of these organizations is to allocate funds, either those solicited as private donations or those already accumulated in an endowment or private fortune, for other agencies that provide actual services. Many of these organizations restrict their grants of funds to groups that provide a narrow range of services of interest to the funding organization. A Jewish federation is likely to make contributions solely to Jewish-affiliated organizations or others that principally serve the Jewish community. The United Way generally provides funding to social service agencies. Some foundations restrict their contributions to organizations promoting services for women, health-care related studies, or arts and humanities agencies.

2. Membership organizations (e.g., Common Cause, the Sierra Club, League of Women Voters)

   These organizations exist primarily to provide services (such as advocacy, information sharing, and networking) for their members, usually with a specialty of expertise.

3. Service agencies (e.g., hospitals, schools, day care centers, family services)

   These organizations exist to provide specific services to the public. They often charge fees on a sliding scale for their services to fund the bulk of their budgets.

Each type of organization operates differently in many significant ways.

The decision to incorporate is a mere formality for most leaders who envision a large organization with employees, contracts, offices, property, and equipment. Corporate status in general, and nonprofit corporate status in particular, provides many advantages. Maintaining an unincorporated organization with annual revenue and expenditures comfortably in five figures is cumbersome at best, if not impossible. It is at the low end of the scale where the decision to incorporate is most important.

It would be ludicrous to consider incorporation for the Saturday morning running group get-together, which collects two dollars from each of its eight members to pay for the refreshments after the run. Yet, when the group expands to three hundred members, dues are collected to finance a race, the municipality demands that the club purchase insurance to indemnify against accidents, and the club wants a grant from an area foundation to purchase sophisticated race timing equipment with the intention of renting it to organizations that are hosting local 5K race fundraisers, then incorporation is clearly the option of choice.

There is no legal requirement that organizations incorporate in order to successfully fulfill their missions of serving the public. However, incorporation provides many distinct advantages, so most organizations will want to accomplish this quickly. Incorporation also has some disadvantages.

Advantages and Disadvantages of Incorporation

1. Limited Liability. Of all the reasons to seek corporate status, this is perhaps the most compelling. Under most state laws, the officers, directors, employees, and members of a corporation, except under very limited and unusual circumstances, are not personally liable for lawsuit judgments and debts relating to the organization. Thus, the personal assets of the organization's executive director or board members are not at risk in the event there is a successful suit against the corporation, or in the event the organization goes out of business while owing money to creditors. Assets of an organization may be minuscule, although the individuals running it may have substantial assets. Corporate status protects those personal assets. Many people will not even consider participating in the leadership of an organization unless their personal assets are shielded by incorporation.

The Congress and the Texaslegislature have enacted laws that are designed to expand the liability protection afforded to nonprofit boards of directors and volunteers (see Chapter 9).

2. Tax Advantages. Income accruing to an individual running an organization is subject to federal, state, and local taxes at the individual rate, which can be substantially more than the corporate rate. In the case of nonprofit incorporation, an organization can be exempt from many taxes, depending upon its type.

For organizations that are charitable, educational, religious, literary, or scientific, 501(c)(3) tax-exempt status is particularly attractive. Many types of charitable institutions, such as colleges and hospitals, which have substantial property holdings, would be taxed beyond their ability to operate if they were denied tax exemptions. Many funding sources, such as government, foundations, and the public, will not make grants or contributions to an organization that is not federally tax exempt under Section 501(c)(3) of the Internal Revenue Code, since this status provides a tax-exemption to the contributor and assures that there is at least some minimal level of accountability on behalf of the organization.

3. Structure, Accountability, Perpetuity, and Legally Recognized Authority. When people and organizations interact with a bona fide corporation, they have confidence that there is some order and authority behind the decision-making of that entity. A reasonable expectation exists that the corporation will continue to honor agreements even if the principal actor for the organization dies, resigns, or otherwise disassociates himself or herself from the organization. They know that there is a legal document governing decision-making (as detailed in the bylaws), succession of officers, clear purposes (as detailed in the Certificate of Formation), a system for paying bills, accounting for income and expenses, and a forum for the sharing of ideas on policy and direction from the corporation's board members. So long as the necessary papers are filed, the organization will continue in perpetuity regardless of changes in leadership. This gives such organizations an aura of immortality, which is seen as an advantage in planning beyond the likely tenure of an individual board chairperson or executive director.

4. Ancillary Benefits. Nonprofit incorporation can provide lower postage rates; access to media (through free public service announcements); volunteers, who would be more hesitant volunteering for a comparable for-profit entity; and the so-called "halo effect," in which the public is more willing to do business with a nonprofit because of a real or perceived view that such an organization is founded and operated in the public interest. Charities are often eligible for free or discounted goods and services, such as computer equipment and software.

5. Strength of Collegial Decision-Making. Decision-making in an autocracy is clearly easier and more efficient than in an organization run as a democracy. Yet, there is a value in making decisions by building a consensus among a majority of members of a diverse, volunteer, community-based board. Members of a board often bring different experience and talents and provide information that would otherwise not be available in making decisions. Issues are often raised that, if overlooked, could possibly result in disastrous consequences for the organization.

Disadvantages of Incorporation

1. Loss of Centralized Control. Many organizations are formed and run by a charismatic leader with a vision of how to accomplish a particular task or mission. Decision-making is enhanced without the distractions of the scores of issues that relate not to the actual mission of the organization but to maintaining the organization itself. The very act of forming a nonprofit corporation can be draining—preparing and filing the Certificate of Formation; negotiating bylaws; finding quality colleagues to serve on a board of directors; hiring qualified staff, if necessary; and dealing with the many issues that emanate from hiring staff, preparing budgets, raising money, and preparing minutes of board meetings. Even finding a convenient time and place where the board can meet to ensure that a quorum is present can pose a troublesome and potentially overwhelming problem at times.

Incorporation is a legal framework that trades off the advantages addressed earlier in this section with some serious disadvantages. Decisions can no longer be made in a vacuum by one person without oversight or accountability, but are legally under the purview of a board of directors. Decisions have to withstand scrutiny of *all* persons on the board, some of whom may be hostile or have personal axes to grind. By definition, boards of directors are committees, and committees often make decisions that are compromises in order to mollify members with divergent viewpoints and competing interests.

For those used to making quick decisions "on the fly" and who revel in not having those decisions subject to second-guessing, modification, or otherwise being meddled with, incorporation can be a personally shackling experience and can dilute one's control over the organization.

2. Paperwork, Paperwork, Paperwork. Even in the smallest nonprofit corporation, the paperwork load related to corporate status can at times be overwhelming. There are deadlines for virtually every filing. Keeping ahead of the paperwork wave requires discipline, commitment, and a sense of humor. Forms get misfiled or lost in the bureaucracy or in the mail.

Failure to handle this paperwork can result in criminal penalties, in some cases. There are penalties for missed filings (e.g., failure to file a timely 990 federal tax return results in a $20/day penalty, up to a maximum of $10,000, or 5% of the organization's gross revenues, whichever is smaller—and $100/day up to $50,000 for organizations with annual gross receipts exceeding $1 million). Even the smallest tax-exempt organization can lose its exemption if it does not electronically file a 990-N e-postcard at least once every three years. As soon as the first employee is hired, the paperwork wave accompanying that addition is substantial.

In the first year, the filings can be intimidating, time-consuming, and frustrating. A new corporation must develop a bookkeeping system that is understandable by the accountant who will perform the audit and prepare the financial reports, pass resolutions, file forms to open up corporate savings and checking accounts, order checks, file tax returns, and pay taxes.

There are many different federal, state, and local taxes, each of which requires its own filing at varying times of the year. A new corporation must also reconcile savings and checking accounts, prepare board meeting announcements and minutes, devise a system to pay bills, and establish a process for the reimbursement of expenses. Other tasks the corporation must accomplish are filing forms to protect its corporate name, preparing an annual report, adopting a personnel policy, purchasing office equipment, renting an office, preparing budgets, writing fundraising letters, and finding and retaining board members.

Few of these tasks have a direct impact on the actual work of the organization, but typically they will consume more time during the initial year after incorporation than does the work related to the actual mission of the organization.

The only consolation is that after a few years, one becomes familiar with the required filings. Then they become routine and just a minor nuisance.

3. Expenses in Money and Time. Significant resources are required to establish a corporation and run it efficiently. No law prohibits running a corporation from one's home with volunteer staff. Legally, the only monetary requirement is to pay a fee to file the Certificate of Formation. Yet, doing so often sets off a chain of events that dramatically increases the organization's complexity. Opening up corporate bank accounts, doing expense reports, filing tax returns, and doing the paperwork described above are difficult to accomplish solely with volunteer labor. Raising the funds necessary to hire a person to do all of this work—in addition to coordinating the actual work of the organization—adds to this burden, and requires even more filing and paperwork.

Many of these tasks would be required even in the absence of a decision to incorporate. One can avoid much of the "wasted" time and energy by keeping "small," but that places a substantial limit on what one can accomplish.

Nonprofits and Private Benefit

Nonprofit corporation status provides many advantages over comparable for-profits. Yet this status is not conferred without a cost. Generally, nonprofits must operate differently and with different motivations than their for-profit counterparts. There is a general legal doctrine that prohibits nonprofits from acting in a manner that results in "private inurement" to individuals, i.e., the transfer of earnings or profits from the corporation to its "owners." The basic principle at work here is that a for-profit is intended to benefit its owners, whereas a nonprofit is intended to further a purpose. Chapter 22 of Title 2 of the Texas Business Organizations Code contains the following:

> Sec. 22.053. DIVIDENDS PROHIBITED. A dividend may not be paid to, and no part of the income of a corporation may be distributed to, the corporation's members, directors, or officers.

> Sec. 22.054. AUTHORIZED BENEFITS AND DISTRIBUTIONS. A corporation may:
> (1) pay compensation in a reasonable amount to the members, directors, or officers of the corporation for services provided;
> (2) confer benefits on the corporation's members in conformity with the corporation's purposes; and
> (3) make distributions to the corporation's members on winding up and termination to the extent authorized by this chapter.

Sec. 22.055. POWER TO ASSIST EMPLOYEE OR OFFICER. (a) A corporation may lend money to or otherwise assist an employee or officer of the corporation, but not a director, if the loan or assistance may reasonably be expected to directly or indirectly benefit the corporation.

(b) A loan made to an officer must be:

(1) made for the purpose of financing the officer's principal residence; or

(2) set in an original principal amount that does not exceed:

(A) 100 percent of the officer's annual salary, if the loan is made   before the first anniversary of the officer's employment; or

(B) 50 percent of the officer's annual salary, if the loan is made in any subsequent year.

Texas law does not preclude the board of directors from serving as the non-profit corporation's employees, provided they are not compensated unreasonably for their services. Yet there is a clear prohibition against the income received by the organization being distributed to these directors in a manner other than as "reasonable" compensation for services.

The term "reasonable" has been generally defined by the courts as compensation that is not excessive compared to individuals with similar expertise and responsibility in the same or similar community. Internal Revenue Service regulations (see Chapter 7) have been promulgated to place restrictions on compensation. However, there is no legal precedent for a doctrine that suggests individuals who work for charities or nonprofits should be paid any less than their for-profit counterparts.

Typically, those who serve on the boards of nonprofit organizations do so without compensation, although paying board members, while frowned upon, is not unheard of.

In the book *Starting & Managing a Nonprofit Organization*, now in a 7th edition (2017), author-attorney Bruce R. Hopkins provides a useful chapter on the issue of private inurement in nonprofits.

There is nothing illegal or unethical about nonprofits selling goods and services and generating income. Nonprofits are becoming more sophisticated in finding new revenue sources to supplant the loss of government funds (see Chapters 16, 22, and 23). Yet, nonprofits are distinguished from their for-profit counterparts by the destination of any profit. Chapter 26 includes a list of many of the important differences between nonprofits and for-profits.

Tips:

- Review Texas's nonprofit laws and decide whether your organization is willing to be subjected to the limitations and accountability required by these laws.

- Avoid incorporating if it is essential to maintain complete control of the organization, and if it is possible to keep the scale of operations small.

- Contact someone who runs a nonprofit corporation of similar size and type envisioned for your organization. Ask questions about paperwork requirements, office equipment, rental space, and the benefits and pitfalls of running such a corporation.

- If leaning toward incorporation, identify potential incorporators/board members who are—

  a. accessible, and not spread too thin among many other competing organizations
  b. potential contributors to the organization
  c. experienced fundraisers
  d. knowledgeable about the issues of concern to the organization,
  e. respected and well-known in the community
  f. experienced in legal, accounting, and nonprofit management issues.

- If you find the requirements of incorporating your own organization too intimidating, consider seeking a fiscal sponsor (see Chapter 10).

Chapter 2
Steps to Incorporation

Synopsis: Organizational leadership must file the appropriate forms with the Texas Department of State's Corporations Section to incorporate an organization. Among important decisions to be made are choosing the corporate name, opting whether to have members, and choosing corporate purposes.

While incorporation is a legal procedure, it does not require the services of a lawyer. However, lawyers with training and experience in Texas nonprofit law can be useful in reviewing, if not preparing, the Certificate of Formation and bylaws that are consistent with both statutory requirements and with the purposes of the organization. There are several sources for the text of these laws.

The first is the 2006 codification itself, the Texas Business Organizations Code (Title 2, Chapter 22). It can be found in county law libraries, some public libraries, many university libraries, and online at: *https://statutes.capitol.texas. gov/Docs/BO/htm/BO.2.htm#2.002.*

Role of Incorporators

Incorporators are those legally responsible for forming the corporation. It is common for one person to serve as an organization's incorporator and do most, if not all, of the work involved. Several persons may sign the Certificate of Formation form as formal incorporators. Some states require more than one incorporator, although Texas is not one of them.

Incorporators frequently play a more active role than just being a name on the Certificate of Formation filing. If they act to promote the interests of the new corporation (e.g., raise funds, recruit personnel, negotiate leases, or purchase property for the organization), their legal status is augmented by the responsibility of serving in a fiduciary capacity. This legal status confers on them the duty to take actions in the best interest of the corporation rather than their own personal interest, and to disclose any conflicts of interest that may occur in their business dealings on behalf of the corporation.

By law, the incorporators make agreements on behalf of the corporation while it is in the process of legal formation. However, these agreements have no legal effect until they are approved by the corporation's board of directors, which assumes authority once the corporation legally exists. As a result, the incorporators involved in these agreements must make it clear to the other party that the agreement is not binding until the corporation exists as a legal entity and its board ratifies the agreement.

Once the Certificate of Formation is filed and the Texas Department of State approves them, incorporators have no formal status, with one exception. They are invited to be present at the organizational meeting required by law, at which the board of directors is selected and bylaws are approved, consistent with Section 22.104 of Chapter 22 of Title 2 of the Texas Business Organizations Code:

> *Sec. 22.104. ORGANIZATION MEETING. (a) After the certificate of formation is filed, the board of directors named in the certificate of formation of a corporation shall hold an organization meeting of the board, either in or out of this state, at the call of the organizers or a majority of the directors to adopt bylaws and elect officers and for other purposes determined by the board at the meeting. The organizers or directors calling the meeting shall send notice of the time and place of the meeting to each director named in the certificate of formation not later than the third day before the date of the meeting.*

> *(b) A first meeting of the members may be held at the call of the majority of the directors on notice provided not later than the third day before the date of the meeting. The notice must state the purposes of the meeting.*

> *(c) If the management of a corporation is vested in the corporation's members, the members shall hold the organization meeting on the call of an organizer. An organizer who calls the meeting shall:*

> *(1) send notice of the time and place of the meeting to each member not later than the third day before the date of the meeting;*

> *(2) if the corporation is a church, make an oral announcement of the time and place of the meeting at a regularly scheduled worship service before the meeting; or*

> *(3) send notice of the meeting in the manner provided by the certificate of formation.*

It is a common practice that the incorporators include members who will be serving on the first board of directors. Thus, care should be taken as to the qualifications of incorporators, since they may continue their association with the corporation as directors.

The Certificate of Formation in Texas *(see: https://www.sos.state.tx.us/corp/forms/202_boc.pdf)* includes the organization's name and that is will be a nonprofit corporation; information about the registered agent; the number, names, and addresses of the initial board of directors—or whether governance will be by the organization's members; whether the corporation will have members; the purpose of the organization; optional provisions (such as what is needed to obtain federal tax-exempt status from the Internal Revenue Service, the name and address of the organizer; and the effective date of the incorporation.

Choosing a Corporate Name

One of the most important and basic decisions in forming a corporation is choosing a corporate name. This name will be the organization's corporate identity, and the image created by it provides the first impression held by those outside of the corporation. "Short" and "descriptive" are two desirable characteristics in a corporate name. Many nonprofit organizations choose a name that gives the connotation of helping, or otherwise doing charitable activities in the public interest, rather than implying a for-profit motive.

If the organization plans to apply for 501(c)(3) status, it should avoid names that would be suitable for organizations whose activities are clearly not eligible for this status. The organization may wish to consider suitable acronyms comprising the first letter of each word of its name, but cute or frivolous acronyms often give an unprofessional impression. It is useful to check if any other organization is using the prospective name by using Internet search engines and the U.S. Patent and Trademark Office's database (see below).

The process of having to change a corporate name after incorporating and operating as a nonprofit often results in time-consuming and costly activities, such as changing the logo (see Chapter 25); reprinting stationery, business cards, checks, and brochures; and changing all of the legal forms relating to the Certificate of Formation, bank accounts, and contracts.

For obvious legal reasons, the name must be unique in Texas, although it is usually legal to adopt a name similar to another existing corporation after receiving permission from that corporation and filing the necessary forms to do so. There are some statutory limitations to names that are approved by the Corporations Section, which can be found in Section 5.051 of the Business Organizations Code (see: *https://statutes.capitol.texas.gov/Docs/BO/htm/BO.5.htm#5.054).*

A name search should be performed with the Corporations Section of the Department of State to ensure that no other corporation, active or inactive, is using an identical or similar name. For a preliminary determination on name availability, you may call (512) 463-5555 or e-mail your name inquiry to the Corporations Section (corpinfo@sos.texas.gov).

The Bureau permits the name to be reserved for $40 for a 120-day period prior to registration as a corporation. Use form 501 (available at: *https://www. sos.state.tx.us/corp/forms/501_boc.pdf).*

Many corporations also choose to do a national name search and take steps to register their names with the United States Patent and Trademark Office as trademarks. This can be done only for those organizations that will be marketing goods and services interstate. The fee is $400 for paper filing and $250 for electronic filing using the Trademark Electronic Applications System (TEAS), which provides registration for ten years, assuming the owner certifies that the trademark has active status. See: *https://www.uspto.gov/learning-and-resources/general-faqs* for requirements to be eligible for a $50 discount by filing a TEAS Plus form. Obviously, if an organization has trademarked its name, it is not available for other organizations, even if that organization is headquartered in another state.

For more information or to obtain the correct forms, contact the Patent and Trademark Office:

U.S. Patent and Trademark Office (USPTO)
Commissioner for Trademarks
U.S. Department of Commerce
PO Box 1451
Alexandria, VA 22313
(571) 272-1000
(800) 786-9199
https://www.uspto.gov/trademarks/apply

Basic information about trademarks can be accessed at: *https://www.uspto. gov/*

Choosing Corporate Purposes

It is generally advisable to state broad corporate purposes in a manner that permits the corporation to grow and change direction without requiring its Certificate of Formation to be amended. However, the purposes should be specific enough to permit the corporation to be eligible for 501(c)(3) status, if this is expected.

The Internal Revenue Service provides guidance on drafting a purpose statement that will facilitate a successful 501(c)(3) eligibility determination. Two examples illustrate clauses that will satisfy the IRS:

1. Charitable and educational purposes within the meaning of IRC 501(c)(3).
2. To grant scholarships for deserving junior college students residing in Gotham City.

"To operate a hospital" is an example of a purpose that is insufficient to the IRS. The explanation provided by the IRS is that the purpose is ambiguous, since a hospital may be exempt or not exempt, depending upon how it is operated.

The IRS provides language that nonprofit organizations may use if they choose a broad corporate purpose consistent with the first example:

> *This corporation is organized exclusively for one or more purposes as specified in Section 501(c)(3) of the Internal Revenue Code or the corresponding section of any future federal tax code, including, for such purposes, the making of distributions to organizations that qualify as exempt organizations under Section 501(c)(3) of the Internal Revenue Code, or the corresponding section of any future tax code.*

A second consideration when devising the purpose statement to facilitate exemption is to provide that the organization benefits an indefinite class of individuals, not specific persons. For example, if the purpose of the organization is intended to be establishing a scholarship fund for members of a specific family orphaned by the COVID-19 pandemic, the purpose should be "to grant scholarships to deserving American students orphaned by the COVID-19 pandemic" rather than "to grant scholarships to the children of John A. Smith."

Research similar organizations and review their Certificate of Formation to obtain ideas on framing your own organization's Certificate of Formation.

Choosing To Have Members or No Members

The Texas Business Code permits the incorporators of a nonprofit organization to choose whether the organization will be governed by its members, or will have no members—and whereby governance will be accomplished by a board of directors.

> *Sec. 22.151. MEMBERS. (a) A corporation may have one or more classes of members or may have no members.*
> *(b) If the corporation has one or more classes of members, the corporation's certificate of formation or bylaws must include:*
> *(1) a designation of each class;*
> *(2) the manner of the election or appointment of the members of each class; and*

(3) the qualifications and rights of the members of each class.

(c) A corporation may issue a certificate, card, or other instrument evidencing membership rights, voting rights, or ownership rights as authorized by the certificate of formation or bylaws.

"Membership" in the legal sense has a different meaning than those in an organization who pay dues. In the context of incorporation, having members refers to providing broad governance authority beyond an organization's board of directors. In general, it is desirable for most nonprofit corporations to have no members. This will ensure that all power and authority will be maintained by the board of directors, and it will prevent the difficult legal problems of expelling an individual member should that occasion arise. It is also expensive and time-consuming to conduct elections, change bylaws, and make major organizational decisions when all members have the legal right to participate. Outsiders, including those who would pay dues in exchange for participating in organizational programs and activities, can still participate in the activities of the nonprofit corporation without being legal members who are entitled to vote on the affairs of the corporation.

As with almost every issue, there are exceptions to this. Many organizations will find it desirable for each participant in the organization's programs and activities to have an equal voice in the internal governance of the organization. Many individuals bristle at the fact that a nonprofit organization's governance is often controlled by a self-selected group of individuals that sometimes are perceived by members to be elitist, paternalistic, or secretive about the organization's affairs. Some feel that having legal members is more egalitarian and democratic.

Additional Provisions

Many corporations that wish to qualify for 501(c)(3) status add one or more provisions to facilitate tax-exemption approval. One such provision is a statement forbidding the corporation from engaging in inurement and partisan political activity on behalf of a candidate or substantially engaging in lobbying. The language for this provision is suggested by the IRS (see: *https://www.irs.gov/charities-non-profits/suggested-language-for-corporations-and-associations*):

No part of the net earnings of the corporation shall inure to the benefit of, or be distributable to its members, trustees, officers, or other private persons, except that the corporation shall be authorized and empowered to pay reasonable compensation for services rendered and to make payments and distributions in furtherance of the purposes set forth in Article _____ hereof. No substantial part of the activities of the corporation shall be the carrying on of propaganda, or otherwise attempting to influence legislation, and the corporation shall not participate in, or intervene in (including the publishing or distribution of statements) any political campaign on behalf of or in opposition to any candidate for public office. Notwithstanding any other provision of these articles, the corporation shall not carry on any other activities not permitted to be carried on (a) by a corporation exempt from federal income tax under section 501(c)(3) of the Internal Revenue Code, or the corresponding section of any future federal tax code, or (b) by a corporation, contributions to which are deductible under section 170(c)(2) of the Internal Revenue Code, or the corresponding section of any future federal tax code

Another provision required for Section 501(c)(3) eligibility relates to corporate dissolution:

Upon the dissolution of the organization, assets shall be distributed for one or more exempt purposes within the meaning of Section 501(c)(3) of the Internal Revenue Code, or corresponding section of any future federal tax code, or shall be distributed to the federal government, or to a state or local government, for a public purpose.

Once the Certificate of Formation are filed and approved, all actions taken on behalf of the Corporation should clearly indicate that they are actions for the corporation and not on behalf of individuals. Otherwise, such individuals may be personally liable for fulfilling the terms of contracts and other agreements, such as paying rent, staff salaries, telephone installation costs, and so on. One way to indicate that persons are acting on behalf of the corporation is to explicitly sign legal contracts and other documents as follows:

(corporate name)
By (individual's signature)
(individual's corporate title)

The Certificate of Formation filing form (Form 202) and other forms referred to in this section may be downloaded from the Department of State's Web site at *https://www.sos.state.tx.us/corp/forms_boc.shtml.* The form needs to be submitted in duplicate, with a $25 filing fee, to:

Department of State
PO Box 13697
Austin, TX 78711-3697

The form may be faxed to (512) 463-5709, but the filer must include Form 807 available at *https://webservices.sos.state.tx.us/forms/payment.pdf* and provide credit card information.

Once processed by the Department, the duplicate copy will be returned and file-stamped.

The department requires an actual street address or rural route box number. It will disapprove applications if a post office box, mailbox service, or telephone answering service is listed as the corporate address.

Form 202 requires the corporate name, the name and address of the initial registered agent, whether the governance of the organization will be vested in a board of directors or its members, the name and addresses of the initial board of directors if governance will be by a board rather than by its members (minimum of three required), the organization's purpose(s), supplemental provisions that may be required to achieve tax-exempt status, the name and address of the organizer, the effective date of the document, and the signature of the organizer. This form may be accessed at: *https://www.sos.state.tx.us/corp/forms/202_boc.pdf*

The department will send a confirmation of the filing of the application only if it receives a self-addressed, stamped postcard or envelope with the filing information.

Other Required Reports

Upon request by the Secretary of State, nonprofit organizations are required to file an informational report not more than once every four years. This form (Form 802) may be accessed at: *https://www.sos.state.tx.us/corp/forms/802_boc.pdf*. This report provides information about the organization's registered agent and registered office, as well as current officers and directors. It may be filed voluntarily. Failure to file a requested report within 30 days from the date the report is sent by the Secretary of State results in the corporation forfeiting its right to transact business in Texas. However, the action will be reversed if the organization files the report within 120 days of the notice of forfeiture. An organization involuntarily terminated under this process may file for reinstatement by filing the informational report and paying a $25 filing fee, but it may find that its corporate name is no longer available.

Corporate Dissolution

When the governing authority of a Texas nonprofit organization (the Board of Directors or the members, as the case may be) have determined that its existence should terminate, or there is an occurrence of an event specified in the governing documents requiring the winding up, dissolution or termination of the organization, chapter 11 of the Texas Business Organizations Code (BOC) provides procedures for doing so. On completion of the winding up process, Form 652 is filed to accomplish this. The fee is $5. for more details, see: *https://www.sos.state. tx.us/corp/forms/652_boc.pdf*

The legal requirements for the involuntary dissolution of a corporation are much more complex. Nonprofits that face legal notices concerning involuntary dissolution need to seek immediate legal advice.

Tips:

- *Review the legal requirements of Texas law for nonprofits (particularly Chapter 22 of Title 2 of the Business Organizations Code) to make sure the organization can and is willing to comply with them.*

- *Have a lawyer review, if not draft, the Certificate of Formation.*

- *Include in the Certificate of Formation additional provisions to enhance the prospects for achieving the appropriate federal tax status if such status is desirable. See Chapter 8 for additional details.*

- *Choose a short and descriptive corporate name.*

- *Check out your prospective name using popular Internet search engines, such as Google (https://www.google.com/), Bing (https://www.bing. com/), and Yahoo! (https://www.yahoo.com/). Having a corporate name that is not unique in the world may not be illegal, but it could be confusing.*

- *Review publications published by the Small Business Administration (SBA) that will help you start up and run your organization. A good place to start is: https://www.sba.gov/business-guide*

- Review publications published by Texas agencies to assist entrepreneurs who wish to start up a nonprofit organization in Texas. Among them is: Forming a NonprofitTax-Exempt Corporation in Texas *(https:// tinyurl.com/27o5wsse)*

Chapter 3
Bylaws

> **Synopsis:** Bylaws provide general policy guidelines for nonprofit corporations. There are statutory provisions that go into effect automatically in the absence of comparable bylaw provisions.

"Bylaws" refers to the code of rules adopted by the board of directors for the regulation or management of the business and affairs of the corporation. Texas nonprofit law requires each corporation to have a set of bylaws:

Sec. 22.102. BYLAWS. (a) The initial bylaws of a corporation shall be adopted by the corporation's board of directors or, if the management of the corporation is vested in the corporation's members, by the members.

(b) The bylaws may contain provisions for the regulation and management of the affairs of the corporation that are consistent with law and the certificate of formation.

(c) The board of directors may amend or repeal the bylaws, or adopt new bylaws, unless:

> *(1) this chapter or the corporation's certificate of formation wholly or partly reserves the power exclusively to the corporation's members;*

> *(2) the management of the corporation is vested in the corporation's members; or*

> *(3) in amending, repealing, or adopting a bylaw, the members expressly provide that the board of directors may not amend or repeal the bylaw*

Texas law provides that the incorporators must schedule an organizational meeting of initial directors for the purpose of adopting bylaws. State law requires that at least three days' notice be given for this organizational meeting.

The term "bylaws" is defined in law to be "the rules adopted to regulate or manage the corporation, regardless of the name used to designate the rules."

Certain provisions must by law be included in bylaws of Texas nonprofit corporations. Beyond legal requirements, corporate bylaws are a necessary and important document, and great thought and care should be exercised as to what will be included in them.

Typical bylaws include provisions governing the following 26 internal procedures and policies of the nonprofit corporation:

1. The purposes of the corporation, consistent with any federal tax law limitation or state laws governing lobbying or other activity;
2. Limitations of liability of directors, consistent with Texas law
3. Types of officers (Texas law requires there be at least one president and one secretary, although the same person may serve as both);
4. Terms, powers, and succession of officers;
5. Location of principal office;
6. Whether the corporation will have members, or whether all powers will be vested in a board of directors;
7. How directors will be selected and how vacancies will be filled,
8. How many directors there will be;
9. Length of terms of board of directors, limits on consecutive terms, and if and how such terms will overlap with other board members;
10. Terms under which a member of the board of directors can be disqualified;
11. Conditions under which the annual meeting and other regularly scheduled board meetings are held, consistent with what is required in Texas law (see: Section 22.153 at: *https://statutes.capitol.texas.gov/Docs/BO/htm/BO.22.htm);*
12. How unscheduled meetings of the board may be called;
13. Terms under which notice of board meetings must occur;
14. What constitutes a quorum for the transaction of business;
15. How many directors are required to approve an action;
16. Whether actions of the board may be ratified through the mail or by conference call, or require directors to be present at a meeting;
17. Power of the chairperson (or president) to appoint committees, and to provide for rules, powers, and procedures of such committees;
18. Whether alternates may be empowered to represent directors, and who selects them;
19. Who is responsible for preparing board meeting minutes;
20. Who is responsible for keeping and reviewing the corporate books, and dispersing corporate funds;
21. How amendments may be made to the bylaws;
22. Terms and conditions regarding compensation, if any, paid to directors;
23. What committees are authorized, and what powers and duties they have;
24. The terms under which the corporation will be dissolved; and
25. Which, if any, parliamentary procedure will be used at board meetings.
26. Whether board meetings may be held by conference call or videoconferencing.

A sample set of bylaws may be found in Appendix A. This sample is a guideline, and should be modified to fit the needs of the organization. It is highly recommended that an attorney either draft the organization's bylaws, or review it before it is finalized to assure its provisions are consistent with Texas law, and are consistent with how the organizers desire to manage and govern the organization.

Legal Requirements for Bylaws in Texas

Texas law provides for some minimum standards with respect to bylaws of nonprofit corporations. For example, every Texas nonprofit corporation must—

- Have a President and Secretary (or officers who perform comparable duties). A single person may not hold both offices.
- Not have meetings organized for the transaction of business unless a quorum is present.
- Must have a board of at least three individuals.

Texas statute provides rules on many of the above bylaw options in the absence of explicit directions in the nonprofit corporation's bylaws. Thus, it is important to place provisions in the bylaws that will be intended to supersede these statutory legal guidelines, if the directors feel that the guidance provided in law is not acceptable to the corporation. In every case, provisions in the organization's Certificate of Formation supersede any contradictory bylaw provisions.

Among the provisions of bylaws that deserve the highest consideration and thought are the following, with some comments about the issues they raise:

Quorum Requirements

A quorum is the minimum number of members or directors required to be present for a meeting to be held for the legal transaction of business. The purpose of a quorum requirement is to assure that actions are taken by a representative number of duly authorized participants rather than by an elite few. Standard advice, in the absence of relying on any statutory requirement, is to set the quorum at the minimum number of people who will be expected to attend a meeting, taking into account emergencies, adverse weather conditions, or conflicts with competing meetings. If the bylaws permit it, board members may participate in meetings and be counted as part of a quorum if they are in communication by speaker phone, by conference call, Skype, or by other internet or electronic technology whereby all board members can hear each other.

Since actions cannot be taken legally at board meetings without a quorum present, it is best to begin with a conservatively low quorum requirement. Then change the bylaws to increase that number as appropriate. Otherwise, it is possible that the corporation will never have a quorum for its meetings, even if the sole purpose of the meeting is to change the bylaws to decrease the number of directors constituting a quorum.

Note, in the absence of provisions in the bylaws or Certificate of Formation regarding quorum requirements, Texas law provides that:

> Sec. 22.213. QUORUM. (a) A quorum for the transaction of business by the board of directors of a corporation is the lesser of:
>
> (1) the majority of the number of directors set by the corporation's bylaws or, in the absence of a bylaw setting the number of directors, a majority of the number of directors stated in the corporation's certificate of formation; or
>
> (2) any number, not less than three, set as a quorum by the certificate of formation or bylaws.
>
> (b) A director present by proxy at a meeting may not be counted toward a quorum.

Voting Rights

Boards need to vote to formally demonstrate that they have taken actions. Many organizations can be effectively run by consensus rather than by formal voting, but even the most congenial and tolerant boards will eventually face issues that will divide them. In the absence of a provision in the bylaws, action may be taken at a board meeting with the approval of a majority of directors who are present at the meeting. Nothing prohibits a two-thirds vote from being required to ensure that actions are closer to representing a consensus. A two-thirds vote may be suggested for changing bylaws, or for changing membership dues requirements. Generally, a majority vote is sufficient for most routine board decisions, and avoids the inability to take positions and actions that can occur as a result of a two-thirds voting requirement.

In the absence of a provision in the bylaws or Certificate of Formation, Texas law provides guidance on voting:

> Sec. 22.159. (b) The vote of the majority of the votes entitled to be cast by the members present or represented by proxy at a meeting at which a quorum is present is the act of the members meeting, unless the vote of a greater number is required by law or the certificate of formation or bylaws.

Selection of Officers

Many organizations are attracted to the democratic notion of offices being opened to all. With such a policy, any director can run for an office, ballots are prepared, and the winner is selected by the majority (or plurality) of voters from the board of directors or the membership at large. Other organizations feel that democracy puts at risk an orderly succession and threatens the existing power structure. Orderly succession can be accomplished by providing for a nominating committee, appointed by the chairperson, which selects a slate of officers. This slate is then perfunctorily approved by the full board. Both systems have their advantages and disadvantages.

Some organizations utilize a third alternative that combines the two. The nominations committee recommends a slate of candidates, but the procedures permit other candidates to run, as well.

Executive Committees

Board meetings may occur at regular intervals, but issues arise in the interim that demand immediate attention. In such cases, it is valuable to have a mandated procedure for taking legally legitimate actions in the absence of board meetings. The mechanism to accomplish this is the executive committee, provided for in the corporate bylaws. The executive committee typically has all of the power and authority of the full board with the following three exceptions:

1. The executive committee cannot fill vacancies on the board.
2. The executive committee cannot adopt, amend, or repeal bylaws.
3. The executive committee cannot have powers inconsistent with the resolution passed by the board establishing it.

Although Texas law does not explicitly authorize executive committees, there is a provision authorizing a management committee that could achieve the same function:

> *Sec. 22.218. MANAGEMENT COMMITTEE. (a) If authorized by the certificate of formation or bylaws of the corporation, the board of directors of a corporation, by resolution adopted by the majority of the directors in office, may designate one or more committees to have and exercise the authority of the board in the management of the corporation to the extent provided by:*
>   *(1) the resolution;*
>   *(2) the certificate of formation; or*
>   *(3) the bylaws.*
> *(b) A committee designated under this section must consist of at least two persons. Except as provided by Subsection (b-1), the majority of the persons on the committee must be directors. If provided by the certificate of formation or*

bylaws, the remaining persons on the committee are not required to be directors.

(b-1) If a corporation is a religious institution and if provided by the corporation's certificate of formation or bylaws, a committee designated under this section may be composed entirely of persons who are not directors of the corporation.

(c) The designation of a committee and the delegation of authority to the committee does not operate to relieve the board of directors, or an individual director, of any responsibility imposed on the board or director by law. A committee member who is not a director has the same responsibility with respect to the committee as a committee member who is a director.

Conference Call and Videoconference Meetings

As of September 2019, nonprofit organizations may explicitly amend their bylaws to permit meetings to be held by conference call or over the internet using popular videoconferencing technology such as Zoom or Skype:

22.002. MEETINGS BY REMOTE COMMUNICATIONS TECHNOLOGY. A meeting of the members of a corporation, the board of directors of a corporation, or any committee designated by the board of directors of a corporation may be held by means of a conference telephone or similar communications equipment, another suitable electronic communications system, including videoconferencing technology or the Internet, or any combination of those means, in accordance with Section 6.002. Acts 2003, 78th Leg., ch. 182, Sec. 1, eff. Jan. 1, 2006. Amended by: Acts 2019, 86th Leg., R.S., Ch. 665 (S.B. 1971), Sec. 17, eff. September 1, 2019. Sec. 6.002. ALTERNATIVE FORMS OF MEETINGS. (a) Subject to this code and the governing documents of a domestic entity, the owners, members, or governing persons of the entity, or a committee of the owners, members, or governing persons, may hold meetings by using a conference telephone or similar communications equipment, or another suitable electronic communications system, including videoconferencing technology or the Internet, or any combination, if the telephone or other equipment or system permits each person participating in the meeting to communicate with all other persons participating in the meeting. (b) If voting is to take place at the meeting, the entity must: (1) implement reasonable measures to verify that every person voting at the meeting by means of remote communications is sufficiently identified; and (2) keep a record of any vote or other action taken. Acts 2003, 78th Leg., ch. 182, Sec. 1, eff. Jan. 1, 2006.

Tips:

- Review Texas law with respect to corporate bylaws. Identify which provisions are required, which provisions apply only in the absence of a different provision in the bylaws, and which act to pre-empt any statutory guideline.

- Give careful consideration to the more important bylaw provisions, such as—

  a. quorum requirements
  b. succession of officers
  c. powers of the executive committee
  d. voting by the board of directors.

- Have an attorney review the bylaws to ensure that they are in compliance with state law, and ensure that the organization's desires with respect to internal decision-making will be consistent with efficient operating procedures.

- Schedule an organizational meeting to approve the bylaws, and distribute a draft of proposed bylaws before this meeting.

- After a final version of the bylaws is approved, provide a final copy of the bylaws to all members of the board of directors.

- Review the Sample Bylaws provided in Appendix B and determine how they might be modified to meet the specific needs of your organization.

Chapter 4
Nonprofit Governance

by Michael A. Sand and Gary M. Grobman

Synopsis: It is a critically important function for nonprofit organizations to find and retain qualified, experienced board members and officers. Board meetings generally have a routine order of business and provide the forum for making organizational policy.

The term "governance" refers to the exercise of authority over an organization that relates to providing direction and control for the purpose of ensuring that it stays true to its mission and achieves its purposes. Governance in a nonprofit organization is entrusted to the board of directors (also often referred to as "board of trustees"). Governance responsibilities include hiring, evaluating, and disciplining the chief staff officer, who may be called the executive director, president, or chief executive officer. Governance is comprised of the structures, responsibilities, and processes that the organization uses to support its mission. It is the process of setting and safeguarding the strategic direction for the organization, and, as described by Mel Gill in his book, *Governing for Results*, includes four principal components:

1. *accountability*—requires that these decision-makers are legally liable for the actions they take, and apply sanctions against those who violate the organization's rules.

2. *transparency*—provides for stakeholder access to reliable information about the organization's operations, including financial information.

3. *predictability*—assures that the organization is in compliance with all laws and regulations, and that the policies of the organization are fairly and uniformly enforced.

4. *participation*—assures that in making decisions, the board members receive wide input with respect to planning, decision processes, and evaluation.

Governance differs from management in that the latter consists of the processes used to *carry out* the strategic leadership of those governing the organization, including the supervision of those who do the work of the organization, such as staff and volunteers. Management is typically reserved for paid staff, although it is, of course, not unusual for a nonprofit organization to have no staff, with all management responsibilities divided up among board members.

Governance and management functions occasionally overlap in organizations, and each one develops its own culture with respect to what responsibilities are those of the board and what is handled by staff. Ideally, there should be a delineation between management and governance functions.

Most nonprofit organizations, particularly those that will seek tax-exempt status from the state and federal government, will formalize their organizational structure by filing corporate papers with the state's corporation bureau. Having a board as a governance structure is a requirement for all corporations. The board is the legally constituted "owner" of a nonprofit organization, and each board member has a fiduciary responsibility to act in the interest of the organization rather than his or her own individual interests.

Types of Boards

As one might expect, nonprofit boards differ substantially with respect to the number of members, the diversity of their composition, the degree to which they get involved in the day-to-day operations of the organization, the committee structures they may have, and the amount of authority they delegate to the executive director. Scholars have attempted to categorize boards into general types, and this section conveys two attempts to classify boards based on general characteristics.

The first, offered by Mel Gill, proposes nine general types:

1. *Operational*—Board members and other volunteers do all of the work of the organization. Organizations with this model are typically newly founded and do not have any staff.

2. *Collective*—Board and staff work together to do the work of the organization, and staff have a strong role in typical governance issues.

3. *Management*—Board members are the primary managers of the work of the organization, but there may be a staff coordinator. The staff report to individual board member managers, who may be committee chairs who are responsible for various organization activities, such as personnel, finances, and service delivery.

4. *Constituent Representational*—Board members are comprised of various stakeholder constituencies, and tend to represent the interests of the organizations who elected them to the nonprofit board.

5. *Traditional*—Oversight of management staff is achieved through functional committees, and staff manage and report to these committees. At times, these committees may be involved in management activities.

6. *Results-Based*—The board sets direction of the organization, and the executive director is charged with achieving the goals set by the board. The executive director is often a non-voting member of the board, has a major role in setting this direction, but is evaluated by the board periodically.

7. *Policy Governance*—Often referred to as the "Carver Model," the board sets general goals and policies, provides some general limitations (particularly relating to ethics), and then gets out of the way and lets the executive director have the freedom to choose the means to achieve those goals. One aspect that distinguishes this model from others is that the board uses ad hoc task forces to assist management rather than permanent committees.

8. *Fundraising*—These boards typically serve primarily to raise money to support the work of the organization.

9. *Advisory*—This type of board is comprised of high profile (and perhaps wealthy) members of the community who rubber-stamp whatever the executive director suggests, and typically have little, if any, role in what is traditionally considered to be governance.

Gill suggests that these board types fall along a continuum. Organizations of the first type (operational) are at one extreme of this continuum, and are small, not complex, and have board members with a high degree of involvement in management activities. At the other extreme of the continuum are those in the ninth type (advisory) where the organizations tend to be quite large, complex, and have board members with minimal day-to-day involvement in management operations. The other types are in the middle, in approximate order along this continuum.

A second typology, offered by Richard Chait, William Ryan, and Barbara Taylor, has three types of boards. It is based on the role that the board members play in dealing with the organization's future.

The three types of governance are:

Type I: Fiduciary—These boards have as their principal focus the stewardship of resources. Its committees are often structured along the lines of their focus, such as fundraising, budgeting, auditing, investments, and program review.

Type II: Strategic—These boards create a strategic partnership with management to plan for the future. They look at the organization's strengths and weaknesses, how the outside environment is changing, and consider modifying the direction of the organization to respond. Type II boards focus more on "big thinking questions" such as "what is the future of the organization when there are likely changes in demographics or service needs?" rather than how much money should be allocated next year for staff conferences, and whether the amount spent this year for that line-item was appropriate—typical Type I questions.

Type III: Generative—These boards spend more time dreaming about the organization's future, thinking "outside of the box" to develop new ways to think about the organization's problems, how to deal with them in new ways (often through brainstorming sessions), and raising existential questions. They may consider problems that do not even exist yet, and where the organization fits into the big picture of accomplishing the core mission for which it was established.

The authors suggest that boards should be engaging in all three types of modes for peak performance, but that most boards tend to engage in one mode more than the others.

Forming a Board of Directors

One important requirement of a nonprofit organization is the formation of a board of directors. The board has the responsibility to set policy for the organization consistent with all applicable federal, state, and local laws and to see that the policies are implemented.

The size of the board should depend on the needs of the organization. If the board's role is strictly policy-making and the policies are implemented by a qualified staff, a small board might be appropriate. However, if extensive board time is required for fundraising or implementing programs, then a larger board is in order.

The number of board members is established in the bylaws. One effective technique is to set a minimum and maximum number of board members and to allow the board to determine its own size within these parameters. Then the board can start small and add members as the need arises. Note that Texas law requires a nonprofit organization to have at least three directors.

The term of board members must be included in the bylaws. Board members should have fixed terms of office. One common practice is for all board members to have three-year terms, with one-third of the members having their terms expire each year. In this way, board continuity is assured. Some boards allow their members to serve unlimited terms; other boards wish to limit the number to ensure new members with fresh ideas.

The election process should also be spelled out in the bylaws.

Many organizations have a nominating or governance committee that is responsible for recommending new board members to the full board. Additional candidates for board membership can be nominated either in advance or from the floor during the election.

The titles, duties, length of term, and process for the election of officers should be spelled out in the bylaws.

Organizational Officers

The elected officers of most organizations are similar:

Chairperson, Chair, or President
Convenes and leads the meetings of the organization. Appoints committee chairs. Either signs checks or delegates this duty to another individual.

Vice-Chairperson, Vice-Chair or Vice-President
Assumes the duties of the Chairperson, president or chair in his or her absence, or upon his or her death or resignation. In many organizations, is given specific responsibilities either in the bylaws or by vote. In some organizations, automatically becomes the next president. Some organizations have more than one; some may have a President-elect.

Secretary
Either takes minutes at the board meeting or approves the minutes if taken by another individual. Responsible for all official correspondence.

Treasurer
Responsible for finances of the organization. Usually makes financial reports to the board and signs checks. The actual responsibilities will depend upon whether the organization has staff who manage fiscal duties.

In some organizations, the officers are elected by the full membership. In others, the board of directors elects its own officers.

Recruiting Good Board Members

Many organizations are finding it more difficult than ever to attract excellent board members. This is due to many factors, such as the large increase in the number of nonprofit boards, the increasing demands of being in the work force, and the fact that upwardly mobile professionals often relocate.

In order to ensure excellence, many nominating committees meet several times during the year rather than just once, to search for potential board members. One effective technique is to strive for a diverse board (see Chapter 14), and to list the types of characteristics desired. Some might be:

- *Expertise*: Some board members should have personnel management, fiscal, fundraising, or legal expertise.

- *Ages*: It is helpful to have older people represented, as well as youth and individuals in between.

- *Races and Religions:* All major races and religions in the community should be represented on a diverse board.

- *Backgrounds:* It would be helpful if some board members had corporate backgrounds, some were government leaders, and others served on boards of other nonprofit groups.

- *Users of the service:* Many boards include representatives of the client population being served.

A short version oft repeated is that nominations committees should seek those who fulfill at least one, and ideally more than one, of the following three W's: wealth, wisdom, and work, but not an over-reliance on any single attribute.

The nominating committee or board development committee can search throughout the year for individuals with these characteristics, who are then asked if they want to be considered for board membership.

Each board should have a list of board member responsibilities. These might include attending board meetings on a regular basis, serving on at least one standing committee, and participating in fundraising. The list of duties should be provided to each prospective board member, and no board member should be elected who will not agree to meet these responsibilities.

Keeping Good Board Members

One technique for keeping good board members is to require all new board members to participate in an orientation program before they attend their first board meeting.

The first step in the process is to review materials that all board members should have received prior to the program. These include—

- articles of incorporation (Certificate of Formation in Texas)
- bylaws
- funding applications
- personnel, fiscal, and other board policies
- annual reports
- names, addresses, phone numbers, and biographical sketches of other board members and key staff members
- list of committees and committee duties
- minutes of the last several board meetings
- audits, budgets, and recent financial statements.

The second step is to hold a meeting with the board chair and the executive director. This provides an opportunity to ask questions about the materials received, visit the staff offices and programs, get an update of current issues, and review board member responsibilities. Other steps to encourage productivity of board members include—

- Give board members specific projects. A board member who serves as the chair of a committee or who has specific fundraising responsibilities is more likely to stay active.
- Keep board meetings interesting.
- Thank board members for their work.
- Have social events periodically, in addition to formal board meetings.

One other technique is to remove unproductive board members quickly and replace them with new and productive ones.

Other ways to increase board productivity include—

- having a policy in the bylaws that missing a specified number of board meetings without a reason will result in automatic dismissal.

- re-electing only board members who have been meeting their responsibilities.
- calling board members who have not been active to ask them if there are any problems. In some cases, the chairperson should ask for their resignation if they do not agree to meet board responsibilities.

Board Responsibilities

There are three functions of the board that are of paramount importance.

Perhaps the most important function of the board of directors is to define and safeguard the organization's mission and values. The board is expected to disapprove any proposed program or change of direction proposed by management, unless it formally votes to approve such a change. The board also should periodically review the programs and operations of the organization to assure they are consistent with the mission, and are effectively meeting the needs for which they were established.

The second most important is to hire (and then periodically evaluate, and if necessary, discipline or remove) the executive director, the chief paid staff person of the organization (who also may be referred to as the CEO, President, or President and CEO), if it has one. The board then makes assignments to that individual and monitors his or her performance. It is appropriate for the board or its Personnel Committee to do a formal performance appraisal of the CEO at least annually. The board approves salary scales and job descriptions for the other staff members, who are hired by the executive director. The board approves the personnel policies for the organization.

And third, the board should be responsible for setting policy with respect to the ethical values of the organization (for example, approving an ethics code), not delegating this important function to management.

Among other typical functions of the board of directors include—

Finance
The board approves budgets for the organization. No funds are expended unless the funds are included in a budget approved by the board. The board approves spending reports, which are submitted on a regular basis.

Fundraising
The board approves plans for special events and fundraising, and board members are expected to participate in these special events.

Planning

Board members approve short- and long-range plans for the organization. They then monitor the effectiveness of the organization's programs to see if they have met the goals outlined in the plans.

Board Development/Nominations

The board selects new board members and adopts procedures to see that excellent board members are selected and continue to serve.

Public Relations

Board members are aware of all of the organization's activities and encourage participation in appropriate activities by the community.

Advising

Board members advise the executive director on policy implementation as requested.

How Boards Function Effectively

Boards set policies through a majority vote of their members at board meetings, unless the bylaws provide otherwise. For boards with staff, one effective method of policy-making is to ask the staff to draft proposed policies. These policies are then sent to a board committee for review.

The chair of each committee should be a board member appointed by the board president. Members of committees are frequently selected by the committee chair and may include non-board members.

All committees are advisory, except that the bylaws may permit the executive committee to act on behalf of the board between board meetings. Once a committee approves a proposed policy, it is submitted to the board for approval. The board may delegate authority to committees to implement some decisions.

Board members who want a policy to be adopted begin the discussion by making a motion that it be approved. If another board member seconds the motion, discussion can begin; if not, the motion fails.

Once a motion is seconded, the chairperson opens the floor for discussion. Members are recognized by the chairperson before they may speak, and they can discuss only the motion on the floor. When the discussion has ended, the chairperson announces that a vote will be taken.

The easiest way to vote is by a show of hands. The secretary can then record the vote. If more than a majority approves a policy, it becomes the board's policy (unless the bylaws provide otherwise). It is the responsibility of the executive director to implement that policy.

The executive director receives instructions from the board at a board meeting. It is improper for individual board members to give assignments to any staff member without prior board authorization.

Holding High-Quality Board Meetings

One key factor in getting and keeping excellent board members is the quality of the board meetings. If board meetings are unproductive, board members tend to be unproductive.

An important technique for improving board meetings is to do as much planning *before the board meeting* as possible.

This might include:

• sending a notice of the date, time, and location of the meeting to the members several weeks before the meeting. Even if the board meets the same day of each month at the same place and time, a reminder notice is important.

• giving the board members the telephone number and email address of the individual (usually the chairperson) to contact if they cannot attend the meeting. This way, the chairperson can get input on important items from individuals who cannot attend the meeting. Moreover, if a quorum will not be present, the meeting can be canceled in advance.

• notifying members of important items to be discussed at the meeting. For major items, information or issue papers might be included in the meeting notice packet.

• including as many written items as possible with the meeting notice rather than distributing them at the meeting. These may include the minutes of the previous meeting and the treasurer's report, for example. Members then have an opportunity to read items before the meeting, and members who do not attend the meeting are kept informed more effectively.

- developing a preliminary agenda before the meeting. Committee chairs who will be asked to report at the meeting should be notified. Background reports should be developed for important issues.

The board meetings should start on time. Once the members know that every board meeting starts on time, it is much more likely that they will be prompt. Each board meeting should start with the distribution of a written agenda. The agenda should be as detailed as possible, listing each separate item on which to be voted.

Once the secretary announces that a quorum is present, the chairperson asks all those present if there are any additional items for the agenda. Thus, there will be no surprises, and the chairperson can run the meeting more effectively. The chairperson has the option of referring new items to committees or postponing items until future meetings.

A typical order of business at a board meeting is as follows:

- *Approval of the Minutes of the Previous Meeting.* A formal vote is needed to approve the minutes. Minutes should be distributed to all members and should not be read aloud at the meeting.

- *Chairperson's Report.* The chairperson should state before each item whether it is informational only or requires board action. The chairperson should remind the members that only policy-making recommendations require board action.

- *Executive Director's Report.* This report should be in writing. If it is lengthy, it should be distributed before the meeting. The executive director should then highlight important aspects of the written report and take questions.

- *Committee Reports.* Committee reports should be in writing unless they are very brief. After giving the report, the committee chair should make specific motions when board action is required. Only policy items require board action; no board action is required when the committee chair is simply providing information.

- *Unfinished Business.* The only items belonging in this section are ones raised at previous board meetings. The chairperson should remind the members when the item was raised originally and why it was postponed.

- *New Business.* Major items of business are discussed as part of the chairperson's report, executive director's report, or committee reports.

At the beginning of the meeting, members are asked if they have additional agenda items, and the chairperson has the option of placing some of these items under New Business.

- *Good and Welfare.* Many organizations provide an opportunity for members and guests to make short announcements, raise issues to be discussed at future meetings, or comment on items of interest.

- *Adjournment.* No formal action is needed. The chairperson announces the date, time, and place of the next meeting, reminds the members of steps to be taken before the meeting, such as committee meetings, and adjourns the board meeting.

After the board meeting, the minutes are sent to board members for their review. The minutes must include a list of attendees and the motions made and votes taken. Additional information may be included at the discretion of the board. Many organizations include only the minimum required, and the minutes do not include individual comments made at the meeting. Although the minutes need not be taken by the board secretary, they should be distributed over the signature of the board secretary.

Relationship Between Board and Staff Members

The board of directors sets policy for the organization. Several examples of the types of policies set by the board are provided above. The only way policy can be set is by a majority vote of the board at a board meeting (unless the bylaws provide otherwise).

The executive director of the organization attends all board meetings, and is responsible for implementing the policies set by the board. The executive director hires other staff members (whose salary ranges and job descriptions often, but not always, have been approved by the board) to assist in implementing these policies.

When an item arises at a board meeting, the chairperson rules whether the item is a policy matter. If so, a vote of the board is required in order for action to be taken. If the item is not a policy matter, no board vote is taken. The purpose of the discussion is to provide guidance to the executive director on non-policy matters.

Certain types of communications between board members and staff members are not appropriate. For example, individual board members may not give assignments to staff members. Assignments are given to the executive director by vote of the board at a board meeting. The executive director is responsible for assigning tasks to other staff members.

Staff members should not complain to individual board members about programs, assignments, or policies. Complaints should be made according to specific procedures established by the board.

When a board member volunteers to help out in the office, that person must be treated as a staff person and no longer wears the "board hat." The executive director remains the person to make assignments to that person.

Parliamentary Procedure

Board meetings of nonprofit organizations may be formally or informally conducted, but its decisions made consistent with law and its bylaws are legally binding and may be enforced by a court. At times, decision-making can be a contentious exercise. Without an acceptance of basic rules for conducting meetings by those who attend, a meeting could become highly dysfunctional, with meaningful decision-making becoming impossible. Members may all decide to speak at once, may disagree on whether a decision has really been made, or may refuse to accept decisions made by the chair. They may become frustrated when they do not feel that their participation has been treated respectfully or that they have been given a fair opportunity to voice their opinions and advocate for their positions.

Over the centuries, a set of standardized, basic rules for conducting meetings fairly has been developed. The standard used by many nonprofit organization boards is based on Roberts Rules of Order, first published in 1874. Henry M. Roberts, a West Point graduate, based his manual on a 15-page set of parliamentary rules he developed to help him, his wife, and others who served on the boards of various nonprofit organizations.

Roberts was influenced by the writings on the topic by Thomas Jefferson (Jefferson's Manual, which still serves as the rules of debate for the U.S. House of Representatives) and others that governed the debates of the Senate. These rules are based on rules of the English Parliament, from which the term "parliamentary procedure" derives its name.

Several other parliamentary procedure manuals are in use, among them the *Standard Code of Parliamentary Procedure* by Alice Sturgess (1950), George Demeter's *Demeter's Manual of Parliamentary Law and Procedure* (1969), and *Modern Parliamentary Procedure* by Ray E. Keesey (1974).

In nonprofit organizations, in which participants volunteer their time, it makes some sense to follow parliamentary procedure a bit more loosely compared to legislative bodies, keeping an eye on the objective of keeping meetings civil and assuring that decisions made by the board truly reflect either a consensus of members, or at least a majority. The more participants there are at a meeting, the more likely that increased formality will be productive.

There are five clear advantages to conducting meetings using parliamentary procedure, including—

1. There are procedures to ending debate, which in some cases could otherwise drag on interminably
2. Everyone with something to say has the opportunity to be heard
3. Debate on any issue remains on topic, and new topics are considered only after there is closure on the previous topic, or there is agreement to postpone closure
4. There is a procedure to reconsider decisions that may have been made in haste and without complete information
5. There are rules to deal with destructive, personal confrontations

Typically, board meetings are conducted by the President (or Chair) of the board. It helps when that individual has a basic understanding of parliamentary procedure, although some organizations will hire a Certified Professional Parliamentarian with specific knowledge of parliamentary procedure to advise the chair (see: *http://www.jimslaughter.com/handouts.cfm* for lots of free resources about conducting a meeting using parliamentary procedure).

Many organizations will indicate in their bylaws that meetings shall use a particular form of parliamentary procedure, such as—

The rules contained in the current edition of Robert's Rules of Order Newly Revised *shall govern the organization in all cases to which they are applicable and in which they are not inconsistent with these bylaws and any special rules of order the Society may adopt.*

For an explanation of Robert's Rules and details about how it works in practice, see the Robert's Rules website at: *https://robertsrules.com/*

Legal Responsibilities of Board Members

Being a board member of a nonprofit organization is not an honorary position. Texas law holds board members accountable for violating accepted standards of conduct and decision-making. Although there may be a gray area with respect to what constitutes illegal conduct, boards may make bad decisions with impunity. They are required, however, to have made those decisions believing at the time that they were in the best interests of the organization rather than themselves, and they were consistent with the organization's mission.

Among the legal duties of board members are—

- Duty of Care. They must take reasonable care when making decisions for the organization.
- Duty of Loyalty. They must act in the best interest of the organization.
- Duty of Obedience. They must act in accordance with the organization's mission.
- Avoid Conflicts of Interest. They must not participate in decision-making in which they have a personal interest that may constitute a conflict of interest.

Texas law (Chapter 22, Title 22, Texas Business Organizations Code) explicitly provides standards with respect to board member accountability:

> Sec. 22.221. GENERAL STANDARDS FOR DIRECTORS. (a) A director shall discharge the director's duties, including duties as a committee member, in good faith, with ordinary care, and in a manner the director reasonably believes to be in the best interest of the corporation.
> (b) A director is not liable to the corporation, a member, or another person for an action taken or not taken as a director if the director acted in compliance with this section. A person seeking to establish liability of a director must prove that the director did not act:
> (1) in good faith;
> (2) with ordinary care; and
> (3) in a manner the director reasonably believed to be in the best interest of the corporation.

"Ordinary care" is defined statutorily as "the care that an ordinarily prudent person in a similar position would exercise under similar circumstances." Compared to other states, this may not be a high standard.

A publication of the Attorney General of Pennsylvania provides similar guidance on the legal duties of board members of nonprofit organizations. *The Handbook for Charitable Nonprofit Organizations (https://www.attorneygeneral.gov/wp-content/uploads/2018/02/nonprofitbooklet.pdf)* includes the following general advice:

When performing their duties, board members, senior management and members of committees must use the degree of care, skill, caution and diligence that a prudent person would use in handling corporate affairs. Decision-makers are required to make reasonable inquiries when analyzing contracts, investments, business dealings, and other matters. An individual who is acting in conformance with this standard will:

- *attend and participate in board meetings on a regular basis;*
- *attend and participate in committee meetings when the individual is a member of the committee;*
- *diligently read, review, and inquire about material that affects the corporation;*
- *keep abreast of the affairs and finances of the corporation; and*
- *use independent judgment when analyzing matters that affect the corporation....*

Board members, trustees and senior management have a fiduciary responsibility when handling finances and investments. That simply means, they must exercise the degree of care, caution and diligence that prudent persons would exercise in handling their own personal investments and finances. Individuals who have or claim to have special knowledge or skills in the area of investment will be held to a higher standard. Fiduciaries who carelessly or negligently invest funds may be personally liable for any losses sustained.

Although the Pennsylvania Attorney General's interpretation of these requirements do not necessarily apply in Texas, they are based on universal legal principles and make sense regardless of the legal standard that might apply in the event the TexasAttorney General feels compelled to intervene when there is misconduct by board members of Texas nonprofit organizations.

Tips:

- Develop a list of typical decision areas that are likely to arise in the course of routine corporate operations and reach a board consensus on whether the decisions should be made by—

    a. the executive director alone;
    b. the executive director, in consultation with the board;
    c. the executive director, in consultation with the board chairperson;
    d. the board alone;

e. the chairperson alone; and

f. a committee of the board.

Review, revise, and update this list annually.

- Consider adopting a policy on the responsibilities and privileges of board members, and include a conflict-of-interest policy. A sample conflict of interest policy is provided in Form 1023 of the Internal Revenue Service, and more information may be found on the Web at: *https://www.irs.gov/pub/irs-pdf/i1023.pdf*

- Become familiar with the basic procedures of *Robert's Rules of Order.*

Chapter 5

Mission and Vision Statements

Synopsis: Mission and vision statements provide a foundation for your organization's future and help keep it focused on the purposes for which it was created. The mission statement includes the core organizational purpose. The vision statement describes the ideal future of the organization. Both are useful in maintaining the stability of organizations.

Every nonprofit organization should have a mission statement and a vision statement. Many nonprofit executives are confused about the difference between the two, and this is not surprising, since organizational consultants disagree among themselves about what they should contain.

The Mission Statement

The mission statement should be a succinct description of the basic purpose of the organization, including the nature of the work to be carried out, the reason the organization exists, and the clients and constituencies it is designed to serve. It may also include some principles and values that are to guide the organization, although these can be enumerated in a separate values/principles statement.

The mission statement serves two main purposes.

First, it is a basic document guiding decision-making for the organization. The mission statement can effectively place a constraint on decision-making that is inconsistent with the organization's core purpose, and thus provide a mechanism for organizational stability. Any decision made by an organization that would result in activities that contradict the mission statement should either not be implemented, or should require a major soul-searching by the organization's board of directors.

A second purpose is to provide the organization's board and staff with a useful short description of the organization. This permits all who work with the organization to be on the same page with respect to its core purpose. The mission statement serves an important public relations function by explaining to important stakeholders, such as funders, government regulators, and clients, what the organization is about.

Many mission statements contain two parts, although the first part is sufficient. The first part is often referred to as the "umbrella," a short overview of the purpose of the organization. For example, the Pennsylvania Jewish Coalition's mission is "to monitor legislative and regulatory developments in Harrisburg that affect Pennsylvania's organized Jewish community."

A second part of the mission statement, which many consider to be optional, provides more detail. One way to do this is to add the following after the umbrella: "In support of this mission, we..." followed by general, bullet-pointed objectives relating to who we are, who we serve, what benefits we provide to those we serve, and how we provide this benefit. For example, objectives that might be included are increasing public awareness about the organization's goals and objectives; meeting the needs of clients; providing quality services; and maintaining relationships with officials from the government, the media, the advocacy community, and the public.

The Vision Statement

The vision statement is related to, but clearly different from, the mission statement. Its purpose is to convey the ideal future of the organization—what it hopes to become in the eyes of its board, staff, and stakeholders. One purpose of the vision statement is to inspire those in the organization to achieve goals. Another is to help frame decisions made by the organization in the context of achieving these goals.

Among the issues that might be appropriate in a vision statement include the organization's place in society, its intended growth, its use of new technology, quality improvement, its reputation in the community, and how the public perceives the organization's effectiveness and efficiency. It also could include how it will serve as a good organizational citizen in the community, a measurement of the degree to which it hopes to contribute to solving (or mitigating) particular social problems, and whether and to what degree the problem is solved as a result of the organization's actions.

One of the best guides on the preparation of mission statements and vision statements is a 1996 book, *A Guide to Strategic Thinking: Building Your Planning Foundation* by George Morrisey (Jossey-Bass).

Examples of Mission and Vision Statements

The following are examples of mission and vision statements:

Mission and Vision Statements of the Pennsylvania Association of Nonprofit Organizations (reprinted with permission):

Mission - PANO amplifies the impact of the community benefit sector through advocacy, collaboration, learning and support.
Vision - PANO envisions vibrant, thriving communities where people reach their fullest potential.

Mission and Vision Statements of The Benton Middle School (Massachusetts) (reprinted with permission):

BMS Mission Statement
Our mission is to cultivate excellence and empower students for life-long success through a student centered learning environment.

Our Vision
A shared expectation of excellence

Vision Statement of California State University, Monterey Bay (CSUMB) (reprinted with permission):

California State University, Monterey Bay (CSUMB) is envisioned as a comprehensive state university which values service through high quality education. The campus will be distinctive in serving the diverse people of California, especially the working class and historically undereducated and low-income populations. It will feature an enriched living and learning environment and year-round operation. The identity of the university will be framed by substantive commitment to multilingual, multicultural, gender-equitable learning. The university will be a collaborative, intellectual community distinguished by partnerships with existing institutions both public and private, cooperative agreements which enable students, faculty, and staff to cross institutional boundaries for innovative instruction, broadly defined scholarly and creative activity, and coordinated community service.

The university will invest in preparation for the future through integrated and experimental use of technologies as resources to people, catalysts for learning, and providers of increased access and enriched quality learning. The curriculum of CSUMB will be student and society centered and of sufficient breadth and depth to meet statewide and regional needs, specifically those involving both inner-city and isolated rural populations, and needs relevant to communities in the immediate Tri-County region (Monterey, Santa Cruz, and San Benito). The programs of instruction will strive for distinction, building on regional assets in developing specialty clusters in such areas as: the sciences (marine, atmospheric, and environmental); visual and performing arts and related humanities; languages, cultures, and international studies; education; business; studies of human behavior, information, and communication, within broad curricular areas; and professional study.

The university will develop a culture of innovation in its overall conceptual design and organization, and will utilize new and varied pedagogical and instructional approaches including distance learning. Institutional programs will value and cultivate creative and productive talents of students, faculty, and staff, and seek ways to contribute to the economy of the state, the well-being of our communities, and the quality of life and development of its students, faculty, and service areas.

The education programs at CSUMB will:

- Integrate the sciences, the arts and humanities, liberal studies, and professional training;
- Integrate modern learning technology and pedagogy to create liberal education adequate for the contemporary world;
- Integrate work and learning, service and reflection;
- Recognize the importance of global interdependence;
- Invest in languages and cross-cultural competence;
- Emphasize those topics most central to the local area's economy and ecology, and California's long-term needs;
- Offer a multicultural, gender-equitable, intergenerational, and accessible residential learning environment.

The university will provide a new model of organizing, managing, and financing higher education:

- The university will be integrated with other institutions, essentially collaborative in its orientation, and active in seeking partnerships across institutional boundaries. It will develop and implement various arrangements for sharing courses, curriculum, faculty, students, and facilities with other institutions.
- The organizational structure of the university will reflect a belief in the importance of each administrative staff and faculty member, working to integrate the university community across "staff" and "faculty" lines.
- The financial aid system will emphasize a fundamental commitment to equity and access.

- *The budget and financial systems, including student fees, will provide for efficient and effective operation of the university.*
- *University governance will be exercised with a substantial amount of autonomy and independence within a very broad CSU system-wide policy context.*
- *Accountability will emphasize careful evaluation and assessment of results and outcomes.*

Our vision of the goals of California State University, Monterey Bay includes: a model pluralistic academic community where all learn and teach one another in an atmosphere of mutual respect and pursuit of excellence; a faculty and staff motivated to excel in their respective fields as well as to contribute to the broadly defined university environment. Our graduates will have an understanding of interdependence and global competence, distinctive technical and educational skills, the experience and abilities to contribute to California's high quality work force, the critical thinking abilities to be productive citizens, and the social responsibility and skills to be community builders. CSUMB will dynamically link the past, present, and future by responding to historical and changing conditions, experimenting with strategies which increase access, improve quality, and lower costs through education in a distinctive CSU environment. University students and personnel will attempt analytically and creatively to meet critical state and regional needs, and to provide California with responsible and creative leadership for the global 21st century.

Vision Statement of the Young Adult Library Services Association, a division of the American Library Association (reprinted with permission).

In every library in the nation, quality library service to young adults is provided by a staff that understands and respects the unique informational, educational and recreational needs of teenagers. Equal access to information, services and materials is recognized as a right not a privilege. Young adults are actively involved in the library decision-making process. The library staff collaborates and cooperates with other youth-serving agencies to provide a holistic, community-wide network of activities and services that support healthy development.

To ensure that this vision becomes a reality, the Young Adult Library Services Association (YALSA), a division of the American Library Association (ALA):

- *advocates extensive and developmentally appropriate library and information services for young adults, ages 12-18;*
- *promotes reading and supports the literacy movement;*
- *advocates the use of information and communications technologies to provide effective library service;*

- *supports equality of access to the full range of library materials and services, including existing and emerging information and communication technologies, for young adults;*
- *provides education and professional development to enable its members to serve as effective advocates for young people;*
- *fosters collaboration and partnerships among its individual members with library and information services that meet the unique needs and interests of young adults;*
- *encourages research and is in the vanguard of new thinking concerning the provision of library and information services to youth.*

Online Resources To Explore:

The Grantsmanship Center: How to Write a Mission Statement
https://www.tgci.com/sites/default/files/pdf/How%20to%20Write%20a%20 Mission%20Statement_1.pdf

Leader to Leader
https://onlinelibrary.wiley.com/journal/15315355

MissionStatements.com
http://www.missionstatements.com/nonprofit_mission_statements.html

Tips:

- Keep your mission statement focused on a narrow, specific purpose, to an extent that your organization will not be seen as potentially duplicative of other organizations in your area. In other words, carve out your own organizational niche, highlighting a unique service or serving a unique population of clients.

- Do not try to put too much into your mission statement; a single sentence is usually sufficient.

- Consider the mission and vision statements of similar organizations. You can find many examples on the internet.

- Periodically revisit your mission and vision statements and determine if they might be constraining your organization from adapting to new environmental conditions.

Chapter 6
Strategic Planning

Synopsis: Formal strategic planning is not for every organization. All stakeholders must be committed to successfully develop and implement a strategic plan. Although such plans require a major investment in money and time and have other institutional costs and risks, the benefits include enhancing the organization's ability to respond to internal and external threats.

Strategic planning is a formalized process by which an organization makes a study of its vision for the future, typically for three years or more from the present. A strategic plan is an important management tool that can help an organization's leaders to consider the effects of advances in technology; changing markets for its services; government funding cutbacks; or the emergence of other organizations (both for-profits and nonprofits) that provide similar, competing services.

An organization's CEO often is frequently so involved with putting out fires and responding to the exigencies of day-to-day operations that it is a luxury to set aside time to think about the position of the organization even a year into the future. An organization's board is often ill equipped to consider changes in structure and operations in the context of a regular board meeting.

Purpose of Strategic Planning

In his 1994 book *The Rise and Fall of Strategic Planning*, Henry Mintzberg lists four reasons organizations do strategic planning: to coordinate their activities, to ensure that the future is taken into account, to be rational, and to control. Strategic planning is designed to suggest remedies for organizational problems before they escalate. Deep cuts in government grants, changes in markets, advances in technology, competition from for-profit businesses, and changes in demographics in an organization's service area all crystallize the need to change the basic way an organization does business. Strategic planning is also a technique to systematically provide an institutionalized process to respond to changes in an organizational environment, whether or not there is a specific problem that needs to be addressed.

Virtually all successful large for-profit businesses engage in a formal strategic planning process. The conventional wisdom is that businesses that do so, regardless of whether they are for-profit or nonprofit, are more successful over time than those that do not. However, Mintzberg cites scores of academic studies that show mixed results as to the benefits of strategic planning in business and industry, and concludes that the value of strategic planning is nebulous at best.

Putting that aside, a periodic strategic planning process provides the framework for a long-term assessment of emerging threats, and the opportunity to develop creative strategies to respond to them. The intent here is not to encourage or discourage nonprofits from engaging in a formal strategic planning process; rather, it is to raise issues to consider in the event that this endeavor, for whatever reason, is under consideration.

Strategic planning requires the investment of both time and money. For most nonprofits, both are scarce. Thus, it is important that an organization's leaders systematically evaluate whether the benefits of preparing, updating, and implementing a periodic strategic plan outweigh the costs. Strategic plan preparation often involves the hiring of an outside consultant; resource-consuming meetings; and the involvement of board members, staff, and other stakeholders for an extended period of time.

The strategic planning process is fraught with danger. The contents of a final strategic plan often are totally at odds with the vision of the organization leader who first suggested preparing one. The planning committee dynamics are often uncontrollable by the people who provide the organization with leadership. An organization's leaders may be uncomfortable sharing with a professional outside consultant the organization's dreams and aspirations, its "dirty little secrets," and proprietary financial projections, and may be even more reticent with community members of the planning committee. Yet, many organizations that successfully complete a strategic planning process improve their performance. Participating board members feel a renewed connection and bond to both the organization and their colleagues. Organizations that do not plan for the future, whether in a formalized process or informal board retreats, often suffer the consequences.

Strategic planning in the for-profit sector has been popular for several decades. In the for-profit world, strategic planning has the advantage of having each member of the committee, virtually by definition, already in agreement on the basic mission of the organization; that is, in short, to make as much profit as possible. There will be differences, of course, as to the methods used to accomplish this. In a nonprofit, there is not always agreement on the mission from the outset. In a hospital situation, for example, some planning committee members may view the mission as providing quality health care to the community. Others may feel it is to teach medical students, advance life-saving technology, increase "market share" by gobbling up other health care institutions, or serve populations not served by other institutions.

In a for-profit setting, the outcomes are easily measurable—net profit and market share are statistics easily compiled. In the nonprofit sector, consumer satisfaction, community benefit, and image in the community often are considered more important than bottom-line net revenue, and they are difficult to measure satisfactorily. In the nonprofit sector, board members may actually be concerned if the institution is making too much net revenue and not providing services to sectors of the market that would clearly result in revenue shortfalls. It is the nature of nonprofits that the institution is not motivated by private profit motive and, in theory, this can create conflicts. As a result of government cutbacks, tensions are mounting within nonprofit boards as they wrestle with difficult decisions concerning how to ease the financial crunch while maintaining traditional markets.

Making the Decision to Develop a Strategic Plan

The motivation for initiating a strategic plan comes from many sources:

Board Members. Board members who have participated in successful strategic planning as a result of their service on other nonprofit boards are often the source for initiating a strategic plan. Board members who run their own businesses or work for for-profit companies that routinely develop strategic plans also may raise this issue. Many who serve on nonprofit boards see strategic planning as a management and governance tool equal in importance to budgeting, and they cannot imagine an organization that does not initiate a formal process to look inward at least once every half-decade.

Funders. Some funders require the development of a strategic plan before they make grants to nonprofit charities. These funders want evidence that their contributions will be used prudently and cost-effectively and will influence the direction of the organization. A strategic plan developed as a result of such a requirement by a funder would obviously highlight changes in the organization's programs that are the direct result of the contribution.

Retirement of a Long-Term CEO. Many nonprofits were started by visionary leaders who ran the organizations from the seat of their pants. This "old school" of doing business may no longer be valid. New leaders, many with MBAs, believe that nonprofit organizations are businesses, and the same management techniques they learned in business school are applicable to the philanthropic sector. The "new school" of doing business recognizes that the bottom line remains the principal concern of the organization, whether or not the bottom line is interpreted as the net revenue at the end of the year or the number of satisfied clients served. The old school organization executive is often skeptical, if not fearful, of strategic planning. Perhaps his or her vision has never been challenged, and a formal process to evaluate from top to bottom, from the mission statement on down, is a threat to executive autonomy. In some cases, that skepticism is justified.

Once a new generation assumes the mantle of leadership, there is motivation to rebuild from the ground up, starting with the mission statement and proceeding, in some extreme cases, to changing the model of the copying machine. A strategic plan is often the vehicle for the new leadership to assert its authority and provide a mechanism for a higher level of executive accountability.

Organization Trauma. More often than not, it is an organizational crisis that triggers the decision for a strategic plan when an organization has no regular process to prepare one. The resignation or firing of a CEO is a traumatic event for any nonprofit. Sometimes, this event has occurred because of underlying unresolved issues and problems that may have developed and been inadequately addressed over many years. In the case of the involuntary separation, the organization's leadership has the opportunity to reshape the organization before a new executive takes over and molds its direction. Other traumatic events that may trigger the initiation of a strategic plan are the loss of a major funder; the establishment of competition from another nonprofit or for-profit; major damage to, or aging of, the organization's physical plant; liability suits; or quantum advances in technology that call into question the future demand for services.

Benefits of Strategic Planning

1. **It permits discussion of issues in a proactive rather than reactive mode.** Usually developed in an atmosphere that encourages creativity and brainstorming, the strategic plan may not only include concrete directions, but also provide an institutional set of core values. In a typical board meeting, there is simply no time to engage in a meaningful discussion about the long-term future of an organization. Many nonprofits are operating on the edge of financial chaos, often one failed grant application away from having to lay off staff or fold entirely.

2. **It requires an action plan to solve real problems faced by an organization.** The action plan is a template that the staff can use to implement the policies and desires of the board. Many CEOs complain that the board helps with solving problems, but fails to provide direction on the core values of the organization. A strategic plan explicitly includes those core values, and assists the CEO in creative strategies for solving current problems and anticipating future ones.

3. **It provides a formal mandate for the reallocation of resources to respond to changing conditions, and the means to obtain additional resources if required.** A successful strategic planning process that develops an aggressive plan to attack problems often energizes a moribund board.

4. **It builds inter-board relationships that might not otherwise exist, and creates a partnership among the board chairperson, board members, staff, funders, and other stakeholders.** Each has a role that is defined in the plan and, if bought into, the added responsibilities increase the available resources of the organization. The social contact that occurs at many board retreats, particularly those designed in bucolic settings away from the hustle and bustle of the organization, cement personal relationships among participants. This improves the bond between the organization and its leadership.

5. **It provides a mechanism for the board, staff, and organization stakeholders to become more informed about the activities and problems faced by the organization.** It promotes, in many cases, a frank discussion by the organization's chief executive of problems that might not be shared in a conventional board meeting context. Many CEOs welcome the process in that it takes a burden off their shoulders and shares it with the organization's "owners" and constituents.

6. **It provides an opportunity to focus on the forest rather than the trees.** It is easy for a CEO to become lost in the mundane issues of personnel, budgeting, fundraising, office management, board relations, and public relations, and virtually ignore issues relating to the actual purpose and mission of the nonprofit.

Costs of Strategic Planning

1. **Money.** Serious strategic planning costs money, a scarce resource for most nonprofits. Many nonprofits recognize that it is useful to have a trained, dispassionate consultant to assist in the planning process. There are costs to schedule planning meetings and travel to those meetings. Many organizations recognize the value of eliminating outside distractions to aid brainstorming, and thus schedule planning meetings at staff retreats held at attractive, isolated campgrounds, conference centers, business resorts, or hotels. There are costs of photocopying and printing all of the planning documents. There are opportunity costs, as well, because staff and board resources are diverted from other duties.

2. **Time.** Any realistic strategic planning process requires the allocation of precious staff and board resources. Meeting preparation, meeting attendance, minutes, preparation of draft and final strategic plans, and hiring a consultant all take time. It is not uncommon for a strategic planning process to take more than a year.

3. **Potential bad will.** As with any process, things can go wrong. Bad group dynamics can result in painful meetings and destructive outcomes. A group may spend an entire four-hour meeting arguing over trivial words in a mission statement. This can be painfully frustrating for committee members more interested in developing an action plan to solve problems. Strategic planning may bring board factions into collision, and meetings can degenerate into a test of wills. This may be healthy in the context of a committee rather than having a drag-out fight at a board meeting, but it means that to have a constructive planning process, personal baggage must be dealt with first. If the final strategic plan is not implemented, board members who participated may feel that the organization wasted their time, and may not be as likely to participate in future efforts, or even may resign from the board. Current staff members may feel threatened that their jobs are at risk, and may look for other employment.

4. **Loss of Initiative.** A formal strategic plan may diminish an executive's initiative and quick response to changing conditions, because the preferred course of action is not in the strategic plan. The strategic plan may become outdated quickly and stifle a more appropriate response to changing conditions that were not anticipated in the plan. In addition, strategic planning often involves the board not just in setting objectives and outcomes, but also in determining the methods that should be used to achieve those objectives and outcomes. Many feel that this is the role of staff, not the board, and making it the role of the board takes away the flexibility necessary for executive staff to function effectively.

A Sample Strategic Planning Model

This chapter gives a cursory review of what a strategic plan is, its costs and benefits, some advantages and disadvantages, and some issues that often arise when nonprofits consider initiating a strategic plan. It is recommended that other specific resources be consulted when exploring the need for a strategic planning process, and several excellent sources are included in the bibliography. The following is one model for developing a strategic plan and is a hybrid put together from several theoretical models.

Step 1. Decide whether to develop a strategic plan.

Consider the costs and benefits mentioned earlier in this chapter, and also the following questions:

- Is there enough time and money to allocate for this planning process now?
- Is the organization prepared to implement whatever plan eventually is approved, or will it sit on the shelf?
- Do we have a commitment from the executive director, board chairperson, board members, and other stakeholders to develop a plan, or will we just be going through the motions?
- Are the organization's short-term problems so overwhelming that the organization is wasting time planning for the future when its continued existence is seriously threatened by current problems?

Step 2. Build the infrastructure necessary to develop a plan.

- **Appoint a planning committee of the board.** Include creative board members, funders, the CEO, chief financial officer, clients, and opinion makers from the community. Consider that any committee of more than 10 becomes unmanageable. Some strategic planners recommend that the entire board serve on the committee.

- **Compile and distribute articles and related material on strategic planning to the entire board.** (For information on reprints or rights to photocopy this chapter or other copyrighted materials, contact the publisher of the material.)

- **Decide on whether the facilitator/consultant will be a board member or a paid or volunteer consultant.** A board member already knows a lot about the organization, its strengths and weaknesses, its personnel, and all other members of the committee. On the other hand, that board member brings with him or her prejudices about colleagues and staff, and often has a point of view or hidden agenda that is not objective. A private strategic planning consultant has the experience to keep the discussion focused and follow the agenda. There are many consultants who have experience working with nonprofit agencies in designing the planning process itself, participating in orientation sessions for the planning committee, serving as a referee for dispute resolution, helping the committee reach consensus when that is desired, neutralizing oppositional or disruptive participants, and providing technical assistance.

A good consultant can organize the process and provide logistical support so the board and staff will not be absorbed by the planning process mechanics. On the other hand, a bad consultant may influence the process beyond what is desirable, and constrain the participation of committee members. One must be careful to ensure that the plan, if written by a consultant, is not a tepid re-write of the plan the consultant developed for a previous client, which may have only minimal relevance to the current client.

It is a good idea to informally survey comparable organizations to check out potential strategic planning consultants. Statewide associations may also be helpful in identifying consultants. Of course, it is vital that any contract between the organization and the consultant spell out exactly what services are required, the timetable, and the level of participation required by the consultant.

Step 3. Decide how many years the strategic plan will cover.

In general, small nonprofits choose a shorter time frame than larger nonprofits, perhaps two-to-four years for smaller agencies, compared to larger institutions, which prepare five-year plans.

Step 4. Put in writing the timetable and the process.

This includes the steps that are required and who is responsible for accomplishing each task. Among the tasks are:

• appointing the committee
• hiring a consultant or facilitator
• leading the orientation of the planning committee
• choosing the meeting site
• scheduling the meetings
• writing the first draft of the plan
• providing the procedures to review and revise the draft
• writing the final plan
• developing the process for the planning committee to approve the final plan
• formulating the review and the process for the full board's approval of the final plan.

Step 5. Prepare a memo on what is expected of the strategic planning process.

This memo to the planning committee should highlight the major problems that are to be resolved by the strategic plan, such as how to review and update the mission statement, how to respond to potential cuts in government funding, how to respond to the new location of a for-profit competitor, how to deal with a change in the demographics of the people in the area served by the organization, and so on. The memo should note whether the planning report should be a consensus document (which does not require unanimity) or if majority rules after all points of view are heard.

Step 6. Have the board endorse the planning process, and allocate funds necessary for it to proceed.

Step 7. Appoint the committee, appoint or hire the facilitator/consultant, send out orientation materials, and schedule the first meeting.

The first meeting

The first meeting is usually an orientation session, which includes some of the following five components:

1. A review of the purpose of the committee, the timetable, future meeting schedule, and meeting the facilitator.

2. A review of the organization's current mission, history, short-term problems, long-term threats, staff resources, programs, activities, strengths and weaknesses, major successes and failures, core values of the organization, financial status, and future commitments. The CEO and CFO should be present to answer questions from the planning committee and to ask questions of the facilitator to establish ground rules for the planning process.

3. An analysis of the needs of the stakeholders, including those currently receiving service, and scenarios about how those needs may change. For example, is the population served by the organization changing demographically? Is government funding likely to drop? Is the community becoming poorer, limiting future fee-for-service revenue and requiring more non-fee revenue?

4. An analysis of institutional limits: population served by geography, age group, and income level.

5. An identification of what in the above can be changed by the organization as a result of strategic planning and what is the result of forces beyond the control of the organization.

The second meeting

The second meeting begins the brainstorming of the committee. This meeting examines the mission statement and reviews potential changes to that statement which—in some cases—might have been unrevised for decades. The facilitator may list various problems on the horizon, with the planning committee serving as a focus group—such as funding problems, changes in markets, competitors, outside threats from changing social, economic, political, or technological conditions, or demand for services. The planning committee is given a homework assignment to come to the third meeting with suggestions for solving these problems.

The third meeting

The third meeting consists of brainstorming on action strategies that will solve the problems identified at the first and second meetings. The facilitator lists each strategy and includes a table with the costs and benefits of each, the probability of success, and the pros and cons. Each strategy for each problem may be ranked based on the committee's assessment as to the value of the strategy.

The fourth meeting

The committee develops an action plan, with a timetable for implementation that includes coming up with the resources necessary to implement the action plan. The plan also includes a procedure to review the progress made in implementing the plan.

In the above model, a draft strategic plan can be accomplished with four three-hour meetings.

In *Managing a Nonprofit Organization,* Thomas Wolff outlines six levels in the linear model of strategic planning. In the linear model, the planning committee considers one level before proceeding to the next. This contrasts with the integrated planning model, which provides for many of these levels to be considered simultaneously, recognizing that the end result is interdependent upon each of the earlier levels.

Level 1. The planners consider the mission statement, which describes the purpose the organization is trying to achieve.

Level 2. Organization goals are developed, providing the general direction in which the organization intends to go.

Level 3. Objectives and targets are set, indicating the outcomes the organization hopes to achieve.

Level 4. Strategies are formulated to meet the objectives and targets. These are the methods and ways the organization plans to achieve those outcomes.

Level 5. An action plan is developed to implement the strategies.

Level 6. An evaluation is performed after implementation, to review whether the outcomes were achieved and whether the strategies were successful.

For example, a hypothetical nursing home might have a planning document that, in an abridged form, is as follows:

Level 1. To provide quality long-term care services to the aging population of Anytown, for the purpose of improving the quality of life for those who need institutional care.

Level 2. To reduce the operating deficit and become the long-term care institution of choice in the community by improving quality of care.

Level 3. Increase non-fee revenue by 50%, and improve the cash-flow situation by taking advantage of accounting productivity. Improve government reimbursement by 25% within three years.

Increase the number of private pay residents from 30% to 50% within the next five years.

Level 4. Hire a development staff member.

Hire a lobbyist to assist the statewide association to advocate for increases in Medicaid reimbursement.

Hire a marketing associate to place advertisements in publications read by active, upscale, middle-aged persons whose parents may be in need of long-term care services.

Level 5. Investigate the feasibility of marketing charitable gift annuities, and hire a consultant by July 15 to develop a program for residents and their families.

Aggressively go after accounts receivable, delay accounts payable for an additional 30 days, eliminate programs that are not profitable, increase fee-for-service revenues; increase fundraising; become entrepreneurial by selling clothing and health care equipment on the organization's website.

Place an advertisement in the newsletter of the state chapter of the American Society of Association Executives to hire a registered lobbyist.

Hire a marketing associate by June 15, and use endowment funds for seed money. Assume the new staff member will generate at least enough income to finance his or her salary.

Level 6. One year after final approval of this report, require the executive director to prepare a progress report on whether the goals outlined in Level 2 are being achieved, and what mid-course corrections to Level 5 are required in order to meet the targets of Level 3.

The process of planning each level can be discussed and refined for two hours or nine months. The parameters differ, obviously, for a hospital with a half-billion dollars in gross revenue, compared to a charity with $50,000 in gross revenue.

The actual plan may be written by the facilitator, the chairperson of the planning committee, or staff in consultation with the board and facilitator. In every case, the planning committee should review a draft of the plan before submitting its final version to the board. The board reserves the power to approve, disapprove, approve with changes, or send the plan back for revision.

Some of the changes that may be recommended by a nonprofit organization strategic plan are:

1. a mission change
2. a change in the character of services provided
3. a plan to expand or downsize staff
4. a plan to expand or sell capital equipment and/or physical plant
5. a plan to expand fundraising
6. a plan to retrain staff
7. a plan to move the organization's location
8. a plan to seek a merger with similar organizations
9. a communications plan to improve or renovate the organization's public image
10. a plan to hire a lobbyist, or form a statewide association representing agencies with similar problems or uncertainties
11. a plan to establish a for-profit subsidiary
12. a plan to seek, or refuse, government grants
13. a plan to liquidate the organization
14. a plan to professionalize the organization, or deprofessionalize it—e.g., a decision by a hospital to substitute nurse aides where registered nurses were used formerly

15. a plan to change the governance of the organization—increase or decrease board membership, change quorum requirements, change voting requirements, change committee structure, change the powers of officers
16. a plan to change the compensation structure to reward and improve productivity
17. a plan to change the organization's market niche
18. a plan to change into a for-profit
19. a plan to modernize the name of the organization.

Some components of a strategic plan may be:

1. a five-year projection of staffing patterns
2. a five-year projected budget
3. sources of revenue to implement changes required by the plan
4. a marketing strategy
5. a schedule for periodically updating the strategic plan
6. a schedule for evaluating whether the plan is being implemented effectively and whether the strategies provided in the plan are successful
7. a physical plant/equipment plan.

Tips:

- Don't let a strategic plan sit on the shelf after investing time and money developing it.

- Know when to let a strategic plan sit on the shelf when conditions have become so turbulent or changed that it would not make sense to follow it blindly.

Chapter 7
Nonprofit Organization Ethics

by Gerald Kaufman and Gary Grobman

Synopsis: Nonprofit charities have a special obligation, both legal and moral, to uphold the highest standards of ethical practice, to be accountable to their boards and the public, to avoid conflicts of interest, and to treat their employees with dignity.

Nonprofit organizations, especially those qualified under section 501(c)(3) of the Internal Revenue Code, occupy a special and unique place in American society. Their uniqueness has many attributes.

All such organizations are supported by the nation's taxpayers: they are exempt from federal and state income taxes. Contributors, for the most part, can deduct their contributions from their federal and state income taxes in most states; they are eligible to have their postage subsidized by the federal government; and many are exempt from state and local sales and property taxes.

Ethics in the Nonprofit Environment

Among the general categories of ethical conflicts that are endemic to the nonprofit sector are accountability, conflict of interest, and disclosure. Specific issues of interest are relationships between board members and the staff; board members and the organization (such as business relationships); self-dealing; charitable solicitation disclosure; the degree to which donations finance fundraising costs rather than programs; the accumulation of surpluses; outside remuneration of staff; the appropriateness of salaries, benefits, and perquisites; and merit pay. For example, pay based on income received rather than mission accomplished is considered unethical. Staff members of charities are under more of an obligation not to exploit their position on staff for personal gain (such as charging a fee for outside speaking engagements on their own time) than their for-profit counterparts. Unlike their for-profit or government counterparts, charities generally are under an ethical, if not legal, obligation not to accumulate large surpluses. Salaries, benefits, and perquisites must be "reasonable," and prior to the promulgation by the IRS of regulations relating to this and other "excess benefit" transactions, the legal requirements applying to these issues were in a gray area.

The following sections include some issues relating to ethics that are appropriate for nonprofit boards and staff to consider.

Accountability

Accountability often is overlooked in discussions about ethics. Because of the unique status of 501(c)(3) organizations, they have a special obligation to the public to be accountable for the results of their activities that justify their tax exemptions and other privileges. Organizations should continually challenge themselves by asking if the outcomes produced are worth the public investment.

Nonprofit boards of directors have a special obligation to govern with integrity. Governing with integrity means that the organization recognizes that it is accountable to the public, to the people it serves, and to its funders. Accountability includes the concept that nonprofit organizations exist only to produce worthwhile results in furtherance of their missions.

In addition, accountability encompasses a core system of values and beliefs regarding the treatment of staff, clients, colleagues, and community. Yet, organizational survival needs too often undercut core values. Although everyone in the organization is responsible, it is the board's ultimate responsibility to ensure that its values are not compromised, and that the activities are conducted within acceptable limits.

Staff will sometimes pursue grants and contracts, or engage in direct solicitation campaigns, for the primary purpose of growing. This subtle issue of accountability is seldom discussed. Boards sometimes ask whether the executive director "grew the organization" as the primary criterion for measuring success. Boards have an obligation to ascertain that all activities support the organization's mission.

Conflict of Interest

A potential conflict of interest occurs any time organizational resources are directed to the private interests of a person or persons who have an influence over the decision to use those resources. Examples might include the leasing of property owned by a relative of the executive director or a board member, the board awarding itself a salary, the organization hiring a board member to provide legal representation, or the executive director hiring a relative or a board member's relative.

A conflict also can occur when the person (or persons) making a decision expects something in exchange from the person in whose favor the decision is made. One example is the case in which an executive director retains a direct mail firm, and the executive director's spouse is hired by that direct mail firm shortly thereafter.

With regard to board members, the cleanest approach is to adopt a policy that does not allow any board member to profit from the organization. It is the duty of every board member to exercise independent judgment solely on behalf of the organization. For example, suppose a board member who owns a public relations business successfully argues that the nonprofit needs a public relations campaign and then is hired to conduct the campaign. The board member's self-interest in arguing for the campaign will always be subject to question.

Suppose, in the above example, the board member offers to do the campaign at cost, and that is the lowest bid. It may be that even "at cost," the board member's firm benefits, because the campaign will pay part of the salary of some staff members or cover other overhead. It may be perfectly appropriate to accept the board member's offer, even though it is a conflict of interest. However, it is absolutely essential that the board have a procedure in place to deal with these types of issues.

Some organizations permit financial arrangements with board members, provided that the member does not vote on the decision. Given the good fellowship and personal relationships that often exist within nonprofit boards, such a rule can be more for show and without substance.

A similar conflict can occur in the awarding of contracts to certain individuals who do not serve on the board. There may be personal reasons for one or more members of the board or the executive director to award contracts to particular persons, such as enhancing their personal or professional relationships with that person.

There are instances in which it is appropriate to have a contract with an insider, such as when a board member offers to sell equipment to the organization at cost, or agrees to sell other goods or services well below market value. Here, too, the organization should assure itself that these same goods or services are not available as donations.

It is essential for the board to confront and grapple with these issues and adopt a written policy to govern potential conflicts of interest, in order to avoid the trap of self-dealing or its appearances. Many potential abuses are not only unethical, but also illegal as a result of the *Taxpayer Bill of Rights 2,* enacted in July 1996 (Public Law 104–168, 110 Stat. 1452).

Disclosures

There is much disagreement within the nonprofit sector regarding how much disclosure is required to those who donate to charitable nonprofits. The first obligation of every organization is to obey the laws and regulations governing disclosure. Nonprofits have a legal and ethical obligation to report fundraising costs accurately on their IRS Form 990, to obey the requirement regarding what portion of the cost of attending a fundraising event is deductible, and to comply with state charitable registration laws and regulations.

Nonprofits face a more difficult ethical issue when deciding how much disclosure to make that is not required by law, particularly if the organization believes that some people may not contribute if those disclosures are made. One controversial example of this is Kiva *(https://www.kiva.org/)*, which many feel does excellent work in facilitating micro-loans to deserving entrepreneurs. But, among other criticisms, the organization has been criticized for making it appear that potential investors choose to whom to make loans, when in most cases, the entrepreneur the investor chooses as a recipient of a loan has already received a loan, and the investor's funds are channeled to others. (See: *https://www.nytimes.com/2009/11/09/business/global/09kiva.html?_r=0)*

In the for-profit corporate world, the Securities and Exchange Commission demands full, written disclosure of pertinent information, no matter how negative, when companies are offering stock to the public. There is no comparable agency that regulates charitable solicitations by nonprofits. Nonprofits must be very careful to disclose voluntarily all relevant information and to avoid the kind of hyperbole that misrepresents the organization.

Another difficult issue is whether fundraising costs should be disclosed at the point of solicitation. The costs of telemarketing campaigns or maintaining development offices are sometimes 80%, or even more, of every dollar collected. Some argue that people would not give if these costs were disclosed. Others argue that if the soliciting organization cannot justify these costs to the public (and in many cases, they are not justifiable), then the organization is not deserving of support.

Accumulation of Surplus

If the funds of a charitable nonprofit are to be used for charitable purposes, what is a reasonable amount of surplus to accumulate? The Wise Giving Alliance has suggested a ceiling of three times the current year's expenses or the next year's budget, whichever is greater.

Organizations should consider the circumstances under which it is appropriate to disclose to prospective donors the amount expected to be used to accumulate a surplus. Clearly, if a major purpose of the solicitation is to build a surplus, that should be disclosed.

Outside Remuneration

Executive directors and other staff often are offered honoraria or consulting fees for speeches, teaching, providing technical assistance, or other work. The ethical issue is whether the staff person should turn the fees over to the nonprofit employer or be able to retain them. Potential conflicts can be avoided if the policy is based on the principle that all reasonably related outside income belongs to the organization. For example, an executive director's honorarium for speaking to a national conference as a representative of the organization or an expert in his or her field would revert to the employer, but his or her fee for playing in a rock band on weekends could be individual income.

The argument for this policy is that the line between the employer's and the employee's personal time is not so easy to draw. An argument against this principle is that employees' usage of their spare time should be of no concern to the employer. Is it ethical for an employee to exploit the knowledge and experience gained on the job for personal gain? Are we buying only time from our employees, or do we expect that we are getting the undivided professional attention of that person?

If the board or executive director is silent on this issue, the assumption is that earning outside income is a private matter. It makes sense to have a clear policy on outside income before an employee is hired.

Salaries, Benefits, and Perquisites

Determining an appropriate salary structure is perhaps the most difficult ethical issue in the nonprofit sector. Ethical considerations arise at both the high and low ends of the salary spectrum.

If an organization is funded by grants from foundations and corporations or by government contracts, the funders can and do provide some restraint on excessive salaries. However, if the nonprofit is funded primarily by individual donations or fees for service, such constraints (other than, perhaps, those relating to the intermediate sanctions regulations of the Internal Revenue Service) are absent.

Boards fall into an ethical trap if they reward executive directors based on the amount of income received, rather than on how well they have accomplished the organization's mission. A board can consider many criteria when setting the salary of the executive director. These include the size and complexity of the organization, what others in similar organizations are earning, and whether the salary is justifiable to the public. Some nonprofits include proportionality in their salary structures by limiting the highest paid to a factor of the lowest paid (e.g., the highest can be no more than three times the lowest).

As a result of enactment of the *Taxpayers Bill of Rights 2*, there are now legal as well as ethical restrictions on paying excessive compensation. Ethical management of employees requires that each person be treated with dignity and respect, paid a salary that can provide a decent standard of living, and given a basic level of benefits, including health insurance coverage. A potential critical conflict arises when a charitable organization working to spread its social values treats its staff in a way that conflicts with its organizational values.

Personal Relationships

Nonprofit organization executives and board members must not engage in sexual harassment, or behavior that makes an employee feel uncomfortable, at best, or threatened and intimidated, at worst. Employees should be treated fairly, which among other things, means that no favoritism should be permitted with respect to work assignments. Discrimination should not be permitted, even if it does not meet the threshold required for legal violations.

Those who supervise employees should not be having any sexual or romantic relationship with those they supervise, consensual or otherwise. Having such relationships is a conflict of interest, and creates the potential for thorny legal and management problems. The organization's policy should be in writing as part of the personnel policy.

Nepotism—the hiring of family members—should be prohibited. Nonprofit executives and board members should seek to keep personal friendships from influencing professional judgment. Managers should not make it difficult for employees to maintain an appropriate work-family balance. Privacy and confidentiality of workers should be respected. A diverse workforce means that cultural differences among staff should be respected to the maximum extent possible (see Chapter 14).

Standards for Excellence

In 1998, the Maryland Association of Nonprofit Organizations initiated an ethics and accountability code for the nonprofit sector entitled *Standards for Excellence®*. Along with the code, the program includes educational components, a voluntary accreditation process, and a basic legal and regulatory review. As a result of several major grants, the program has been expanded beyond Maryland to include nonprofit support organizations five other states— Alabama, Delaware, Ohio, Oklahoma, and Pennsylvania. These are known as "Replication Partners." There are also national Replication Partners, according to the program's website— Center for Public Justice, Sacred Sector, Center for Nonprofit Advancement, The Arc of the United States, the American Nurses Association, Momentum Nonprofit Partners, and the Leadership Roundtable. The Santa Clara University Markkula Center for Applied Ethics is a Regional Replication Partner. The National Standards for Excellence Institute administers the program for all partners and for nonprofits in states that do not have a licensed partner.

The 67 performance standards for both research best practices and legal and regulatory requirements are grouped in six areas:

- Mission, Strategy, and Evaluation

- Leadership: Board, Staff, and Volunteers

- Legal Compliance and Ethics

- Finance and Operations

- Resource Development

- Public Awareness, Engagement, and Advocacy

The focus of the program is to provide education and resources to encourage nonprofits to adopt ethical and legal practices. Organizations choosing to become accredited demonstrate that they adhere to the standards by participating in a 3-phase review process, which includes peer reviewers examining all practices. The process includes submitting an application documenting their compliance with the standards, as well as paying a fee and moving through the 3-phase review process. Once the peer-review panel affirms that the organization meets the standards, the statewide Standards for Excellence Committee does a final review and approves the organization. The organization receives a Seal of Excellence, with the expectation that having the Seal will provide the organization with increased credibility with donors and grantmakers. Organizations desiring to ensure that all legal and regulatory components are in place may apply for the Basic Legal and Regulatory Review and become recognized as "Standards Basics" approved organizations. Organizations achieving approval under Accreditation or "Standards Basics" receive national recognition on GuideStar.org. Organizations are accredited for an initial 3-year period, must reapply for a 3-year renewal, and then may renew for 5-year periods. There is a process for accredited organizations to have that accreditation revoked if they are found to have violated standards after an investigation by the program.

The full set of standards for national certification can be found at: *https:// standardsforexcellence.org/Home-2/code*

Among the standards are:

- The board should have stated performance expectations and hold board members accountable for attendance at meetings, participation in fundraising activities, committee service, and awareness of program activities.

- On average, over a 5-year period, a charity should assure that the fundraising revenues as compared with expenses have a greater than 3:1 ratio.

- Fundraisers, whether or not they are employees or independent consultants, should not be compensated based on a percentage of the amount raised or some other commission formula.

- Nonprofits must be aware of and comply with all applicable federal, state, and local laws. This may include, but is not limited to, complying with laws and regulations related to IRS filing requirements, governance, human resources, licensing, financial accountability, taxation, valuation of in-kind gifts, unrelated business income, document retention and destruction, related entities, data security, accessibility, fundraising, lobbying, and advocacy.

Taxpayer Bill of Rights 2—Intermediate Sanctions

The *Taxpayer Bill of Rights 2* was signed into law by President Clinton on July 30, 1996. The principal purpose of this law is to punish individuals affiliated with charities and social welfare organizations who are participating in financial abuses, and to provide the government with a sanction other than simply revoking the charity's exemption status. The law also includes expanded public disclosure requirements for annual federal tax returns.

Previous law required charities to make their 990 tax returns available for public inspection, but did not require that copies be provided. The law was changed to require that if a person requests a copy of the 990 in person, it must be immediately provided for a reasonable fee for copying. If the request is made in writing, it must be provided for a reasonable copying and postage fee within 30 days. Organizations that make these documents "widely available," such as posting them on the internet, are exempt, although they still must make the document available for public inspection. The law expands the disclosure that must be made on the 990, adding information about excess expenditures to influence legislation, any political expenditures, any disqualified lobbying expenditures, and amounts of "excess benefit" transactions.

The law raises the fine for failure to file a timely 990 from $10 per day to $20 per day, with a maximum of $10,000. Higher fines apply to organizations with gross receipts over $1 million.

Both state and federal law have prohibitions against "private inurement"—permitting a charity's income to benefit a private shareholder or individual. Legislation at the federal level was enacted to define what constitutes a prevalent form of private inurement and to refine the definition of a private shareholder. It aims to respond to alleged financial abuses by some organizations perceived as providing unreasonable compensation to organization "insiders."

To curb financial abuses, the law authorizes the IRS to impose an excise tax, 25% in most cases, on certain improper financial transactions by 501(c)(3) and 501(c)(4) organizations. The tax applies on transactions that benefit a "disqualified person," defined as people in positions to exercise substantial influence over the organization, their family members, or other organizations controlled by those persons.

Disqualified persons include voting members of the board, the president or chair, the CEO, the chief operating officer, the chief financial officer, and the treasurer, among potential other officers and staff. The benefit to the disqualified person must exceed the value that the organization receives in order to be subject to the tax. To avoid problems, tax experts are advising organizations to treat every benefit to a director or staff person as compensation, and reflect these benefits in W-2s, 1099s, and their budget documents. Seemingly innocent benefits, such as paying for the travel and lodging expenses for a spouse attending a board retreat or a health club membership for an executive director, may trigger questions about excess benefit. Luxury travel could be considered an excess benefit.

Compensation is considered reasonable if it is in an amount that would ordinarily be paid for similar services by similar organizations in similar circumstances. The term "compensation" is defined broadly, and includes severance payments, insurance, and deferred compensation.

Most of the provisions relating to intermediate sanctions apply retroactively to September 14, 1995, the date the legislation was first introduced. Steep additional excise tax penalties, up to 200% of the excess benefit plus the initial 25% excise tax, apply for excess benefit transactions that are not corrected in a reasonable amount of time. An excise tax may also be applied to an organization's managers (a term that is meant to include an officer, director, trustee) who approve the excess benefit transaction in an amount of 10% of the excess benefit, up to $10,000 maximum per transaction.

Although these excise taxes apply to individuals and not to the organizations themselves, there is nothing in this law that prohibits organizations from paying the tax or purchasing insurance to cover an individual's liability for the tax penalty. However, if the organization does purchase this insurance, the premium must be considered compensation to the individual. This insurance could become the basis for an excess benefit if total compensation to the individual, including this insurance, exceeds the fair market value that the person provides to the organization in exchange for the total compensation that person receives from the organization. It makes sense to consult an attorney who is knowledgeable about the *Taxpayer Bill of Rights 2* if there are any unresolved issues that would make an organization's directors and staff vulnerable to an IRS audit.

The Internal Revenue Service published draft regulations on this section of the Revenue Code in the *Federal Register* on August 4, 1998. Final regulations were published in the *Federal Register* on January 23, 2002.

The final regulations provide more examples of situations that might be faced by charities. One change in the final regulations is that they permit organizations to rely not only on the advice of their attorneys (as was a feature of the draft regulations), but also on the advice of other outside consultants, such as their accountants.

Codes of Ethics

A code of ethics is a systematic effort to define acceptable conduct. Ethical behavior in the workplace is enforced through the use of codes of ethics, codes of conduct, ethicists, ethics committees, policies and procedures relating to ethical dilemmas, and ethics training.

Codes of ethics may be general or specific, aspirational or idealistic, coercive or legalistic, and apply to members of a profession, an organization, or an association representing a class of organizations. Codes of ethics may be a simple list of ten golden rules or a lengthy, codified system of procedures and ideals such as the one adopted by the National Association of Social Workers. It may have the force of law (such as a statutory ethics code for public officials), be a collection of principles that are not law but are morally binding, or simply provide a system of symbolic principles for meaningful communication.

Codes of Ethics for public officials are fundamentally different from codes for nonprofit organizations, and codes for nonprofit organizations differ equally from those for government officials or private business persons. Yet they share many elements.

In recent years, there has been a trend toward turning nonprofit management into a recognized profession, with credentialing becoming available for fundraising executives, association managers, and nonprofit organization managers. Organizations such as the Association of Fundraising Professionals (AFP), the

American Society of Association Executives (ASAE), and the National Council of Nonprofits—and the state and local chapters of these organizations—have sought to professionalize their memberships.

Unlike government (which has the taxing power) and for-profit business (which generates revenue through market transactions), charities generate much of their revenue through nonmarket mechanisms such as seeking donations—in the form of contributions from the public and grants from foundations and government. This form of revenue generation offers a ripe area for fraudulent practices, and many of the ethics-related principles that differentiate nonprofit organizations from their government and private sector counterparts focus on this area.

Until 2003, there were two major ethical codes focusing on fundraising standards for charitable organizations. The first, which was developed during the late 1980s and went into effect in 1992, is the National Charities Information Bureau's (NCIB) Standards in Philanthropy. Almost all of these ethical standards would have been meaningless in anything other than a nonprofit context. The standards were not enforceable by law, but served as a guide to both donors and those who run the charities. The standards were grouped into nine areas:

1. Board Governance
2. Purpose
3. Programs
4. Information
5. Financial Support and Related Activities
6. Use of Funds
7. Annual Reporting
8. Accountability
9. Budget

Another code, the Council of Better Business Bureau's Standards for Charitable Solicitations were first published in 1974.

In 2001, NCIB merged with the Foundation of the Better Business Bureau and its Philanthropic Advisory Service (PAS). The new organization, the Better Business Bureau's Wise Giving Alliance, developed an updated code, published in March 2003. In 2007, the BBB rebranded its charity resources with a "Start With Trust" campaign. Charities that meet its standards are now referred to as "BBB accredited charities." The 20 standards that comprise this influential ethics code can be found at: *https://www.give.org/charity-landing-page/bbb-standards-for-charity-accountability*

Among the most controversial aspects of this code is the provision that calls on charities to allocate at least 65% of their donations for program expenses, spending no more than 35% of related contributions on fundraising. This is a higher standard than either the NCIB (60%) or the BBB's Philanthropic Advisory Service (50%) had enforced prior to the merger.

In December 2009, the Wise Giving Alliance announced that it was temporarily loosening its standards because of the severe recession. For the fiscal years ending in June 2008-2010, organizations still qualified for the Wise Giving Alliance stamp of approval if the organization spent at least 55% of donations on program expenses and no more than 45% on fundraising (Hall, 2009). As of 2020, the standard is back to a minimum of 65% for program expenses and a maximum of 35% for fundraising expenses.

Other standards in this code provide for regular assessment of the CEO's performance, establishment of a conflict-of-interest policy, the completion of a written assessment of the charity's performance at least every two years, and standards protecting donor privacy. The new standard frowns upon accumulating unrestricted net assets available for use that exceed either three times the amount of the past year's expenses or three times the current budget, whichever is higher.

The national professional association of fundraisers also has an ethics code. The Statement of Ethical Principles of the Association of Fundraising Professionals (AFP) was adopted in 1991 when that organization was known as the National Society of Fund Raising Executives (NSFRE). AFP "exists to foster the development and growth of fund-raising professionals and the profession, to promote high ethical standards in the fund-raising profession and to preserve and enhance philanthropy and volunteerism." This code was amended in 2015 and expanded to 25 principles, which can be viewed at:

https://afpglobal.org/sites/default/files/attachments/2019-10/ CodeofEthics_ENGLISH_Oct2019_FINAL.pdf

AFP's ethics code consists of a set of general ethical principles, introduced by a preamble that recognizes the stewardship of fundraisers and the rights of donors to have their funds used for the intent they expect.

Many of these principles are deontological, and would be appropriate for any type of organization, such as to "foster cultural diversity and pluralistic values, and treat all people with dignity and respect" and "value the privacy, freedom of choice and interests of all those affected by their actions." Some of the principles are appropriate for public organizations, such as having an obligation to "safeguard the public trust," and others are parochial to the profession, such as to "put philanthropic mission above personal gain," and "affirm, through personal giving, a commitment to philanthropy and its role in society."

One year after the adoption of the AFP principles, the organization adopted its "Standards of Professional Practice" and incorporated them into its ethics code. Its 25 principles are mostly in the form of "members shall" and "members shall not."

A statement within the Code notes that violations "may subject the member to disciplinary sanctions, including expulsion, as provided by the (AFP's) Ethics Enforcement Procedures."

Some of these standards are perfunctory, such as "members shall comply with all applicable local, state, provincial, federal, civil and criminal laws." Others are general and broad, with implications that are not easily subject to interpretation, such as "Members shall not exploit any relationship with a donor, prospect, volunteer or employee to the benefit of the member or the member's organization." Among issues raised by the standards are conflicts of interest, truthfulness, privacy, and financial accountability.

Another issue raised in the principles that is of current interest in a number of professions is the standard that "Members shall not accept compensation that is based on the percentage of charitable contributions...."

Some states have expressly prohibited lobbyists from signing contingency fee contracts in which they are paid only when they are successful in getting a bill or amendment passed by the legislature. The theory is that such contracts encourage lobbyists to engage in efforts that go beyond the boundaries of acceptable behavior. On the other hand, contingency fees are routine for attorneys in civil cases. It is also not unusual for professional fundraisers to be paid a percentage of the amount they raise. Many in the field find that this practice promotes unethical solicitations (e.g., presentations that exaggerate facts, minimize disclosure, and other behavior to intimidate and harass potential donors), and it is interesting that a major professional organization such as the AFP has taken an unequivocal position in opposition to compensation based on the amount a fundraiser raises. This is an example of a teleological approach to ethics, in that there is nothing inherently unethical about basing compensation on "performance."

A 2001 White Paper published by the Association of Fundraising Professionals (AFP) with an excellent discussion about this issue can be found at: *https://afpglobal.org/ethicsmain?itemnumber=734*

In February 2004, Independent Sector adopted a *Statement of Values and Code of Ethics for Nonprofit and Philanthropic Organizations*, and recommended that it serve as a model. The statement identifies a set of values to which nonprofits may subscribe, including commitment to the public good, accountability to the public, and commitment beyond the law. It also outlines broad ethical principles in the following areas: personal and professional integrity, mission, governance, legal compliance, responsible stewardship, openness and disclosure, program evaluation, inclusiveness and diversity, and fundraising. The full text of the most current version, adopted by the Board in June 2020, can be accessed at: *https://independentsector.org/wp-content/uploads/2016/12/Code-of-Ethics-2020.pdf*

Ethical Dilemmas

There are circumstances that staff and board members of nonprofit organizations can identify in which there is a clear choice about how to behave. We know it is clearly unethical (and illegal) to embezzle funds that belong to our organizations. We know it is unethical (and usually illegal) to lie to or otherwise deceive potential donors to manipulate them to give. And we know it is unethical (and illegal) to make false statements on our 990 tax returns to make our organizations' performance appear better than it really is. These are just a few examples of situations in which there is little doubt about the choices we can make between doing the right thing and the wrong thing.

Yet, there are often circumstances in which there is some ambiguity about what one's behavior should be, even if the individual has an absolute commitment to behaving ethically. This can occur when there are two or more important ethical principles in conflict, and behaving in a manner that honors one principle may bring about conflict with honoring a different ethical principle that may be equally important.

For example, a co-worker may come to you to discuss a problem, and ask you to swear beforehand that you will keep what he says in total confidence, and you agree. Then, that coworker shares information that you feel ethically compelled to share with your board chair, or even law enforcement authorities, to avoid potential harm to the organization or to individuals. In this example, one principle, "preserving confidentiality," might conflict with another, the "duty to report." You have to make a choice not between doing the right thing and doing the wrong thing—as would be the case in deciding whether or not to divert organization resources to one's personal benefit. Rather, you must make a choice between doing the right thing or doing another right thing when one cannot reasonably do both.

Regardless of which choice one makes, there is at least one ethical principle that would be violated.

This is what is known as an ethical dilemma—a situation in which there is a conflict between honoring two moral principles, and one cannot act in a way that satisfies one of them without not satisfying the other.

Acting with loyalty and in the best interests of one's organization is considered ethical. Being a whistle-blower when that organization is acting unethically itself is also considered ethical behavior. It is considered ethical to act in the best interest of your stakeholders (duty of care), and also ethical to let them make decisions for themselves (self-determination). How should you act when they have made a choice, and you strongly feel that this choice is not in their own interests? These are common examples of two ethical principles colliding.

Resolving Ethical Dilemmas

There are many standard models that ethicists have developed to make decisions about one's behavior when facing an ethical dilemma. One popular model is called RESPECT, developed by Yeo and Moorhouse in 1996, and is an acrostic for:

- Recognize the moral dimensions of the problem.
- Enumerate the guiding and evaluative principles.
- Specify the stakeholders and their guiding principles.
- Plot various action alternatives.
- Evaluate alternatives in light of principles and stakeholders.
- Consult and involve stakeholders as appropriate.
- Tell stakeholders the reason for the decision.

A model I like just a bit better is attributed to Frederic Reamer, modified slightly for the purpose of this discussion. It is comprised of the following steps:

- Identify the ethical issues that are controversial.
- Identify those who will be affected by the decision.
- Identify the potential courses of action, and the pros and cons of doing each.
- Analyze how each stakeholder might be affected, and how the decision is or is not consistent with one's values, one's organization, and one's profession.
- Consult others who are not affected about the dilemma for some input and advice.
- Make the decision, and document it.
- Follow up and evaluate the result of the decision.

It might not be unusual for a party adversely affected by a decision made by a nonprofit organization leader to contest it in some way. By following a standard model, it is more likely that the decision can be justified. This is certainly welcome if one finds himself or herself on the witness stand in a criminal or civil trial having to defend a decision one has made in response to a situation in which any course of action could be questioned on legal or ethical grounds.

Conclusion

There are many other ethical issues that nonprofit organizations will confront on a regular basis, such as: personal use of office supplies and equipment; personal use of frequent flier mileage; the extent of staff and board diversity; and the use of private discriminatory clubs for fundraisers, board meetings, or other events. The list is endless.

What is important is that nonprofit organizations proactively engage in discussions about ethics and values on a regular basis, recognizing that the charitable nonprofit sector has a special obligation to uphold the very highest standards. Boards of directors of charitable nonprofits have an important role in this regard. Boards cannot play a more important role than assuring that nonprofits are accountable, and that they operate as mission- and value-driven organizations.

Many who choose to work in the nonprofit sector do so because the stated values of the sector and their personal values are in harmony. It is critical that such people be vigilant against the erosion of those very principles that attracted them to the work.

Only in this way can the public be assured that the charitable nonprofit sector remains worthy of its privileges and that the sector continues to occupy its special and unique place in our society.

Tips:

- Challenge yourself and your organization to hold yourself up to the highest ethical standards, avoiding even gray areas of conflicts of interest and appearances of conflicts of interest.

- When in doubt, ask yourself, "How would I feel if my family and friends read about this on the front page of the daily newspaper?"

- Obtain salary surveys published by the Texas Society of Association Executives (TSAE), and determine whether anyone in the organization has an unreasonable salary (see: *https://www.tsae.org/*.

- Demand that all business relationships with the organization be at "arm's-length," and obtain at least three bids on any work that costs at least $1,000, even if a board member claims that he/she will provide the product/service at cost.

Chapter 8
Section 501(c)(3) Tax-Exempt Status

Synopsis: Federal 501(c)(3) tax-exempt status is valuable not only because of the tax advantages to the nonprofit corporation, but to the organization's contributors. Corporations with this status may not substantially engage in lobbying or engage in partisan political activities.

After filing the Certificate of Formation, achieving 501(c)(3) status should be the principal objective for virtually all nonprofits organized and operated for religious, charitable, scientific, literary, or educational purposes, testing for public safety, fostering national or international amateur sports competitions, and preventing cruelty to children or animals.

The federal regulation implementing Section 501(c)(3) tax-exempt status states (Reg. §1.501(c)(3)-1(d)):

>   *(d) Exempt purposes. (1) In general.*
>   *(i) An organization may be exempt as an organization described in section 501(c)(3) if it is organized and operated exclusively for one or more of the following purposes:*
>   *(a) Religious,*
>   *(b) Charitable,*
>   *(c) Scientific,*
>   *(d) Testing for Public Safety,*
>   *(e) Literary,*
>   *(f) Educational, or*
>   *(g) Prevention of cruelty to children or animals.*
>
>   *(ii) An organization is not organized or operated exclusively for one or more of the purposes specified in subdivision (i) of this subparagraph unless it serves a public rather than a private interest. Thus, to meet the requirement of this subdivision, it is necessary for an organization to establish that it is not organized or operated for the benefit of private interests such as designated individuals, the creator or his family, shareholders of the organization, or persons controlled, directly or indirectly, by such private interests...*

Federal 501(c)(3) tax-exempt status confers five major benefits to the organization:

1. The nonprofit will be exempt from federal income taxes other than unrelated business income taxes (UBIT).

2. Persons contributing to the nonprofit can take a deduction on their own income taxes for their contributions.

3. Many major donors (such as United Ways and certain foundations) will not make contributions to organizations that do not have 501(c)(3) status.

4. The designation of 501(c)(3) status indicates a minimal level of accountability, policed by the Internal Revenue Service, which is a useful governmental stamp of approval of the charitable activities of the organization.

5. In some states, including Texas, qualifying 501(c)(3) organizations may elect to self-insure for purposes of complying with unemployment compensation laws.

There are four major disadvantages:

1. A 501(c)(3) may not engage in partisan political activity on behalf of political candidates.

2. Such organizations may not substantially engage in lobbying or propaganda.

3. Such organizations have a higher level of accountability, and are required, as must all 501(c) exempt organizations, to make copies of their 990 tax returns available in their offices upon request.

4. There is a substantial application fee, and this fee is not refunded if tax-exempt status is denied.

Although not always the case, most incorporators of nonprofits have some altruistic motive for incorporating. The motives of the incorporators cannot be for personal gain. As one might expect, the motives are usually of an "eleemosynary" nature, i.e., related to charity.

Many nonprofit corporations are formed because a person or group of persons is frustrated with the lack of government action to solve a societal problem that, in that person's view, should be solved by government. Congress historically has recognized that government cannot do everything for everybody, even when the cause is just. Instead, Congress provides an opportunity for citizens to form organizations to do the activities themselves. They are rewarded by having certain privileges and subsidies, such as the tax-exemption, provided that the activity falls within a statutorily enumerated list of activities.

Section 501(c) of the Internal Revenue Code lists more than 20 classes of activities that can qualify a nonprofit corporation for tax-exempt status. A list of these classes is provided on page 112. Only one of these classes, 501(c)(3), permits a tax deduction for contributions made to organizations in that class, and requires that such organizations not engage in substantial lobbying or propaganda activities, or in political activities that advance the cause of candidates.

501(c)(3) status is not granted pro forma. Because of this, 501(c)(3) status is prized, and it is viewed by many in the public as a stamp of approval by the federal government. The fact is that 501(c)(3) status does not necessarily imply government's endorsement of the organization's activities. In FY 2019, the Internal Revenue Service granted 86,383 (c)(3) applications, denied 39, and took "other" action on 8,829. many of which were eventually approved after additional information was provided.

Successful application is facilitated by having certain provisions in the organization's governing documents. These provisions are discussed on pages 35-38.

Differences Between Private Foundations and Public Charities

Public charities and private foundations are both granted tax-exempt status under Section 501(c)(3) of the Internal Revenue Code. However, Section 509(a) differentiates organizations that receive their income from a broad range of public sources from those organizations that receive their income principally from one, or a limited number of sources plus investment income. Private foundations pay a federal tax on net investment income, must meet a minimum annual threshold for making distributions of their assets to charities, and are flatly prohibited from lobbying. To be considered a public charity rather than a private foundation, an organization must pass a public support test enforced by the IRS. There are two such tests, one of which must be passed for the organization to be considered a public charity. The test is based on financial data for a four-year period. If one test is passed, the organization will qualify as a public charity for the following two years. For information about these tests, see: *https://www.irs.gov/pub/irs-pdf/p557.pdf*

Nonprofits that don't fit neatly into the public-serving or member-serving category are the 375,000 religious congregations, about 80% of which do not register with the IRS or file a 990 federal annual tax return because there is no requirement to do so. While these congregations exist primarily to serve their members, their tax treatment is as if they primarily serve the public. In fact, nonprofit organizations are not required by law to file for exempt status with the Internal Revenue Service provided they have a recognized creed or form of worship, are "sacerdotal" in character, carry on regular religious services, and operate for other than private gain.

There are several commercially available guides for filling out the Form 1023 in a manner that will maximize your chances for your application to be approved. Among them are:

How to Form your Own Non-Profit Corporation (12th Edition, published June 2015) by Anthony Mancuso (Nolo Press, 950 Parker Street, Berkeley, CA 94710).

How To Apply for 501(c)(3) Status—Form 1023-EZ

In July 2014, the IRS announced it had approved a Form 1023-EZ, enabling most organizations to file a smaller, streamlined application for 501(c)(3) tax-exempt status. It may be accessed at: *https://www.irs.gov/pub/irs-pdf/f1023ez.pdf*

This form, as is the case for the full 1023, must be filed online as of January 2020 at *pay.gov*. The form is just three pages, compared to 26 for the traditional 1023, although there is a 26-question worksheet found in the instructions that must be included. Filing is accomplished exclusively online, using pay.gov. Approval of these applications is also much quicker than those that file the traditional Form 1023. The reduced filing fee that applies to small organizations, currently $275, applies to Form 1023-EZ filers, a $325 savings compared to filing the 1023. Organizations intended to be eligible for filing this form are those with actual or projected gross receipts of under $50,000 annually for any of the current or either of the next two years, and assets of under $250,000. Churches, hospitals, universities, credit counseling organizations, organizations that do not have a mailing address, and limited liability companies (LLCs) are not eligible. Full instructions providing additional requirements may be accessed at: *https://www.irs.gov/pub/irs-pdf/i1023ez.pdf*

The IRS estimates that up to 70% of applicants for federal charitable tax-exempt status are eligible to file the 1023-EZ form. Some organizations are reporting that they receive approval from the IRS within two weeks, compared to a response of several months for those who submit the traditional form. The IRS says to expect a decision in 3-6 months.

How To Apply for 501(c)(3) Status—Traditional Forms

As of January 2020, the filing must be submitted online at *pay.gov*. To apply, an organization needs the following forms and booklets from the Internal Revenue Service:

- Form 8718—*User Fee for Exempt Organization Determination Letter Request* (for organizations that have had annual gross receipts averaging not more than $10,000 during its preceding four years, or new organizations that anticipate averaging not more than $10,000 during its first four years). This form may be downloaded at: *https:// www.irs.gov/pub/irs-pdf/f8718.pdf*
- Form SS-4—*Application for Employer Identification Number* This form may be downloaded at: *https://www.irs.gov/pub/irs-pdf/fss4. pdf*
- Form 1023—*Form for applying for 501(c)(3) tax-exempt status* This form may be downloaded at: *https://www.irs.gov/pub/irs-pdf/f1023. pdf*
- Instruction booklet for applying for 501(c)(3) tax-exempt status This publication may be downloaded at: *https://www.irs.gov/instructions/ i1023*
- Publication 557—*Tax-Exempt Status for Your Organization* This publication may be downloaded at: *https://www.irs.gov/pub/irs-pdf/ p557.pdf*

The above forms and booklets also may be obtained at any local IRS office.

IRS's instruction book accompanying Form 1023 previously estimated that it takes an average of nine hours and 39 minutes to complete the basic form and several more hours to complete supplemental schedules. It also takes an additional five hours to learn about the law and how to complete the forms. The current version (January 2020) of the instructions notes "The time needed to complete and file this form will vary depending on individual circumstances." It is advisable to be as careful as possible in completing the forms, since the wrong phrase can result in denial.

Some organizations are exempt from having to file the 1023. Among them are:

1. those that will have gross receipts of less than $5,000 annually

2. bona fide religious institutions

3. certain groups affiliated with a parent organization that already has tax-exempt status and will send a letter extending its exemption to them

4. organizations eligible to file Form 8718 (see above).

The Internal Revenue Service expects that an application for 501(c)(3) status will be filed within 27 months after the end of the month in which the Articles of Incorporation (Certificate of Formation in Texas) are filed. If the organization files on time and the application is approved, 501(c)(3) status will be retroactive to the date of the Certificate of Formation. There is a form to file if the 27-month deadline is not met. For more information about this option, see IRS Publication 557.

Completing the Application

The best advice for filling out Form 1023 is to carefully read the instruction booklet and follow the directions. It sounds obvious, but many fail to do that and are surprised by delays in having their applications approved for organizations that are obviously qualified for 501(c)(3) status. Beyond that, however, here are four tips that experts offer to assist you.

1. Avoid an organizational name that would raise a red flag to an IRS examiner.

2. Have all governing documents (e.g., Certificate of Formation and bylaws) include the language suggested in Chapter 2 with respect to corporate purposes, propaganda and lobbying, and distribution of assets upon dissolution.

3. Have an organizational conflict of interest policy that is consistent with what appears in the instruction booklet to IRS Form 1023 (or that can be found at: *https://www.irs.gov/pub/irs-pdf/i1023.pdf*).

4. Provide a three-year budget that makes sense. First, it should be consistent with the fee schedule you are seeking, i.e., should average less than $10,000 per year if you want to pay the $275 application fee rather than $850. IRS examiners know you cannot possibly predict with any precision what your revenue and expenses will be for your completely new organization three years in advance. They just want something realistic. How does one do this? Experts suggest two approaches. The first, the expense approach, is you set the organization's goals, calculate what it would cost to accomplish those goals, and then develop a plan that raises that amount of money. The second, the revenue approach, involves estimat-

ing the amount of revenue you can reasonably expect to generate for the organization, through fundraising, membership dues, sales of goods and services, and grants. Then you decide how that amount of money could be responsibly spent. A third approach is to blend these two approaches. With either approach, make sure that the source of funds is broad enough to justify exemption as a public charity. If you receive funding from only a handful of sources, you may be eligible for tax exemption, but as a private foundation rather than as a public charity. See below for an explanation of the differences.

Fees

There is a $600 application fee to file Form 1023, *Application for Recognition of Exemption.* New organizations expecting gross receipts of not more than $10,000 for each of the first four years, or existing organizations that have not had gross receipts of that amount in each of the last four years, can qualify for a reduced fee of $400 by filing Form 8718, *User Fee for Exempt Organization Request.* Form 1023-EZ filers (see page 108) pay $275, reduced from $400 in July 2016. Filers pay by credit card at *pay.gov.*

Timetable

You can expect a form letter from the IRS within a few weeks of its receipt of your application acknowledging that it was received. Organizations that file an application requiring minimal decision-making by the IRS or that do not require a follow-up letter from them are processed in six-ten weeks. This applies to about half of applications. On the average, about 60% of all applications are quickly approved. Less than 1% of applications are quickly denied. About a quarter of applications are neither approved nor disapproved, but include the granting of tax status different than the category applied for, those sent down from the IRS's Cincinnati Office (located in Covington, KY) to the IRS headquarters in Washington for more work, and those awaiting a response to inquiries for more information, among other reasons.

Tax-Exempt Status Other than 501(c)(3)

The Internal Revenue Code provides 28 other categories of tax-exempt status besides 501(c)(3). Those who wish to file for tax-exempt status under section 501(c) for other than 501(c)(3) need to request Package 1024 from the IRS. Note: You can download this package, and all other common IRS forms and instruction booklets at: *https://www.irs.gov/*

Among the other categories are:

501(c)(4)—civic leagues, social welfare organizations

501(c)(5)—labor, agricultural, or horticultural organizations

501(c)(6)—business leagues, chambers of commerce, trade associations

501(c)(7)—social clubs

501(c)(8)—fraternal beneficiary societies

501(c)(9)—voluntary employee beneficiary associations

501(c)(10)—domestic fraternal societies and orders that do not provide life, sick, or health benefits

501(c)(11)—teacher retirement fund associations

501(c)(12)—benevolent life insurance associations and other mutual businesses

501(c)(13)—cemeteries and crematoria

501(c)(14)—credit unions

501(c)(15)—mutual insurance companies

501(c)(16)—farmers' co-ops

501(c)(17)—unemployment compensation benefit trusts

501(c)(20)—prepaid group legal services organizations

501(c)(25)—title holding corporations or trusts.

With limited exceptions, these organizations have the same federal tax benefits as a 501(c)(3). One major difference is that with few exceptions, contributors cannot deduct the amount of their donation from their personal income tax payments. For many of these organizations, there is no limitation against lobbying activities, and most are permitted to engage in partisan political activity (although there may be a substantial federal excise tax associated with political expenditures).

A Short History of Tax-Exempt Status

In ancient times, government, whether secular or non-secular, recognized that certain activities assisted the role of government and were deserving of tax exemptions. A passage in the Bible (Ezra 7:24) provides that "it shall not be lawful to impose toll, tribute, or customs" upon certain priests and their staff. Several thousand years ago, some of the best land in the Nile Valley was set aside tax-free by the Egyptian pharaoh for the priests of Osiris.

Modern tax-exemption law has its roots in England, with the passage of the Statute of Charitable Uses in 1601. Current U.S. tax-exemption law draws its roots from an 1891 court case in Britain *(Commissioners of Income Tax v. Pemsel)* that provided a judicial definition of charity strikingly similar to the American legal standard.

The modern federal tax-exemption can be traced to 1863, when the income of religious organizations was exempted from a corporate tax enacted to finance the

Civil War. The Wilson-Gorman Tariff Act of 1894, the first general U.S. corporate income tax, imposed a 2% flat tax and statutorily exempted charitable income. Section 32 of this Act extended this exemption to charitable, religious, educational, fraternal, and some savings and loan institutions. It was eventually declared unconstitutional and subsequently repealed. It did, however, serve as the precedent for exempting organizations that were for "charitable, religious, or educational purposes." The Revenue Act of 1913, passed after the 16th Amendment was ratified, included identical language (Arnsberger, et al., 2008). The Revenue Act of 1917 included a tax deduction for contributions made to charitable organizations.

A 1924 Supreme Court case, *Trinidad v. Sagrada*, ruled that for purposes of tax-exempt status, the destination of the funds, rather than the source, was the key determinant. This case involved a religious order that sold food, wine, and other goods to support its school, mission, church, and other operations. Thus, tax-exempt organizations were permitted to run profit-making enterprises provided that the net profits were funneled to tax-exempt purposes. This policy was revised by Congressional enactment of an "unrelated business income tax" (UBIT) in 1950. The rationale for this was that charities were seen as competing unfairly with for-profit enterprises, the most celebrated case of which was New York University's ownership of a macaroni factory.

From 1909 to the present, many other categories of tax-exempt status were added by federal statute, including labor, horticultural and agriculture organizations (1909), business leagues, chambers of commerce, scientific organizations, and mutual cemetery companies (1913), public utilities, social clubs, land banks, title holding companies, and farming associations (1916), societies for the prevention of cruelty to animals (1918), foundations and community chests (1921), and homeowner associations, fishing associations, and organizations that promote national and international sporting competitions (1976).

The Tax Reform Act of 1969 established an explicit category for private foundations, defined them as either operating or nonoperating foundations, provided for an excise tax on their investment income, and required minimum distributions to be made annually by nonoperating foundations.

Restoring Tax-Exempt Status

In 2010, the IRS informed hundreds of thousands of small nonprofit organizations that they were in danger of losing their federal tax exemptions because they had not complied with their legal obligation to file the 990-N e-postcard. This filing for tax-exempt organizations with gross income of $25,000 or less annually was authorized by the *Pension Protection Act of 2006*. The Act requires organizations to lose their exemptions automatically if they fail to file for three consecutive years.

With perhaps as many as 320,000 organizations missing the May 17 filing deadline, the IRS offered a one-time extension in filing, providing organizations that missed the deadline the opportunity to comply by October 15, 2010. According to the IRS, 275,000 organizations had their exemptions automatically revoked in 2011 and posted their names on a website with a searchable database at: *https://www.irs.gov/charities-non-profits/tax-exempt-organization-search*

In 2014, the IRS issued Revenue Procedure 2014-11 to provide a streamlined process for affected organizations to have their exemptions restored. For more information, see: *https://www.irs.gov/pub/irs-drop/rp-14-11.pdf*

Tips:

- Before filing an application for exempt status, review Chapter 2 for provisions that should be in your organization's governing documents.

- Consider reviewing the Interactive version of Form 1023 that can be accessed at *https://www.stayexempt.irs.gov/home/starting-out/interactive-form-1023-prerequisite-questions*

- Make sure you are not eligible for the discounted filing fees available to smaller organizations before sending a $600 check to the IRS.

- Consider developing a conflict of interest statement (see Chapter 7) and providing it to the IRS with other organization documents. There has been anecdotal evidence that some IRS application examiners, but not all, are requiring such a statement.

- Consider using the IRS Cyber Assistant online application process to apply for 501(c)(3) status, when and if it becomes available, to qualify for a further discount on the application fee.

Chapter 9
Liability, Risk Management, and Insurance

Synopsis: Nonprofit organizations, like all others, are exposed to risk in a variety of areas. Staff members, volunteers, clients, and members of the general public may suffer injuries while participating in or attending an organization's activities. The nonprofit may be sued for a variety of alleged wrongful acts, from unemployment discrimination to negligent supervision to breach of fiduciary duty. Every nonprofit organization should consider how it will minimize its risks, even though state and federal laws provide some protection to nonprofit organizations.

Murphy's Law has many variations and corollaries. In its simplest form, it states, "If something can go wrong, it will." And at the worst possible time. No one can foresee catastrophic events, and even if one could, it is virtually impossible to protect a corporation against all possible eventualities.

A nonprofit corporation, like a business corporation, should do everything in its power to mitigate the effect of claims against it. Like any other type of business, nonprofits could suffer personal injury or property damage claims caused by floods, fire, theft, earthquake, wind damage, building collapse, and slips and falls, just to name a few possibilities.

Legal claims against corporations tend to be of the low-incidence, high risk variety. These claims do not happen very often, but when they do, the results can be disastrous for the organization and its leadership.

Nonprofits are exposed to legal risks in many other areas. They engage in typical business transactions on a routine basis. They post on social media sites. They arrange for conventions, seminars, and other meetings. They publish newsletters. They also are employers with the attendant risk that hiring, advancement, or firing decisions may be challenged based on contract rights, discrimination, or fraud.

Some nonprofit corporations, particularly associations of members and member organizations, are vulnerable to member suits. These organizations may have ethics codes with enforcement procedures for alleged violators, industry standards, or professional credentialing or licensure that could be challenged by members. Associations could be targeted with anti-trust law violations for certain practices that may appear on the surface to be in the interest of their members. The adjudication of decisions made by such a nonprofit could be challenged if it is perceived to be unfair by a member. I was reminded of this when the National Football League recently changed its corporate status from a 501(c)(6) tax-exempt corporation to a for-profit. The organization was constantly in the spotlight for various suits against it by its members.

Liability of Officers, Directors, and Other Volunteers

Nonprofit corporation volunteers may suffer from the same potential liability for actions in performance of their duties as individuals involved with business corporations. Furthermore, as managerial people, volunteer officers and directors of nonprofit corporations are bound by the same basic principles governing conduct as are directors and officers of profit-making business corporations. They owe a fiduciary duty of reasonable care and the duty to act in the best interests of the corporation and its members. This involves a duty of loyalty or good faith in managing the affairs of the corporation (see Chapter 4).

Generally, this duty requires individuals to use due care in the performance of their duties for the corporation, to act in good faith in the best interest of the corporation as a whole and not for the interests of some but not all of the members. It also entails a requirement to avoid activity or transactions in which the individual has a personal interest.

In short, in this litigious society, courts are tending more and more to impose responsibility on officers, directors, and volunteers of nonprofit corporations—including hospitals, charities, and educational institutions—for anti-trust problems, tort liability, and similar areas of liability exposure.

Several other factors contribute to increasing liability exposure for nonprofit organizations, according to Melanie Herman, a nonprofit risk management expert.

First, federal and state laws, such as expansion of the 1964 *Civil Rights Act* and the *Health Insurance Portability and Accountability Act of 1996* have fueled an increase in lawsuits against organizations.

Second, nonprofits (as is the case with all other types of organizations) routinely collect and store personal information of their stakeholders. Cyberhacking has reached epidemic proportions. The news about the 2017 hacking of Equifax in which the accounts of 147 million Americans was believed to be compromised is evidence of the vulnerability we face.

People Inc., a large New York state-based social service agency serving individuals with intellectual disabilities with employment, health care, outreach, and recreational programs, was victimized by a hacking incident in 2019. The organization disclosed that up to 1,000 of its clients may be affected by the breach that may have involved the loss of names, addresses, Social Security numbers, financial information, medical data, health insurance information, and other government identification of its clients.

Third, the sector is engaging in business activities to an increasing degree to fund their programs, and this may accelerate even more with the government funding cuts to social programs at all levels of government.

And finally, but related to the three above, nonprofit organizations are engaging in partnership agreements with other organizations. These agreements are typically consummated with a formal contract that has procedures for resolving disputes that may involve litigation.

Civil and Criminal Liability

Nonprofit organizations have two types of liability to worry about. The first, tort liability, is intended to require someone who causes damages to another person to "make them whole" by compensating them. The damage may have been intentional or unintentional, but the action that caused the damage usually, but not always, does not fall to the level of being a crime. An example might be when an employee is the victim of employment discrimination and sues the organization for not taking appropriate action as an employer. If the plaintiff can prove in court that the organization violated the law, monetary damages such as for back pay, including punitive damages, could be awarded.

The other type is criminal liability. When a staff member of my professional association, ARNOVA, was accused of embezzling nearly $50,000 from the organization in 2012, he was charged with a crime, convicted, and sent to jail. He was also ordered to make restitution to the organization for his embezzlement.

A civil trial has a standard of "preponderance of the evidence." A criminal trial has a standard of "beyond a reasonable doubt." Those losing a civil trial are ordered by the judge to pay monetary damages, and may pay court costs. In contrast, if the defendant is convicted in a criminal trial, the defendant may face a prison sentence.

A perpetrator of sexual harassment, for example, may be liable for both tort liability and criminal liability. The first is intended to compensate the victim for damages. The second is intended to punish the perpetrator.

In dealing with liability suits, the courts generally consider the degree to which the action that caused the damage was intentional, and whether the damage would have been avoided if the defendant had acted in a reasonable manner. Courts also consider the context of the action—for example, even a nonprofit organization has a higher standard with respect to avoiding harm that may result in the transportation of their clients. A court may consider a higher standard to apply if the client is paying for a service.

Volunteer Protection Act

At the federal level, the *Volunteer Protection Act* (VPA) was signed into law by President Clinton in July of 1997, with an effective date of September 16, 1997.

The intent of the law is to provide limited legal immunity for the volunteers of charities who are involved in accidents that occur in connection with their charitable service. The VPA provides some protection, but there are some limitations to its applicability. Among these limitations are—

- protection applies only to volunteers—those who do not receive compensation for their services other than reasonable reimbursement of their expenses. Directors and officers are covered if their compensation is $500 annually or less.

- protection applies only in cases in which the volunteer was acting within the scope of his or her volunteer responsibilities at the time of the incident.

- the liability limit does not apply if the volunteer was required to be licensed or certified to perform an activity, and that volunteer lacked such certification or licensing.

- the liability limit does not apply if the person intentionally caused harm to others or showed flagrant indifference to the safety of those who were injured.

The immunity does not extend to harm caused by the operation of a motor vehicle, crimes of violence, activities not authorized by the charity, hate crimes, civil rights violations, damage resulting from the use of alcohol or drugs, or sexual offenses. The law encourages states to grant liability immunity to nonprofit organization volunteers who are acting in good faith and within the scope of their official duties.

Even if a nonprofit organization is liable for injuries caused by its volunteers, there is nothing in the act that prohibits the nonprofit from taking action against a volunteer who was directly responsible for damages, and recovering money paid by the nonprofit organization in claims. The act does provide for some limits of non-economic losses, such as punitive damages, that may apply to the volunteer, unless the damage caused was the result of willful or criminal misconduct, or conscious, flagrant indifference.

Texas Statutory Nonprofit Liability Limitations

The Texas Charitable Immunity and Liability Act was enacted into law in 1987 (Texas Civil Practice & Remedies Code Ann § 84.001 to .008). It provides limited immunity to charitable organizations, which the law defines as —

> *any organization exempt from federal income tax under Section 501(a) of the Internal Revenue Code of 1986 by being listed as an exempt organization in Section 501(c)(3) or 501(c)(4) of the code, if it is a corporation, foundation, community chest, church, or fund organized and operated exclusively for charitable, religious, prevention of cruelty to children or animals, youth sports and youth recreational, neighborhood crime prevention or patrol, fire protection or prevention, emergency medical or hazardous material response services, or educational purposes, including private primary or secondary schools if accredited by a member association of the Texas Private School Accreditation Commission but excluding fraternities, sororities, and secret societies, or is organized and operated exclusively for the promotion of social welfare by being primarily engaged in promoting the common good and general welfare of the people in a community;*

> *(B) any bona fide charitable, religious, prevention of cruelty to children or animals, youth sports and youth recreational, neighborhood crime prevention or patrol, or educational organization, excluding fraternities, sororities, and secret societies, or other organization organized and operated exclusively for the promotion of social welfare by being primarily engaged in promoting the common good and general welfare of the people in a community, and that:*
> *(i) is organized and operated exclusively for one or more of the above purposes;*
> *(ii) does not engage in activities which in themselves are not in furtherance of the purpose or purposes;*
> *(iii) does not directly or indirectly participate or intervene in any political campaign on behalf of or in opposition to any candidate for public office;*
> *(iv) dedicates its assets to achieving the stated purpose or purposes of the organization;*
> *(v) does not allow any part of its net assets on dissolution of the*

organization to inure to the benefit of any group, shareholder, or individual; and

    (vi) normally receives more than one-third of its support in any year from private or public gifts, grants, contributions, or membership fees...

There are a few other types of organizations that are included within this law, which can be found at: *https://statutes.capitol.texas.gov/Docs/CP/htm/CP.84.htm*

The statute grants these volunteers of these organizations limited civil immunity relating to "any act or omission resulting in death, damage, or injury if the volunteer was acting in the course and scope of the volunteer's duties or functions, including as an officer, director, or trustee within the organization."

This immunity does not apply to any act or omission arising from the operation or use of any motor-driven equipment, including an airplane. It also does not apply to "an act or omission that is intentional, wilfully negligent, or done with conscious indifference or reckless disregard for the safety of others."

Texas state law is strewn with other statutes that provide limited civil liability to more narrow groups of volunteers, including youth council volunteers (Texas Code § 61.096), higher education volunteers (Texas Code § 51.937), volunteer firefighters (Texas Code § 78.001), food donation volunteers (Texas Code § 76.004), alternative dispute resolution volunteers (Texas Code § 154.055), child abuse investigation volunteers (Texas Code § 261.106), child advocacy volunteers (Texas Code § 264.407), child welfare volunteers (Texas Code 40.061), and protective services for the elderly and and disabled volunteers (Texas Code § 48.054).

Insurance for Nonprofits and Nonprofit Personnel

There are various forms of coverage that nonprofits may consider as they look for ways to finance insurable risks. The Nonprofit Risk Management Center has published a comprehensive guide on insurance for nonprofits and provides detailed information on a wide range of coverages available to and purchased by nonprofits. The $30 Guide, *Coverage, Claims and Consequences: An Insurance Handbook for Nonprofits,* is available at: *https://www.nonprofitrisk.org/products/*

The most commonly purchased coverages are discussed below:

Commercial general liability insurance—Commercial general liability or CGL policies cover liability exposures that are common to all organizations. The policy actually includes a combination of three separate coverages, each with its own insuring agreement and exclusions: Coverage A (general liability), Coverage B (personal injury and advertising injury liability) and Coverage C (medical payments). The most common CGL claims against nonprofits are third party claims alleging bodily injury or property damage. While most CGL policies are based on standard wording available from the Insurance Services Office (ISO), there are dozens of different policies available to nonprofits and many more exclusions, endorsements, and other provisions that add or delete coverages. For example, one nonprofit may purchase a CGL policy that provides coverage for its special events, while another nonprofit may choose a policy that includes protection against suits alleging sexual abuse.

Commercial property insurance—*Property insurance* covers risk of loss to an organization's buildings or personal property. Coverage usually includes buildings, personal property of the insured, personal property of others on site and in the insured's possession.

Crime coverage—Many nonprofits purchase crime coverage, typically a package of policies that protect an organization against intentional theft by insiders, as well as theft of assets by third parties. Crime coverage generally includes a fidelity bond (also called employee dishonesty coverage) plus a basic menu of other coverages.

Directors' & officers' liability insurance—D&O insurance provides coverage against wrongful acts which might include actual or alleged errors, omissions, misleading statements, and neglect or breach of duty on the part of the board of directors and other insured persons and entities. Many D&O policies include employment practices liability coverage, protecting a nonprofit against claims alleging improper or illegal employment practices.

Professional liability insurance—Also known as malpractice coverage or errors and omissions (E&O) coverage, professional liability insurance protects against claims alleging negligence in the delivery of (or failure to deliver) professional services, such as medical services, counseling, legal services and more.

Workers' compensation and employers' liability insurance—Workers compensation coverage covers expenses an employer is mandated to pay by state statute to cover specific benefits for employee injuries. Employers' liability insurance protects employers from employee-related suits that are separate from WC claims.

Personal or Professional Individual Insurance Coverage

These federal statutory provisions and many state laws provide some protection to individuals involved with nonprofit corporations. Nonetheless, many nonprofit corporations purchase either directors' and officers' (D&O) insurance to cover directors and officers, or a broader type of policy sometimes referred to as professional liability insurance, to protect not only officers and directors but all association volunteers and staff. The value of this insurance is not only to pay for substantiated claims that arise against the organization and its leadership. It also will provide the funds to defend against frivolous or otherwise unsuccessful lawsuits.

There is not much standardization with respect to what D&O insurance covers or does not cover. Consequently, organizations need to review every provision carefully and understand what they are buying. They need to consider deductibles and other out-of-pocket expenses they may have to incur before receiving benefits. Some of the more common exclusions are—

- *Dishonesty exclusion:* This is a provision that excludes coverage when a "finding in fact" is that the director or officer engaged in dishonest, fraudulent, or criminal conduct. Some policies may trigger this exclusion even when there are simply allegations of such conduct rather than a "final adjudication" by the court that such conduct did occur.

- *Insured vs. insured exclusion:* This provision excludes coverage when one director of an organization sues another director of that organization in many, but not all, cases. The intent of this provision is to limit fraudulent collusion between directors to tap insurance benefits.

- *Reimbursement after the fact:* Some D&O insurance policies only provide benefits after the claim has been resolved. Some policies will advance the funds needed to defend a claim, which can be vital in mounting an effective defense.

Although premiums for this type of insurance continue to be high, it is expected that the decrease in exposure afforded by recent state and federal laws will result in lower claims, and, eventually, lower premiums. How much should you expect to pay? The Nonprofits Insurance Alliance *(https://insurancefornonprofits.org/ coverages/nonprofits-own/flat-rate-do/)* offers flat rate policies for organizations without employees for $600 for $1 million in coverage, and those with employees should expect to pay several thousands of dollars, but premiums vary widely, based on the number of employees covered and the amount of coverage.

Board Member Decision-Making

The Board of a nonprofit organization "owns" the organization in trust for the public. Ultimately, the board is responsible for assuring that the organization complies with all laws, and it is the board, not staff, that is responsible for protecting the assets of the organization. There are few cases in which board members have been found liable for making reasonable, good-faith, arm's length decisions even when hindsight has demonstrated such decisions were "bad." More likely, board members have been liable for decisions that involved self-dealing, obviously taken with criminal intent, or were just plain "stupid." As Dr. Carter McNamara writes in *Some Legal Considerations for Board Members (https://managementhelp. org/boards/liabilities.htm)*, "Directors must attend most board meetings, not just on occasion. Absence from a board meeting does not release the director from responsibility for decisions made. A pattern of absence may indeed be presumed to increase an individual's liability because she/he cannot demonstrate a serious dedication to the obligations of the position."

McNamara further states that board members are more liable for taking no action than for taking the wrong action for the right reasons. His advice is sage when he suggests that board members should be vigilant against something that smells "fishy" and should not always assume that the information they receive is accurate.

Risk Management

The term "risk management" refers to management strategies an organization can use to enhance the safety of its stakeholders, such as clients and employees; minimize its exposure to litigation; protect its assets; and maintain its reputation. One step is to engage in a continuing planning process and implement a risk management program. Among the steps of a typical planning process are—

1. Identify potential exposure and risk to the organization's personnel, property, clients, funding, and reputation.

2. Evaluate and prioritize potential risks.

3. Develop strategies to minimize these risks.

4. Periodically evaluate and update a risk management plan.

The Nonprofit Risk Management Center has developed resources to help nonprofits assess and manage their risks. See: *https://nonprofitrisk.org/*

Strategies to Minimize Exposure to Lawsuits

What can a nonprofit organization do to minimize its exposure to lawsuits? Among the strategies risk management experts suggest are—

1. *Make sure that every agreement entered into on behalf of the organization is in writing and signed by all parties.* It should provide a clear

description of what is expected from both organizations, deadline schedules and sanctions for when these deadlines are not met, all payment amounts and schedules, the contract duration, what happens when the contract expires, and how disputes will be resolved.

2. *Carefully and methodically document all personnel actions, particularly disciplinary actions and evaluations of job performance.* Suits by disgruntled employees are among the fastest growing type of suits experienced by organizations.

3. *Become familiar with all federal and state laws that apply to employers in general and nonprofit organizations in particular.* Particularly worthy of attention are laws relating to employment discrimination, sexual harassment, wages and benefits, liability of volunteers, and wrongful discharge.

4. *If you find that the risk of offering any particular program or activity imposes an unacceptable risk, simply don't offer that program or activity.* This may be the strategy of choice if your organization does not have the funds to adequately train and supervise workers or if you typically hire low-salary, entry-level workers rather than those with experience who require higher salaries. Can you afford state-of-the-art, professionally installed equipment, or are you forced to rely on donated materials constructed by volunteers? Many nonprofits make society better for all of us *because* they are willing to stick their necks out and provide a needed service when neither government nor the private sector is willing to do so—but there needs to be constraints on acceptable risk.

5. *Modify the activity or the work processes involved to reduce liability exposure.* There may be a creative way to change how a program is applied that may make it safer. It may require having more staff supervise a particular activity, or have those with particular training or certification administer services.

6. *Pool the risk by passing it on to insurance companies or other third parties.* Respond to risk exposure by purchasing insurance to cover potential losses of specific programs and activities, or general activities of the organization and its employees and leaders. Another strategy is to have a third party indemnify the nonprofit for damages against the nonprofit that may have occurred because of the actions of that third party—such as from a caterer who is hired to cater an event sponsored by the nonprofit.

7. *Share the risk, or pass it on to another organization that is better prepared to deal with the increased liability exposure.* For example, an organization may choose to outsource some aspect of a program that is inherently risky, such as client transportation, to a for-profit provider that already has sufficient insurance to cover potential losses. The exposure to potential costly accidents with experienced, licensed, and trained drivers who are employed by that for-profit would likely be preferable to using the nonprofit organization's volunteers. Doing this would certainly cost more, but the peace of mind might well be worth that cost.

While these strategies are excellent suggestions, they cannot militate against the need to have basic general liability insurance to cover personal injury and property damage claims. Organizations are likely to also benefit from purchasing directors' and officers' (D&O) insurance to protect volunteer leadership from personal legal claims.

Government has recognized the public benefit of reducing the liability exposure of nonprofit organizations, in the same way that the doctrine of *sovereign immunity* has reduced the exposure of governmental authorities to many types of lawsuits. Over the years, volunteers for nonprofit organizations have benefited from the protection of federal and state laws designed to limit their liability exposure, although the protection provided is quite limited.

General Business Insurance

Employee lawsuits, floods, fire, theft, earthquakes, wind damage, building collapse, loss of business income, pollution, riot, lightning, war, landslides, nuclear contamination, power failures, falls, electrocution...the possibilities for natural disasters, accidents, and crime are endless. Fortunately, generic business insurance policies will protect a corporation from all of these, plus scores of other potential, but unlikely, occurrences.

If the organization is willing to accept a reasonable deductible (an amount of damages the corporation pays before benefits are provided on the remaining amount of damages), a policy may cost as little as a few hundred dollars. It is a worthwhile investment to make, if only for peace of mind.

Most policies include paying for defending corporate leaders in the event they are sued for whatever reason relating to business activity. Prices for basic insurance are competitive. A nonprofit organization should have liability and medical expenses coverage of at least $500,000, and the policy should cover the legal costs of defending and settling suits against the corporation and its staff.

Cyber Liability Insurance

Nonprofit organizations, as with their for-profit counterparts, are increasing reliant on electronic data for storing confidential and otherwise sensitive data. These systems are vulnerable to hacking, viruses, denial of service attacks, and ransomware attacks. A surge of ransomware attacks hit hospitals in the fall of 2020, and other nonprofit organizations also would be brought to their knees if subjected to extortion. Even if an organization pays the perpetrator to restore its access to data, the data breach could result in court suits from those injured by the release of confidential data. Cyber liability insurance covers financial losses that result from data breaches and other cyber events. Most cyber policies include both first-party and third-party coverages. First-party coverages cover expenses the organization incurs such as having to inform its clients of the breach and how they should respond, or having to hire experts to restore the lost data. Third-party coverages apply to expenses resulting from claims against those who claim injury from the release of the information.

Depending on the policy, coverage may include any extortion payments made by the organization or even costs related to the loss of reputation the organization might have in the event of a data breach.

As with other forms of liability insurance, there is no standard policy, and there are opportunities to tweak any individual policy to meet the customized needs of the organization.

Interest in these policies appears to be growing. According to NetDiligence, *(https://netdiligence.com/cyber-claims-study-2020-report/)* there were more than 3,500 cyber claims made to insurance companies it analyzed between 2015 and 2019, many of which were nonprofit organizations.

Workers' Compensation Insurance

Every state, including Texas, has a workers' compensation law. The purpose of workers' compensation is to provide income to workers injured on the job and to pay their medical bills. In exchange, the employee gives up the right to sue the employer.

Participation in the state program is voluntary for Texas private employers. If an employer chooses to participate the organization will either purchase a workers' compensation policy from a private insurance company licensed by the Texas Department of Insurance, be certified by the Department to self-insure, or join a self-insurance group from an organization certified by the Department. If an employer chooses not to cover their employees, they must still meet certain compliance standards. For example, they must post written notices in the workplace informing their employees that they do not have workers' compensation insurance. They must inform new employees that they do not have this insurance coverage. If they do purchase insurance, they must inform their employees within 15 days of the policy's effective date. They must still report workplace injuries, illnesses, and fatalities with the Texas Division of Workers' Compensation (DWC). For more information, see: *https://www.tdi.texas.gov/pubs/factsheets/employerrr.pdf*

Unemployment Compensation Insurance

The unemployment compensation program in Texas is a job insurance program. Its purpose is to provide some limited protection against loss of income for workers who lose their jobs through no fault of their own. Section 3309 of the Federal Unemployment Tax Act enables 501(c)(3) organizations to opt out of the tax system and reimburse the state only for unemployment claims the state has paid out to the nonprofits' former employees. Statistically, most nonprofit organizations do better by choosing this reimbursable method, i.e., they pay less in benefits than they would in paying taxes for the insurance. Bona-fide religious organizations are exempt from the law. Employers who pay at least $1,500 in total gross wages in any calendar quarter or pay at least one employee for a minimum of one hour a day during 20 different weeks in a calendar year must register with the Texas Workplace Commission and create a tax account. 501(c)(3) organizations that have at least four full- or part-time employees for 20 different weeks in a calendar year must also register. The state tax is only on the first $9,000 paid to an employee by an employer during a calendar year. Employers file quarterly wage reports and taxes must be filed and paid by the last day of the month following the end of the calendar quarter.

For more information, see: *https://www.twc.state.tx.us/businesses/unemployment-tax*

Texas Workforce Commission
101 E 15th St, Rm 665
Austin, TX 78778-0001
Call 800-832-9394 and choose option 1, or call 512-463-2699
tax@twc.state.tx.us

Online Resources to Explore:

Carter McNamara's Guide to Business Insurance
https://managementhelp.org/businessinsurance/index.htm

The Grantsmanship Center's Managing Risks in Hiring and Firing
  https://www.tgci.com/articles/managing-risks-hiring-and-firing

Nonprofit Risk Management Center
  https://nonprofitrisk.org/

Tips:

- This chapter provides an introduction to some of the liability concerns facing nonprofits. Seek legal counsel before making any organizational decisions with respect to changing policy that could affect your exposure to liability, or about any liability suits and claims.

- Be certain you have an up-to-date personnel policy manual and that it includes a sexual harassment policy. Take steps to enforce these policies. While the policies should be customized to the needs of your organization, samples can be found online.

- Provide detailed job descriptions even for volunteers. Some provisions of the federal immunity law apply only in cases in which volunteers are engaged in activities within the scope of their duties.

- Make sure that all volunteers are certified or licensed if they engage in activities that require certification or licensing for paid staff.

- If your organization transports clients, verify that volunteers have vehicle insurance and that all insurance policies for vehicles owned by the organization will cover damages caused by volunteers while driving those vehicles.

- If you serve on a board and disagree with a board decision being made at a board meeting that you feel may result in unreasonable increased liability exposure to you or your organization, ask that your objections be recorded in the minutes.

- Shop around for directors' and officers' insurance. Check to see if any policy you are considering will insure directors and officers for more than civil lawsuits.

- Make sure that those who hire employees are familiar with the questions they can and cannot legally ask (see Chapter 12).

Chapter 10
Financial Management

Synopsis: All nonprofit corporations must keep certain financial records and create reports of their financial condition. There are three standards of financial verification used by accountants to verify financial data—audit, review, and compilation, with the audit being the highest level of scrutiny. Line-item and program budgets are the two major forms of budgeting utilized by nonprofit corporations. Nonprofit organizations must institute financial management systems to assure they will operate efficiently and effectively, and to minimize waste, fraud, and abuse.

Some of the most critically important duties of an organization's board and staff are to take steps to pay its obligations, invest its money, and plan for its financial future. Imagine the consequences that may occur if an otherwise "perfect," respected organization finds itself unable to meet its payroll because a large check anticipated from a funder failed to arrive in time before it could be deposited. An organizational culture that condones stealing—whether in the form of allowing office supplies or organization vehicles to be requisitioned for personal use, using credit cards to make personal purchases, or even not penalizing the use of an organization's copy machines for personal use—may experience a hemorrhage of organizational resources that could be fatal during tough economic times. Buyers who steer purchases to their relatives and friends rather than make dispassionate business decisions that are in the organization's best interest are subjecting the organization to a hidden "tax." Both board and staff leadership have a fiduciary duty to act in the best interests of the organization rather than in their own personal interest, and to manage the financial affairs of the organization prudently. To do otherwise is not only dangerous to the long-term health of the organization, but is both unethical and illegal as well.

An organization's board and staff leadership are not the only sources of pressure to make its operations more "business-like," and assure that each dollar expended is necessary and used effectively to further the organization's mission. Government and private funders are increasingly demanding efficiency, cost effectiveness, and outcomes that demonstrate real, measurable progress toward achieving program goals. The press has perhaps become more vigilant about monitoring the voluntary sector since high profile scandals involving institutions such as the National Rifle Association, Liberty University, American University, the United Way of New York City, the Association for Volunteer Administration, and the American Red Cross have made headlines. The Madoff financial scandal of 2008 resulted in the crippling or demise of hundreds of nonprofit organizations.

Nonprofit organizations are increasingly operating in a competitive environment not dissimilar to their for-profit counterparts. They compete for grants and donations, for board members, contracts, volunteers, media coverage, and qualified staff. Failure to manage the financial affairs of an organization can be catastrophic, resulting in bankruptcy, cutbacks of services, layoffs, involuntary merger/takeovers, and dissolution.

Where the transfer of money is involved, there are always ethics and accountability issues of which to be aware. As a result of high profile financial scandals in the nonprofit sector, the elimination of waste, fraud, and abuse in nonprofit organizations is not simply a public relations problem. In 2004, the Finance Committee of the U. S. Senate launched an initiative focusing on devising changes to laws that affect how the sector will develop, whether its historical tax exemptions will be secure, and what disclosure will be required to assure the highest level of ethics and accountability of these organizations that are ostensibly formed for the public good rather than any individual pecuniary interest. Obviously, the financial management practices of the sector are among the prominent areas under scrutiny.

As this is being written, there is a climate of increased demand for human services and fewer resources to pay for them from all levels of government (see Chapter 27). Competent financial management is the glue that can hold a nonprofit organization together during tough times.

How Nonprofit Financial Management Differs From Private Sector Financial Management

The private sector's general goal is to make a profit for the organization with the highest return on investment (ROI), and it uses financial management as a tool for that purpose. In contrast, a nonprofit organization uses financial management to make the optimal use of resources to achieve its mission(s) and accomplish its goals. Rather than trying to maximize profit, a nonprofit organization seeks to maximize the production and delivery of goods and services, consistent with demand, to those who for one reason or another, cannot receive those goods and services from either government or the marketplace. It may be that this is because they cannot afford the market cost of the services. Or it could be because the organization provides collective goods that the government either chooses not to provide, or chooses to subsidize nonprofit organizations that will. Nonprofit organizations also advocate for various causes, knowing that they will never generate any direct income from providing advocacy services.

Generally, nonprofit organizations experience more of a political process in virtually every aspect of financial management compared to a private sector organization. Those involved in that political process are typically more diverse demographically and are not always on the same page with respect to the principal goal of the organization. In theory, the goal of for-profit organizations is to make as much profit as possible. A nonprofit organization may have many competing goals, some of which may be in conflict with each other. For example, a nursing home may want to increase its share of private-pay patients compared to those whose care is financed by Medicaid, but want to become the institution of choice for those who need care for Alzheimer's disease.

Because of the public benefits granted to nonprofit organizations, particularly those with 501(c)(3) tax-exempt status, the degree of accountability for funds is somewhat higher than for for-profit organizations. Such organizations are entrusted with the care of people, many of whom are vulnerable and who have not voluntarily chosen that organization to receive services in the marketplace. There is an implicit acceptance by the public and government agencies that ethical standards are higher for such organizations than would apply to their for-profit counterparts (although many would argue that all organizations should have equally high ethical standards, regardless of their sector). Even with this being the case, there is no federal government regulatory authority over the financial management of nonprofit organizations comparable to that which the Securities and Exchange Commission (SEC) has over stock-issuing corporations. Such an agency might "impose uniform accounting standards on public charities, disseminate information on the financial conditions of organizations, and create channels through which donors, volunteers, clients, and community members could access and use this information," as Peter Frumkin has suggested in his book, *On Being Nonprofit*.

Components of Financial Management

Among the activities encompassed by financial management, are a sequence of related activities, including planning, programming, budgeting, financing, controlling, and evaluating.

Planning involves assessing the organization's current and likely future situation, surveying its strengths and weaknesses, setting out its goals and objectives, and developing a roadmap to achieve them. See Chapter 6 for an in-depth discussion of strategic planning. There are financial implications to changes in market conditions, new competitors, new laws and regulations, additional paperwork requirements (such as might be required by a new government or foundation funder), and an increase in the demand for services—both an increase in the number of clients and an increase in the level of services required by each client—resulting from changing social, economic, or political conditions.

Programming is the scheduling of the activities the organization needs to engage in to make its goals become a reality. In this phase, the organization creates distinct programs. A program is defined by Carter McNamara as "a collection of organizational resources that is geared to accomplish a certain major goal or set of goals," Prudent financial management requires that financial data be segregated by program, so that the performance of each program can be independently evaluated. This is particularly important to nonprofit organizations, as funders—and to an increasing degree, donors as well—want their grants and donations used for a particular purpose that may be only one small part of the overall operations of the organization.

The "program" is intended to achieve a particular outcome. Resources are sought from government, foundations, and the public to finance any net loss that the agency would incur by conducting that program, whether or not fees are charged to those who benefit directly from program services.

Budgeting is the process for allocating expenditures to each program. A budget is defined as an itemized summary of estimated or intended expenditures for a given period, often for a given fiscal year. A "fiscal year" is a one-year period at the end of which all accounts are reconciled, and for which the one-year budget applies. It does not necessarily coincide with a calendar year. For example, the federal government's fiscal year begins on October 1. Many states begin their fiscal year on July 1.

Typically, an organization's budget is not only a document to control the activities of subordinates, but it is also a political document. A budget, either directly or indirectly, indicates the priorities of the organization. Annual budget documents in all three sectors usually indicate what was spent during the previous fiscal year, what is being spent during the current year, and what is proposed to be spent for the next fiscal year. Stakeholders reading the budget get a sense of the direction the organization is heading with respect to each of its programs, whether it is growing or declining, from where it is planning to get its funds, and its general financial health. One gets a sense from the budget about whether the organization is more comfortable outsourcing or performing tasks with its own personnel. Those who prepare organizational budgets should look at it in its entirety and think about what message it is sending. For more details about budgeting, see pages 144-147.

Financing includes the activities necessary to obtain the resources needed in the budget. It may include borrowing from financial institutions to start new entrepreneurial ventures, or perhaps using endowment funds to serve as startup capital. It typically involves managing cash flow to assure that the organization has enough funds to pay its obligations, and policies relating to managing its cash and other assets. Fundraising, investment of surplus revenues, management of endowment funds, and use of funds generated by for-profit subsidiaries are among the activities that are included in the financing phase of the financial management cycle.

Controlling includes the development of a system that assures that the programs envisioned in the plans are being carried out appropriately. It also provides for feedback to warn when a program does not measure up to its expectations so that mid-course corrections can be implemented to get it back on track. Included in this phase of operations are policies to assure that the organization's assets—such as equipment and supplies, inventory of goods, and cash—are protected from inappropriate use or distribution. Most importantly, this includes systems that are designed to measure whether the implementation of programs is consistent with budget plans and projections, and to have procedures in place to expand, contract, or otherwise modify program operations when their performance differs from what was anticipated by the budget and planning documents. The basic accounting system; expense account policies; policies designed to minimize waste, fraud, and abuse; and the general Management Information System (MIS), if the organization has one, are among the systems that fall under this phase.

According to Thomas McLaughlin, there are six elements of an internal control system.

1. *Control Cues.* This involves management and leadership sending signals, both overt and covert, of proper ethical behavior, and training staff in appropriate control policies that promote accountability.

2. *Policy Communication.* This entails having written policies and procedures for accountability and ethics related issues when you can, but in the absence of that, being able to communicate to employees what is acceptable and what is not by email, texting, interoffice memo, or voice mail.

3. *Segregation of Duties.* This involves breaking up work duties so that one person does not have total dominance over a portion of the financial system. For example, it might make sense for the person ordering the good or service, filling out the purchase order, writing the check, signing the check, mailing the check, and receiving the ordered goods to be different people within the organization. This becomes a challenge for organizations with only a few employees, but even for a one-person office, a system of checks and balances needs to be developed.

4. *Record-keeping.* This relates to documentation and recording of all financial transactions. Among ways nonprofits try to minimize their vulnerability to internal fraud and abuse is by using a reliable payroll service, contracting out accounts receivable, and taking advantage of those financial institu-

tions willing to do cash management for organizations. Of course, doing so increases the organization's vulnerability to external fraud and abuse.

5. *Budgets.* The budget is perhaps the best strategy to control behavior, since if there are no funds in the budget, it is difficult for spending to occur that has not been planned for and preauthorized.

6. *Reporting.* McLaughlin's view is that "you only need five financial reports to control the average nonprofit corporation" (p. 207): the balance sheet, revenue and expenses, aged accounts receivables, cash flow projection, and utilization reporting (which generally, refers to how many people are using the organization's services, and to what extent). By looking at these reports periodically, a manager ostensibly can see trouble spots.

Evaluation provides data on whether the programs are accomplishing what they set out to do. It involves validating the efforts of what is working and providing enough information to eliminate components of programs, or entire programs, when it is determined that they are not working. Many funders require the independent evaluation of the specific programs they fund as a condition of the grant. Since the popularity of the "reinventing government" movement and outcome-based management, nonprofit organizations are under increasing pressure to evaluate programs based on outcomes rather than the more easily measured outputs (see Chapter 30 for more on this topic). Regardless, systems to collect data that facilitate evaluation that are in place at the beginning before a program starts operating make evaluation easier than having to start from scratch after the program has been operating.

Generally, it is considered more efficient if all of the functions described in this financial management cycle are administered by one person. In smaller organizations, the executive director is responsible for all of the tasks involved that are described above. Larger organizations, however, will have one person (typically with the title of Chief Operating Officer or Chief Financial Officer) who will have these duties. In the case of the latter, as some high-profile criminal and civil cases have shown with respect to the for-profit sector, it is expected that there will be sufficient communication between the CEO and the CFO or equivalent. The CEO is ultimately responsible for the health of the organization, and simple ethics require that the CEO maintain a close watch over the financial affairs of the organization even if a subordinate staff member maintains day-to-day control over the financial operation of the organization.

Controls for Waste, Fraud, and Abuse

There are two general classifications of systems that are used to control waste, fraud, and abuse in nonprofit organizations. The first is to discourage these before they occur. The second is to assist in discovering them after they have occurred. The traditional method of thwarting waste, fraud, and abuse *before* they occur consists of—

1. *The independent auditor's annual audit and the annual management letter.* The management letter is an opportunity by the auditor(s) to point out any deficiencies seen in the operations of the organization that affect financial accountability and ethical concerns directly to the board. When you get a management letter that cites chapter and verse with respect to internal control problems, you need to deal with it (and quickly!). This requires a plan of corrective action that is approved by the board before implementation.

2. *Internal controls of the organization.* This consists of a system of checks and balances to assure that no one person (or perhaps even more than one) can control assets without appropriate accountability. This involves the requirement that expenditures be preauthorized by a responsible organization official in accordance with predetermined policies affecting disbursements. All expenditures are recorded by the accountant/bookkeeper, with appropriate documentation for the expenditure becoming part of the file. That financial officer has the responsibility to raise any questions about the expenditure. Oversight might include pre-audit checks of all purchase orders and vouchers, and review by someone other than the person requesting them before a payment is made, and separating those who order goods and services from the organization from those who receive the goods and services. It also might include spot checks of credit card transactions, long distance and 900 number telephone bills, and cell phone accounts to assure that no personal expenses are charged to the organization.

3. *Policies requiring large orders of goods and services to be put out for bid.* This includes related policies that discourage purchasers from dividing up orders into small increments in order to undermine this policy. This does not necessarily mean that the organization must prepare a formal *Request for Proposal* (RFP) for every large purchase. But it should mean that quotes should be obtained from several qualified vendors and contractors for large purchases.

4. *Ethics policies that apply to organization resources are distributed to individuals.* These policies might apply to credit cards, copying machines, telephones, internet accounts, cell phones, and organization vehicles, for example. Those authorized to make purchases need to have an arms-length relationship to the vendor. These ethics policies would also include what is acceptable with respect to receiving gifts. For example, those who authorize company purchases would be prohibited from accepting gifts from suppli-

ers other than *de minimus* gifts such as calendars. More substantial gifts, such as a box of cookies, would have to be shared with everyone in the organization. (The free vacation to Las Vegas as a thanks from the vendor to the organization's purchaser would have to be declined.) An ethics policy should also cover the issue of gifts made to staff members from those who receive services. All ethics policies should be reviewed at least annually and updated as appropriate.

5. *Training all employees on how to deal with the elimination of waste, fraud, and abuse.* The philosophy inherent in this method is that it is difficult to deal with a "bad" behavior when an individual might not have a clear sense as to what that might be in every case. The training should include procedures for staff to report suspected cases of fraud.

6. *Severe penalties for violating the organization's policies.* This involves written policies that require those found to have stolen from the organization be fired and referred to criminal authorities, or otherwise appropriately sanctioned by reprimand or suspension if the violation is in a gray area.

7. *Record keeping about all assets and taking a periodic inventory.* This is important so that when something is missing (such as a lap-top computer), an investigation can commence quickly.

8. *Electronic protection of records.* The purpose of maintaining backups is so that there remains an electronic trail, if not a paper trail, in the event of a fire or flood that destroys paper records.

Methods used to find occurrences *after* they have occurred include—

1. Determining when an employee has suddenly adopted a high lifestyle beyond his/her known income.

2. Investigating when it becomes suspected that purchasers are funneling purchases to personal friends or relatives, or receiving expensive gifts from suppliers.

3. Taking swift action when there appears to be missing documentation, "lost" organization checks, or an increased backlog in recording transactions.

4. Randomly reviewing credit card transactions for personal expenses charged to the organization's account.

5. Determining which expenses seem too high compared to what they have been historically, particularly when it is difficult to account for that with a reasonable explanation.

Basic Financial Statements

For a sample, actual document that summarizes the financial position of a nonprofit, the Association for Research on Nonprofit Organizations and Voluntary Action (ARNOVA) see Appendix F. There are four basic financial statements that are prepared by the organization's accountant:

1. *Balance sheet (Statement of Financial Position).* The purpose of the balance sheet is to demonstrate the financial position of the organization at a certain point, typically the end of a fiscal year, by comparing its assets (what the organization owns) to liabilities (what the organization owes). Current assets consist of the monetary value of what is owned by the organization other than long-term assets, including the cash in the checking account and cash equivalents such as certificates of deposit; accounts receivable (minus the value of those receivables that are not likely to be collected, called "bad debts"); pledges receivable; grants receivable; the current value of its investments (stocks, bonds, and other marketable financial assets); inventories of goods; and prepaid expenses and other deferred charges (such as, for example, a fully-paid life insurance policy that covers more than one fiscal year). Fixed assets (including the value of land, buildings, and equipment owned by the organization that has a life of more than a year) are those that are not likely to be converted into cash at any time in the near future, such as stocks and bonds or real property owned by the organization.

   Liabilities are debts that the organization owes to those outside of the organization. Current short-term liabilities include accounts payable, grants payable (for those nonprofits that make such grants), taxes owed but not yet paid (such as sales taxes collected and UBIT—unrelated business income taxes— that apply even to those organizations that are tax-exempt), and current loans. Long-term liabilities include long-term loans, bonds, and mortgages. The report is called a balance sheet because assets and liabilities are brought into balance in the "bottom line" as a result of merging liabilities with the "net assets," also referred to as "fund balance"—the net value, the net worth, or the equity of the organization at that point in time.

2. *Income Statement.* Income statements consist of three parts, showing revenues, expenses, and the net difference between these two (positive if there

is a profit, negative if there is a loss). That net difference can be distorted when an organization is on a cash basis of accounting, and there are either expenses or revenue paid out (or taken in, as the case may be), in a different accounting period. The accrual method of accounting overcomes this flaw (see page 142). Categories of income may include grants; donations; income from fees for services; income from for-profit subsidiaries; and sales of land, buildings, and equipment. Expense categories may include salaries, supplies, depreciation on buildings and equipment, administrative, general and fundraising expenses, and other expenses. The statement usually includes a line at the bottom comparing the net profit of the current year to the previous year, and the amount of this profit that has aggregated over time (called the "fund balance").

3. *Statement of Changes in Financial Position.* This statement typically includes the amount of cash from revenues; the amount of cash expenditures (and the difference between the two as net revenue or net loss); expenses from purchases of land, equipment, and income from the sale of these; and income from loans and bonds. The "bottom line" on this statement shows the net profit or loss and the cash balance, as well as how that cash balance compares to the previous year.

4. *Form 990—Return of Organization Exempt From Income Tax.* This annual information form has been required by the Internal Revenue Service since the 1940s. It applies to most federally tax-exempt organizations with gross revenues of $25,000 or more. Organizations with gross revenues of less than $100,000 and total assets of less than $250,000 may elect to file the short version of the form, 990-EZ. And smaller organizations are required to file a 990-N, which provides contact information, but does not disclose any financial data.

The 990 filing deadline is four and a half months following the organization's fiscal year. Organizations are required by law to provide a copy of their Form 990 to anyone who requests it, although organizations that make their returns "widely available," such as by posting their 990s online, are exempt from this requirement. The organization may charge a reasonable copying fee (none if the requester provides his or her own copying equipment on site) and actual postage costs. Form 990, last revised in 2020, requires detailed disclosure relating to Revenue, Expenses, Changes in Net Assets or Fund Balances (Part 1); Statement of Functional Expenses (Part 2); Statement of Program Service Accomplishments (Part 3); Balance Sheets (Part 4); a list of officers, directors, trustees, and key employees that includes salary information (Part 5); and "Other" information that includes information about lobbying, fundraising, unrelated business income, in-kind donations, among other issues (Part 6). The fine for not filing this return is $20 per day, not to exceed the lesser of $10,000 or 5% of the gross receipts of the organization for the year. For large organizations (those with annual gross receipts exceeding $1 million), the penalty is $100 per day up to $50,000.

Small organizations (those with revenue under $25,000 annually) must file a 990-N e-postcard at least once every three years, or they will automatically lose their federal tax exemptions, a requirement of a 2006 federal law.

Fund Accounting

Separate accounting records are maintained for each fund of a nonprofit organization. The nonprofit establishes each of these funds to meet a specified purpose. A small-sized nonprofit might only have a single fund, called the general fund, operating fund, or unrestricted fund. Larger nonprofits may have several funds in addition to this general fund. Among the most common are—

Endowment Fund. A permanent endowment fund assumes that the financial principal remains unspent, but that the interest earned on this fund may be spent for either any purpose or a restricted, specified purpose.

Fixed Asset Fund. This fund includes the fixed assets of the organization and liabilities associated with the physical plant (both purchase and maintenance). Pledges to construct new facilities are included in this fund.

Restricted Funds. It is not unusual for donors to specify how their donations must be used. If the board does not have the power to use donations for any purpose it chooses, the donations are placed in a restricted fund and reported in a separate accounting statement of Income, Expenses, and Changes in Net Assets. Some nonprofits have funds established for each major donor.

Accounting rules tend to get somewhat complex and legalistic. Some donations have conditions attached before they can be counted on by the charity. Two examples of these are bequests and matching pledges. Rather than being included as assets in fund accounting, these donations are often disclosed as footnotes in the financial reports.

Cash-Flow Analysis

Nonprofit organizations, as with other organizations, benefit from performing a cash flow analysis. The analysis is designed to answer the questions of how much cash the organization needs to pay its obligations at each point in time, and when and from where is it coming at each such point in time. This analysis is necessary because revenue, such as that coming from grants, is not always received before expenses need to be paid. A year-long grant may be paid in monthly installments. For organizations that write paychecks every two weeks, there are three payrolls rather than two every third month.

Utility bills (such as for heating in the winter and cooling in the summer), may be seasonal. The organization's annual fundraiser may create a spike in donations in May, a month or so before the end of the fiscal year. In short, a budget may balance appropriately based on a year of revenue and expenses. If the expenses are incurred mostly before the income is received, the organization may find itself unable to pay its obligations. A cash-flow analysis will look at how revenues and expenses project each month, and determines whether there is a problem with having enough cash in the bank to write checks for obligations when they need to be written. When there is a problem identified, there are often strategies for dealing with it. Some payments can be made in installments. Purchases can be put on a credit card until enough cash comes in. Accounts payable could be delayed a month or so in order to catch up or the organization could seek a loan.

What is the FASB?

The Financial Accounting Standards Board (FASB) is the independent, private-sector, nonprofit organization that establishes financial accounting and reporting standards for public and private companies and nonprofit organizations that follow Generally Accepted Accounting Principles (GAAP). The Financial Accounting Foundation (FAF), another private nonprofit, supports and provides oversight, administration, financing, and appointment of the FASB and the Governmental Accounting Standards Board (GASB). The collective mission of these three organizations "is to establish and improve financial accounting and reporting standards to provide useful information to investors and other users of financial reports and educate stakeholders on how to most effectively understand and implement those standards."

Its accounting standards are promulgated with an open, participatory process, and are recognized by government agencies with statutory authority to enforce organizational accountability, including the Securities and Exchange Commission, and professional associations such as the American Institute of Certified Public Accountants. Indeed, although the board is independent of all government and professional associations, the FASB consists of seven full-time members appointed by the board of the FAF.

There are two important standards issued by the FASB that apply to nonprofit organizations.

FASB Statement 116 and Statement 117 were issued in June 1993, and apply to all charities with at least $5 million in assets and $1 million in annual expenses and generally is required to be adopted for financial statements for fiscal years beginning after December 15, 1995. Statement 116 sets standards with respect to accounting for contributions made and received. Among changes in policy made by this statement is that donor pledges that are unconditional are counted as assets even though no actual payment on the pledges has been received. For a summary, see: *https://www.fasb.org/st/summary/stsum116.shtml*

FASB Statement117 establishes standards for financial statements of nonprofit organizations. It requires, among other standards, that nonprofit organizations provide a statement of financial position, a statement of activities, and a cash-flow statement. Organizations must report total assets, liabilities, and net assets in a statement of financial position; report the change in an organization's net assets in a statement of activities; and report the change in cash and cash equivalents in a statement of cash flows. The main theme of SFAS 117 is to take into account the presence or absence of donor restrictions, and group an organization's funds into three categories: permanently restricted, temporarily restricted, and unrestricted, applicable only to the organization's net assets. For a summary, see: *https://www.fasb.org/st/summary/stsum117.shtml*

Sarbanes-Oxley

The *American Competitiveness and Corporate Accountability Act,* commonly known as the Sarbanes-Oxley Act, was enacted by the Congress in 2002 as a response to corporate financial scandals, such as those at Enron, Arthur Anderson, and Global Crossing. Generally, this act does not apply to nonprofit corporations, although two provisions—those relating to protecting whistle-blowers and the destruction of litigation-related documents—do apply to both for-profit and non-profit corporations. Note that Texas has its own whistleblower protection law, the *Texas Whistleblower Act,* which can be found in Section 554.001 et seq. of Title 5.

Bookkeeping

Both state and federal law require corporations to record all expenses and income in an organized format. This can be done manually or by using one of many popular computer programs.

Several basic decisions must be made with respect to record-keeping. First, the corporation must decide on the period of its fiscal year. Federal law requires the Form 990 nonprofit tax return to be filed within four-and-a-half months after the end of the fiscal year (technically, by the 15th day of the fifth month after the end of the fiscal year), that alone can determine when to begin the fiscal year. Other factors to consider are the fiscal years or the announcement dates of grants of major funding sources, using a calendar year for simplicity, or beginning the fiscal year as soon as the first corporate income has been received.

A second issue is in deciding whether the bookkeeping system will be on a "cash" or "accrual" basis. Cash basis financial reporting recognizes a transaction the date income was actually received and deposited and when expenditures were made. The "accrual" method recognizes a transaction when it is made, i.e., when supplies are ordered, not when they are received. The "accrual" method factors in "accounts payable" (when the organization owes someone money, but has not actually sent them a payment) and "accounts receivable" (when there is a legal obligation to pay the organization something in the future, but the organization has not yet received payment). Most novices find the cash basis easier and simpler. The accrual method, on the other hand, gives a more realistic picture of the actual financial situation of the organization, and thus complies with generally accepted accounting principles.

The "cash" vs. "accrual" decision should be discussed with the organization's accountant, or whoever is likely to prepare the tax returns and annual financial report. This is the time when the foresight of placing a certified public accountant or two on the board of directors can pay dividends.

Some funding agencies may have their own unique financial reporting requirements to qualify for grants.

Levels of Financial Verification

There are three levels of financial verification. In descending levels of scope and scrutiny, they are audits, reviews, and compilations. The level of financial verification required is often determined by the nature and source of funding for the organization. Many government grants explicitly require a minimum level of financial verification in their contracts. Such a contract may be a "pass-through" of funds from another source, and the original source may need to be tracked down to determine whether it has its own requirements. For example, a nonprofit organization may receive a grant from a United Way, but the funding is provided by a state government. As a result, the United Way may require financial reports from the nonprofit organization that will permit it to comply with its own reporting requirements to that state government grantor.

It is wise to request all financial reporting information, in writing, from any contracting agency that provides the organization with grant funds.

All of the three financial verification levels require that all organizational funds be segregated by the appropriate organizational accounts (and, of course, from the accounts of other organizations) and all transactions be accounted for. It is never good organizational policy to sign over an incoming check payment to a third party. Instead, deposit the check into the organization's account and then write a new check to the third party. Although ignoring this advice may save the time of making a deposit and writing a check, it will result in a loss of "paper trail" necessary to determine who paid what to whom, when, and for what.

In the absence of an overriding requirement in a contract, federal, state, and local governments require an audit report when the funds in the contract are $100,000 or more in any single year. State and local governments generally require a review if funding is between $25,000 and $100,000 annually. If funding is less than $25,000, a compilation report is usually acceptable.

Audit Report

The highest level of financial verification, an audit, is a complete arm's-length verification of the accuracy and reliability of account statements and financial reports. Records are systematically examined and checked to determine how they adhere to generally accepted accounting principles, management policies, and other stated policies. The purpose of independent audits is to eliminate bias, self-interest, fraud, and unintentional errors. What does the auditor do?

The auditor will request information from individuals and institutions to confirm bank balances, contribution amounts, conditions and restrictions, contractual obligations, and monies owed to and by your organization. The auditor will review physical assets, journals and ledgers, and board minutes to ensure that all activity with significant financial implications is adequately disclosed in the financial statements. In addition, the auditor will select a sample of financial transactions to determine whether there is proper documentation and whether the transaction was posted correctly into the books. In addition, the auditor will interview key personnel and read the procedures manual, if one exists, to determine whether or not the organization's internal accounting control system is adequate. The auditor usually spends several days at the organization's office looking over records and checking for completeness.

Although an auditor can never obtain *absolute* proof of the representations made in a financial statement, the standard used is that of a "reasonable man" (or woman) who has "adequate technical training and proficiency as an auditor," according to the American Institute of Certified Public Accountants. Auditors have a professional code of ethics to ensure their independence from the management of the nonprofit organization they are auditing. Although they are paid a fee by the corporation, they are considered to be responsible to the public rather than to their corporate clients.

Many government agencies have audit requirements for recipients of their grants, as do many foundations and other umbrella fundraising organizations, such as United Ways and Jewish federations. Audits are often required by major umbrella fundraising organizations unless the revenues are relatively small.

Review

A second standard of financial verification, called a "review," is the application of analytical procedures by the accountant to the financial data supplied by the corporation. It is substantially narrower in scope than an audit. Much of the information supplied by the corporation is accepted at face value, although there may be a spot check to see if there are any glaring errors or inconsistencies between expenses recorded and the checks that are written. The examination of internal control and the proper allocation of income and expenses is similar to that of an audit report. Unlike an audit, the review will not include a formal auditor's "opinion" as to the compliance with generally accepted accounting principles.

Compilation

The third level of financial reporting/verification, a "compilation," calls only for the proper classification of assets, liabilities, fund balances, income, and expenses, from information supplied by management. Third-party verification of assets and liabilities is not required, although internal supporting documents may be used in their place. "Spot checks" are employed only when the accountant is aware of inconsistencies in other areas of the examination. As in a review, the accountant will not render an "opinion" on the accuracy of the report.

In the absence of legal requirements, it is good policy for nonprofits that expend more than a few thousand dollars to have at least a review. Many nonprofits have certified public accountants on their boards who may be willing to arrange for a review of the corporation on a *pro bono* basis.

Budgeting

Some nonprofits can exist for years using volunteer labor, donations of stamps, in-kind printing and other services, and have no need to raise money or make any expenditures. Others are more likely to have some staff and pay office rent or, if not, still have expenditures for workshops, postage, printing, telephone, and other typical corporate expenses.

The annual budget document is the blueprint for both spending and income. A poorly conceived budget can lead to the corporation's demise. On the other hand, a well-conceived, realistic budget can be the catalyst for program planning that provides a corporate life for many fruitful years.

Line-item and program budgets are the two major types of budgeting used by nonprofit corporations. Each has its advantages and disadvantages.

Line-Item Budget

The line-item budget is as it says—a list of various categories and the amount the corporation expects to spend for each category. Corporations, from the largest to the smallest, have some of the same categories in a line-item budget. Among the most common are:

- salaries
- consulting services
- professional services
- taxes
- fringe benefits
- telephone/wireless
- postage
- printing and photocopying
- travel
- workshops and conferences
- bank fees
- dues
- subscriptions and publications
- data processing
- equipment
- equipment maintenance and repair
- legal services
- insurance
- rent
- office supplies
- maintenance and repairs
- security services
- utilities
- bookkeeping and payroll services
- Web hosting services
- advertising
- miscellaneous

As an expense is incurred, its amount is entered in a journal prepared for this purpose, coded by its expense category. At the end of each month, the amounts of each category are aggregated on a ledger sheet called a "monthly summary."

The monthly totals should be compared with the budget for each category to determine whether spending patterns are consistent with the budget. For example, an organization can have "annual conference" as a program, and include all expenses associated with it included, such as printing, postage, advertising, travel, consulting, and so on. Or as an alternative, the individual expenses of the conference for printing and postage could be included in the organization's regular printing and postage line-items.

The advantage of a line-item budget is the ease of assigning every expenditure. A dollar spent on paper clips is an expense for "supplies," and a dollar spent on Web hosting is an expense for "Web hosting." The disadvantage is that it is not always clear how much can be saved by eliminating any particular program of an organization, because the expenses of that program are subsumed within many different line-items, such as would be the case with the example of an annual conference.

Program Budget

The second type of budget is called a program budget. The program budget also contains various line-items, but the difference is that each program of a nonprofit, such as conferences, newsletter, membership, or publications, has its own budget within it.

For example, if the organization is having a conference, then the conference itself has a budget. Printing, postage, and telephone costs are attributed to the conference. Printing and postage costs may be associated with another program as well, such as a newsletter.

The advantage of the program budget is that one can quickly determine the incremental savings that will accrue to the organization if a particular program is eliminated. The disadvantage is that it is not easy to allocate overhead costs—such as the CEO's salary and rent—to various programs.

It is not unusual for nonprofits to combine the two types of budgeting—to have a general line-item budget, but to allocate some spending in all categories to certain programs. For small nonprofits, line-item budgets are the easiest to prepare and follow, but program budgets provide better information.

The Budget Process

Each organization is likely to develop its own budgeting process, which evolves over time based on the personalities of its staff and board, the stability of its funding streams, the needs of outside stakeholders, and other factors. The following is one possible model.

Step 1. Begin the budgeting process at least three months before the start of the organization's fiscal year, allowing enough time for the board to approve the final budget after having the opportunity to provide feedback.

Step 2. Review all programs and management achievements. Compile a comparison of estimated costs to actual costs, which is called a "variance."

Step 3. Make estimates of expenses for commitments made for the upcoming year (in salaries, new programs, capital expenses) that did not require funding for the current year, such as new programs and the expansion of existing programs approved in the organization's strategic plan.

Step 4. Make estimates of expenditure increases resulting from predictable budget items, such as salary inflation adjustments and merit increases, rent, utilities, insurance, and other categories that grow as a result of inflation rather than expansion of services or programs.

Step 5. Make estimates of income—including estimated contributions, grants, fees, the sale of goods and services, and investment income.

Step 6. Adjust spending and income based on the organization's ability to build surpluses or incur deficits, but avoid making adjustments in income based on the need to balance a budget. The reason is that spending is more likely to be controllable compared to income.

Step 7. Submit the budget to the board for approval.

Step 8. Periodically adjust the organization's budget and resubmit changes to the board as new information is received.

Expense Reimbursement

Organizations incur expenses. Many of these can be paid conveniently by corporate check. Many others can be paid by corporate credit card, which is particularly useful for travel expenses. For reasons of good financial management, it is not atypical for newly formed organizations to require two signatures on checks. This is not unreasonable for recurring expenses that can be processed well in advance, such as paychecks, rent, major equipment purchases, and taxes.

Requiring two signatures does present problems when making small, but reasonable, on-the-spot purchases. An expense reimbursement system should be designed to provide protection against one person making unilateral, capricious decisions on spending, but needs to be flexible enough to keep the organization from being hamstrung when trying to pay $25 for office supplies.

One suggestion is to set up an "imprest account" to pay routine office expenses, requiring only one signature. The authorized person (such as the executive director) has a reasonable sum to disburse from this checking account, which is entirely separate from the "master" checking account. The imprest account is replenished from the master checking account using a check that requires the usual two signatures, only upon a review by the chairperson or treasurer (or both) of what was expended—including supporting documentation, such as receipts. This account should provide an amount needed not only to pay reasonable expenses for the month, but enough to cover expenses for part of the following month, since several days or weeks may elapse during the processing of the expense report.

The organization's leadership should provide general guidelines as to what types of expenses are acceptable for reimbursement and what expenses should be absorbed by the staff. For example, hotel accommodations in any city can range from $60-$300. A dinner can be purchased for $5 or $75. Many organizations refuse to make decisions concerning what is appropriate, and instead provide a per diem allowance—a flat payment that is expected to pay reasonable travel expenses for each one-day period. The staff member then must absorb costs that go beyond this amount.

Many other expense issues arise that require board policies. How much should staff be reimbursed for mileage? What if a spouse attends a conference with a staff member and shares a room, resulting in an incremental cost increase? How will expenses be reimbursed that cannot be directly documented with a receipt, such as tips or parking meter expenses?

All of these issues can be resolved on an ad hoc basis, but it is useful to think about the nature of expense reimbursement before it creates problems. Many organizations have failed because their budgets were depleted by discretionary spending in the absence of an expense policy.

Document Retention and Destruction Policy

Every nonprofit organization should have a written document retention and destruction policy that addresses the responsibilities of board members, staff, volunteers, and contractors who have access to the organization's records and data. No one expects an organization to retain and store every official document in perpetuity. But the unavailability of important documents could have serious adverse consequences.

Certain documents should not only be retained permanently, but also be readily accessible. Among these are the Certificate of Formation, bylaws, and IRS Determination letters; tax returns; financial statements; board resolutions; board minutes; insurance policies; audit reports; personnel records; bank statements; and documents relating to occupancy of offices (such as leases, mortgages, and deeds).

Other documents should be retained for a reasonable amount of time, such as cancelled checks, wire transfer records, credit card records, and other financial transaction records; invoices; contracts; sales tax records; newsletters and other organization reports; records relating to programs and activities; and correspondence, including emails. Availability of storage capacity used to be a major constraint on how many documents should be retained and for how long. Electronic storage has made it much easier to retain almost everything, if one has a good system to retrieve what one is trying to find.

The IRS provides some guidance with respect to how long financial documents need to be retained—found in the instructions to the Form 990.

The organization's records should be kept for as long as they may be needed for the administration of any provision of the Internal Revenue Code. Usually, records that support an item of income, deduction, or credit must be kept for a minimum of three years from the date the return is due or filed, whichever is later. Keep records that verify the organization's basis in property for as long as they are needed to figure the basis of the original or replacement property. Applicable law and an organization's policies can require that the organization retain records longer than three years. Form 990, Part VI, line 14, asks whether the organization has a document retention and destruction policy.

The organization also should keep copies of any returns it has filed. They help in preparing future returns and in making computations when filing an amended return. However, depending on circumstances, the IRS may expect to have access to records beyond the minimum of three years referred to in this guidance. And each state also has individual requirements.

For an example of a document retention and destruction policy, see: *https://www.multiplyinggood.org/National%20Site/Who%20We%20Are/Financials/Destruction%20&%20Retention%20Policy.pdf*

Investment Policy

According to the National Center for Charitable Statistics, public charities earn 4.8% of their revenues from investments, providing a small, yet significant supplement to revenues from service fees and donations. There are thousands of organizations that live hand-to-mouth, struggling day-to-day with making ends meet, and allocating virtually all of their meager resources to keeping the organization afloat. They may only have a checking account, often not bearing any interest. They can only dream of a day, which may never come, when the organization can move beyond that to have a steady source of income from investments with a diverse portfolio of stocks and bonds. At the other end of the spectrum is Harvard University, which, through the Harvard Management Corporation, manages an endowment valued at $40.9 billion as of the end of FY 2019, and other investments.

Most nonprofits fall somewhere between these two extremes. They may have a nest egg of modest revenue surpluses, which is certainly appropriate to have for times when costs exceed revenues. Putting surplus revenue into a certificate of deposit is safe, but over the long term, other strategies have shown to provide a much better return. Many nonprofits receive gifts of assets in the form of bonds, equities, royalties from intellectual property, real estate, valuable goods that can appreciate in value, and other investment instruments. It takes work to manage them. Lots of issues arise in how these assets are managed.

It simply makes sense for organizations to have a formal investment policy that spells out the board's policy with respect to the following six issues:

1. Goals and Objectives—What rate of return are we expecting to achieve from investments?
2. Payout—How will we be using the return from investment for the operating budget of the organization?
3. Diversification—What is our philosophy with respect to "asset allocation," the extent to which we do not put all of our investment eggs in one basket?
4. Management—Who will be responsible for investment management, for reporting and updating the status of investments, and for overseeing/evaluating the results achieved?
5. Risk—How much risk are we willing to accept to meet the goals and objectives we have in #1?
6. Ethics and Values—Are there certain investments we will consider prohibited because they are not consistent with our organization's values?

For sample organization investment policies, see: *https://www.councilofnonprofits.org/tools-resources/investment-policies-nonprofits*

Fiscal Sponsorship

Social entrepreneurs often face a difficult dilemma once they decide to run with an idea to improve the quality of life for their communities. If they create a formal organization, they face spending countless hours building its infrastructure and complying with all of the legal requirements described in Chapters 2 and 3. Yet, if they choose to go it alone, they suffer the consequences of not being able to accomplish as much as they could by having a formal organization, and face the reluctance of donors to make donations to them. Grantors seldom are willing or able to fund individuals, and donors are often wary of making donations to organizations that do not qualify as 501(c)(3)s and permit those donations to be tax-deductible.

There is a third option beyond these two alternatives that is increasingly attractive, but relatively obscure—finding a fiscal sponsor. Perhaps this is not as obscure at first glance. Perhaps the majority of scientific research is carried out by individuals who are affiliated with universities. The grantor makes a tax-deductible check out to the university, and the university passes along most of the grant to the individual researcher and handles all of the administration.

This model can be, and has been, adapted for social entrepreneurship. A social entrepreneur, instead of creating his or her own 501(c)(3) tax-exempt organization, approaches an existing tax-exempt organization to serve as the fiscal sponsor. The entrepreneur becomes in effect an employee of that fiscal sponsor. The sponsor receives the grants and donations on behalf of the program being carried out by the entrepreneur, provides a salary and benefits, handles all financial transactions, and provides financial oversight over the program. The donors receive their tax benefits, and the entrepreneur is free to devote his or her energies to the program rather than administration.

One barrier to doing this is finding a willing fiscal sponsor. Among those that might be considered are those with an interest in supporting the mission of the program you plan to pursue. This might include foundations, United Ways or similar umbrella fundraising organizations, institutions of higher learning, professional societies, museums, health agencies, labor unions, religious institutions, and arts organizations.

Of course, if you choose this route, you must be willing to relinquish some control over the organization. Technically, you would be an employee of the fiscal sponsor, and the board of the fiscal sponsor is the de facto "ruler" of your organization rather than yourself. The agreement between your organization and the fiscal sponsor needs to be in writing and quite clear as to the responsibilities of each party. You will want everything spelled out about what control you will have, and whether you will have the ability to spin off your organization as a separate, independent organization in the future, should you desire to do so.

For a comprehensive online guide to considering whether to structure your organization via the fiscal sponsorship model, see the Foundation Center's tutorial at: *https://learning.candid.org/resources/knowledge-base/fiscal-sponsorship/*

Online Resources to Explore:

Business Owner's Toolkit: Small Business Guide
https://www.bizfilings.com/toolkit

Guidestar—Nonprofit Reports
https://learn.guidestar.org/update-nonprofit-report?search=false&search=false

Carter McNamara's All About Financial Management in Nonprofits
https://managementhelp.org/nonprofitfinances/index.htm

Nonprofit Good Practice Guide
https://philanthropynewsdigest.org/on-the-web/nonprofit-good-practice-guide

Board Source/Independent Sector: The Sarbanes-Oxley Act and Implications for Nonprofit Organizations
https://independentsector.org/resource/sarbanes-oxley-act-and-implications-for-nonprofits/

Tips:

- Before choosing either a cash or accrual basis of accounting, verify that your organization is not required to adopt the accrual method because of government or funder requirements.

- If you are not the individual performing the accounting, yet are legally responsible for their accuracy, periodically examine the organization's books to see if there are any inconsistencies, or whether they are being kept sloppily.

- Have clear, written policies that inform staff about how they need to avoid diverting organizational resources for personal use and the penalties for doing so.

- Create a document retention and destruction policy (see pages 148-149) that is customized to the needs of your organization. Keep duplicate paper and electronic copies of important financial records, and store them at an alternative physical site and/or "in the cloud."

Chapter 11
Personnel

Synopsis: Nonprofit corporations with staff should have a written personnel policy. There are a number of state and federal laws that apply to nonprofits that have employees and many standard forms that must be filed to comply with these laws.

Whether a nonprofit corporation has one salaried employee or hundreds, a written personnel policy can prevent disputes that, in some cases, can destroy an organization even before it gets off the ground. A personnel policy for a small organization will be less complex than that of a large one. It is advisable to review personnel policies of several organizations of similar scope and choose among the provisions that are most sensitive to your organizational needs. It is not necessary to reinvent the wheel, but *having* a wheel is important.

Qualified and trained personnel are an organization's most prized assets. Staff members need to feel that the organization is flexible enough to respond to their individual needs. Conversely, the organization must have the ability to operate efficiently, effectively, and economically, and to treat all employees fairly and equally. A balance must be attained, and each organization can best determine for itself where the balance lies.

Before hiring the first employee, among the issues to consider and to develop policies for are:

- Should staff be paid employees of the corporation, or should the corporation hire a consultant? (See pages 169-170)
- What will be included in staff job descriptions?
- How much should each staff member be compensated? Should a staff person be paid on a salaried basis or by the hour?
- If an office is established, what should the office hours be, and where should the office be located?

It may be advisable for the organization to have a personnel committee. Its role is to study the issues raised in this section; develop a personnel policy for ratification by the board, if appropriate; and to serve as the adjudicating body to resolve grievances by employees.

Personnel Policies

After a decision is made to hire employees, some of the issues to consider for inclusion in a personnel policy are the following:

1. **Hiring policies**—How should job vacancies be advertised? Will there be affirmative action to recruit minorities? Should the search be national, statewide, regional, or local? Should current employees be given preference in hiring for vacant positions? Is a pre-hiring physical examination required?

2. **Firing policies**—What are the conditions that permit dismissal without appeal, such as "for cause"? Will there be severance pay? Will placement services be provided? Will notice be given of unsatisfactory job performance before dismissal?

3. **Probationary periods of employment**—Should there be a period of probation during which an employee can be terminated without access to any grievance procedure or will not be entitled to receive benefits, including leave?

4. **Sick leave and vacation**—How many days will be allowed? Can they be accumulated and, if so, how? Will a doctor's note verifying illness be required?

5. **Holidays**—Which holidays are paid holidays and which are optional? What is the policy with respect to the observance of religious holidays?

6. **Personal days**—How many personal days will be permitted, and will they be accumulated? If not taken, will they carry over? Can they be "cashed in" upon retirement?

7. **Overtime policies**—Which classes of employees are eligible for overtime pay? Is overtime mandatory if requested by the organization? Will overtime be compensated in salary or compensatory time?

8. **Compensatory ("Comp") time**—Should comp time be granted in lieu of overtime pay? Should surplus comp time be required to be used for routine doctor and dentist appointments rather than for sick leave?

9. **Full-time vs. part-time status**—How many hours per week qualify the employee for benefits?

10. **Health insurance**—What *must* be offered to comply with the *Affordable Care Act*? Is there a group plan? Will gross salary be increased if an employee is covered by the health insurance policy of a spouse and elects not to be covered by the organization?

11. **Pension**—How long does it take for an employee to be vested? What is the employer and employee contribution required?

12. **Life insurance and other benefits**—Is there a menu from which to choose?

13. **Employee evaluation**—Who performs the evaluation? How often will the evaluation be performed? Under what conditions may employees exercise their legal rights to examine their files? Who has access to personnel files?

14. **Merit salary increases; cost-of-living increases**—What are the criteria used for salary increases, and how often and by whom are salaries reviewed?

15. **Continuing education benefits**—Are they offered? Who has authority to approve requests? What are the time and cost limitations? When do employees become eligible? What types of courses are eligible for reimbursement?

16. **Staff training/orientation**—Is there a formal review for new employees concerning staff personnel policies? What type of training will be provided and who will provide it?

17. **Maternity leave**—What documentation is required? What is the maximum leave the employee may take without losing her job?

18. **Bereavement leave**—How long will such leave be, and which relatives will be included in the policy?

19. **Family and medical leave**—For what purposes will this leave be granted? What documentation is required to accompany a leave request? Will the leave be paid or unpaid? What will be the effect on unused sick leave and vacation (see #17)?

20. **Pay for jury duty, military leave**—What is the organization's policy?

21. **Sabbatical leave**—After how many years will employees qualify, for how long, and will this be paid or unpaid leave?

22. **Expense reimbursement documentation**—How will expenses be filed and what expenses are eligible? Is there a flat per diem rate for out-of-town travel or reimbursement? What amount will be reimbursed for mileage?

23. **Notice required for resignation**—What is the minimum notice required, and what are the sanctions for not complying?

24. System for resolution of employee grievances—May employees appeal to the board of directors? Is there a committee for this purpose?

25. Disciplinary sanctions for rule-breaking—Is there provision for suspension with or without pay?

26. Prohibition against secondary employment—What types of outside earned income are prohibited or permitted?

27. Telephone policy—What is company policy concerning personal calls at work, including reimbursement by the employee for toll calls or personal use of cell phones provided by the organization?

28. Payroll—Will salary be provided weekly, every other week, or monthly?

29. Use of the internet—What is the policy for using the organization's internet account for personal use, during working hours, and after working hours? Are there limitations on what employees may post on their personal social networking sites about work-related issues?

30. Personal Relationships—What types of personal relationships are not permitted among staff, or which may need to be reported to determine if there is a conflict of interest?

31. Dress Code—Is there a dress code? What is and is not permitted?

Although the issues may seem overwhelming, a small organization may only need basic policies such as hours of operation, vacation and sick leave policy, benefits provided, and holidays. The rest can be determined on an ad hoc basis by the executive director, in consultation with the board's chairperson and/or the personnel committee, if there is one.

Required Postings in the Workplace

Texas has laws and regulations requiring all employers to post in the workplace posters available from the Texas Workforce Commission to inform their employees about rights they have under state law. Among these are posters relating to the Workers' Compensation Program, the Uniformed Services Employment and Reemployment Rights Act, the Fair Labor Standards Act, the Employee Polygraph Protection Act, and the Occupational Safety and Health Act. Employers subject to the Texas Payday Law must also display an information poster. Employers liable under the Texas Unemployment Compensation Act must display a poster that includes information about both unemployment compensation and the Texas Payday Law. Every employer with 15 or more employees, and smaller employers with federal grants and contracts must post the notice entitled "Equal Employment Opportunity Is the Law," which contains information about the Equal Employment Opportunity/Americans with Disabilities Act laws. Posters may be printed out from links found at *https://www.twc.texas.gov/businesses/posters-workplace.* For more information about what may be required to be posted in your specific circumstances, contact the Texas Workforce Commission's Texas Labor Law unit at 800-832-9243 or 512-475-2670.

Major Federal Laws Affecting Employers

Taxpayer Bill of Rights 2 (P. L. 104-168)

This law was enacted on July 30, 1996, but its provisions relating to excessive income are retroactive to September 1995. It includes "intermediate sanctions" provisions that authorize the Internal Revenue Service to levy excise taxes on excessive compensation paid out by 501(c)(3) and (c)(4) organizations, and to penalize nonprofit managers who authorize such compensation. The law also provides for increased public disclosure of financial documents.

Fair Labor Standards Act of 1938 (52 Stat. 1060, 29 §201 et seq.)

Enacted in 1938, the law provides for a minimum wage, controls child labor, and requires premium pay for overtime for workers paid less than $684 per week ($35,568 annually), with that threshold to be updated in January 2021.

Equal Pay Act of 1963 (P.L. 88-38, 29 § 206)

Requires that men and women performing equal work be paid equally.

Civil Rights Act of 1964 (P.L. 88-352, 28 §1447, 42 §1971, 1975a-1975-d, 2000 et seq.)

Prohibits discrimination, including employment discrimination, on the basis of race, color, religion, sex or national origin. Includes prohibition of certain questions being asked by prospective employers at job interviews.

Equal Employment Opportunity Act of 1972 (P.L. 92-2615 §5108, 5314-5316, 42 §2000e)

Amends the Civil Rights Act by expanding employment anti-discrimination protection relating to race, color, national origin, sex, religion, age, disability, political beliefs, and marital or familial status.

Age Discrimination in Employment Act of 1967 (P.L. 90-202, 29 §621 et seq.)

Prohibits discrimination against persons age 40-70, as revised by the 1978 amendments.

Immigration Reform and Control Act of 1986 (P.L. 99-603, 7 §2025 and other references)
Requires employers to certify that their workers are not undocumented, and prevents discrimination on the basis of national origin.

Employee Retirement Income Security Act of 1974 (ERISA) (P.L. 93-406, 26 § 37 et seq., 29 §1001 et seq., and other references)
Requires accountability and reporting related to employer pension plans.

National Labor Relations Act of 1935 (49 Stat 449, 29 §151 et seq.)
Authorizes workers to form unions and other collective bargaining units.

Pregnancy Discrimination Act of 1978 (P.L. 95-555, 42 §2000e(k))
Amends the Civil Rights Act (which prohibits discrimination on the basis of sex) to change the definition of "sex" to include "because of or on the basis of pregnancy, childbirth, or related medical conditions."

Drug-Free Workplace Act of 1988 (P.L. 100-690, 41 §701 et seq.)
Requires organizations receiving federal grants to certify that they will provide a drug-free workplace, notify their employees of actions taken against those who violate drug laws, and establish a drug-free awareness program.

Americans With Disabilities Act of 1990 (P.L. 101-336, 29 §706, 42 §12101 et seq., 47 §152, 221, 225, 611)
Prohibits discrimination and ensures equal opportunity for persons with disabilities in employment, state and local government services, public accommodations, commercial facilities, and transportation. It also mandates the establishment of TDD/telephone relay services.

Family and Medical Leave Act (P.L. 103-3, 29§2601 et seq.)
Requires businesses with 50 or more employees to provide certain workers with up to 12 weeks annually of family or medical leave to care for a sick spouse, child, or parent, or to care for a new child.

Uniformed Services Employment and Re-Employment Rights Act of 1994 (P.L. 103-353, 38§4301-4304).
Protects the job rights of individuals who voluntarily or involuntarily leave employment positions to undertake military service and prohibits employers from discriminating against past and present members of the uniformed services and applicants to the uniformed services.

The Patient Protection and Affordable Care Act of 2010 (P.L.111-148, 29§1558).

Among many other requirements, requires employers to report the value of health care benefits to employees on W-2s, requires nonprofit hospitals to meet certain criteria to maintain their federal tax exemptions, and provides small tax-exempt organizations with a refundable tax credit to subsidize the cost of providing health insurance to their employees, specifically targeted for low- and moderate-income individuals. Most of the provisions apply to employers of 50 or more full time equivalent employees.

The Health Insurance Portability and Accountability Act of 1996 (HIPAA) (Public Law 104-19, 110 Stat. 1936)

Requires health care providers and organizations, as well as their business associates, to develop and follow procedures that ensure the confidentiality and security of protected health information when it is transferred, received, handled, or shared. It also provides the ability to transfer and continue health insurance coverage for millions of American workers and their families when they change or lose their jobs.

Texas Laws Affecting Nonprofit Employers

The Texas Law Enforcement Telephone Solicitation Act (LETSA)(Business and Commerce Code, Title 10, Section 303.001 et seq.)

Regulates certain law enforcement related organizations that engage in telephone solicitation in the State of Texas.

The Public Safety Solicitation Act (Texas Occupations Code, Title 11, Section 1803.001 et seq.)

Requires certain public safety organizations, public safety publications, and their solicitors and/or independent promoters to register, pay a fee, and post a bond with the Secretary of State.

The Charitable Raffle Enabling Act (Occupations Code, Chapter 2202, 2202.001-2002.058 et seq.)

Permits "qualified organizations" to hold up to two raffles per calendar year, with certain specified restrictions.

The Veterans Solicitation Act (Texas Occupations Code, Title 11, Section 1804.001 et seq.)

Requires certain veterans organizations to file a registration statement with the Secretary of State and pay a fee. If the veterans organization uses a solicitor, the organization must post a surety bond with the Secretary of State.

Texas Child Labor Law (Texas Labor Code, Chapter 51, Section 51.001 et seq.)

Ensures that a child is not employed in an occupation or manner that is harmful to the child's safety, health, or well-being.

Texas Business Organizations Code, Nonprofit Corporations (Chapter 22).

Contains codified statutes that apply to all nonprofit corporations in Texas.

Charitable Volunteer Immunity (Tex. Code § 84.004)

Limits the civil liability of volunteers who are serving as an officer, director, trustee, or direct service volunteer of a charitable organization for an act or omission resulting in death, injury or damage if the volunteer was acting within the scope of duty.

Texas Commission on Human Rights Act (Texas Labor Code, Chapter 21, 21.001 et seq.)

Prohibits employment discrimination because of race, color, disability, religion, sex, national origin, or age.

Lobbyist Registration (Texas Government Code Title 3, Section 305 et seq., Legislative Branch)

Requires persons receiving compensation or who spend money to advocate the passage or defeat of legislation to register with the State Ethics Commission, and to disclose certain expenditures and contacts.

Texas Minimum Wage Act (Texas Labor Code, Chapter 62.001-62.205)

Sets the Texas minimum wage for non-exempt employees at the federal minimum wage.

Texas Workers' Compensation Act (Texas Labor Code, Title 5, Sections 406.001 et seq.)

Provides for a worker's compensation program.

Unemployment Compensation Act (Texas Labor Code, Sections 201-001201.101)

Provides for unemployment compensation to workers who lose their jobs through no fault of their own.

State Forms

1. AP-201—Texas Sales and/or Use Tax Permit. All organizations, including those that are exempt from paying sales taxes on their purchases, must collect and remit sales tax on all goods and taxable services they sell. It takes about four weeks to receive the permit. Organizations may apply for the permit online at: *https://comptroller.texas.gov/taxpermit/*

2. Form C-1—Employer's Status Report for Unemployment Compensation. This is used for employers to register with the Texas Workforce Commission for liability assessment under the Unemployment Compensation Insurance Act. Registration may be accomplished online at: *https://comptroller.texas.gov/taxes/ file-pay/*. The PDF of this form may be accessed at: *https://www.twc.texas.gov/ files/businesses/c-1-employers-registration-status-report-twc.pdf*

3. Form 802—Nonprofit Organization Periodic Annual Report. This periodic report lists the names and addresses of all directors and officers of the corporation. The Office of the Secretary of State may require a domestic nonprofit corporation or a foreign nonprofit corporation registered to transact business in this state to file this report not more than once every four years. Instructions at:
https://direct.sos.state.tx.us/help/web%20filing%20instructions%20form%20 802(0711).pdf

4. Form 202—Certificate of Formation, Domestic Nonprofit Organization. This form, filed with the Secretary of State, governs the formation of a nonprofit corporation and sets forth the provisions required or permitted to be contained in the certificate of formation, which provides for the incorporation of the organization.

5. Form AP-205—Application for Exemption. Charitable Organizations. This form is filed with the Texas Comptroller of Public Accounts to request exemption from Texas sales tax, hotel occupancy tax, and franchise tax, if applicable.

6. Form AP-207—Application for Exemption. Educational Institutions. This form is filed with the Texas Comptroller of Public Accounts to request exemption from Texas sales tax, hotel occupancy tax, and franchise tax, if applicable.

7. Form AP-209—Application for Exemption. Religious Institutions. This form is filed with the Texas Comptroller of Public Accounts to request exemption from Texas sales tax, hotel occupancy tax, and franchise tax, if applicable.

8. LETSA Registration Form. This form is used to register solicitors under the Law Enforcement Telephone Solicitation Act (LETSA) with the Attorney General.

9. Form REG—Lobby Registration. This form is used to register as a lobbyist with the Texas Ethics Commission. Online registration is required, but the form can be viewed at: *https://www.ethics.state.tx.us/forms/lobby/*

10. Form 50-115. Application for Charitable Organization Property Tax Exemption. This form must be filed with the appropriate office in the county in which the property is located. See: *http://www.hayscad.com/PA/forms/50-115.pdf*

Standard Federal Paperwork for Corporations with Employees

1. Form SS-4—Application for Employer Identification Number—This is the first form to be filed when starting a corporation. Once this form is filed, the Internal Revenue Service will establish an account for the organization and assign a federal tax number (EIN). This number will be the organization's account for paying taxes and is requested by other government authorities for tax purposes. It is requested by most foundations and grant makers, as well. This form should be filed at least a month before the number is needed. To obtain this form, call the IRS toll-free at 1-800-829-3676 or access it at: *https://www.irs.gov/pub/irs-pdf/fss4.pdf.* Organizations may apply for an EIN online at *https://www.irs.gov/businesses/small-businesses-self-employed/apply-for-an-employer-identification-number-ein-online*

2. Form W-4—Employee's Withholding Allowance Certificate—Each employee must file with the employer a copy of form W-4, which documents the number of exemptions and additional federal withholding. The information in the W-4 enables the employer to calculate how much should be withheld from gross salary (not including state and local withholding). Note: Due to changes in the law, taxpayers can no longer claim personal exemptions or dependency exemptions. The 2020 Form W-4 no longer asks an employee to report the number of withholding allowances that they are claiming because of changes in the tax law that eliminate the personal and dependent exemptions.

3. Circular E—Employer's Tax Guide—Employers need to obtain a copy of this publication (call toll-free 1-800-829-3676 to request this guide or access it at: *https://www.irs.gov/publications/p15)* to calculate the amount of federal income tax withholding, Social Security withholding (for calendar year 2020 set at 6.2% of gross wages up to $137,700), and Medicare withholding (for calendar year 2017 set at 1.45% of gross wages, without any ceiling). The amount of wages needed to earn a Social Security credit is $1,470 in 2021. Workers thus will need to earn $5,880 in 2021 to earn the maximum four credits for the year. Most workers need 40 credits to be eligible for retirement benefits (see *https://www.ssa.gov/pubs/EN-05-10072.pdf* for more information about Social Security credits).

4. Form 1099-NEC. There is a new Form 1099-NEC to report nonemployee compensation paid in 2020. It replaces Form 1099 MISC. The 2020 Form 1099-NEC was due February 1, 2021. This form must be filed if the organization pays more than $600 in the calendar year to those who are not direct employees, such as independent contractors. One copy is given to the individual on or before January 31.

5. Electronic Federal Tax Payment System (EFTPS)—As of 2011, employers must use electronic funds transfer to make all federal tax deposits (such as deposits of employment tax, excise tax, and corporate income tax). Generally, electronic fund transfers are made using the Electronic Federal Tax Payment System (EFTPS). Employers may arrange for a tax professional, financial institution, payroll service, or other trusted third party to make electronic deposits on their behalf. For more information on what forms are required and how they are electronically submitted with payments, see: *https://www.eftps.gov/eftps/*

6. Form 941—Employer's Quarterly Federal Tax Return—Each quarter, the IRS requires reconciling federal tax payments that were deposited for the previous quarter. The final line will indicate if the corporation owes any payments to the IRS. With limited exceptions, employers must submit their return and payment using the Electronic Federal Tax Payment System (EFTPS) unless their total payment for the current quarter or previous quarter is not more than $2,500.

7. Form 940—Employer's Annual Federal Unemployment (FUTA) Tax Return— Nonprofit organizations other than those with 501(c)(3) status are subject to FUTA taxes. This form must be filed if more than $1,500 was paid in wages during any calendar quarter or if the organization had one or more employees at any time in each of 20 calendar weeks during the previous two calendar years. The tax rate for 2020 was 6.0% of the first $7,000 paid to each employee. Businesses receive a credit on the amount of unemployment taxes paid to their state. Quarterly tax deposits may be necessary, depending on the amount owed. These deposits are made in the same way as federal quarterly withholding deposits. If payments are more than $500, the payment must be submitted using the Electronic Federal Tax Payment System (EFTPS).

8. Form W-2—Wage and Tax Statement—This statement is given to all employees on or before January 31. It details their gross salary and amounts withheld in federal, state, and local taxes during the previous year.

9. Form W-3—Transmittal of Income and Tax Statement—This return looks like a Master W-2, and aggregates information for all employees. It is filed with the Social Security Administration, accompanied by one copy of each employee's W-2.

10. Form 990—This is the tax-exempt nonprofit corporation's tax return.

11. Form 990-T—This is a supplement to the tax-exempt nonprofit corporation's 990 tax return that reports gross income of $1,000 or more from unrelated business income during the fiscal year.

12. Form I-9—This form is kept by the employer for each worker to certify that the worker is a citizen, national, or alien legally authorized to work in the United States.

Tips:

- Don't ever be "too busy" to comply with the law and fill out all of the paperwork.

- Make a copy of your organization's Form 990 Annual Tax Return available on your website to avoid having to make copies for members of the public who request their own personal copies.

- Download posters that by law must be posted in the workplace by all employers. See: *https://www.dol.gov/general/topics/posters#workplace-posters* to access resources.

Chapter 12
Hiring, Evaluation, and Firing

Synopsis: Nonprofits have options for staffing their agencies. A planning process is necessary when hiring and firing employees, and there are legal requirements for doing so. A regular evaluation process for staff and the executive director is recommended. There is a continuum for disciplining employees short of termination.

Few can argue with the view that a nonprofit's human capital is its most important resource.

The executive director influences the direction, morale, image, and financial stability of an organization. Yet, even the least senior employee can have a significant impact, negative or positive, on the organization. Employees can be creative, nurturing, versatile, ingenious, inspiring, and team-building. Or they can be disruptive and destructive—infecting morale, and creating scandal that can ruin the reputation of a charity that took decades to foster.

The scandal involving the United Way of America's CEO, William Aramony—convicted in 1995 on 25 counts of engaging in fraudulent practices and generally living lavishly at the organization's expense— is just one example of how a single individual can stain an entire sector. The shock waves from the New Era Philanthropy scandal are continuing to be felt. The forced resignation of the American Red Cross's chief executive in 2001, blamed in part on an alleged policy of deceptive fundraising, made front page news.

More recent allegations against the CEOs of the National Rifle Association and Liberty University have damaged the reputations of both organizations.

As our society becomes more litigious, poor performance by an employee can have disastrous consequences. Many human services nonprofits that work closely with aging populations, children, and people with disabilities have had experience defending the actions of their employees in court, and they are at risk for damage suits that run in the millions of dollars. In some cases, poor staff performance may be a matter of life and death for at-risk clients. The responsibility for choosing staff in a nonprofit should not be taken lightly.

Each hired employee is an investment by a nonprofit not only in the salary paid to him or her. The chemistry of an organization is changed by a new hire, and bad hiring decisions can haunt an organization for many years or destroy it completely.

In recent years, nonprofits have lost the image of having certain characteristics, compared with their for-profit counterparts. That image often viewed nonprofits as—

- less hierarchically structured
- less willing or able to fire non-productive employees
- more informally managed
- paying less and providing fewer benefits for longer hours
- more altruistically managed, with less emphasis on the bottom line
- more interested in their employees' personal satisfaction.

Evidence shows that this stereotype is no longer valid, or that it is at least becoming frayed at the edges. Nonprofits today face the same competitive and financial pressures to succeed as their for-profit counterparts. Nonprofits are becoming more comfortable hiring MBAs and those with for-profit business experience to manage their enterprises, whereas once social science degrees were the educational pedigree of choice.

Hiring Employees

Many of the jobs available in the nonprofit sector are equally available in the for-profit sector. For example, both often require a CEO, accountants, legal staff, supervisors, receptionists, Webmasters, human resources specialists, social media managers, government relations personnel, public relations officers, administrative assistants, and secretaries. In many of these jobs, the actual tasks performed by nonprofit employees are quite similar to those performed by for-profit employees.

Regardless, it is important to recognize that those who apply for jobs offered by nonprofits may retain the stereotypical image. It is useful to consider whether a prospective employee may have an unreasonable expectation of working for a nonprofit organization. This can be assessed during the job interview.

Hiring requires a positive attitude, which is often missing on the part of the hirer. First, if the hiring is being done to replace an employee who was fired or resigned, the hirer often is distracted by the disruption caused by the separation. The hirer often is in a position of having to perform a task that is not pleasant—putting aside current responsibilities to conduct the job search and interview. Few, if any, managers enjoy this process.

Before embarking on hiring a new employee, it is useful to do some planning that addresses some considerations:

- What are the tasks and duties the new employee will perform?
- Are these tasks absolutely necessary?
- Could someone already in the organization perform these tasks? Do these tasks require special education, professional credentials, and/or experience that are currently lacking in the staff?
- Can we obtain these services through means other than hiring an employee?
- How long will it take to hire a new employee, and will these duties still be required after that time?
- How will these tasks change over time?
- What level of productivity can we expect of this new hire?
- Which support services will this person require? For example, will we also have to hire a secretary or administrative assistant?

Options—Advantages, Disadvantages, Legal Considerations

Organizations must choose among various staffing options, and each has its advantages and disadvantages. Among these options are—

Hired Staff—The Sunday newspaper classifieds and online job boards are usually filled with hundreds of job listings from nonprofit organizations that have decided to hire full-time staff.

> **Advantages**: Employees have the most stake in the organization; they tend to be loyal, may work additional hours, and can be flexible in doing tasks not in the job description when necessary.

> **Disadvantages**: Employees must be paid even when work is not needed, require payroll taxes and expensive benefits, and are paid for vacations and when sick—possibly disrupting work flow.

Paid Contractors—private for-profit companies and individuals market their services to nonprofits to perform tasks that are intended to obviate the need for hiring full-time workers.

> **Advantages:** The nonprofit does not have to withhold employee income, Social Security, Medicare, state and local taxes, or pay unemployment and Social Security taxes. Contractors can be hired for short-term or long-term projects and can be terminated easily, do not require year-round benefits (although the equivalent is often built into the contract price), and do not obligate payment by the nonprofit unless the job is completed successfully. The contractor may have skills and resources that the nonprofit would not otherwise be able to afford, except on a temporary basis.

Disadvantages: Hiring a paid contractor may be legal only under certain limited circumstances. The Internal Revenue Service Publication 15-A *(Employer's Supplemental Tax Guide)* provides details on the score of factors that indicate whether an individual is considered an employee or an independent contractor. This publication is available for download from the IRS *(https://www.irs.gov/pub/irs-pdf/p15a.pdf)*. Independent contractors sometimes charge steeply in that they must cover overhead and marketing, as well as make a profit.

Volunteers—Unsalaried workers, some of whom may be there not solely because they are altruistic and want to help, but because they may be fulfilling educational requirements or disciplinary requirements ordered by a court.

Advantages: They do not require a salary, and they are there not for a paycheck but, with some exceptions, because they want to be.

Disadvantages: They do not have the paycheck as motivation, generally work fewer hours than employees, and may leave the organization on short notice.

Temporary Hires— hiring people for short-term employment without a promise that the employment will continue beyond a certain date.

Advantages: They permit the organization to respond to short-term or seasonal fluctuations in workload.

Disadvantages: The recruitment and administrative burden of temp workers can be substantial.

Outsourcing to another organization—either contracting with an employment service for temporary workers, or contracting with an outside organization to perform the functions. One example is a payroll and accounting service, which could perform services otherwise done by a staff bookkeeper.

Advantages—The organization can avoid the expense and administrative burden of hiring employees.

Disadvantages—Outsourcing is often more expensive on an hourly basis than would be the case if a person were hired temporarily.

Process in Hiring

Search Process. Many nonprofits, through their personnel committees, develop a procedure for hiring new employees. Search committees are often authorized by the board to develop job descriptions, prepare job notices, cull through résumés to identify several candidates to interview, and recommend a candidate to the board. Others delegate the process entirely to the executive director—unless, of course, the search is for an executive director. In either case, the basic steps remain the same:

1. **Prepare a job description.** The job description is a useful planning document for the organization. It also allows prospective employees to decide if they are interested in, and capable of, performing the duties expected of them.

2. **Prepare a job notice.** The job notice provides standard information, such as job title, description of the job, education and/or work experience required, salary range, deadline for application, and the person to contact. Decide whether the notice will request applicants to send résumés or file applications provided by the organization.

3. **Advertise the job.** Jobs may be advertised in daily newspapers, trade journals and publications, the newsletter of a state association, through the State Job Service, with educational institutions, online through the internet at general employment sites such as Indeed (*https://www.indeed.com/*), Monster *https://www.monster.com/), Career Builder (https://www.careerbuilder.com/)*, and, most importantly, internally. There are online job boards that target nonprofit sector employment, such as Idealist *(https://www.idealist.org), The Chronicle of Philanthropy (https://www.philanthropy.com/)*, and *Philanthropy News Digest (http://philanthropynewsdigest.org/jobs)*. Many nonprofit organizations also include a current job opportunities listing on their own websites and social networking pages, as well.

4. **Review the applications.** Develop a process for reviewing and ranking applications to decide who will be invited to interview. Remember to send a letter to those not interviewed, informing them that they were unsuccessful.

5. **Interview candidates.** The interview should be a dialogue, not a monologue by the interviewer. Let the candidate talk, so the interviewer can make judgments about how articulate the candidate is. It is useful to be friendly, ask a few softball questions first, and perhaps make a comment about something interesting on the résumé, such as a hobby, professional association membership, or award. Ask about any years that appear to be missing from the résumé.

There are questions that should be asked by the interviewers, and questions that by law cannot be asked. Among the questions that may be asked are:

- What background and experience make you feel you would be suitable for this particular position?

- What has attracted you to apply for a position with this organization?

- What experience, education, or background prepares you for this position that makes you feel you would be suitable for this position, and would separate you from other applicants?

- Do you have experience using the software packages used by this organization?

- What former employers or teachers may be consulted concerning your abilities?

- What are your long-term professional goals?

- What are the two or three things that are most important to you in a new professional setting?

- What motivates you to perform? How do you motivate those who work with you or for you?

- What were some of the most important accomplishments in your previous position, and what did you do that was special to achieve them?

- Describe a situation in which you had a conflict with another individual, and explain what you did to resolve it.

- Are you more comfortable working with a team on a group assignment, or by yourself?

- What are your significant strengths and weaknesses?

- Why are you shifting direction in employment?

- Where do you see yourself professionally in five years?

- How do you feel about your current/previous employer(s)?

Among questions that may *not* be asked are:

- questions relating to an applicant's race, sex, sexual orientation, national origin, religion, or age

- questions relating to the applicant's physical and mental condition that are unrelated to performing the job

- questions that provide an indication of the above, such as the number of children the applicant has, the applicant's maiden name, child care arrangements, height/weight, whether the applicant is pregnant or planning to have children, the date the applicant graduated from high school, and whether the applicant is a Sabbath observer

- whether the applicant has ever been arrested or convicted of a crime, without proof of business necessity for asking.

The Texas Workforce Commission plays an important role in Texas in enforcing anti-discrimination laws in the state. For more information, contact:

Texas Workforce Commission, Civil Rights Division
101 East 15th Street, Suite 144T
Austin, Texas 78778
(512) 463-2643
(888) 452-4778 (Toll Free)
https://www.twc.texas.gov/

6. **Select the best-qualified candidate.** This is different from selecting the best candidate. The best candidate within the pool of applicants may be identified easily, but if that person is not quite up to the task, it is a mistake to hire him or her. It is better to begin the search again, or try to find another way to have those duties performed without taking a chance that a bad hiring decision will harm the organization, perhaps irreparably.

7. **Verify information from the résumé and interviews; investigate references.** By law in some states, employers may not refuse to hire an employee based on a prior criminal conviction, unless that conviction specifically relates to the prospective employee's suitability for employment.

Even in that case, the applicant must be informed in writing of a decision based on that, in whole or in part. For some nonprofit jobs, particularly those involving children, state law requires a State Police background check.

It is not unusual for job candidates desperate to make their résumés stand out to embellish their educational or professional qualifications. A few telephone calls can ferret out many of these. This is a wise investment; someone who is dishonest enough to falsify qualifications on a résumé is likely to be just as dishonest when it comes to other professional issues. Investigating references can often turn up reasons for not hiring someone. It is good practice to request permission from the applicant to check references and to contact previous employers. Although a candidate may refuse for personal reasons to permit contact with a previous employer, it is sometimes, but not always, an indication of a flawed relationship.

Among the questions that are appropriate when contacting prior employers are:

- How long did the applicant work for you?

- What was the quality of work of this applicant?

- What level of responsibility was the applicant given?

- How did the applicant get along with coworkers?

- Did the applicant show initiative and creativity? In what ways?

- Was the applicant a self-starter, or did he or she require constant supervision and direction?

- Was the applicant punctual?

- Is there anything you can tell me that would be relevant to my decision to hire or not hire the applicant?

8. **Make an offer to the candidate and negotiate salary, benefits, and other terms of the offer.**

9. **Put the offer in writing once the offer is successful.** Use a contract, if necessary or desirable. Once the contract is signed or the offer is otherwise accepted, notify other candidates that they were not successful, and arrange to orient the successful candidate.

Evaluation

Periodic staff evaluations are an important tool for executive directors and human resource managers to communicate important information to staff and obtain valuable feedback. One principal purpose of these evaluations is for the executive director to convey to the employee, in a measurable way, how well that employee is performing with respect to each of several areas of the position. This process is useful to both parties. Most employees want to do as well as they can, and the staff evaluation is an opportunity for the executive director to share potential shortcomings that might otherwise have been difficult to communicate.

The staff evaluation is an opportunity to focus on both strengths and weaknesses. Weaknesses are not necessarily the fault of the employee. In areas where improvement is needed, the executive director can suggest strategies, such as on-the-job training, mentoring, continuing education, and additional supervision, which can assist an employee in improving performance. Many nonprofit executives are reticent about approaching the subject of poor employee performance, and many employees are unaware that their managers feel that improvement is necessary. A regular staff evaluation can put in motion a series of positive steps that assist the employee in addressing shortcomings that might otherwise fail to be communicated. For problem employees, the staff evaluation is an opportunity to formally point out shortcomings in advance of disciplinary action or firing.

Staff evaluations are generally an annual affair, often scheduled a few weeks into a new calendar or fiscal year, or a month before or after the Annual Meeting.

In a typical staff evaluation process, certain questions are addressed, regardless of whether the evaluation is a simple 15-minute, informal meeting between the manager and employee or a formal process that involves filling out survey instruments that become a part of the employee's permanent personnel record and are the basis for merit salary increases.

There are many different formats, but many organizations have a formal personnel policy that requires all staff members to be evaluated (typically by the executive director, if the organization is small enough), with a written memo summarizing the results of an evaluation interview. The memo is shared with the employee, who signs it, acknowledging that it has been read, but not necessarily agreeing to the content. In many evaluation processes, the employee is provided an opportunity to respond in writing to any of the criticisms included in the evaluation, and this is included with any evaluation that is placed in that employee's personnel file.

Issues to be addressed should include:

- What goals were the employee expected to accomplish, and how successful was the employee in accomplishing these goals?
- What could have been done by the organization to help the employee accomplish more toward meeting these goals?
- What were the areas that the evaluator found to be the employee's strongest and weakest areas?
- What can the employee suggest to assist him/her to improve in those weak areas?
- What goals are expected to be accomplished before the next employee evaluation?
- How well has the employee gotten along personally with colleagues?
- How well has the employee worked with colleagues as a team to accomplish organizational goals?
- Has the employee shown loyalty to the organization by cheerfully taking on tasks when needed that may not have been in the job description?
- Has the employee favorably represented the organization outside of work?
- Has the employee demonstrated professional work habits by arriving on time, taking reasonable lunch and break time, and not being unnecessarily absent?
- What can the employee share about organization policies, procedures, and work processes that could be improved?

Evaluation of the Executive Director

The task of evaluating the Executive Director is relegated to the Board of Directors. A formal process to evaluate the executive director is appropriate annually. It can be performed by the Chair, the Personnel Committee, or a group designated by the Board that could consist of an ad hoc committee of board members. While an interview with the executive director is a major component, an evaluation of the executive director should also include feedback from staff members, grantors and other contributors, organization clients, and other stakeholders.

Some of the areas that may be evaluated include—

- success of the executive director in furthering the stated mission and vision of the organization and implementing the organization's strategic plan
- financial management, including adherence to board-approved budgets, fundraising, and maintenance of financial viability of the organization
- ability to maintain and improve staff morale and teamwork

- ability to communicate with the board, staff, clients, donors, lawmakers and regulators, and the public
- success in maintaining and improving public trust in the organization
- success in collaborating with other organizations
- maintaining a highly ethical, credible, organization.

Firing Employees

The loss of one's job is often the most stressful and traumatic event in a worker's life, with the exceptions of the death of a close family member or divorce. For most managers, having to fire someone is unpleasant at best, and can be traumatic. In many cases, it represents a failure not just by the affected worker but also by the organization.

Managers must be careful about how the firing is done; employee lawsuits over firings are becoming more common. When a nonprofit is unionized, even firings for the most egregious offenses may be challenged. It is also important to make sure that there is authority to fire. For example, the board chairperson may not fire the executive director without authority from the board, unless the bylaws provide for that. The executive director may not fire the communications director, for example, unless the organization's bylaws, policy of the board, and/or job description of the executive director make it clear that he or she has this authority.

Planning Issues

Before firing an employee, it is important to do some planning. Among the issues to consider are how to deal with the workload performed by the fired employee; the effective date of the termination; what to tell coworkers about the action; how to ensure that the employee will not take away sensitive files and other materials; what to tell the employee about health and life insurance continuity, pension, and other benefits; how to deal with separating personal property and organizational property; how and when to terminate email addresses and passwords; how much severance pay to offer; and whether any letter of recommendation will be provided.

When to Fire

It is usually appropriate to summarily (without warning) fire an employee for gross misconduct that threatens the organization. Examples of this are drinking on the job, being convicted of a serious criminal offense, the willful destruction of organizational property, stealing from the organization, or causing harm to others (such as clients or other employees).

Most unacceptable behaviors that eventually result in dismissal are not as abrupt, and it is only after the manager has attempted a series of mitigation efforts that have failed that the employee is told to leave. Among these behaviors are unexplained absences, chronic tardiness, insubordination, laziness, and general poor job performance. Many nonprofit managers are close to their employees and shy away from taking appropriate disciplinary action. They need to realize that the health of the organization requires discipline and that they are getting paid to ensure that the organization functions. Problem employees inhibit otherwise productive coworkers.

Discipline Short of Firing

Poor performance on the job may be the result of many factors. These might include personal problems of the employee, miscommunication by the manager, or the employee's lack of skills—for whatever reason—required to perform the task. Each of these has a remedy and, if the manager is flexible, dismissal can be avoided.

For example, the birth of a child or serious illness of a spouse or other close family member can leave a valued employee temporarily unable or unavailable to perform job duties. Some time off, flextime, counseling, or temporarily decreasing duties can all help. Continuing education can improve job skills. Improving communication from the manager, either through "coaching" on how to do the job better, or at least providing some feedback on what is going wrong, can prevent the necessity to terminate an employee. Most employees want to do well, and many believe they are doing well but are never told that their professional work is actually considered poor by those who evaluate and manage them. For some employees, however, discipline is required.

Discipline Continuum

1. **Verbal communication.** Short of the gross misconduct referred to in the beginning of this section, this should always take the form of informal communication by the manager. It should be verbal, one-on-one, and definitely not in front of coworkers. The manager should explain the problem and seek an explanation from the employee of what the manager can do to help improve the worker's ability to perform. In many cases, this will be enough. Make a notation in your records when this communication occurred and what was said, and whether the employee acknowledged the problem and agreed to improve his or her performance.

2. **Written warning.** If there is no appropriate response to the verbal communication (e.g., the employee continues to show up to work late or misses reasonable deadlines), a written memo outlining the problem should be shared with the employee. It should not be accusatory, but should state that the employee is engaging in behavior that is unacceptable, needs to be changed, and that this memo follows up on a verbal communication.

3. **Written formal warning.** This involves a formal memo to the employee from his or her immediate supervisor, similar to the written warning, but notes that this new memo will become a part of the employee's permanent personnel file. The memo should make clear that the person's job may be in jeopardy unless there is significant progress measured by a certain date, and that this progress will be evaluated on or shortly after that date.

4. **Suspension without pay.** Some employees just will not comprehend the seriousness of being late or being disruptive unless there is a real financial penalty attached. A one-day suspension, without pay, makes it clear that the manager has authority to take action and that permanent suspension (i.e., firing) is possible.

5. **Firing.** This is the last resort. In a larger nonprofit, this may actually have a beneficial effect on other employees if they feel that the employee being fired is hurting the organization. In the smaller organization, firing is rarely beneficial in the short term; a poor employee is often much more productive than no employee at all.

In a nonprofit organization, firing should always be for cause. It is not appropriate to fire your administrative assistant who has been faithful, loyal, and productive for 10 years just because the daughter of your college professor moved to town and needs a job, even if the administrative assistant has a contract that provides for employment "at will."

Even if there is no avenue for the fired employee to appeal, a nonprofit manager should be convinced that the firing is called for and could be defended in a court of law, if necessary. Some managers may actually have to defend the firing in court or before a grievance panel of some kind, such as a human relations commission. In recent years, courts have considered "wrongful discharge" suits and have awarded damages to fired employees who were dismissed unfairly.

How to Fire

1. It is common courtesy to make sure that the fired employee is the first to know, other than those up the chain of command who must know or be consulted first to obtain dismissal authority.

2. Fire the person in private, in a one-on-one situation or with other supervisors present, as appropriate.

3. Explain to the person why he or she is being fired, and point out the previous attempts to reach accommodation. Do not turn the meeting into a debate or let the person plead for his or her job. By this time, it is counterproductive to rescind the decision. Explain that the purpose of the meeting, in addition to letting the person know about the firing, is to share important information about policies, procedures, and benefits.

4. Explain applicable company policies, procedures, and benefits, such as severance pay, outplacement services, the effective date of the firing, when to turn over keys and files, and COBRA benefits. COBRA (the Consolidated Omnibus Budget Reconciliation Act of 1985) permits employees who retire, are laid off, who quit, or who are fired for reasons other than gross misconduct to continue to qualify for group health coverage for up to 18 months after termination, provided they pay the premiums. At this time, the manager may make suggestions about other jobs.

5. If appropriate, arrange for an exit interview, permitting the employee the opportunity to share information about the organization, job description, coworkers, job function, and so on. Although this exit interview may not always be pleasant, the information provided may be invaluable.

Tips:

- Make sure your policy is clear on what is permitted with respect to using the computer and internet service provided by the organization, both on organization time and personal time while in the office. For example, use of the computer to retrieve, store, or disseminate pornography should be expressly prohibited. Other policies should address other prohibited uses, such as visits to gambling sites, playing games, looking for other jobs, forwarding copyrighted material, hacking into the system, or using the organization hardware and/or software for other illegal purposes.

- Consult an attorney to resolve particularly sticky personnel matters.

- Keep good records of employee misconduct and what you did at every step to address the problem.

- Treat all employees as you would like to be treated if you were in the same position.

- Keep calm, even if the employee you are disciplining starts yelling, screaming, or crying.

- Consider the advance of technology on your personnel policies. Revisit your formal document at least annually.

Chapter 13
Volunteers

Synopsis: Volunteers are a crucial strength for nonprofits. They can be highly motivated and can save organizational resources. There are significant disadvantages, as well. Managing volunteers requires many of the responsibilities of managing paid staff.

Nonprofit organizations rely on volunteers to perform organizational functions, ranging from receptionist to board chairperson. Indeed, the term "voluntary sector" is a working synonym for "nonprofit charities."

Nonprofit organization budgets rarely permit salaries for all needed employees. During times of economic uncertainty, nonprofit organizations are particularly vulnerable to budget cutbacks, ironically at the very same time that the demand for their services increases. Using volunteers is an effective way to stretch limited organizational resources, build community support, improve communications, and tap hard-to-find skills.

The changing demographics in recent decades—more single-parent households, more two-parent working families, more women in the workforce, an increased incentive to continue working to maintain income rather than retiring—demand that volunteer recruitment, training, support, and recognition change to meet new realities.

National statistics validate the view that volunteering continues to be popular, despite a slightly declining trend. According to Independent Sector, nearly 77.4 million Americans averaged about 89 hours of volunteer service during 2019 worth an estimated $187.7 billion, based on an estimate that each hour is worth $27.20.

Volunteerism is alive and well in the United States. New public-private sector initiatives are strengthening the institutions that promote volunteerism. Partnerships are developing in schools, colleges, religious institutions, and the private sector. Successful volunteer programs tap "non-traditional" sources of volunteer strength. More and more, these partnerships are being directly encouraged by government.

Federal legislation signed on September 21, 1993, the *National and Community Service Trust Act* (P.L. 103-82), provides incentives to promote volunteerism among the young and not-so-young, and to pay them living and educational stipends, as well.

President Bush spoke to the nation about changes to the federal budget he would propose in the wake of the September 11th terrorist attacks. In his January 29, 2002 State of the Union address, the President proposed establishing a new "U.S. Freedom Corps," which would also expand volunteer opportunities (see the Corporation for National & Community Service website at: *https://www.nationalservice.gov/serve).* On April 27, 2006, President Bush issued an Executive Order requiring every federal agency to designate one staff member to serve as a liaison for volunteer community service.

In April 2009, President Obama signed into law the *Edward M. Kennedy Service America Act.* It authorizes a 5-year, $5.7 billion national and community service bill that triples the AmeriCorps program over an 8-year period. The law also authorizes transferable $1,000 education grants to those 55 years of age and older who perform community service activities. See: *https://www.nationalservice. gov/about/legislation/edward-m-kennedy-serve-america-act*

On May 23, 2017, President Trump submitted his first budget request to Congress. It proposed a total elimination of the Corporation for National and Community Service. On February 10, 2020, the President's FY 2021 budget request included $81.6 million to provide for the "orderly shutdown" of the Corporation.

Texas is an active participant in the AmeriCorps, Senior Corps, and Social Innovation Fund, programs of the national Corporation for National and Community Service (CNCS). For FY 2015, CNCS committed $51.3 million to support Texas communities' national service efforts. For more information, contact:

OneStar Foundation
9011 Mountain Ridge Drive, Suite 100
Austin, TX 78759
Phone: 512-287-2035
Email: cindy@onestarfoundation.org
http://www.onestarfoundation.org

Benefits and Considerations of Having Volunteers

Among the benefits of using volunteers are:

1. They do not require salaries or fringe benefits. Although this is the most obvious advantage, there may be other financial savings, as well.

2. They are often highly motivated. Volunteers are there because they want to be, not because it is their livelihood. If it was "just a job," volunteers might be somewhere else.

3. They can speak their minds without fear of loss of a livelihood. Volunteers can often be a useful sounding board. They are often less shy about speaking out than a paid employee might be.

4. They may bring skills to the organization that it otherwise may not be able to find or afford.

5. They may have a network of community contacts who may be a source of contributions, expertise, prospective staff, or additional volunteers.

Other considerations are:

1. Just because volunteers are not on the payroll does not mean that the organization incurs no costs. Volunteers need telephones, work space, equipment, supplies, desks, and virtually everything else besides a paycheck. Training and orientation costs are just as high as for salaried workers.

2. Volunteer retention is often a problem. The opportunity for paid employment elsewhere may influence a volunteer to leave, and family commitments or other duties may intervene. A volunteer can be easily captured by competing interests.

3. Volunteers, just like paid staff, dislike dull, repetitive, uninteresting work. They are more likely to do something about it quickly than would paid staff.

4. Volunteers are generally available for fewer hours per day. Many, such as students, volunteer for specific time periods and for short terms. They often require more hours of training and supervision per hour of productive work than employees.

Volunteer Job Description

Individuals are more likely to volunteer to assist an organization if they have specific information about the tasks they are being asked to perform. Before requesting volunteer assistance, develop a detailed job description that includes at least the following information:

- examples of duties to be performed
- specific skills or training needed
- the location where the duties will be performed
- the hours per week required
- the time period (e.g., weeks, months) the duties will be performed
- the supervision or assistance that will be provided
- the training that will be provided.

Volunteer Recruitment

Steve McCurley & Rick Lynch, in their wonderful 2011 book, *Volunteer Management* (Third Edition), provide a typology of volunteer recruiting strategies:

1. *Warm body recruitment*—seeking volunteers from as wide a pool as possible. This is done by distributing brochures and posters, using PSAs, using the organization's website, and contacting organizations who have lots of members. Advantage: This technique is good for finding volunteers for short-term assignments, such as a running race fundraiser. Disadvantage: You typically do not have much time to learn whether the prospective volunteer is honest, dependable, or otherwise suitable for the job. Example: Putting up posters around town seeking volunteers to hand out water for a YMCA-sponsored 5K.

2. *Targeted recruitment*—identifying a particular group of people who are most likely to be suitable for the volunteer position. These groups are targeted both by the message in the communication and the media by which it is communicated to maximize the probability that they will be exposed to it and respond. Advantage: You are more likely to identify someone with the right combination of skills. Disadvantage: You are limiting the pool of individuals from which to recruit. Example: Approaching a local computer club to find a volunteer to create a website for the YMCA's 5K road race.

3. *Concentric circles recruitment*—using current volunteers to find replacements and/or additions. Advantage: It does not require much work on the part of the volunteer coordinator to ask the person opting out to find someone who will take over. Disadvantage: The person who did the volunteer job last year may have a really good reason why he/she would not encourage someone to do that this year! Example: Asking last year's race director to find a replacement for this year's race.

4. *Ambient recruitment*—recruiting volunteers through a particular group who have a high affinity for that group, such as a particular school, business organization, religious congregation, or profession. Advantage: A group of

volunteers from one particular organization will feel a bond, and would likely feel that volunteering on behalf of their group will improve the image of their organization. Disadvantage: Someone still must work with the group to make sure everyone understands their roles, will work together, and will not spend their entire time socializing with each other rather than performing the work for which they volunteered. Example: Sending an email to everyone who is a member of the local Young Professionals Association asking for race volunteers.

5. *Brokered recruitment*—finding volunteers through a third party, such as a local volunteer center, a website that has volunteer listings, a corporate volunteer office, or a similar office whose responsibility is to coordinate the placement of individuals willing to volunteer. Advantage: The organization gets exposure to a pool of willing volunteers, who are likely searching for an assignment that fits their needs with respect to type of work, geographical location, and cause. Disadvantage: You may get folks volunteering for a specific task who are not suitable to the organization. Example: Partnering with the local running club, and offering its members a $5 discount on race registration if the organization provides 40 volunteers.

Active recruiting is required to maintain a dedicated volunteer pool. Some strategies nonprofit organizations use to recruit volunteers are—

- They pass around a sign-up sheet at community speaking engagements where potential volunteers can indicate their interest. Be sure to provide space for addresses, telephone numbers, and email addresses, as well as to indicate specific skills or interests.

- They include information about volunteer opportunities in any public relations brochures, media stories, newsletters, and public service announcements. Many local newspapers have a regular column devoted to nonprofit organization volunteer opportunities.

- They ask users of the organization's services if they would like to volunteer, if this is appropriate.

- They target solicitation of potential volunteers to groups in the community that are likely to have time to share. Retired people, schoolchildren, and groups sponsored by places of worship are excellent sources for volunteers.

- They post volunteer opportunities on their websites and on general sites that permit the posting of volunteer opportunities, such as IdeaList *(https://www.idealist.org)*.

Interview potential volunteers as you would potential employees. Be sure their interests are compatible with the organization's. Find out what their motivation is for volunteering. Is it to perform a service or advance a cause? Is it to develop marketable job skills and make contacts? Is it to have a place to "hang out"?

A volunteer can have the same organizational impact, negative or positive, as a paid staff member.

Tell potential volunteers about the organization and obtain basic information about them, such as their skills, training, and interests. Ask about their time availability. Once satisfied that the right volunteer is matched with the right job, review the volunteer job descriptions with them and ask them if they are ready to volunteer for specific assignments.

The fact that a person is willing to work for free does not automatically make him or her the best candidate for the "job." The organization should not lower its standards in any way. Make sure that expectations are clear and the volunteer's performance is reviewed.

Where practical, organizations should screen volunteers thoroughly and require references, including police background checks, particularly for those positions where the volunteer might be in close contact with children. Organizations should seek diversity in their volunteer mix for the same reasons this is desirable for paid staff (see Chapter 14). And it goes without saying that organizations should avoid discrimination on the basis of any aspect of individuals that are protected by laws relating to paid employment. Organizations should avoid giving volunteers only the work that paid staff feel it is beneath them to perform. Paid staff should be a part of the process for recruiting and supervising volunteers, and making sure that the volunteer job description is meaningful to potential volunteers.

Organizations should have written volunteer policies and share them with volunteers during the recruitment/interview process. See *https://nonprofnetwork. org/Resources/Documents/Sample%20Volunteer%20Management%20Policies.pdf* for a sample volunteer policy.

Volunteer Orientation

Make certain every volunteer receives a complete orientation before starting to work. In some instances, a group of volunteers may participate in a formal volunteer orientation program. In other situations, a one-on-one orientation at the work site is appropriate. Make sure to include—

- an overview of the organization's mission
- a description of the specific task to be performed
- confirmation of the hours required
- a statement of whom to contact if help is needed
- the individual to contact if an assignment cannot be completed as scheduled.

Rewards

Although volunteers do not receive a paycheck for their services, they should receive other types of payment. Remember to thank them for the work they perform. Both informal thanks and periodic formal award and recognition ceremonies for volunteers are appropriate. Encourage volunteers to attend training programs to update their skills. Include them in the organization's social events. Remember that extra "payments" to volunteers will pay off in effective service to the organization.

Virtual Volunteering

A growing number of organizations are harnessing a new source of volunteers—those unable or unwilling to work on site, but who are eager to work for their favorite cause from their home or work computer. Virtual volunteering has obvious advantages for those who are elderly, disabled, caretakers, or those who otherwise are restricted in their mobility or willingness to travel to a volunteer site. For many others who are too busy or otherwise unable to commit to a specific time and place for their volunteering, this non-traditional method opens up opportunities. Virtual volunteering has appeal to those who are too busy to make a commitment, but have the ability to fit in volunteer work from home on an ad hoc basis—provided they have a computer and internet access.

The benefits of virtual volunteering were featured in a November 5, 2020 print article in the *New York Times,* which included links on the electronic version of the article to organizations that offered pandemic-related virtual volunteer opportunities.

Virtual volunteers are being used to design and update websites, prepare newsletters, manage social media, respond to requests for information, research reports, and prepare advocacy materials. Although there are some limitations involved in virtual volunteering (such as no hands-on supervision or the lack of face-to-face interaction), advances in technology are providing opportunities for people who otherwise would not make a commitment to volunteer. An eye-opening feature by Jayne Cravens on virtual volunteering can be found at: *http://www.coyotecommunications.com/volunteer/ovmyths.html*

Impact Online, an organization founded in 1994, administers a Virtual Volunteering Project. You can find information about how to begin, and you can even locate volunteers at this site, which can be found at: *https://www. volunteermatch.org/*

Online Resources To Explore:

IdeaList
https://www.idealist.org

Carter McNamara's Managing Volunteer Programs
https://managementhelp.org/staffing/volunteers.htm

A-Z Volunteer Management Library
https://www.energizeinc.com/a-z

Tips:

- Interview all prospective volunteers.

- Make sure you clearly define duties and expectations, and review their performance.

- Have a policy for volunteer termination or reassignment, just as you would for paid employees.

- Consider having a formal awards ceremony for volunteers.

- Perform an "exit interview" with volunteers who leave or are terminated.

Chapter 14
Diversity, Equity, and Inclusion

Synopsis: Nonprofit organizations are learning how to respond to demographic changes affecting their governance leadership, workforce, donors, and clients by changing their policies to promote diversity, equity, and inclusion. There are substantial benefits to doing so in terms of productivity and promoting a culture in which all stakeholders can feel comfortable.

After decades of minimal progress, nonprofit leaders are still struggling with how to assure their organizations permit all individuals the opportunity to participate. Lately, the media have focused more attention on this aspect of nonprofit management, and programs of nonprofit management are adding this to their curricula. Concepts such as "implicit bias," "microaggressions," "institutional racism," "structural racism," and "gender identity" are among those being talked about more and more at board meetings and in classrooms (Independent Sector, 2016).

As with the government and for-profit sectors, the nonprofit sector has lagged behind in providing both economic progress and leadership opportunities for People of Color.

The high-profile deaths of unarmed, Black citizens at the hands of white police officers (and others) have thrust these issues again in the public spotlight. The Black Lives Matter movement has motivated nonprofit organization leaders to reexamine their own policies and those of government that some have charged contribute to the institutional racism that continues to marginalize people of color. The term "diversity, equity, and inclusion" (DEI) has entered the lexicon to indicate there is value to providing equal opportunity to all, and making everyone feel comfortable leading, working for, and receiving services from organizations of each sector. And as one reviews the literature, it is difficult, if not impossible, to refute that the current business culture of every sector, including the nonprofit sector, favors the dominant white culture, even as the United States inexorably moves toward a population that will, according to the U.S. Census Bureau, have a population by 2044 where white persons are a minority (Colby & Ortman, 2015).

Diversity

The term *diversity* typically is used to refer to how different a group of people, such as nonprofit organization board members, staff, clients, and funders (who often play a direct or indirect role in shaping the organization's policies) is with respect to their race, religion, ethnicity, or gender. Some definitions consider expanding this to include other demographic characteristics, such as age, national origin, socio-economic status, education, marital status, sexual orientation, political affiliation, disability, or language. A definition of Independent Sector includes "diversity of thought: ideas, perspectives, and values" (Kapila, Hines, & Searby; 2016).

This broader definition seeks to capture the reason why diversity is beneficial in many cases to the ability of an organization to make decisions that are sensitive to the needs of a broad range of stakeholders, not as likely if decisions are being made by a group of people who have the same backgrounds. It would not be unusual for a board that is predominantly white, politically conservative Republican, highly educated, and upper-class, to have a member who is male, Black, politically conservative Republican, highly educated, and upper-class, for the purpose of "checking a box" and having a diverse board. Yet, that may defeat the purpose of having a diverse board, because the perspective of that Black board member may be similar to that of his colleagues.

People of Color represent 30% of the American workforce, yet only 18% of non-profit staff and 22% of foundation staff are People of Color (Fernandez & Brown, 2015). And racial minorities are concentrated at the lowest end of the leadership hierarchy of both staff and board membership. As documented in the 9th and latest (2017) BoardSource report Leading with Intent, 90% of Board chairs and 90% of nonprofit organization CEOs are white. And these eye-opening statistics have changed little since BoardSource first began surveying the sector about diversity issues back in 1994.

One possible explanation for this is that people of color are less interested in working for the nonprofit sector than whites. However, the data indicate otherwise.

As in the first Race to Lead report, more people of color aspire to become nonprofit leaders than their white counterparts, and the 2019 results show the gap between the two groups is widening. In contrast to three years prior, people of color were substantially more likely to state that race is a barrier to their advancement, while white respondents were more likely to agree that their race provides a career advantage. (Building Movement Project, 2019)

This lack of diversity in the sector is reflected not only in racial composition, but other demographic categories. For example, a 2018 study sponsored by The Center for Effective Philanthropy found that CEOs responded that their organizations were not diverse with respect to sexual orientation (26 percent), gender identity (42 percent), and disabilities (59 percent). About 73% of all nonprofit employees are women, yet only 45% of nonprofit CEO roles are held by women, according to Emily Patz of DonorPerfect (2018). When it comes to pay, female nonprofit CEOs make just 66% of male salaries, she adds.

White individuals were the CEOs of 90% of nonprofits, chaired the boards of 90% of nonprofits, and comprised 84% of board memberships, according to a report of BoardSource, and this has changed minimally since that organization's first survey in 1994 (BoardSource, 2017). As Anastasia Reisa Tomkin writes,

> The statistics are not new, and neither are they shocking. We've been having this conversation for at least the past 15 years, and funny enough, it's still just that—a conversation. But that's one of the key pillars of modern polite white supremacy, isn't it? The uncanny ability to talk in circles about an issue, without ever taking action on the issue. In fact, the conversation is glorified as though it were the action itself. Organizations introducing and discussing the racial gap in nonprofit leadership is seen as the equivalent of doing the work to bridge the gap. Why is it that nonprofits are still over 80 percent white-led? Why does that number increase to 90 percent when it comes to the 315 largest nonprofits in the country? ... (W)hite supremacy in a basic definition, means white people having the most access to and control over money, resources and people. If we sift through the centuries from slavery through segregation and ask whether there has been any distinct transference of wealth and power to black and brown people, the answer would be a resounding no. Today, in the age of mass incarceration, which affects more black people than slavery ever did, white people still create and maintain the unjust laws, they still own the prisons and jails, and they still hold the majority of positions of power to enact their skewed version of justice. (Tomkin, 2020)

The original *Race to Lead* report was published in 2016. The 2020 update of this report (Race to Lead Revisited) showed minimal progress with three key findings:

Race to Lead Revisited confirms findings in the original report that people of color have similar leadership qualifications as white respondents, and more people of color aspire to become nonprofit leaders than their white counterparts. The report also shows that despite the growing attention paid to diversity, equity, and inclusion in nonprofit organizations, there are entrenched disparities that privilege white people and white-led organizations in the nonprofit sector. The third major finding from the report shows that extensive DEI efforts across the sector appear to have increased awareness of race and racism, but have not yet translated into significant change or more equity in how people of color experience their organizations or the nonprofit sector.

One consequence of the 2020 high-profile incidents of police brutality against Black and Brown persons that galvanized a public outcry and filled streets with protesters, both white and of other races, has been to again put the lack of diversity of the nonprofit sector leadership on the agenda. There is a growing consensus that ending discrimination against marginalized groups that keeps them from participating in the sector is not only a matter of fairness, but also enhances the quality of decision-making.

There is little question that the many cases of injustice suffered by marginalized populations, often recorded on cellphones exposing horrific actions that would have been considered unlikely to have occurred had they not been captured and preserved to be replayed over and over again on our TV screens, have raised the consciousness of white America. The Black Lives Matter movement, founded in response to the acquittal of the individual who shot and killed Treyvon Martin, an unarmed Black teenager, has focused national attention on the extent to which marginalized populations are discriminated against (Biography.com, 2020, Blacklivesmatter, 2020).

Advantages of Board and Staff Diversity

Increasing diversity of a nonprofit organization's board and staff results in benefits for both the organization itself and the public it serves, according to many experts who have studied this. Among them are:

- Brainstorming and decision-making groups that include people with psychological differences are more creative, leading to better group problem-solving (Future State, 2017).

- There is scientific evidence that having a diverse staff drives innovation. Among the reasons is that "(W)hen minorities form a critical mass and leaders value differences, all employees can find senior people to go to bat for compelling ideas and can persuade those in charge of budgets to deploy resources to develop those ideas" (Hewlett, Marshall, & Sherbin, 2013).

- Recruiting diverse workers increases the pool of creative talent from which nonprofit employers may choose. And it is more likely that creative, qualified individuals might not even apply for opportunities if they perceive that the organization does not value diversity of the workforce. Even workers who are part of the dominant demographic group are often less attracted to workplaces that are not diverse. "A majority of workers in the United States want teams which are more diverse. Sharing the same space with similar people is viewed as boring and dull," writes Louise Gaille, a personal finance writer on the Vitanna.org website. (Gaille, 2018).

- Organizations, nonprofit or for-profit, that are diverse can market their goods and services more effectively to all groups of consumers (Future State, 2017).

- A 2017 survey of CEOs, COOs, and HR directors from U.S.-based major foundations and nonprofits found that more than 90% of survey respondents believed that diversity led to increased organizational creativity (Center for Effective Philanthropy, 2018). The same survey found that these respondents also reported other benefits of diversity, including making the organization more connected to their communities, leading to better management and employee relations, harnessing additional fundraising networks, and increased productivity.

- A similar survey of nonprofit CEOs and board chairs, sponsored by the Indiana University Lilly Family School of Philanthropy, in partnership with Johnson, Grossnickle and Associates and BoardSource, surveyed nonprofit CEOs and board chairs on the role of diversity in board engagement. Nonprofit CEOs who had boards with higher percentages of women reported that those boards tend to be more engaged, committed, and involved, and were more engaged in advocacy activities (The Indiana University Lilly Family School of Philanthropy Project Team, 2018).

- Lack of diversity can result in potential donors being turned off who might otherwise be supportive financially. It may well have been true decades ago that women and Other marginalized groups lacked both power and financial capacity, but this stereotype is no longer valid (Koenig, 2016).

But even if you are not convinced of the benefits of having a diverse board and staff, resistance can come with a substantial penalty. The United Way of Central Ohio, according to a report in the *Columbus Dispatch*, "plans to include 'board diversity' as part of the criteria in its next grant-application process. Charities seeking funding from the United Way will need to have diverse boards or a board-approved plan for achieving diversity" (Price, 2019).

Disadvantages of Board and Staff Diversity

In fairness, it should be pointed out that communications among a diverse board and staff have the potential to result in conflict. Language barriers, cultural differences, political tensions, and bigotry and prejudice can contribute to creating a difficult work environment. Organizations need to be vigilant about tensions that may exist in the workplace as a result of less than productive communications among workers with different backgrounds. For a more detailed discussion of this, see:

https://vittana.org/22-advantages-and-disadvantages-of-diversity-in-the-workplace

https://www.bartleby.com/essay/Advantages-And-Disadvantages-Of-Group-Diversity-PK2Z2VZS4FF

https://brandongaille.com/8-pros-and-cons-of-diverse-teams/

Strategies to Address Board Diversity

Consider the following:

- Analyze available demographic data on the U.S. Census Bureau website about the geographic area served by your organization, and make your board more representative of the population it serves.

- Engage in a board retreat with the topic focused on how to improve board diversity, which can be led by a paid consultant with expertise or simply a member of the board with an interest in DEI issues.

- Consider adding board members based on knowledge, experience, and political connections to unrepresented groups without regard to their financial capacity to make donations.

- Expand methods of recruiting new board members beyond one of the most used techniques of asking departing members to suggest and recruit a replacement, which often results in that member suggesting someone who has a similar or identical background.

- Request prominent members of the community who are from underrepresented groups to assist in identifying qualified candidates to serve on the board.

- Ratify through board action policies and procedures that will promote board diversity, such as might be found at the Bloomerang website described in the Activities section of this chapter.

Strategies to Improve Staff Diversity

- Ensure that recruitment goes beyond insider recommendations. If an organization is not diverse, those within the organization are much less likely to recommend others who may be qualified who would improve the diversity of the organization—not because of prejudice, but simply because they don't know many individuals unlike themselves.

- In surveys, many nonprofits report that they favor recommendations from staff over other recruitment strategies. However, if your employees are mostly white, they may be more likely to have, and therefore endorse, mostly white friends or professional acquaintances, says Allison Brown, a consultant at Community Wealth Partners, a company that helps nonprofits create strategies to carry out their missions. A 2014 survey found that 75 percent of white Americans have no minorities in their social networks with whom they discuss important matters, notes Ms. Brown, who has reviewed outside research on implicit bias on behalf of her firm, in part to develop practices to eliminate any bias in its hiring process. That suggests that leaving recruitment purely to endorsements from colleagues will limit who gets their foot in the door, she says (Sandoval, 2017).

- Pay a living wage and offer health insurance. This is a matter of human rights and distributive justice, and will also attract more candidates.

- Share job openings widely, including media that are more likely to be accessible to diverse populations. Advertise positions that include in the job description having a sensitivity to staff diversity, emphasize experience and ability to meet job requirements over formal education, and don't ask applicants for salary history (which often works to the detriment of women and People of Color).

- Promote diversity in internship opportunities. Hosting interns is a good way to identify future personnel.

- If you are using a search firm, hire one that can demonstrate a record of providing opportunities to those who are from diverse communities (Wyllie, 2018).

- Recognize that age diversity in board and staff also promotes positive benefits in decision-making and collaboration. There are major differences in the perspectives of board members and staff who were born during different generations (Bridges, 2020). For example, if board members and staff leadership are predominantly of one age cohort, they may not have the sensitivity to understand the needs of staff, clients, and other stakeholders who have aging parents, young children, different career advancement expectations, work-personal life balance expectations, financial needs, and flexible office and service delivery hours. For example, it is apparent that there are major differences in how Baby Boomers (born between 1946 and 1964), Generation X (born between 1965 and 1980), Millennials or Generation Y (born between 1981 and 1996), and Generation Z (born since 1997) view how to approach appropriate behavior with respect to coping with the pandemic.

Equity

The term *equity* refers to "the fair treatment, access, opportunity, and advancement for all people, while at the same time striving to identify and eliminate barriers that have prevented the full participation of some groups. Improving equity involves increasing justice and fairness within the procedures and processes of institutions or systems, as well as in their distribution of resources. Tackling equity issues requires an understanding of the root causes of outcome disparities within our society" (Kapila, Hines, & Searby, 2016).

There are many examples of pervasive inequities system-wide with respect to nonprofit organizations. Some examples are—

- nonprofit hospitals that act to increase their net revenue by jettisoning "unprofitable" emergency rooms and clinics in underserved areas and re-locating those resources to more lucrative suburban locations (Williams, 2019, Galewitz, 2015).

- nonprofit institutions of higher learning that pay their part-time instruc-tors, many with PhDs, so little to teach that many qualify for food stamps and other public assistance (Wessler, 2015).

- nonprofit foundations that allocate a federally required minimum of their assets as grants, and support types of organizations that predominantly serve the interests of economic, social, and political elites—such as sym-phonies, the ballet, public television, opera companies—with fundraising galas compared to organizations that address basic social needs, such as food banks, homeless shelters, and free clinics (Gamboa, 2008, Reich, 2018).

Equity in nonprofit organizations is not just a "nice thing to do." There is clearly a cost to organizations that engage in discrimination, in terms of decreased productivity and increased costs, in addition to losing the creativity that is brought by leadership and line employees from diverse backgrounds. One classic study about the costs of discrimination was conducted in the early 1970s by Florida State's James Gwartney and Charles Haworth, who collected and analyzed data about the impact of desegregation of baseball teams during the period 1947-1956. They documented that teams that discriminated less against Black players won more games and had higher attendance (1974). More recently, economists sought to place a dollar cost to workplace discrimination and concluded that the monetary costs in the U.S. were an estimated $64 billion annually. This amount included the costs of losing and replacing the more than two million workers who left their jobs because of perceived unfairness relating to how they were being treated at work.

Among the direct costs of losing employees include hiring temporaries, re-cruitment advertising, severance agreements, background checks, drug testing, relocation costs, training the replacement employee, signing bonuses, the time lost in interviewing candidates, and the exposure to lawsuits such as wrongful termination (Burns, 2020). Indirect costs can include the effect on worker mo-rale and productivity of workers who are not being subject to unfair practices by management.

Even though Title 7 of the Civil Rights Act protects workers from discrimination because of their race and gender, among other characteristics and a landmark June 2020 opinion by the U.S. Supreme Court (U.S. Supreme Court, 2020) expanded this protection to sexual orientation and gender identity, many racial, gender, and sexual minorities are still often treated as second-class citizens in the workplace. Many otherwise qualified workers leave their organizations because of how they are treated. The costs in both time and money of recruiting and training replacements is substantial. Exposure to discrimination lawsuits can be an avoidable burden to a nonprofit on a tight budget. Employees who feel subjected to harassment or unfair treatment are less productive and absent more from work (Burns, 2012).

Inclusion

The term *inclusion* refers to "creating environments in which any individual or group can be and feel welcomed, respected, supported, and valued to fully participate. An inclusive and welcoming climate embraces differences and offers respect in words and actions for all people" (Kapila, Hines, & Searby, 2016).

Nonprofit organizations risk having their board members leave, their staff seek employment elsewhere, and their clients look for alternatives to access services if they fall short on being inclusive to all.

Making improvements targeted to increasing inclusion is not as easy as it sounds. In the context of managing a nonprofit organization, one needs to be careful implementing changes in policies designed to make an organization more inclusive, as explained by Justin "Jay" Miller," Dean of the College of Social Work of the University of Kentucky. What may be a good-faith effort can backfire without serious planning and a recognition that changes made may appear to be cosmetic and, in the end, be counterproductive.

> *Inclusion, in an idealistic sense, refers to intentionally engaging with difference. Inclusion initiatives aim to foster norms and cultures that ensure a sense of belonging among all people in a particular system or community. At the intended core, inclusion revolves around value, respect, and empowerment.*

> *From a pragmatic standpoint, though, inclusion looks far less idealistic. Inclusion, in its real-life form, is strikingly incongruous to quixotic notions of equality and celebrating difference. Efforts at inclusion typically start with an administrator or committee and include some semblance of assessment, training, and targeted hiring practices aimed at improving workplace cultures. These efforts, typically, include additions—rather than excavate systems.*

*Although (usually) done with laudable intentions, the impact of inclu-
sion is akin to putting a Band-Aid on a deep wound. It may look pretty;
it may cover up temporarily. It may even serve a better-than-nothing
purpose. But, eventually, the wound gapes open and requires deeper
attention.*

*This implementation of inclusion has notable limitations and can even
exacerbate the problems....*

*Making environments welcoming is not ONLY about changing prac-
tices, policies, and procedures. It is about changing people. Expansive
practices recognize that changing the former does not necessarily lead
to change in the latter. So the lesson here? Avoid being paternalistic
and consult with groups you are trying to include about how best to
approach this sensitive subject. (Miller, 2020)*

Strategies to Promote Inclusion

• Change your organization's environment to make it more supportive and
welcoming. For example, in regard to gender identity and expression, implement a policy to ask transgender staff, clients, and constituents which
pronouns they use and address them by those pronouns. Reconstruct and
re-sign an adequate number of restrooms to make them gender-neutral.
Consider health insurance policies that will cover the medical costs for
non-binary employees that are transitioning (Bridges, 2020).

• Inventory where your grants go (in the case of foundations) and where your
services go (in the case of operating foundations and traditional charities).
Do funding and services disproportionately benefit white organizations and
clients, possibly because of implicit bias? Are there any outreach efforts
made to expand your organization's catchment area to communities with
large populations of People of Color that are not currently served? Are job
openings advertised widely enough or are staff openings filled by recommendations from current board members and staff who may not have diverse
social and professional networks? As pointed out by Adalia Fernandez and
Allison Brown, 75% of whites do not have People of Color in their social
networks (2015).

• Collect some data on how your organization is addressing diversity, equity,
and inclusion issues, and set some goals. As pointed out by Rahsaan Harris,
CEO of the Citizens Committee for New York City, "If you're not measuring
it, you have no way of knowing if you're being successful or not. If you're
not measuring what you're doing with regard to inclusion and diversity,
then it's never going to get better" (Harris and Stiffman, 2020).

Concepts Relating to Diversity, Equity, and Inclusion

Implicit Bias. Implicit bias, a form of what is called stereotyping, refers to unconscious bias about a member of a social group. Social psychologists Mahzarin Banaji and Tony Greenwald first coined the term implicit bias in the 1990s. In 1995, they published their theory of implicit social cognition, which asserted that individuals' social behavior and biases are largely related to unconscious, or implicit, judgments. Their famous research studies during the 1990s using Implicit Association Test (IAT) confirmed their theory (Berghoef, 2019).

Tokenism. Tokenism is "the practice of making only a perfunctory or symbolic effort to do a particular thing, especially by recruiting a small number of people from underrepresented groups in order to give the appearance of sexual or racial equality within a workforce" (Lexico, 2020). Avoiding tokenism is an important consideration in efforts to make a workforce more diverse. This is the case not only because tokenism is despicable, but also because those individuals who are being used as pawns often are put into a work environment that is not welcoming, and made to feel that they are there only to "check a box" rather than being viewed as a qualified, valuable employee.

Affirmative Action. This term refers to "an active effort to improve the employment or educational opportunities of members of minority groups and women" (Merriam-Webster, 2020). Affirmative action is intended as a response to the deleterious effects of past discrimination and increase the representation of historically disadvantaged groups, including women and People of Color. Affirmative action strategies can range from simply publicizing job openings widely enough in venues where People of Color and female candidates are likely to hear about the openings, to requiring that at least a minimum number of women and People of Color be interviewed, to providing a preference in judging candidates who are female and/or People of Color. For more on this, see: *https://www.referenceforbusiness.com/management/A-Bud/Affirmative-Action.html#ixzz6Th0DxrFB*

Systemic racism. Systemic racism, also referred to as structural racism or institutional racism, refers to culture, policies, and institutions that create disparities for People of Color with respect to education, employment, treatment by the criminal justice system, health care, housing, political power, and wealth. The concept traces itself to the writings of sociologist and civil rights leader W. E. B. Du Bois (1868-1963), and the term itself surfaced during the civil rights movement in the 1960s (Yancey-Bragg, 2020).

Microaggression. Microaggressions are "the everyday verbal, nonverbal, and environmental slights, snubs, or insults, whether intentional or unintentional, which communicate hostile, derogatory, or negative messages to target persons based solely upon their marginalized group membership." (Wing, 2010). First used in the 1970s by a Harvard Medical School psychiatrist to describe the "subtle insults" between white and Black students, the target of such comments often feels marginalized and unable to determine whether it was intended or not, and not sure how to respond, if at all. For example, a white person may compliment a Black person as being "well-spoken" or "clean cut" in a manner that suggests the white person thinks that most Black people do not have these characteristics, and that the Black person is an exception. These types of comments uttered by those who don't consider themselves as racist are often considered racist by those who hear them. When people are educated about the harm caused by microaggressions, they may be more likely to avoid them when communicating with others.

The Coronavirus Pandemic and Diversity, Equity, and Inclusion

I am writing this chapter in the middle of 2020, when we are in the midst of the greatest health care crisis in recent American and world history. A pandemic is spreading out of control, the American and world economy is in a free-fall, and government at all levels is unwilling or unable to take coordinated action to respond rationally to the challenge. The nonprofit sector is facing perhaps the largest and most compelling challenge in its history.

The fallout from the economic catastrophe accompanying the pandemic has become an existential challenge for thousands, if not hundreds of thousands, of nonprofit organizations. The largest nonprofits—such as hospitals and educational institutions—are facing revenue losses from which they may never recover unless they reinvent themselves (Carey, 2020; Fernandes, 2020; Thys, 2020). Smaller nonprofits, including many that have survived by depending on grants and donations from individuals, are finding that their revenue sources are drying up, more than they did during "normal" economic downturns. For those that survive, they will consider the massive changes they undergo as a "new normal." Many will simply disappear.

And at the same time, the nonprofit sector is often the last resort to provide the services that the public needs during times of crisis. Many nonprofits are overwhelmed, and their staff demoralized by deteriorating conditions within their organizations exacerbated by the disruption of their personal lives fearing layoffs and pay cuts if they are able to retain their jobs. The American Cancer Society eliminated 1,000 jobs directly attributable to the effects of the pandemic, and other nonprofit health care providers are at risk (Fuerte, 2020; Brooksbank, 2020).

It is perhaps a very inconvenient time to deal with the issues of diversity, equity, and inclusion. But there is perhaps no better time than now.

It has been well-documented that this pandemic has disproportionately affected marginalized populations (Centers for Disease Control and Prevention, 2020;

Hazeltine, 2020). Black and Brown citizens are more likely to die from COVID-19. They are more likely to be "essential workers" and thus required to leave their homes to deliver services, and less likely to be able to work from home. They are more likely to be paid less than their white counterparts, less likely to have a job that provides paid sick leave—and thus are disproportionately penalized for staying at home when they are sick—and are more likely to be among the first laid off during budget challenges.

> *The emergency triggered by COVID-19 lays bare the structural failures of a nation where the most vulnerable continue to be the worst hit. To realize the promise of equity, every policy and investment must provide significant, sustained support to the people hurting most; and serve as a bridge to creating an equitable economy, an inclusive and compassionate society, and a strong, accountable democracy. (PolicyLink.org, n.d.)*

The Race to Lead Revisited report has documented the connection between racism and the pandemic: "...a worldwide pandemic, renewed grief and outrage over the continued killings of Black people by police and vigilantes, and a deepening recession have even more sharply exposed fault lines of who holds power and privilege and who is treated as expendable," aptly states the connection between the pandemic and institutional racism in the nonprofit sector in the introduction to its latest research report (Building Movement Project, 2019, p.1).

"In nonprofits, both the board and CEO have leadership responsibilities," says Shamima Ahmed, PhD, a professor at Northern Kentucky University. "Studies have found that oftentimes a CEO coming from a minority group faces challenges to lead and gain respect from a pre-dominant white staff. Many such leaders leave the agency due to that. So, the sector has to engage in conscious and proactive strategies not only to recruit qualified minority CEOs, but also to make sure that the agency is ready to support such leaders and help him or her to succeed. I also think that the nonprofit sector's leaders have a responsibility to engage in dialogue and advocacy to promote DEI as an important pillar in our community," she adds, "And that means not only focusing internally but also externally when communicating with their stakeholders."

Online Resources

Bloomerang—DEI Nonprofit Organization Essential Resources
https://bloomerang.co/resources/dei/

Nonprofit Learning Lab DEI Resources
https://www.nonprofitlearninglab.org/dei

Nonprofit Leadership Alliance Resource Library
   https://www.nonprofitleadershipalliance.org/leaderosity-learning-library

Note: The full references in this chapter appear in *For Further Reading and References* section of this Handbook, Chapter 14, starting on page 191.

Chapter 15
Charitable Solicitation Registration

> **Synopsis:** With limited exceptions, Texas is one of the few states that that does not require charities to register before soliciting contributions. A Unified Registration Statement is available, which is accepted by 36 states and the District of Columbia, to streamline submissions, although Texas is not among them. The Charleston Principles provide guidance on regulation with respect to internet fundraising regulation.

Texas is one of the few states that does not require charitable organizations that solicit contributions in the state to register and provide financial reports. There are three statutes that provides exceptions to this—*The Texas Law Enforcement Telephone Solicitation Act, The Public Safety Solicitation Act,* and *The Veterans Solicitation Act.* But just because Texas does not require registration, charitable organizations in Texas routinely solicit potential donors in other states, and must comply with the registration and reporting requirements in those states. This chapter provides useful information to assure that your organization can keep its fundraising operation in full compliance.

The Texas Law Enforcement Telephone Solicitation Act

The full text of this law can be accessed at: *https://statutes.capitol.texas.gov/ SOTWDocs/BC/htm/BC.303.htm.* The purpose is to regulate certain law enforcement related organizations that engage in telephone solicitation in Texas. Actual government law enforcement agencies and organizations are explicitly excluded. The law applies to a "commercial telephone solicitor," defined as "a person whom a law enforcement-related charitable organization retains to make a telephone solicitation, directly or through another person under the direction of the person retained. The term does not include a bona fide officer, director, or employee of, or volunteer for, a law enforcement-related charitable organization."

The law defines "Law enforcement-related charitable organization" as "a person who solicits a contribution and is or purports to be established or operating for a charitable purpose relating to law enforcement. The term includes a nongovernmental law enforcement organization or publication and survivors of law enforcement officers killed in the line of duty. The term does not include a governmental law enforcement agency or organization."

Those to whom this definition applies must register annually with the Attorney General, provide financial reports, pay a $50 annual registration fee, and post a $50,000 surety bond.

The Public Safety Solicitation Act

This law requires certain public safety organizations, public safety publications and their solicitors and/or independent promoters to register, pay a $500 annual registration fee and post a $10,000 surety bond with the Secretary of State. "Public safety organization" is defined as—

> ...a nongovernmental organization that, in a manner that reasonably implies that *the organization is composed of law enforcement or public safety personnel or that a contribution, purchase, or membership will benefit public safety personnel, uses the term 'officer,' 'peace officer,' 'police officer,' 'police,' 'law enforcement,' 'reserve officer,' 'deputy,' 'deputy sheriff,' 'constable,' 'deputy constable,' 'fireman,' 'firefighter,' 'volunteer fireman,' 'emergency medical service provider,' 'civilian employee,' or any other term:*
>
> *(A) in its name;*
> *(B) in a publication of the organization; or*
> *(C) in a solicitation for:*
> *(i) contributions to the organization;*
> *(ii) membership in the organization;*
> *(iii) the purchase of advertising in a publication of the organization; or*
> *(iv) the purchase of products or tickets to an event sponsored by or for the benefit of the organization by a solicitor.*
> *(4) "Public safety personnel" means employees or volunteers of a public safety organization, including:*
> *(A) firefighters;*
> *(B) emergency medical service providers; or*
> *(C) civilian employees of a public safety organization.*

The law places limitations on what types of organizations may engage these solicitors on behalf of the organization, such as the percentage or amount of members who are actually public safety or law enforcement employees.

Oral and written solicitation materials must include—

(1) the name of the public safety organization registered under Section 1803.053, if an organization is involved;

(2) a statement that the promotion is independent of affiliation with any public safety organization, if a public safety promoter is involved;

(3) the name of any public safety solicitor employed;

(4) a general statement of the use of net funds received; and

(5) the name, street address, and statewide toll-free telephone number established under Section 1803.102 (800-648-9642) that a person may use to obtain from the Secretary of State additional information on the public safety entity, public safety publication, or public safety solicitor.

The above is a summary of this law. The full text may be accessed at: *https:// statutes.capitol.texas.gov/SOTWDocs/OC/htm/OC.1803.htm*

The Veterans Solicitation Act

This law requires certain veterans organizations to file a registration statement with the Secretary of State and pay a fee. If the veterans organization uses a solicitor, the organization must post a surety bond with the Secretary of State. Among the definitions in the law are—

(1) "Veteran" means a person who has served on active duty in the armed forces of the United States or in the state military forces as defined by Section 437.001, Government Code.

(2) "Veterans organization" means a formally or informally formed nongovernmental entity that:

(A) purports to include or represent veterans; or

(B) includes a term in its name leading a reasonable person to assume the organization is associated with veterans or concerned with veterans' issues.

(3) "Veterans organization solicitor" means a person who receives monetary compensation for solicitation services for a veterans organization and who solicits:

(A) a contribution of financial support or a purchase of goods or services for a veterans organization in person, by telephone, or by mail; or

(B) membership in a veterans organization from an individual who is not a veteran.

A veterans organization may register and use a veterans organization solicitor only if the organization consists of individual members of whom at least 90 percent or 500, whichever is less, are veterans; and who have signed membership agreements with the organization.

The annual registration fees are $150 for the organization and $500 for the solicitor. The surety bond that must be posted by the organization ranges from $1,000-$25,000, depending on the number of counties solicited. The surety bond that must be posted by the solicitor ranges from $5,000-$25,000. Both the organization and solicitor must file annual reports with the Secretary of State. The report by the organization is due each January 15, if it received more than $500 in the previous calendar year. The filing fee is $50. The solicitor must file this report if he/she raised more than $5,000 for the previous calendar quarter. The filing fee is $50. The report is due at the end of each calendar quarter.

During each oral and written solicitation, the solicitor must disclose "The secretary of state has on file important information about persons that seek contributions in the name of veterans, and the number to call about that information is the Solicitation Information Hotline 800-648-9642."

The above is a summary. The full text of the law may be accessed at: *https:// statutes.capitol.texas.gov/SOTWDocs/OC/htm/OC.1804.htm*

Regulation in Other States

All but 11 states in the United States—Delaware, Idaho, Indiana, Iowa, Montana, Nebraska, Nevada, South Dakota, Texas, Vermont, and Wyoming—regulate charitable fundraising. State laws requiring charities to register and to provide information about fundraising activities to the government is not a recent development—for example, the Pennsylvania General Assembly enacted a law to regulate fundraising back in 1919.

Many states during the 1980s and 1990s enacted tough laws regulating charitable solicitation. This trend was motivated by abuses in virtually every state in which unscrupulous organizations posed as charities. Engaging in deceptive practices, these organizations generated contributions from the public that were intended for charitable purposes. Some of these organizations took names similar to those of reputable charities and diverted most, if not all, of the proceeds of their solicitation to line the pockets of private individuals. Other abuses involved professional fundraising organizations that solicited business from bona fide charities, offering to raise funds in exchange for an unreasonably large percentage of the contributions received. Even if the charity received a minuscule percentage of what was raised and the charity benefited—it was at the expense of an unwary public.

Abuses such as these continue to this day. State laws have made it tougher for deceptive practices to occur, and have given law enforcement officials new authority to take action to enjoin illegal or deceptive fundraising activities. On May 5, 2003, the U.S. Supreme Court unanimously decided a case *(Illinois Ex Rel. Madigan v. Telemarketing Associations, Inc.)* that validated the authority of Illinois state regulators to

CHARITABLE SOLICITATION REGISTRATION

regulate the fraudulent practices of telemarketers who attempt to raise charitable funds. The case involved a telemarketer in Illinois who diverted 85% of the funds raised to his own pockets rather than for charitable purposes.

Perhaps as importantly, these state laws have provided the public (and the media) with easy access, often a toll-free telephone call or mouse click on a website away, to information about charities, their leadership, and how much of the money contributed is actually funneled to the charity and used for charitable purposes.

Although most of these laws are weak in prescribing a minimum threshold on the percentage of donations required to be actually put to use for charitable purposes (rather than paying the expenses of professional fundraisers), the public policy philosophy is more along the lines of "a little sunlight is the best antiseptic."

One can find similar patterns, although each state that regulates charitable solicitation has its own law, regulations, and forms for registration, registration renewal, and expense/fundraising reporting. Many states also require registration and reporting for professional solicitors and fundraising counsels, and they require those who make their living in this manner to post a bond with the state.

For charities that raise funds in more than one state (on the internet or by direct mail, for example), complying with the requirements of each state can be problematic, expensive, and time-consuming. For several years, national and regional charities legitimately have complained about the impracticality of keeping up with the legal requirements for solicitation law compliance. An innovative project, the Unified Registration Statement, has addressed this concern.

The Unified Registration Statement

The National Association of Attorneys General and the National Association of State Charity Officials have developed the Unified Registration Statement (URS). The purpose of the URS is to provide a standardized reporting form that charities can use when they are required to submit information to many different states with respect to charitable solicitation activities. This document can be downloaded from the internet at: *http://www.multistatefiling.org*

Although each state regulating charitable solicitation maintains the practice of providing its own individual registration form, 36 states and the District of Columbia will accept the URS for registration purposes—all but three of the states (Colorado, Florida, and Oklahoma) that require registration. Fourteen of the 37 jurisdictions that accept the URS (Arkansas, California, District of Columbia, Georgia, Maine, Minnesota, Mississippi, North Carolina, North Dakota, Tennessee,

White Hat Communications | 209

Utah, Washington, West Virginia, and Wisconsin) also require a supplemental filing. These supplemental forms are not extensive and are available on the internet as an appendix to the URS forms (see: *http://www.multistatefiling.org/#no_states*).

Charities may print out the form, in the format of a PDF file, directly from the internet (or save it for printing out later), fill in the information, and file it with each participating state. Instructions are provided at the website for printing or saving the file. A version of the form in HTML can be reviewed on the website, but this version is not acceptable for printing out and submitting to state regulatory offices.

The URS is continually updated and improved in response to comments provided by participating charities and state regulators. As of February 2021, the latest version of the form was 4.02, which was made public in March 2014. The following website provides details about the latest version:

http://www.multistatefiling.org/#version

As of January 2021, the District of Columbia and the following states accept the URS for registration: Alabama, Alaska, Arizona, Arkansas, California, Connecticut, Georgia, Hawaii, Illinois, Kansas, Kentucky, Louisiana, Maine, Maryland, Massachusetts, Michigan, Minnesota, Mississippi, Missouri, New Hampshire, New Jersey, New Mexico, New York, North Carolina, North Dakota, Ohio, Oregon, Pennsylvania, Rhode Island, South Carolina, Tennessee, Utah, Virginia, Washington, West Virginia, and Wisconsin. Colorado, Florida, and Oklahoma do not accept the URS.

Each state has individual exemptions and exclusions from registration requirements based on, for example, the type of organization or the amount of fundraising conducted annually. Also, each state requires different supporting documents to accompany the URS and charges an individual registration fee. Charities may still submit the state's individual registration form, but most charities soliciting in several states that accept the URS find it much more convenient to submit the standardized form.

The general Unified Registration Statement, version 4.02, consists of three pages of questions. It requests:

- general information about the charity
- whether there was a previous legal name used
- information about misconduct by the organization's officers, directors, employees, or fundraisers

- a list of states where the charity is registered and the dates and type of solicitation conducted
- information about the organization's federal tax status
- methods of solicitation
- information about the purposes and programs of the organization for which funds are being solicited
- the names, titles, addresses, and telephone numbers of officers, directors, trustees, and principal salaried executives
- information that describes relationships (such as financial interest or relationship by blood, marriage, or adoption) between organizational leaders and professional fundraising organizations, suppliers, or vendors
- information about felonies or misdemeanors committed by the organization's leaders
- the names of those who are responsible for custody and/or distribution of funds, fundraising, financial records, and those authorized to sign checks
- banks where funds are deposited, along with the account numbers and bank telephone numbers
- the name and address of the accountant/auditor
- the name and address of the person authorized to receive service of process
- whether the organization receives financial support from other nonprofit organizations, shares revenue with other nonprofits, whether anyone owns an interest of 10% or greater in the organization, and whether the organization owns a 10% or greater interest in any other organization (and explanations for all of these)
- whether the organization uses volunteers or professionals to solicit directly to the public
- a list of professional fundraisers, solicitors, fundraising counsels, or commercial co-venturers accompanied by information about their services, compensation arrangements, contract dates, dates of the campaign, and whether these persons/organizations have custody or control of donations
- the amount paid to these persons during the previous year.

It also requests financial information about the charity, including:

- contributions in the previous year, program service expenses, fundraising expenses in the previous year, management and general expenses
- fundraising costs as a percentage of funds raised
- fundraising costs plus management and general costs as a percentage of funds raised
- program services as a percentage of total expenses.

Note that the URS can be used only for registration and registration renewal, but not for the annual financial reporting required by almost all states that regulate charitable solicitation. A standardized reporting form for annual financial reporting is being developed.

State Regulation of Fundraising on the Internet

The use of the internet for fundraising has raised legal questions that previously were not relevant. For example, is a charity in Texas that is not registered in Utah violating the Utah solicitation law if it puts a general solicitation on its website and receives contributions from someone in Utah? This area of law is not clear, and it will likely take several years, if not decades, for a body of case law and statutory law to provide guidance to charities wrestling with these questions.

Beginning in the late 1990s, the National Association of Attorneys General (NAAG) and the National Association of State Charity Officials (NASCO) began meeting to reach a consensus national policy on how states should appropriately regulate charitable solicitation conducted over the internet. The public dialogue on this issue began in Charleston, S.C. at the October 1999 NAAG/NASCO annual conference. In September of 2000, NASCO released a draft proposal of model state guidelines and posted it on the internet. The final version was approved by the NASCO Board in March 2001, and can be found at: *http://www.nasconet.org/wp-content/uploads/2018/04/Charleston-Principles.pdf*

Charities that shied away from putting solicitation information on their websites for fear of attracting out-of-state enforcement proceedings can breathe a bit easier and feel comfortable reposting this information. Charities that took the time and effort (and considerable expense) to register in all of the 39 states and the District of Columbia requiring registration may reconsider if the extent to which they solicit falls within the thresholds of these principles. And charities that target their internet solicitations to out-of-state residents, either via their Web pages or email, should be put on notice that these direct and indirect solicitations will, rightfully so, be treated the same as charitable solicitations conducted by conventional media.

The *Charleston Principles* consist of a preamble and four broad principles, each with subprinciples. Here is a synopsis:

The *preamble* lays out the general purpose of the document, recognizing that although most charities provide valuable services, fraud and misuse of contributions are significant problems, and oversight by state regulators is a reasonable function of government.

Principle 1 underscores that using the internet for fundraising is legitimate and should not be discouraged. However, since state laws vary and technology is still developing, the application of these principles by individual states may change and, in any case, is not binding upon any state.

Principle II provides that states should be enforcing the law against charities that use the internet to mislead or defraud those in any state, regardless of which state the charity calls home.

Principle III is divided into two parts—principles applicable to charities soliciting contributions in the state where they are based, and those that apply to solicitations and donations in a foreign state. A charity that uses the internet to conduct solicitations in its home state is required to register in that state, as it would be with conventional solicitations.

It is the wording of the second part of this principle that *could* have been drafted in a manner problematic to charities but, perhaps, strikes the right balance between over-regulation and no regulation. It provides that—

> *An entity that is not domiciled within a state must register in accordance with the law of that state if: Its non-Internet activities alone would be sufficient to require registration; The entity solicits contributions through an interactive Web site; and (e)ither the entity: (s)pecifically targets persons physically located in the state for solicitation, or {r} eceives contributions from the state on a repeated and ongoing basis or a substantial basis through its Web site; or (t)he entity solicits contributions through a site that is not interactive, but either specifically invites further offline activity to complete a contribution, or establishes other contacts with that state, such as sending e-mail messages or other communications that promote the Web site, and (t)he entity satisfies Principle III.B.1.b. (2)*

(Note: III.B. 1.b.{2} relates to specifically targeting persons in another state or receiving contributions from the state on a repeated and ongoing or substantial basis through a website.)

Principle III also defines terms used above. "Interactive" refers to sites that have the capacity to accept donations by obtaining funds directly from a contributor, such as via credit card or electronic funds transfer. The principles do not provide specific guidelines on what thresholds of donations trigger regulation; states are encouraged to set thresholds for what is meant by "repeated and ongoing or substantial."

Another section of this principle responds to the issue of charity portals that solicit funds from the public, often providing a list of every charity that is on the Internal Revenue Service's Master List. The principle proposed on this issue is that if state law technically requires such a charity to register as a result of receiving donations from that portal, the state should exercise "prosecutorial discretion" and not enforce that law. Also, companies that pledge to devote a portion of the sale of a product or service to a charity or for a charitable purpose, often referred to as "cause marketing," should not be exempt from state registration requirements.

Finally, those who merely provide administration, support, or technical services to charities, such as processing Web donations, should not be required to register, provided they do not actually solicit donations. However, the principle includes a statement that "Compensation for services based on the amount of funds raised may be a strong indication that entity is doing more than simply providing technical services."

Principle IV addresses general issues relating to easing the administrative burden of multi-state filing for those charities required to do so consistent with these principles. It encourages charities to post their Unified Registration Statements, completed federal tax exemption applications, and their last three 990s online.

Tips:

- If you know that your organization is not in compliance with charitable solicitation regulations, consider "turning yourself in" rather than being "caught red-handed." Most state regulators are more interested in bringing nonprofit organizations into compliance than punishing them. Your organization's penalty, if any, is more likely to be reduced if you make a good faith effort to correct past abuses or noncompliance.

- Take advantage of the Uniform Registration Statement if you are able to do so.

Chapter 16
Fundraising

Synopsis: One aspect of nonprofit organizations that differentiates them from their government and for-profit counterparts is the need, in most cases, for donations from the public to support their activities. The basic rule of fundraising is to ask—ask the right people at the right time in the right way. There are many conventional and creative ways to raise funds for a nonprofit organization.

ASK.

The rest of what is needed to know about fundraising—the amount to ask, whom to ask, when to ask—are technical details that will be expanded upon in this chapter. However, the simple task of asking for funds for an organization is the major point of this chapter, since it is rare, though not unheard of, that funds are sent to an organization unsolicited.

How Much To Fundraise

There are enormous differences in the recommended fundraising techniques if one is trying to raise $10 million for a new hospital wing compared to $1,000 to finance the costs of filing Certificate of Formation, 501(c)(3) application, and a some rolls of first-class stamps. There also are many similarities.

First, the organization must start with a reasonable budget plan (see Chapter 10). How much is needed to finance the organization's first-year activities? Will it have paid staff? Staff salaries, benefits, and payroll taxes generally are the largest line-items in any budget. The next decision that determines the order of magnitude in an organization's budget is whether the organization will have an office, which requires rent, telephone, furniture, equipment, and supplies.

A good practice is to prepare three budgets:

1. A "low-end" budget, which assumes a minimum level to get the organization off the ground. The organization would cease to function if revenue did not cover expenses in this budget.

2. A "middle-end" budget, which is as realistic as possible and considers the likely availability of funds for the year, and

3. A "high-end" budget, which is optimistic enough to assume the organization can pay for almost anything it seeks to do.

In asking for money, one should tailor the "pitch" to the demographics of the contributors. It helps to understand the motivation of the contributors, as well. People give money for a reason. It may be they share the organization's motivation for starting up. It may be they feel guilty because otherwise they would not be doing anything to address a problem. It may be they desire power in the organization that they can get only by contributing. They also may be looking for ways to get a tax deduction, align themselves with a popular cause, or they seek immortality (such as by contributing an endowed chair or building wing with their name on it). They may be contributing to an organization because they want a particular organizational leader to be their friend or to contribute to their own favorite cause. Or perhaps none of these—they are simply participating in a 5K fundraiser or "ice bucket challenge" for fun without even thinking about the sponsoring charity.

The most successful fundraising is done by requesting contributions from people who have money to give away, who both know and respect the organization (or someone on its board or staff), and who are given reasons for contributing that are sensitive to their private motivations. Many organizations select some board or advisory committee members based on their ability to tap funds from their friends and associates. Many of their friends will write a check to virtually any cause solely because that influential board member picked up the telephone and asked them to do so.

The donations of board members are often an important source of revenue for new organizations. Many organizations will identify members of the community to serve on their boards because of their willingness and ability to make substantial financial contributions, rather than having governance expertise.

Board members are usually—but not always—delighted to donate when asked, recognizing that the organization, to be successful, does need some start-up funding, and it would make them look foolish if the organization is stillborn as a result of lack of seed money. It is not unusual for external funding sources to consider the extent to which board members make contributions. Therefore, the participation percentage of board member contributions may be as important, or more so, as the dollar amount raised from them.

IRS Substantiation Rules

Most states require organizations to register before they raise funds for charitable purposes (see Chapter 15). However, states are not the only source of government regulation of charities. The federal *Omnibus Budget Reconciliation Act* (OBRA), enacted in 1993, imposed requirements on charities and donors with respect to substantiation of donations made beginning with the 1994 tax year. The law requires charities to provide a contemporaneous written acknowledgment of contributions of $250 or more; the donor may not take a charitable tax deduction without having such a written acknowledgment.

The practical effect is that charities send these statements routinely to their donors as a part of a "thank you" letter. The written acknowledgment must include the amount of cash paid or a description of property transferred by the donor, a statement of whether the donor received goods or services in exchange for the donation, and a good-faith estimate of the value of such goods and services, if any.

Additional requirements of this law apply in cases when charities provide goods or services in exchange for the donation. If the donation is in excess of $75, the charity must provide a written a statement to the donor that the deductibility of the donation is limited to the excess of the amount donated over and above the value of the goods and services provided, and an estimate of the value of these goods and services provided by the charity. For example, if a 501(c)(3) organization holds a fundraising dinner and estimates that the costs for catering and entertainment are $45 per person and the charge is $100 per ticket, federal law requires disclosure to ticket holders that they can deduct a contribution of $55 per ticket purchased. IRS Publication 1771 provides examples of fact situations that require this disclosure.

Final regulations issued in December 1996 by the IRS provided some guidance to charities on several issues. First, charities may ignore benefits provided to members that can be used "frequently," such as gift shop discounts, free or discounted parking, or free or discounted admission to the organization's facilities or events. Second, there are safe harbors (examples that an organization can follow and avoid violating the law) for benefits of minimal value. One safe harbor permits a donor to deduct the entire value of the contribution if the benefit received has a value less than 2% of the contribution or $106, whichever is less. For example, a $1,000 contributor may receive a T-shirt and mug as a thank you gift without tax penalty to the donor, provided these gifts have a value of under $20.

A second safe harbor applies in the case of small contributions when the benefit received is relatively small. This applies to contributions of at least $56.50 when the value of the benefit provided to the contributor is less than $11.30.

The dollar thresholds mentioned above are for calendar year 2021. Each year, the IRS adjusts these numbers (referred to as the "de minimis threshold amounts") for inflation. Current thresholds can be obtained by downloading Publication 1771 from the IRS website *(https://www.irs.gov/pub/irs-pdf/p1771.pdf)* or by calling 877-829-5500.

The regulations require charities to provide written substantiation of a donation to volunteers who wish to claim as a deduction the cost of unreimbursed expenses of $250 or more. They also require that institutions such as colleges that raise money by offering their alumni the right to purchase hard-to-get athletic tickets must consider 20% of the payment for the tickets as the fair market value for the right to purchase the tickets. This amount may not be deducted on the alumni's tax returns as charitable contributions.

Many gray areas remain with respect to substantiation issues, and advocates for the charitable community continue to complain that the IRS has not been totally clear in providing guidance on the regulations implementing substantiation requirements.

Sources of Funding

Among potential sources for funding other than via the Internet, which is discussed in detail in Chapter 22, are:

1. Umbrella Fundraising Groups (e.g. United Ways, Jewish Federations, Catholic Charities, Women's Way, and similar organizations)

In addition to providing an important source of funding, membership in a federated fundraising organization provides added visibility and community endorsement. This is especially important for agencies that lack name recognition.

Although membership in a federated fundraising organization carries no iron-clad guarantee that funding levels will be sustained or increased (especially in a recessionary and highly competitive fundraising environment), member organizations fulfilling needs that are a priority to the funding agency can count on relatively stable funding.

Although members sometimes chafe at accountability, program, and fundraising requirements imposed by umbrella organizations, few would trade their federated funding for total independence.

2. Foundations

Major foundations usually require written proposals, many of which can be time-consuming to prepare. There is also a time lag between when the application is submitted—and perhaps, a response to questions from the foundation on issues that were not adequately covered by the application—and when the "check is in the mail."

Many smaller foundations are managed by the philanthropists themselves who establish the foundations for tax purposes. The benefactor may write a check as soon as the request for funds is received.

Most foundation proposals can be prepared by someone without special training or education. The trick is to research the kinds of organizations and activities of interest to the foundation and tailor the grant application to that information. It is also vitally important to tailor it to the application guidelines of the foundation, since many proposals are rejected on technical grounds even before they are judged on their substance.

Many local libraries have sections devoted to foundation fundraising, including research materials with the names, addresses, and type of funding provided by each foundation.

Foundations are responsible for only a small percentage of philanthropy. However, the individual gift may be quite substantial, and the awarding of a major gift by a name foundation can have benefits beyond the financial reward. It can serve as a catalyst for other grants and give the beneficiary organization increased credibility.

3. Direct Mail

The key to direct mail fundraising is a mailing list of people who are likely to consider making a contribution. Professional services sell mailing lists categorized by various interests and demographics. Organizations may wish to send a few newsletters to such a list, and then follow up with a direct mail appeal.

If an organization is a membership organization, its members should be among the first to receive an appeal for voluntary contributions. After all, they have already indicated their interest in the organization's activities and are most likely to know what the organization is doing and how its funds are spent.

Others to include on solicitation lists are—

* persons who benefit from the service provided by the organization and families of such persons, provided this is appropriate
* individuals who are in attendance at speaking engagements
* persons who make contributions to similar organizations.

Successful fundraising letters often appeal to some basic instinct that will make the reader have an irresistible urge to run to his or her checkbook and write a check to the organization. Appeals that honestly portray the needs of the organization and the importance of the services it provides are a basic component of direct mail letters. Among the most popular are those that appeal to:

- *Guilt.* They make people feel guilty that they are not participating in solving some urgent problem.

- *Affiliation.* They appeal to the need to belong to an organization that is doing something worthwhile.

- *Self-interest.* They find some way to show that by helping the organization, donors' own lives will be improved in some way.

- *Ego.* They make prospective donors feel they are wonderful people only if they make a contribution.

- *Idealism.* They appeal to the idea that the world or community will be a better place for everyone, and only a chosen few selfless people will help this cause.

- *Religious obligation to give to charity.* Religious organizations have relied on this for years, but many secular organizations find this line of appeal equally effective for certain target audiences.

4. Businesses

Many organizations receive operating funds and in-kind contributions of services, equipment, and supplies from businesses in their communities. These businesses include—

- employers of board members

- suppliers of goods and services to the organization

- businesses that make contributions to other nonprofit organizations in the community

- businesses that sell goods and services to board members, organizational members, or clients

- major employers in the community.

Rather than visiting a business "cold," organizations sometimes find it effective to involve representatives of businesses in the organization's program before asking them for funds. Among ways they do this are:

- They have business representation on the board.

- They establish a "business advisory committee" consisting of local businesspeople.

- They invite business representatives to an "open house" to see the organization in action.

- They place business representatives on the organization's mailing list, and send them the newsletter and newspaper clippings about the organization's accomplishments.

- They invite business representatives to speak to the organization's board or membership about their products and services.

Many business corporations have established foundations that are specifically staffed to consider funding applications from charities.

5. Telephone Solicitation

Similar to direct mail, telephone solicitation is effective if done with the right list of names and correct telephone numbers. A college making calls to its alumni using student volunteers will certainly have a much better response than if it makes calls at random. Similarly, an organization is well served if it can tailor calls to those with a likely interest in its purpose.

6. Text Giving Solicitation

Also referred to as "text-to-give" or "text-to-donate," sending cellphone texts is becoming the modern version of telephone solicitation (see #5). Fewer and fewer people continue to even have land lines. And more and more people (including myself) won't answer them unless they recognize the name of the person or organization calling on caller I.D., even when the number appears to be local—as many calls from telephone solicitors spoof a local telephone exchange or are otherwise phishing attempts or other unwelcome or fraudulent calls. Millions of donors, and potential donors, are tethered to their cellphones. Using text-to-giving apps meets donors where they are with the ability to almost effortlessly text an immediate donation.

Using a text-giving commercial platform, charities receive a unique telephone number from the provider. The charity selects a specific keyword that donors use to text a donation. Within seconds, the software automatically sends to the donor a text confirming the request to donate with a link to indicate the amount. First-time donors receive a short donation form with payment information. The text message has "donate" and "send" buttons, and the platform securely processes the donations. Successful charities share their keyword and text number on all marketing communications. One provider (Snowball) has a demonstration site where you can see how this works—text the word "gala" to 5054124891. Other popular platforms are OneCause, Double the Donation, QGIV, Pledgling, Gesture, and Accelevents. These providers typically charge an annual fee, a percentage of the amount processed, and a small fee per transaction. Some waive the annual fee for charities that don't need all of the bells and whistles they offer.

7. Government Grants

During the 1980s, federal government grants to nonprofits, particularly for social services, plummeted. Yet, there are millions of dollars in federal and state grants available to nonprofits that still go begging for takers. The trick is to identify the source of funds and determine eligibility.

Assistance Listings, formerly known as The *Catalog of Federal Domestic Assistance,* is available in many libraries. It can also be found on the internet, in searchable format, at *https://beta.sam.gov/help/assistance-listing.* This document provides a summary of available federal grants and the qualifications and conditions for applying.

Government grants usually are accompanied by lots of paperwork and operational requirements, some of which may be inconsistent with the manner in which an organization intends to operate. Some analysts view a 1991 U.S. Supreme Court decision (*Rust v. Sullivan*) as clearing the way for the federal government to impose even greater restrictions on how government funds may be spent. If you are applying for government grants, learn about any additional requirements in order to be in compliance with law.

A new administration in Washington has taken over in 2021 and is facing a massive cut in revenue as a result of the pandemic and increased need for countercyclical spending on top of a $3 trillion budget deficit for the fiscal year that ended in September 2020. States and local governments are reeling from revenue shortfalls, as well, but are unable to borrow in the same manner as the federal government does routinely in times of crisis. Other than pandemic-related programs, it is not likely that there will much of an expansion of government grant-making for the foreseeable future.

8. Revenue Generation Other Than Voluntary Contributions

The following are examples of strategies used by nonprofits to increase income:

- newsletter subscriptions
- newsletter and website advertising
- annual fundraising dinner
- reception for a famous person or someone well known in the field of expertise of the organization/testimonial dinner
- sale of publications
- fees for services to clients
- sale or rental of mailing lists (make sure the buyer will use the list in a manner consistent with the organization's goals and not resell it to others)
- small games of chance (provided they comply with state regulatory laws)
- wills and bequests
- social events (e.g., bus trips to sports events)
- newspaper advertising to request contributions
- in-kind donations
- card calling (using board and organizational members to do peer one-on-one solicitation)
- fees from workshops and conferences
- sale of exhibit space at workshops and conferences
- special fundraising events such as bake sales, flea markets, and running races
- auctions of donated items (including those from celebrities) conducted over the internet or at a live event
- participating in crowdsourcing websites to finance specific programs, such as Kickstarter (*https://www.kickstarter.com/*) and Indiegogo *(https://www. indiegogo.com/)*
- use of online personal fundraising pages to generate donations from friends of stakeholders
- events similar to the ALS's "ice bucket challenge" (see page 287).
- encouraging your stakeholders to create birthday fundraisers on Facebook (see: *https://www.facebook.com/fundraisers?birthday&source=help_center_how_to_create_birthday_fundraiser).*

Searching for Funding Sources Online

Government agencies at all levels, foundations, and corporations have billions of dollars to give away each year to support the missions of worthy charitable organizations. Some of these grants come with substantial strings attached, and others can be used for almost any reasonable purpose. What they have in common is that information about these funding sources is usually posted on the websites of the funders, in addition to being available in databases that are often searchable by categories that will help you target your search.

It wasn't too long ago that nonprofit organizations were comfortable with budgeting thousands of dollars for thick directories of these funding opportunities. Now, many of these directories are available for a reasonable fee on CD-ROM, by subscription on the internet, or for free at scores of websites. If you are looking for funding from such grantors, you need to know about these sites, which will save you countless hours of search for the funds you need.

Of the more than $449 billion raised by charities in 2019, perhaps only a third or so comes from sources other than individual donors, such as foundations run by individuals, families and corporations, community foundations, and corporate giving programs. Yet, there remains a certain caché to having a grant come from a prestigious foundation, providing your organization with instant credibility. The internet has made it much easier to identify potential funders, using online directories and databases that are searchable by the funder's program priorities, geography, and type of support. Today, every major foundation has a website, as do many of the smaller ones. Among typical documents posted are mission and values statements, annual reports, newsletters, grant opportunities, biographies of staff and leadership, funding priorities, guidelines and deadlines, information about previous grants made (including amounts of funding awarded), and, to an increasing degree, application forms that can be submitted electronically.

Identify most likely funding sources

The first objective in a search for funding sources is identifying potential grantmakers that have a history of awarding grants in your charity's area of interest in your geographical area. Among the obvious targets are—

- *Private foundations*—non-governmental organizations with an endowment derived principally from a single source (individual, family, or corporation) that makes grants for charitable purposes
- *Corporate giving programs*—grant-making programs within a for-profit business
- *Public foundations*—charities that make grants to unrelated organizations and individuals
- *Community foundations*—charities that make grants to organizations within a specific locality or region
- *Government*—federal, state, regional, and local governments.

Identify foundation funding

Many nonprofit organizations depend on foundation support to maintain their programs. But with all the progress offered by the internet, foundations will not come to your site to give. Despite that, grant writers were among the first to benefit from the access the internet provided them to look for and approach foundations whose objectives match their missions and to manage the process of applying for grants.

Through the Foundation Center's (Candid) website *(https://candid.org/)*, grantseekers can find a particular foundation or research those most likely to be attracted to their programs by areas of interest, type of funding, or the geographical region they support. The Foundation Directory, long a vital resource for fundraisers, is available online here (subscription required).

Fundraisers can read a foundation's guidelines on its website and learn how to apply. Many allow proposals to be sent online or by email. The internet provides a convenient way to ensure that you are sending the best possible proposal, and it helps foundation staff, as they have to answer fewer questions. Fundraisers should always consult a foundation's website before contacting a program officer with questions. It is wise to become intimately familiar with a foundation by reading through its site before and during the process of applying.

Foundation staff frequently complain when charities call with questions that were clearly answered on their website. Demonstrate to them the courtesy of looking there first. At the same time, while it has become increasingly possible to find a grant and apply for it entirely online, this is not recommended. Make "personal" contact with the grantmaker before applying. Tell the staff if you found useful information at the site. This should be done by telephone or letter. However, follow-up email requests for information or responses to questions are perfectly acceptable.

Some of the information you can find at a foundation's website includes announcements about grants the funder has already made, contact information, strategic plans, annual reports, and other documents you will find useful in crafting your proposal. You can often find useful information from the grantmaker's federal tax return (usually a 990 or 990PF) at such sites as Candid *(https://www.guidestar.org/)* or Charity Navigator *(https://www.charitynavigator.org/)*. The searchable Nozasearch database *(https://www.nozasearch.com/Services.aspx)* offers a free or low-cost service for grantwriters looking for funding sources. You can also use popular search engines such as Google *(https://www.google.com/)* to find general information about the grantmaker, those that have received funding from it, and the grantmaker staff.

Thank and acknowledge support

Cultivate a strong relationship by publicly acknowledging foundation support on your organization's website. Do this in much the same way as you might your individual donors, through donor listings, or even a dedicated page or online press release announcing the gift and describing the foundation's history and matching objectives. If you have done this, be sure to let the foundation know how you have acknowledged its support.

Access free and low-cost databases

Want to search community foundations by state? Point your browser to: *https://www.tgci.com/funding-sources* to tap into the Grantsmanship Center's database. You can find grant sources organized by topic (e.g., children and youth, recreation, arts & cultural activities, and the aged) at: *https://libguides.lib.msu.edu/c.php?g=96743&p=622547*

Visit the Candid *(https//candid.org*—see "finding funders") for searchable databases that help identify potential funding sources. Here you can find basic information about thousands of private and community foundations, including their assets, amount of grants, contact information, and website address.

The Chronicle of Philanthropy has a subscription-based database that includes information about all foundation and corporate grants published in that publication since 1995. If you are a subscriber to the print version (a must read for all who need to, or want to, follow what is happening in the nonprofit sector), you can use the search engine free for searches involving the last two issues.

Government Grants

Assistance Listings, formerly known as The *Catalog of Federal Domestic Assistance (https://beta.sam.gov/),* has been available free online in a searchable format since the mid-1990s. The latest version of this website has much more useful information for grantseekers than was available a decade ago, including a database on more than 2,000 federal grant assistance programs, as of December 2020. Here you can find access to the print editions, and find federal government grants offered in your organization's niche using a keyword search.

Grants.gov, launched in October 2003, takes the online search for federal government funding to a higher level. The objective of this site is to level the playing field so all eligible organizations, regardless of their size or grantsmanship sophistication, can have a fair opportunity to receive federal grants. The site directs grant seekers to more than 1,000 funding programs offered by 26 grant-making federal agencies that aggregately award over $400 billion annually to state and local governments, academia, nonprofits, and other organizations. It not only makes it easier for organizations to find grants of interest, but also streamlines the paperwork needed to apply for them and permits the entire process to be conducted online. All application forms, financial report data in support of organizational audit and performance measurement activities, grant management procedures, and information about grant programs have been standardized across these participating organizations.

The site hosts everything an organization needs to find, apply, and manage a federal grant. Even grant notifications are made electronically. Site visitors download forms, work on them offline, and then submit completed applications electronically, saving hours of time and money. The site is divided into sections that help you engage in a six-step process, consisting of finding grant opportunities of interest, downloading the grant application package, registering with a Central Contract Registry, registering with a credentials provider, registering with grants.gov to submit grant applications, and logging on. There is even a toll-free number to use to request assistance. This site is the first place to go if you have any interest in federal grant funds.

Other places to look for information about federal government grants include—

https://www.fundsnetservices.com/searchresult/8/Government-Funding. html
https://www.councilofnonprofits.org/tools-resources/how-start-nonprofit

Don't forget that many states, counties, and individual municipalities also make grants to nonprofit organizations. They often have searchable websites that can help in identifying funding opportunities.

Finding Corporate Support

Corporate funding sources that are not foundations do not file a 990. However, there are databases, some free and some subscription, which permit you to check them out as well. Among them are EDGAR *(https://www.sec.gov/ edgar/search-and-access)* and D&B Hoover's *(https://www.dnb.com/products/ marketing-sales/dnb-hoovers.html)*. Edgar includes all filings of publicly-traded companies with the SEC since 1994. The annual filing, form 10-K, includes a lot of basic financial information, some of which may be of use to fundraisers. D&B Hoover's includes information on both public and private companies. Some of the basic information can be viewed for free, but more detailed documents and databases require a subscription. There are other, less well known, sources for information about corporations of use to grantseekers, such as David Lamb's Prospect Research Page *(http://www.lambresearch.com)*, which has plenty of links to corporate information. You can also find corporation information at Yahoo! *(see https://finance.yahoo.com/).*

Of course, you will want to visit the corporation's website and learn more about its products and services, financial information, annual reports, newsletters that may provide details about how the organization is involved in its community, and biographies of key leadership.

Find in-kind donations

One thing that distinguishes corporate giving from its non-business counterparts is the willingness to make in-kind donations of company-produced products. Corporations give a staggering amount of products to charity. According to a survey of 150 of the largest corporations conducted by *The Chronicle of Philanthropy,* as much as 30% of total giving by these organizations consisted of in-kind gifts, more than $1 billion in 1999. The same survey conducted five years later found that two individual pharmaceutical companies, Pfizer and Merck, each reached or exceeded this amount in in-kind donations. And, in 2009, this survey found that Oracle (software), Comcast (cable, telephone, internet), and Abbotts Laboratories (pharmaceuticals), Eli-Lilly (pharmaceuticals), Bristol-Myers Squibb (pharmaceuticals), Microsoft (software), IBM (software), and Johnson and Johnson (consumer products, medical devices, pharmaceuticals) joined those two companies in donating at least $100 million in in-kind products and services with such in-kind donations comprising at least 60% of their total charitable donations.

Several intermediary websites have sprung up to find matches between corporations willing to provide such in-kind donations and charities that can put the products to good use. In 2016, Goods360 *(https://good360.org/* formerly known as Gifts-in-Kind)* alone distributed an estimated $400 million worth of goods, partnering with firms such as Office Depot, Gillette, IBM, Avon, and General Motors (each of which was honored with a "Light of Hope" Award for its efforts). According to the organization, more than 57,000 charities currently benefit from these donations. The website provides an easy way for 501(c)(3) organizations to register, and there is no annual registration fee. If a donor does not cover these costs, there is a shipping and handling cost to receive goods.

Many organizations depend on corporate support. Corporate investment in nonprofits is based on entirely different motivations from individual philanthropy. Corporations are looking for mutual benefits. Some corporations support programs in their communities hoping that community building activity will strengthen and support their workforce. Others seek marketing benefits and value associations with organizations whose cause and good name will encourage consumers to purchase their products or services. Corporate fundraisers need to be skilled and knowledgeable in both building good relationships with corporations and helping their organizations think creatively about how they can benefit commercial enterprises.

Design your website to facilitate corporate support

Perhaps the internet's primary value for corporate philanthropy is in visitor traffic. The fundraiser's internet strategy must touch on both the organization's website and the corporation's. Banner ad space or recognition of corporate sponsors on an organization's website is important. Conversely, allowing companies to use your logo and name on their site will have a similar beneficial value, spreading the name of your organization and information about its mission to the company's stakeholders.

Some organizations develop a corporate sponsors page, typically linking logos to the corporation's website. These can link specifically to pages at the company's site that talk about your work, creating a "two-way street" for Web surfers. The company page might focus on the link between the particular product or service and the organization's mission. For example, a company selling baby care products might wish to be identified with an organization providing services related to infant health or child welfare.

These relationships tend to be active partnerships. Therefore, a Web strategy should be particularly dynamic—relating perhaps the regular progress toward the organization's goals with the success of the fundraising relationship.

Employee Giving Programs

Another form of corporate giving is the employee giving program. Companies with large numbers of employees may encourage them to support a particular organization with which they have a relationship. Employees may give individually or participate in fundraising events. Large nonprofits may also seek support from their own employees.

Because workplace giving operates as a special campaign, it may be worth creating a separate Web page for this, including integrating the option to give online and reporting progress to date toward a particular goal.

Hiring a Consultant

There are hundreds of honest, hard-working, professional fundraising consultants who will, for a fee, provide an organization with fundraising advice or even handle all of its fundraising. There also are hundreds who are not reputable.

Most states regulate this industry, and there are opportunities to obtain information about consultants before making a hiring commitment. State associations of nonprofit organizations may be helpful in identifying candidates. Since most states require these fundraising consultants to register, the public may look at these records (some states post reports online) or contact organizations that have hired them to see if they are pleased with the services being provided.

Donation Acceptance Policies

In the fall of 2019, a major fundraising scandal embarrassed many nonprofit organizations, including Massachusetts Institute of Technology (MIT). The MIT media lab was accused of accepting large donations from Jeffrey Epstein, a convicted sex offender, and covering up their contacts with him. Other organizations, including Harvard University, had to make decisions about whether to return money previously donated by Mr. Epstein, who died in prison in August of that year.

The scandal renewed a conversation in the nonprofit community about the ethics of accepting or returning donations that included several types of controversy. Among them are situations when the donor wants to donate money obtained from illegal activities (tainted money), whether the money to be donated is by someone whose behavior is unacceptable (tainted donor), and the situation when the donation was made prior to the donor's behavior becoming unacceptable.

Organizations should have a formal, written policy governing which gifts (both money and goods) will not be accepted, and the process used to adjudicate disputes. Gifts should not be accepted from those who have values at odds with the organization's gift policy. Included in this policy should be provisions dealing with contributions—

- from those convicted of major crimes

- when the gift is unlikely to have any value to the organization

- when the donor places restrictions on the gift that are unacceptable (such as requiring it be used for illegal or unethical purposes)

- when the donor's intent is to exploit the brand of the charity to an extent that is unacceptable, and not in the best interests of the charity.

For sample gift acceptance policies, see: *https://tinyurl.com/y5xu2ode* and *https://www.gcfdn.org/Portals/0/Uploads/Documents/Policy_General_Development.pdf*

Online Resources To Explore:

Association of Fundraising Professionals
   https://afpglobal.org/

PayPal Giving Fund (formerly known as MissionFish)
   https://www.paypal.com/givingfund/

Fundraising.com
   https://www.fundraising.com/

Carter McNamara's Nonprofit Fundraising and Grantwriting
   https://managementhelp.org/nonprofitfundraising/index.htm

Tips:

- Review other organizations' solicitation materials and identify those presentations that can serve as an effective model for solicitation.

- Keep a file of newspaper clippings about benefactors in the community and others who would have a potential interest in the work of the organization. A few well-placed and well-timed telephone calls can be effective in reaching these influential people.

- Involve everyone in the organization in the fundraising effort. It is not prudent to isolate fundraising from the programs the organization funds.

- Always thank each donor, regardless of the amount received. A $5 check from an individual may have required as much personal sacrifice as a $1,000 check from a wealthier contributor.

Chapter 17
Writing Effective Grant Proposals

by Michael A. Sand

> **Synopsis:** Grant applicants should research the grantor before applying. They should not deviate from the format of the grant application except with express permission. There is a formula to follow for effective grant applications that, among other components, emphasizes the needs of the community rather than the needs of the applicant.

Competition for government, corporate, and foundation grants is increasing. At the same time, funding from government sources for human services is shrinking, and the demand for human services is skyrocketing.

In response, charities are becoming more sophisticated in the ways they seek alternative sources of funding. Many are hiring development staff with specialized training and experience in obtaining grants. Others without the resources to make such a major investment are forced to do what they can. The purpose of this chapter is to provide a framework for the preparation of proposals for those without substantial grantsmanship experience.

It is often useful for grant seekers to develop the attitude that the relationship between them and the grantors is collaborative. True, all of the wonderful plans you have in mind will never come to fruition without the funds. However, the grantor needs the creativity, dedication, staff resources, and vision provided by the grant recipient. A grant proposal that is seen as simple begging is not as likely to be as successful as one that encourages the grantor to become a partner in an effort that will have substantial benefits to the community.

Before embarking on a costly and time-consuming search for grants, verify that the purpose of the grant is consistent with the organization's mission. Some organizations apply for grants simply because the money is available and obtainable, and they have a plan to win it. However, a successful grant application may result in the organization losing its focus if the grant is inconsistent with its direction.

Even if the grant's purpose is consistent with the mission, consider whether the project is viewed as constructive by an organization's stakeholders, such as members of the board, clients, and staff. It may be useful to convene a focus group to gauge whether the grant would truly be beneficial to the organization and its clients.

In addition, organizations should consider cash-flow issues, grant eligibility, the politics of the grant, and the source of the grant. The check from the funder may arrive months after the organization has committed itself to hiring staff and paying other project costs. Is a source of funds available until the grant funds are received? Are there laws or other grant requirements that must be adhered to that, for any reason, you are unable or unwilling to honor? Have the grants being applied for been promised informally in advance to other organizations? Does the grantor have a reputation for making unreasonable demands on the organizations it funds?

Researching the Grantor

Once you believe a funding source may have funds available, do not begin to write the grant application until you have tried to find out the answer to several questions. Try to obtain an interview with a representative of the funder before beginning to fill in the funding application. In any case, you should have the following information before beginning the proposal-writing stage:

1. The application format

Why write a 30-page application when a three-page application would have been funded? Why write a three-page application and not get funded when a 10-page proposal would have been accepted? Many government agencies will send you a *Request for Proposal* (RFP) that will outline exactly what should be included in the application. Many larger foundations will provide specific instructions.

If you are given written instructions by a funding source, do not deviate from these instructions without permission. One major reason grants do not get funded is that the writer does not follow the instructions to the letter. Even minor deviations can make the proposal ineligible. If you believe a particular instruction does not apply to your situation, request written permission from the funder to make changes.

2. Motivation of the funding source

Many funding sources specialize in awarding grants for specific purposes. An organization will not receive a grant from such a funder unless the proposal clearly is responsive to the vision and mission of the funding organization. When applying for a government grant, for example, obtain and study the legislative history that led to a funding appropriation. When applying for foundation funds, be sure to obtain the donor's funding instructions. Many corporate and family foundations have a priority listing of the types of programs they fund and will be glad to share this information.

3. The amount of funds awarded by the grantor per award, and the amount of total funds awarded

This will be extremely helpful information if you can obtain it. In many instances, a government agency has a specific allocation of funds for a particular program. Large foundations set specific priority areas and make general allocations in the priority area. Foundation directories provide information about the priority areas of grantors and are available in most public libraries. It is senseless to develop a grant application if the funds awarded by the source are too small for the organization's program needs.

4. Successful applications that were funded in previous funding cycles

Perhaps the best indicator of the types of funding applications that will be successful is a review of actual applications that have been funded. A strong argument can be made that government agencies have an obligation to provide you (as a taxpayer) with copies of funded applications. Although you may have to review the applications at the agency's headquarters or pay for duplication, you should be able to review past grants.

Many foundations will provide a list of the previous year's grants and the total of each. You can contact a funded organization and ask for a copy of its application. Although lists of past grants are often difficult to obtain from businesses, many annual reports and business newsletters include a list of grants that have been awarded as well as their sources.

5. The names of individuals making the funding decisions and their backgrounds

When writing a grant application, it is important to know who will be reviewing it. If the reviewers have extensive expertise in your field, you will not have to define every term. In many instances, however, a foundation trustee or a business official on the allocations committee will not have any knowledge of your particular field. You will then have to carefully explain your services in layman's terms, spell out every abbreviation, and define each technical term you use.

6. The criteria used in making the grant selection

Knowing the selection criteria can be crucial in determining how to write a grant. Many grantor agencies have limited amounts of funds and will give preference to smaller grants. Others will make the selection based on non-cost factors and then negotiate the cost of the proposal. Knowing whether it will be helpful or harmful to have political officials contact the grantor agency is important information.

Sections of a Grant Application

1. Cover Letter

Many grant applications specifically request a cover letter and define what information should be included. If this is not expressly prohibited by the grant application format, write a short cover letter on the organization's stationery that:

- is addressed to the appropriate individual at the grantor agency, making sure the name, title, agency name, and address are absolutely correct

- contains a one-sentence description of the proposal

- provides the number of participants, jobs obtained, or other units to be funded by the grant

- lists the total amount of funds requested

- provides the name, address, and telephone number of the individual at the requesting organization the grantor can contact to request additional information.

2. Executive Summary

Include in this section a succinct summary of the entire proposal.

3. Introduction

Provide important information that may not otherwise appear anywhere else in the grant application. Items you might include are—

- your organization's mission
- how long you have been providing the type of service included in this program
- a brief history of your organization
- your capability of operating the kind of programs they fund efficiently and effectively
- if there are eligibility requirements in the proposal, a statement that you are eligible to receive the funds
- IRS Section 501(c) tax-exempt status determination letter
- outline of letters of support from past clients, representatives of cooperating agencies, and legislative officials. (The letters them-

selves should be included as appendices to the application.)
- statement of how you will obtain funding for the program at the end of the grant period.

4. Need

For a grant to be funded, the organization must demonstrate the need of individuals in the community for the service to be provided. What is the extent of the need and how is the need documented? The need described should be the need of the individuals in the community for the services, not the need of the organization. Rather than stating, "We need a counselor because our organization doesn't have one," or "The funds for the one we had were cut back by the government," estimate the number of individuals who need counseling services. The need should be the need in your coverage area. Although national or statewide figures might be given, if you serve a particular county, the estimate of need for that county should be provided.

The need should be the need for the particular service you are providing. If you provide services for victims of domestic violence, for example, the estimated number of victims of domestic violence should be provided, rather than unemployment figures or other available statistics. The need should be quantified. How many individuals do you believe are eligible for the particular service you provide in your coverage area?

Common sources of data are—

a. **Census Data**—Make certain you are using data from the most recent census. In most cases, earlier data are outdated.

b. **County Planning Departments**—Call the office of your county government to find the telephone number of your county's planning department.

c. **State Agencies**—The Departments of Education, Health, Labor, and Human Services, or their equivalents, are all excellent sources of data.

d. **Local Governments**—Local police departments are excellent sources of crime data, and local school districts can provide educational information.

e. **Self-generated Data**—In many cases, you can provide the data from sources within your organization. Sources might include—

- waiting lists
- letters from potential clients requesting a service
- letters complaining that a particular service is not in existence
- testimony at public hearings
- information obtained from questionnaires administered to present clients asking them to list other services they might like
- community surveys.

5. Objectives

Objectives are the proposed results of the project. Objectives should have the following characteristics:

- They are measurable. How many individuals do you estimate will participate in your program?

- They are time-based. How many individuals do you estimate will participate in your program in the next three months? In the next year?

- They are realistic.

The information needed to measure objectives can be obtained as part of the program funded by the grant. Do not list objectives in your proposal that are impossible to measure.

6. Project Description

Here is where you will outline your program. An easy way to remember what to include are the 6 W's of program writing:

- **Who?** Who are the clients? How are they selected? What are the restrictions (e.g., age, income, geographic)? Who are the staff members?

  If you are asking the funding source to pay for new staff members, include a job description and a qualifications statement that lists the education, experience, and other job requirements. If you are applying for funds to continue existing staff, include a résumé and a biographical statement for each staff member.

- **What?** What services will be provided? What will be the benefits of this program? What are the expected outcomes? For educational programs, include a course outline. You may include relevant sections of an operations manual. For other programs, a narrative outlining the services would be appropriate. Still others might provide a "day in the life of a client." What outreach efforts will be made?

- **Where?** Where will the services be provided? Give the addresses of all main and field offices. If you will be obtaining new space with the program funds, what type of space are you seeking?

- **When?** What are the hours that services will be provided? On which days during the year will services be provided? It is also useful to provide a timetable for project implementation.

- **With whom?** What other agencies are participating with you in the provision of services? For example, include agencies referring clients to you. Outline the agencies to which you refer clients. It is important to obtain letters from the other agencies confirming any relationships you describe.

- **Why?** Why are you providing these services rather than alternatives? Are you utilizing any unique approaches to the provision of services?

7. Budget

If it is not clear from the grant application forms, ask the funding source how much financial detail is required. Many businesses, for example, may only require the total amount you are going to spend. On the other hand, most government agencies require a line-item budget that includes a detailed estimate of all funds to be spent. Such a budget might be set up to include the following:

- personnel costs (salaries, fringe benefits, consultants, and contract services)

- non-personnel costs (travel, office space, equipment, consumable supplies, and other costs such as telephone, postage, and indirect costs)

Some grantors may require your organization to contribute a matching share. If you are permitted to include in-kind or non-cash expenditures, use the same budget categories as above. In the personnel category, for example, you would list the worth of the time volunteers are contributing to your program. In the non-personnel category, you would include the market value of the equipment donated to your program.

8. Evaluation

Inform the funding source that you will be conducting an evaluation of the services you are providing.

- **Detail who will participate in the evaluation process.** Outline the participation of board members, staff members, clients, experts in the substantive field, and representatives of the community in the evaluation process. Some grantors require an independent evaluator.

- **Explain what will be evaluated.** List some of the issues the evaluation team will consider. For example, the evaluators will review whether the need was reduced as a result of providing the services. Were the objectives met? Were the services provided as outlined in the Project Description section? Will the budget be audited by an outside firm and, if not, who will review the receipts and expenditures?

- **Specify what type of evaluation will be provided.** Provide in as much detail as you can how the program will be evaluated. If formal classes are provided, include the pre- and post-test you will use to evaluate them.

  If a client questionnaire will be used, attach a copy to the application. Describe how the program data will be reviewed in the evaluation process. Include a description of the audit or the process you will use to review the budget items.

9. Conclusion

In no more than two or three paragraphs, summarize the proposal's main points and the reasons the community will be improved as a result of successful completion of the project.

When you have finished writing your grant application, ask yourself the following questions before you send it to the funding source:

- Is the application free of the jargon of your field?
- Are all abbreviations spelled out the first time you use them?
- Have you followed all of the instructions in the Request for Proposal (RFP)?

- Are all words spelled correctly? Remember that your computer's spell-checker only tells you that the words you use are spelled correctly and in English, not that they are the correct words for the context.
- Is your application interesting to read?
- If you were the grantor agency, would you fund it?

Finally, get the application in the hands of the grantor well before the deadline. The fundraising field is replete with horror stories about multi-million-dollar proposals that were not even considered because someone put the application in the mail and it did not arrive until well after the deadline.

If the application is mailed, make sure there is enough postage. It is highly recommended that applications be either hand-delivered or sent by a trackable, overnight courier, such as FedEx, UPS, or Airborne Express. Make several office copies before submitting the original, and be sure that you provide the number of copies requested by the grantor.

Online Resources to Explore:

USA.Gov
https://www.usa.gov/business

Grants.gov
https://www.grants.gov/

The Grantsmanship Center—Funding Resources
https://www.tgci.com/funding-sources

Council on Foundations
https://www.cof.org/

Candid (The Foundation Center/Guidestar)
https://candid.org/

Tips:

- Before applying for a grant, check to see if the grantor has a website, which will not only tell you something about that organization and contact information, but may also provide information about prior grants approved, what procedures are required to apply for funds, and, often, the application forms in downloadable format.

- Double-check your proposal for spelling and grammar, that all pages are included in the proposal (i.e., the last page was not left in the copy machine as a result of making a copy of the submission for your files), that the correct number of copies is provided, and that all attachments are included.

- Hand deliver your grant proposal, or use a trackable, reliable delivery service. Track the package to see if it has arrived prior to the deadline. This is not the time to save a few dollars by putting your proposal in the mail.

- Even if your proposal is rejected, send a short thank-you letter to the funder for the opportunity to submit the proposal. Express a willingness to maintain a relationship with respect to future funding opportunities.

- Be careful what you wish for; you might get it. Begin thinking about how to administer a grant even before you apply for it. You may decide that the stress of winning a particular grant might be too much for your organization.

Chapter 18

Marketing

Synopsis: Marketing is an appropriate, if not essential, activity of nonprofit organizations that need to sell goods and services, and to develop a mix of desirable goods and services to support their missions. Nonprofits market by shaping an attractive message, and delivering that message through a variety of methods, including print and electronic advertising, social media, special events, and direct mail. A formal marketing plan can be effective in implementing a strategy to increase an organization's marketing success.

The American Marketing Association defines the term "marketing" as "the activity...and processes for creating, communicating, delivering, and exchanging offerings that have value for customers, clients, partners, and society at large." It includes that function of the organization that communicates with the organization's consumers about their goods and services, determine their needs, meet these needs, and build a program of communications to keep them informed about what the organization offers.

A narrower definition of nonprofit marketing can be: activities of a nonprofit organization, including developing and improving its services, that are designed to result in a transaction between two entities (for our purposes, the organization and either another organization or an individual) to exchange money for goods or services provided by that nonprofit organization. Funds derived from this transaction may be used for any legal purpose consistent with the organization's mission, including paying overhead or expanding the availability of its goods and services to those who may not be able to pay the full cost.

Nonprofit marketing also includes those activities in which money is not exchanged, but the activities are designed to increase the accessibility of the organization's services. For example, when a museum that offers free admission designates funds for advertising for the purpose of increasing its reach into the community, it is also engaging in marketing. Even those who accept an offer of free admission will likely avail themselves of the museum's cafeteria and perhaps its gift shop, contributing to the organization's net revenue, putting aside any benefits a free admission policy might have on contributions. Nonprofits also engage in marketing when they seek volunteers using traditional marketing techniques.

There are two major components to marketing—developing the message that needs to be communicated, and delivering that message to the target through some medium. Both of these components are crucial to the success of any marketing campaign. Organizations that take marketing seriously engage in research prior to the campaign to collect data on what message should be communicated, and which is the most effective way to have that message delivered. Advances in technology, particularly the Web, social media, email, blogging, and texting, have enhanced the opportunities for nonprofit organizations to connect with their stakeholders in ways that these stakeholders find are the most comfortable.

Introduction to Nonprofit Marketing

It was not that long ago that few, if any, nonprofit organizations thought it was appropriate to engage in the traditional marketing campaigns that were considered essential by for-profit business organizations. Many nonprofit leaders felt that engaging in these activities was not consistent with the spirit of being a nonprofit. Mission was paramount, and keeping a vigilant eye on the "bottom line" was a secondary, yet necessary, annoyance. Times have changed. Today's modern nonprofit CEOs often brandish an MBA and are quite comfortable using terms such as "return on investment," "market share," "branding," "profit center," and "SWOT analysis"—terms one never used to hear from those who led nonprofit organizations.

An active marketing program is now not only acceptable for nonprofit organizations, but one is virtually required to keep pace in the turbulent business environment of the sector—particularly among the mega-nonprofits such as institutions of higher learning and hospitals. Some of these organizations have annual budgets in the billions of dollars and market their services with the same aggressiveness as their for-profit competitors.

A strong case can be made that a nonprofit organization is obligated to do what it can to sustain itself, particularly during times when it is threatened by declining donations and government support during economic downturns. A strong marketing program helps an organization acquire the revenues it needs to grow and provide more free and subsidized services than it might otherwise have the capacity to provide.

This book maintains the perspective throughout that nonprofit organizations have many things in common with their for-profit counterparts. One of these is that neither type of organization can take for granted that simply offering services will generate enough "business" to provide financial stability for the purpose (in the case of a for-profit) to generate profit or (in the case of a nonprofit) to generate net revenue to expand services and make up for possible deficits. Both types of organizations typically engage in activities to offer a mix of goods and services for which there is sufficient consumer demand to justify offering them. They communicate with these consumers about the availability of these goods and services.

They communicate information about themselves that builds trust with potential customers. And they promote the value of their particular services compared to any competition they might have. These activities are the essence of marketing.

If you recall our discussion of the diversity of the nonprofit sector in the introduction to this book, there is no monolithic model for financing the operations of nonprofit organizations. It is not unusual for a nonprofit organization to obtain its revenues through three major sources of income—a mix of grants, private contributions, and fees for goods and services. To a lesser extent, investment income provides an additional source of revenue. The proportion of these three major sources of income varies by subsector, according to statistics compiled by the Urban Institute in its report, The Nonprofit Almanac.

One conclusion that can be drawn from these data is just as meaningful today as it was decades ago—the modern charity depends substantially more on the sale of goods and services for its revenue than one might expect. In fact, of the 310,000 plus charitable organizations included in the survey database of the National Center for Charitable Statistics, through a review of 990 and 990EZ tax returns, only about a fifth of their income came from donations in the form of private contributions and government grants.

There is no way to interpret this other than to marvel at how important the sale of goods and services is to the financial health of nonprofit organizations. Fundraising is important, of course, and certainly fundraising for some organizations underwrites virtually all of their operating expenses. But to an increasing extent, this situation is unusual. Imagine how long a typical nonprofit hospital, university, nursing home, family service agency, or day care center could survive financially if it had to depend totally on donations to meet payroll and provide for other expenses.

Nonprofit organizations received more than $449.6 billion in donations in 2020, according to Giving USA, and nonprofit organizations engage in increasingly sophisticated strategies to augment their donations. The same is true with marketing, and even more important with revenues from the sale of goods and services approaching a trillion dollars annually. It is common sense that a dollar in revenue that comes from the sale of goods and services has the same value in paying a staff member's salary as a dollar raised in contributions. Putting aside the effects of the economy, the amount of donations made to charities tends to be quite stable over long periods of time. However, organizations that fail to engage in effective marketing strategies to respond to competition, respond to consumer needs, and trumpet their positive attributes may find that their total revenues shrink despite increases in donations.

Differences Between Nonprofit Marketing and Fundraising

Marketing shares much in common with fundraising. One aspect that differentiates the two is that fundraising implies a relationship whereby a donor makes a gratuitous contribution to the organization without an expectation of anything substantially tangible received in return, and does not benefit directly from the donation any more than someone who does not make a donation. Marketing, on the other hand, implies a transaction in which the organization seeks to convince an individual or organization to make a voluntary exchange of money for goods and services provided by the organization, and the organization can use these funds without any strings attached. The lines between fundraising and marketing are certainly not as black and white as this, but I see this as an important distinction.

There are certainly many techniques in Chapter 16 on fundraising that apply to marketing goods and services. Similarly, there are techniques described in this chapter that are equally relevant to a fundraising campaign.

What Nonprofits Market

The following is a typology of what nonprofit organizations market conceived by Stacy Grau with each followed by real-life examples from my own experience:

- Services and programs—A day care center seeks to find enough children of appropriate ages for which to provide services by placing an advertisement in a local ethnic newspaper.

- Goods—My alma mater's gift shop tries to sell me t-shirts and rocking chairs emblazoned with the school's logo, and tries to sell my son an expensive frame for his diploma.

- Experiences—A symphony orchestra arranges for its assistant conductor to have a pre-concert lecture providing background about the featured composers and artists.

- Concepts—A state-wide conservative think tank prepares and runs a television spot in markets in my state to advocate for state legislation that would prohibit teacher unions from using union dues to finance partisan political activities, thus improving the organization's name recognition.

- Group benefits—A leading organization for senior citizens (in this case, the AARP) markets benefits such as discounts at restaurants and inexpensive car insurance to its membership.

To the above list, one of my ARNOVA colleagues, Martin Berg, who teaches nonprofit marketing at the University of Illinois-Chicago, adds: "Personal satisfaction—In the wake of a devastating hurricane, thousands send money to the Red Cross for no other reason than that they feel a responsibility for their fellow humans. The only "product" they receive in return is the donor's own satisfaction—the warm glow of knowing they could help someone else."

We all have seen firsthand similar marketing efforts by nonprofit organizations, many of which are designed to contribute to net revenues (which, in the for-profit context, would be referred to as "profit"). A Jewish Community Center holds an open house, offering the public free access, so prospective members can check out the fitness center facilities. A local hospital has a booth set up at a 5K race to offer free blood pressure screenings and body fat analysis for the purpose of funneling new patients to its outpatient clinics, and provides free pens at the booth with the name of the hospital prominently printed on them. These marketing efforts by "charities" no longer seem as strange as they might have in years past.

How Nonprofits Market

A few decades ago, nonprofit organizations had a short menu of options to deliver their message to the public. There were a limited number of TV and radio stations on which to advertise. The print media were also limited. Many of today's options of choice for message delivery, such as YouTube, blogs, podcasts, electronic newsletters, Facebook, Twitter, email, texting, and the Web, did not even exist then.

Among the more conventional methods to communicate a marketing effort are described by Dr. Grau—

- *Paid media.* Traditional media used by nonprofits to communicate their messages include both paid and free placements on radio and television outlets, newspapers and magazines, and other outlets such as highway billboards and transit vehicle advertising. Traditional advertising has the advantage of being subject to some targeting of the market the organization wishes to reach. In most cases (magazines and billboards being salient exceptions), traditional advertising can be prepared quickly and reach a wide audience in a short time. Many broadcasters will even offer to help an organization prepare a public service announcement without charge.

- *Commercial media.* This refers to communications prepared by the organization that are sent to media outlets with the hope (but not the requirement, as would be the case with paid media), that the message will be communicated. Included in this are press releases, Op-Ed articles, and blog and podcast interviews in which the organization makes an effort to convince others with market reach to provide some "air" time.

- *Owned media.* This refers to media owned by the organization such as in-house magazines, newspapers, newsletters, messages on its buildings and vehicles, its website, and other media for which the organization can control (such as its Facebook page, blogs, discussion boards, and podcasts).

- *Direct Marketing.* Perhaps of most use by nonprofit organizations to hawk their goods and services is direct marketing. This approach includes contacting individuals directly, typically through the mail, by telephone, by email, and door-to-door. The major benefit of this strategy is that unlike television and radio ads, a mailing can be targeted to those who purchased goods and services from the organization in the past. The communication can be customized to appeal to a particular segment of one's market. The obvious disadvantage is that direct marketing can be costly compared to mass broadcasting. One strategy organizations engage in to facilitate these efforts is to methodically collect names, addresses, telephone numbers, and email addresses of as many individuals as possible who come in contact with the organization, and to note the nature of that contact. This database becomes invaluable for both marketing and fundraising efforts.

- *Event Marketing.* Nonprofit organizations often sponsor events, such as golf tournaments, 5K road races, casino nights, and other events that are designed as fundraisers, but can have marketing benefits, as well. In an article in *The Chronicle of Philanthropy* (May 10, 2007), the author criticized organizers of 5K races for charity that often spent more money on directing the race than was raised. There was a backlash to this article that illustrated the fact that conducting these and other special events had substantially more benefits to the organization than simply raising funds for the cause. Among these benefits is giving visibility to both the organization and the mission it supports.

- *Social media.* Any credible marketing plan by nonprofit organizations these days must have a social media component, with Twitter and Facebook accounts on center-stage. In the past, organizations could be comfortable with making a sizable investment in encouraging potential donors and clients to "like" their Facebook page, and be assured that all of these "likers" would be able to view any and all posts made, with the potential that these viewers would share the posts with their "friends." This is no longer the case, and organizations who engage in this strategy are finding that they may need to allocate funds in their budget to purchase advertising to assure that more of their likers are able to see these posts in their newsfeeds. Beyond this, purchasing advertising on social media sites is generally low cost, and technology has improved the capacity of any message to be targeted to any particular demographic the organization seeks to reach with its message.

The advantage of making social media the centerpiece of any nonprofit marketing campaign is the apparently high cost-benefit of this marketing strategy, as well as its speed. A good communication to a relatively small group of supporters has the ability to "go viral," as recipients of a Facebook post or a tweet have the ability to share (in the case of Facebook) or retweet (in the case of Twitter) to relay the communication to those who otherwise have no relationship with the organization. Facebook and Twitter accounts are free, and a single individual with social networking savvy can create an effective organizational marketing campaign at little or no out-of-pocket cost. Social networking marketing can be coordinated with YouTube videos, organizational website content, and traditional marketing efforts.

In their 2010 book, *The Dragonfly Effect,* Jennifer Aaker and Andy Smith suggest a framework for effective marketing by nonprofit organizations with respect to social media. This framework has value in the context of general nonprofit marketing, as well. The authors suggest a 4-component framework, beginning with engagement, defined as "truly making people feel emotionally connected to helping you achieve your goals." This connectedness is achieved through "storytelling, authenticity, and establishing a personal connection." Ethical organizations must be careful to assure that what they promise in their marketing campaigns are consistent with what they deliver, or risk harm to their reputations.

Branding

The term "branding" refers to an organization's total image, and includes all of the factors that distinguish it from its competition. Among these factors are its reputation, its logo, its taglines (such as the United Way's "Thanks to you, it's working"), its particular print fonts (Coca Cola has one of the most recognized examples), particular colors (the ubiquitous pink that shows up in breast cancer marketing and fundraising efforts), and tchotchkes (such as the Livestrong yellow wrist band). Branding connects the organization to its customers, clients, and the public, in powerful ways. When I participate in the American Cancer Society's "Relay for Life," I feel comfortable my donation will be used to advance the cause of fighting cancer rather than lining the pockets of some for-profit fundraiser. Its logo (view it at: *https://www.brandsoftheworld.com/logo/american-cancer-society*) is one of the most recognized in the nonprofit world, and its brand image is high in the rankings of the most valuable in the world, based on public perception of the organization, media coverage, and the percentage of revenue from direct public support.

The concept of the value of branding is not simply an academic exercise; some try to calculate how much the value of an organization's brand directly or indirectly contributes to the amount of revenue it nets and can be measured in the billions of dollars. (See: *https://www.marketingcharts.com/industries/pharma-and-health-care-9591.)*

An intriguing 2009 study/article by Cone and Intangible Business concluded that the YMCA had the most valuable brand, worth almost $6.4 billion. Interesting enough, the organization rebranded itself as the "Y" beginning in 2010. The Salvation Army and the United Way trailed with $4.7 billion and $4.5 billion respectively. One conclusion that can be drawn from this type of analysis is that everything an organization does affects the value of its brand. For example, a new charity's brand value can skyrocket if it can convince a popular celebrity to actively endorse it. And at the other end of the spectrum, a charity's brand value can plummet when it is involved in a scandal, as was evident by the scandal of the United Way in the late '90s, and the more recent scandal involving the charity started by Lance Armstrong, the Lance Armstrong Foundation.

The case involving the Lance Armstrong Foundation, at one time the fastest growing U.S. charity and one of the most respected, will be studied for years. No one suggests that the Foundation itself was involved in any unethical activity. But its founder's eventual admission of unethical conduct unrelated to the activities of the charity resulted in clear damage to the charity's brand. The board of the organization took steps to, at first, distance itself from its iconic founder, and then completely severed its relationship with Mr. Armstrong, even changing its name to the Livestrong Foundation in November 2012.It may take decades (as was the case with the United Way of America scandal involving its national CEO, William Aramony) to regain its stature as one of the most respected charities in America.

Donors clearly prefer to buy goods and services from an organization with a trusted brand. Doing so eliminates much of the uncertainty that any net revenue will be used for good. It also is useful in creating a strong bond between a donor or consumer and the organization.

Rebranding

The Lance Armstrong Foundation rebranded itself as a result of scandal. The March of Dimes is also a classic example of rebranding—as a result of success. This nonprofit organization had an almost universally recognizable and positive brand, and it launched a successful campaign to rebrand itself in the 1950s. A survey had indicated that 83% of the U.S. could identify the March of Dimes, which for decades had a stellar reputation in helping find a cure for the dreaded polio virus. With success in finding a cure for polio through the application of effective vaccines, the organization changed course to focus on preventing birth defects. There was a longer lead time, as the public's perception of the organization lagged with respect to its new mission. The organization launched a marketing campaign, mostly through advertising targeted to those who were the most likely donors. This campaign was tested in one particular community to collect data on which appeal was the most effective.

Demographics

When considering the startup of a new program or expanding an existing one to offer goods and services, it is important to consider how demographics will affect success or failure. The term "demographics" refers to the characteristics of a particular group of people that might be served by the organization. Demographic factors typically considered in marketing include income, gender, race, age, religion, political affiliation, and ethnic origin. An organization's goods and services are likely to have much more appeal to one particular demographic group compared to another. With limited resources, marketers will be wise to target their communications to those most likely to purchase them, i.e., engaging in market segmentation.

Market Research

Market research includes activities designed to collect and analyze data that will enable the organization to make good decisions with respect to how to market its goods and services. Among the questions that are often the focus of this research are those affecting the four "p's" related to marketing, also referred to as the "marketing mix":

- product (what goods and services to offer)
- price (how much to charge)
- promotion (how to shape the communication with potential buyers)
- place (what media to use to communicate).

Stacy Grau suggests that market research provides information about what is going on with respect to the organization's sales (descriptive research), why it is going on (explanatory research), and what is likely to occur if the organization pursues one particular marketing strategy compared to another (predictive research).

Many of the techniques used in market research are the same ones organizations use to improve their fundraising. Among them are focus groups, surveys, interviews, and analysis of the organization's web and social media pages. Organizations need to know basic information, such as which demographic groups are more likely to use their services, and why, so that their marketing communications can be targeted to appeal to these groups. Conversely, it is helpful to know why certain demographic groups who might benefit from them are not using the organization's services. A special effort can be made to change marketing materials and the method of delivery of those communications. Many smaller organizations do not have much capacity to conduct formal market research. But if they begin a new program or service without a good sense of whether there is sufficient demand for it, the resulting loss of net revenue could threaten the viability of all other programs conducted by the organization.

Even organizations that have too few resources to pay a marketing research firm or to launch a traditional research effort can benefit from low-cost technology strategies. Focus groups can be conducted online using Google+ Hangouts. Survey instruments can be prepared, disseminated, and analyzed using free or inexpensive Web-based services such as Survey Monkey *(https://www.surveymonkey. com/)*. Interviews can be conducted using the chat feature of a social networking site or applications that can be added inexpensively to the organization's website.

Feedback can be obtained using information gleaned from in-house discussion boards. There is certainly benefit to hiring professionals who are trained to find valid answers to research questions and collect and analyze data, avoiding threats to validity that might not be understood by those who are not trained to do this. For many organizations, this is unrealistic. Collecting and analyzing data, even though convenience surveys and the collection of anecdotal comments about the organization's goods and services, is an essential part of any marketing program. "Listening to your customers" gives you a heads-up when something is not going right. Many of your stakeholders will not be shy in complaining, or making helpful suggestions, to improve their transactions.

Among other considerations for marketing are having an effective media relations program (see Chapter 21), engaging in cause-related marketing (see pages 255 and 345), and using special events to communicate the availability of the organization's goods and services to its target markets.

Marketing Plan

A marketing plan can consist of a couple of pages of material or be as involved as a comprehensive strategic plan. It does not need to be costly. A basic marketing plan needs to set goals and objectives, a list of what needs to be done to accomplish those objectives, a time frame, a budget, who will be doing the work, and how the plan will be evaluated. You can find basic nonprofit marketing templates on the Web that can provide a more comprehensive framework for advancing your organization's marketing program. One of these can be found at: *https://blog.hubspot.com/marketing/marketing-plan-template-generator*

This template, prepared by Getting Attention's Nancy Schwartz, features a nine-component plan that includes the following:

- Goal—This is the main goal you hope to achieve with this plan, and goals relating to communications needed to achieve that. An example would be to increase the net revenue of a Jewish Community Center (JCC) without compromising quality.

- Objectives—This includes 3-5 specific and measurable steps you wish to take to achieve that goal. Examples might be to capture more market share for the JCC's fitness facility, improve the reputation and quality of the organization, and increase the registration of children in the JCC's day care program, using an aggressive social media campaign.

- Target Audience—This section covers who the JCC is trying to reach, and what it wants them to do. Examples might be to reach those in the area who have children under six, young professionals who are looking to keep fit and meet people in the area who share their interests, and seniors who have a strong connection to their ethnic community and who may be interested in providing donations to the Center and the community.

- Best Strategies—Examples might be to communicate with every household in a 10-mile radius that has a child under 6, update the exercise equipment in the fitness center, and offer a package of membership fees that will offer free fitness classes to parents with children who are cared for in the day care center.

- Tactics—This includes actual actions that could be taken to meet the goals and objectives, and is where good brainstorming sessions can pay dividends. Examples might include advertising day care services in the local parenting magazine, having a wine and cheese party every Thursday evening following the evening spin classes and offering discounts to members of the Young Professionals organization, and having health fairs for seniors at the JCC. Tactics also include shaping the message to reach the target audience, using the most appropriate mix of media. For example, communicating with the young people about the fitness center would involve totally different tactics than communicating with the seniors, considering research validates the obvious conclusion that these groups of people typically receive their information in divergently different ways.

- Roles and Responsibilities—Executing a marketing plan takes substantial staff time. This aspect of the plan includes who will be responsible for composing the communications, placing the advertisements, updating the website, preparing intake, and training staff to carry out the plan.

- Step-by-Step Work Plan—This is the guts of the marketing plan—what has to happen, when, and by whom.

- Budget—This spells out in detail how much this plan will cost for staff training, print and Web advertising, website management, consulting, and so on.

- Evaluation—This final component considers how the results of implementing the plan will be evaluated and what data will be collected and analyzed.

See the following websites for additional resources on developing a marketing plan:

https://www.networkforgood.com/nonprofitblog/nonprofit-marketing-plan-organization/#.U6u7BLHBfwA
https://www.entrepreneur.com/article/43026
http://www.quickmba.com/marketing/plan/

Some Strategies Included in a Marketing Plan

Among the more generic strategies that might typically be found in a marketing plan are the following:

- redesigning the logo to make it more recognizable and memorable

- targeting a specific demographic group that otherwise is underrepresented in accessing the organization's services

- offering a different menu of the organization's services at different locations

- changing the services offered to respond to changes in demand

- pricing services to be more competitive and offering discounts

- having a conference with an exhibit hall or offering workshops to not only generate revenue, but also to improve the visibility of the organization

- expanding the service area where a program is being offered

- bundling the offering of services (e.g., purchase a gym membership and also receive free access to the swimming pool)

- approaching businesses with preferential partnerships for their employees to access the service

- offering long-term contracts for selected organizations that benefit from the services offered

- changing the delivery of the service to make it more convenient for those who might otherwise not be able to access the service

- harnessing the power of QR Codes (see page 256) to push information to your stakeholders and promote donations.

Strategic Planning and SWOT Analysis

Marketing planning needs to be a part of an organization's strategic planning process, if it has one (see Chapter 6). Many organizations will engage in one particular planning exercise called SWOT Analysis, an acronym for Strengths, Weaknesses, Opportunities, and Threats. The first two are analyses of aspects that are internal to the organization. This part of the process, according to Stacy Grau in her book *Marketing for Nonprofit Organizations*, looks at the organization's "capabilities, expertise, technology, financial stability, staff stability, donor base, volunteer base, board of directors, public image, social impact, program effectiveness, leadership, history, relationships, successes and failures." The last two analyze the environment in which the organization funds itself, and include factors that are external to the organization—such as the regulatory and legal climate, the organization's competition, changes in demographics, potential partners and collaborators, culture, and the advance of technology and how they affect the organization. For more on how a SWOT analysis is performed, see: *https://bizfluent.com/about-6588184-nonprofit-swot-analysis.html*

Cause-Related Marketing

Many nonprofits partner with for-profit organizations to endorse products and services that are consistent with the mission of the nonprofit organization, and which may provide substantial revenue. The term "cause-related marketing" was first used in 1983 by American Express, which engaged in this strategy to improve its market reach and raise funds for the Statue of Liberty restoration project (GrantSpace, n.d.). Cause-related marketing is discussed in more detail in Chapter 23. The benefits to the for-profit organization are well-documented. There are additional benefits that accrue to participating nonprofits beyond any financial remuneration they might receive, such as additional exposure for the organization. Organizations should be careful, however, to assure that any agreements they sign explicitly spell out what is expected from each partner.

Online Resources to Explore:

Constant Contact Marketing Resources
  https://blogs.constantcontact.com/nonprofit-marketing/

MarketingProfs
  https://www.marketingprofs.com/resources/

Nonprofit Marketing Guide

  https://www.nonprofitmarketingguide.com/resources/

Tips:

- . If you are using interactive media such as YouTube to market a controversial message, be prepared for comments, either orchestrated or not, that respond negatively to your message, such as is the case with the Commonwealth Foundation message illustrated on page 246.

- Consider whether your organization has the capacity to serve all of those who want to participate if your marketing plan is wildly successful.

- Setting up an organization's Facebook page is a good first step in using social media. It is free and easy to do. A step-by-step guide on adding a "donate now" button can be found at: *https://itstillworks.com/add-donate-now-button-facebook-8517198.html*

- Make sure you are in compliance with do-not call laws if you are using the telephone to sell goods and services. Typically, these laws provide exemptions for charities soliciting donations, but do not for calls selling goods and services.

- Beware of mission drift with marketing efforts. Consider whether it makes sense to market the organization's goods and services to those who are most likely to be able to afford them while neglecting those who may not.

- Explore the benefits of using QR Codes in your marketing materials. More and more nonprofits are using QR Codes to push information to their stakeholders. QR Codes are two-dimensional bar code images. When scanned by a smartphone, a link is opened to a website, a text is sent, or a phone number is dialed. QR Codes can be created for free at many different websites (for example, for free at sites like *https://www.qrcode-monkey.com/*

- Make an effort to collect names, phone numbers, email addresses, text numbers, and addresses of everyone who attends events of the organization. Use this to send out fundraising appeals, newsletters, text-to-give appeals, and invitations to future events.

Chapter 19
Lobbying

Synopsis: Lobbying by nonprofit corporations is not only legal, but should be encouraged. There are effective strategies for communicating with legislators in person, by letter, or by telephone. All states require lobbyists to be registered and report expenditures.

Lobbying is the time-honored tradition of communicating with elected or appointed officials for the purpose of influencing legislation and other public policy. The word itself derives from the tenure of President Ulysses S. Grant, who used to hang out in the lobby of the Willard Hotel a few blocks from the White House, and listen to individuals seeking favors.

In recent years, the term has developed a pejorative character as the public, justified or not, perceives special interest lobbyists as using their influence to work against the public interest. This general mistrust of lobbyists has been exacerbated by a corruption scandal that rocked the nation's Capital in 2006 involving the lobbying efforts of Jack Abramoff, an independent lobbyist, with close ties to Congressional leaders and the White House.

Organized lobbying is an effective way to communicate an organization's views on a pending issue, to promote a favorable climate for those served, and to directly influence the outcome of decision-making. Lobbyists are employed by organizations who view themselves as working in the public interest—speaking for the poor and disenfranchised, improving the environment, establishing programs to serve the disabled, or expanding government support for vital human service and community needs.

Whether referred to as "advocacy," "government relations," or "lobbying," it is a right afforded by the First Amendment to the U.S. Constitution relating to freedom of speech, as well as the right to petition to redress grievances. Many of the public policy decisions made in Washington, state capitals, and cities and towns have a direct effect on nonprofit organizations and the client interests they serve.

Many nonprofits are expressly created to advance one cause or another whose fate is considered by a government body.

Texas Legal Requirements for Lobbying

Lobbying the executive and legislative branch of state government is regulated in accordance with Chapter 305 of the Texas Government Code. Registration and reporting is required by individuals and organizations once they achieve a threshold for either spending on lobbying activities, or receive compensation for engaging in lobbying activities. The lobbying regulates only direct communications—contact with officials in person, by telephone, telegraph, or letter. A comprehensive lobbying guide is available online from the Texas Ethics Commission at: *https://www.ethics.state.tx.us/data/resources/guides/lobby_guide.pdf*

The following is a summary of legal requirements.

Texas Registration Requirements

Compensation Threshold

Those who receive or are entitled to receive more than $1,560 in any calendar quarter as compensation or reimbursement to lobby must register with the Commission, unless their lobby activity constitutes no more than 40 hours of that person's compensated time during that calendar quarter, including preparatory activity (the so-called incidental lobbying exemption). Personal expenses for that individual's own transportation, lodging, and food and beverage do not count toward this threshold. Reimbursement for most office expenses also do not count toward the threshold.

Expenditure Threshold

Those who spend more than $780 in a calendar quarter for lobbying activities must register. The expenditures that count toward the expenditure threshold are those that benefit a state officer or employee or the immediate family of a state officer or employee, that are made to communicate with a state officer or employee to influence legislation or administrative action, and that fall into one of the following six categories: transportation and lodging; food and beverages; entertainment; gifts; awards and mementos; and the attendance of a state officer or employee at a political fundraiser or charity event.

A nonprofit organization may be required to register as a lobbyist if it exceeds either the compensation threshold or expenditure threshold. It may nonetheless avoid registration if all activity otherwise reportable by the organization is reported by one or more registrants. The registration fee for organizations exempt under

501(c)(3), (c)(4), and (c)(6) is $150, and $750 for other organizations and individuals. Registration is required no later than five days after the communications are made that trigger the registration requirement. Registration is accomplished online, although there are provisions for paper filings (Form REG) for those unable to register online. Registration includes an indication of whether reporting will be on a monthly or annual basis. Annual reporting is available to those who expect to expend less than $1,790 during the calendar year.

Texas Reporting Requirements

Lobby activity reports are due by the tenth day of each month covering activities for the preceding calendar month. The form used is Form LA, which is submitted electronically. Expenditures are reported by the following categories: transportation and lodging; food and beverages; entertainment; gifts other than awards and mementos; awards and mementos; expenditures made for the attendance of a state officer or employee at a political fundraiser or charity event; and mass media expenditures.

The reports include spending attributable to the following groups (other than mass media spending): expenditures for state senators; expenditures for state representatives; expenditures for elected or appointed state officers, other than state senators or state representatives; expenditures for legislative agency employees; expenditures for executive agency employees; expenditures for the immediate family (spouse and dependent children) of a state officer or employee; expenditures for guests (when invited by a state senator, a state representative, other elected or appointed state officers, a legislative agency employee, or an executive agency employee); and expenditures for events to which all legislators are invited.

The lobbying law also provides some restrictions on making bribes; conveying cash gifts and loans; providing transportation and lodging for ceremonial events or pleasure; providing food, beverages, and entertainment to an official when the lobbyist is not present; and spending on gifts, awards/mementos and entertainment. In most cases, it is illegal to be compensated based on the success of a lobbying effort to pass or defeat legislation (so-called contingent fee compensation).

The physical address of the Commission is at: 201 East 14th St., 10th Floor Austin, TX 78701 For more information, contact:

Texas Ethics Commission
P. O. Box 12070
Austin, TX 78711-2070
512-463-5800
https://www.ethics.state.tx.us/

For more information about either executive branch or legislative branch lobbying, contact:

Lobbyist Registration Office
111 W. Madison Street
Room G-68
Tallahassee, FL 32399-1425
(850) 922-4990

Federal Legal Requirements for Lobbying

The *Lobbying Disclosure Act*, PL 104-65, was enacted on December 19, 1995, and provides major changes in registration and reporting requirements for lobbying the Congress and the Executive Branch. The law also includes a provision (Section 18) that places restrictions on the lobbying by nonprofit civic leagues and social welfare organizations, among others, which receive federal funds. The effective date of the act was January 1, 1996. Minor changes were made by the *Lobbying Disclosure Technical Amendments Act of 1998*. On September 14, 2007, President George Bush signed into law the *Honest Leadership and Open Government Act*, which made substantive reforms affecting lobbying, a response to a major scandal. The new law makes major changes in lobbying reporting requirements, gift disclosure, and travel financed by lobbyists:

- Lobbying disclosure forms are now required to be filed quarterly rather than semi-annually.
- Thresholds for reporting lobbying expenses have been reduced.
- Information requirements for reporting and disclosure have been expanded.
- New reports are required relating to political contributions made by, or transferred to politicians by, lobbyists.
- With some exceptions, gifts to members of Congress and their staff from lobbyists are prohibited.
- With some exceptions, lobbyists, or organizations that employ them, may not pay for the private travel of members of Congress or their staff.
- Lobbyists may not participate in privately funded Congressional travel.

The *Lobbying Disclosure Act* was further amended when President Donald Trump signed into law the *Justice Against Corruption on K Street Act* (a.k.a., the JACK Act) on January 3, 2019. That law required all registrations and all quarterly activity reports to include—

"for any listed lobbyist who was convicted in a Federal or State court of an offense involving bribery, extortion, embezzlement, an illegal kickback, tax evasion, fraud, a conflict of interest, making a false statement, perjury, or money laundering, the date of the conviction and a description of the offense."

The *Lobbying Disclosure Act* defines "lobbying contact" as—

any oral or written communication (including an electronic communication) to a covered executive branch official or a covered legislative branch official that is made on behalf of a client with regard to—

(i) the formulation, modification, or adoption of Federal legislation (including legislative proposals);

   (ii) the formulation, modification, or adoption of a Federal rule, regulation, Executive order, or any other program, policy, or position of the United States Government;

   (iii) the administration or execution of a Federal program or policy (including the negotiation, award, or administration of a Federal contract, grant, loan, permit, or license); or

   (iv) the nomination or confirmation of a person for a position subject to confirmation by the Senate.

It defines "lobbyist" as—

any individual who is employed or retained by a client for financial or other compensation for services that include more than one lobbying contact, other than an individual whose lobbying activities constitute less than 20 percent of the time engaged in the services provided by such individual to that client over a six month period.

A packet of materials, including a copy of the *Lobbying Disclosure Act,* registration and expense reporting forms, instruction booklets for filling out the forms, and answers to frequently asked questions, can be obtained by contacting—

Secretary of the Senate
Office of Public Records
232 Hart Senate Office Building
Washington, D.C. 20510
(202) 224-0758

Unless they are self-employed, individual lobbyists do not register with the House and Senate. The law requires registration by lobbying firms, defined as entities with one or more employees who act as lobbyists for outside clients. A separate registration is required for each client. A typical nonprofit that has one or more employees who engage in lobbying activities is required to register, provided that its expenses attributable to lobbying exceed $13,000 in a quarterly period. Registration is required no later than 45 days after a lobbyist first makes a lobbying contact or is employed to do so, whichever comes earlier. To register, the organization must electronically file a Form LD-1 in duplicate with the Secretary of the Senate and the Clerk of the House:

Secretary of the Senate	Clerk of the House
Office of Public Records	Legislative Resource Center
232 Hart Senate Office Building	B106 Cannon House Office Building
Washington, D.C. 20510	Washington, D.C. 20515
(202) 224-0758	(202) 226-5200

Registration discloses general information, a description of the registrant's business or activities (e.g., social welfare organization), and a list of employees who act or are expected to act as lobbyists (an employee is not considered to be a lobbyist if he/she spends less than 20% of his or her time lobbying). Also disclosed are an indication of the issues to be lobbied (selected from a list of 76 general categories, such as "welfare"), and the specific issues to be addressed, including specific bill numbers or executive branch activities.

Online forms and instructions can be found at: *https://lobbyingdisclosure. house.gov/*

Expense Reporting Requirements

Registered organizations are required to file two semiannual expense reports each year. Each semiannual report is required no later than 45 days after the end of a semiannual period beginning on the first day of January and the first day of July of every year in which a registrant is registered. One copy each must be filed with the Secretary of the Senate and the Clerk of the House. Organizations employing lobbyists must report whether their lobbying expenses were less than $10,000, or more. If lobbying expenses were more than $10,000, the organization must make a good-faith estimate, rounded to the nearest $20,000, of its lobbying expenses during the reporting period.

Organizations must also file a separate sheet on each general lobbying issue that was engaged, specific information about each bill or executive branch action, houses of Congress and federal agencies contacted, and the name and title of each employee who acted as a lobbyist. Online forms and instructions can be found at: *https://lobbyingdisclosure.house.gov/lda.html*

Effective Strategies for Lobbying and Advocacy

- Get to Know Legislators—Give them the information they need to help the nonprofit organization meet its objectives.

- Identify Key Contacts—Survey the organization's network to discover who has a personal or professional relationship with key public policy decision-makers, and who contributes to political campaigns.

- Target Decision-Makers—Pay special attention to legislative leadership, the majority and minority chairpersons of relevant committees, and their staffs.

- Use Local Resources—Identify constituents connected to the organization, such as board members and organization members. Match them with their legislators, and assign them to meet with these particular legislators on issues of concern to the organization.

- Schedule Lobby Days—Many nonprofit organizations and other groups schedule a Capitol Lobby Day. Such events typically include a briefing on an important pending issue by the organization's executive director, a rally and/or press conference in the Capitol, scheduled office visits to local legislators and legislative leadership, and a closing session conducted by the organization's staff to exchange information gleaned from those visited.

- Schedule Press Conferences—Nongovernmental organizations can hold press conferences in the Capitol or on the steps of the Capitol.

- Circulate Petitions—Although viewed as one of the least effective forms of lobbying, the presentation to a legislator or government official of a petition signed by thousands of persons is a worthy "photo opportunity" and may get some coverage.

- Present Awards—Many nonprofit organizations present a "Legislator of the Year" or similar award to recognize key legislators for their interest in the issues of concern to that nonprofit. These awards further cement a positive relationship and ensure continued access to that legislator.

- Arrange Speaking Engagements—Most legislators are delighted to receive invitations to address groups of their constituents. Such gatherings provide opportunities to educate the legislator on issues of interest to the organization through questions and comments from the audience.

- Request Public Hearings—Public hearings held by a legislative committee provide an opportunity for media coverage, a forum for an organization's point of view, and a way to galvanize support for an issue. Having an organization's clients fill a hearing room sends a clear message to the committee members and staff. Although it is true that the suggestion by a committee chairperson to hold hearings on an issue may be a strategy to delay or kill a bill, public hearings can nevertheless be utilized by the organization to focus attention on an issue. A hearing can generate public and media support. It can provide a forum for improving the proposal, thereby minimizing opposition to the legislation.

501(h) Election

The U.S. Congress in 1976 enacted a law that expanded the rights of nonprofits to lobby. However, it was not until August 30, 1990, that the IRS and Treasury Department promulgated final regulations to implement this law. In the preceding 14 years, there had been a pitched battle between nonprofits and the Congress. Nonprofits fought diligently to preserve their rights to lobby under the Constitution and the 1976 law. Some in the executive branch also sought to deny those rights. The principal issue is the definition of the term "substantial," since the law prohibits 501(c)(3) nonprofits from carrying on "substantial" lobbying activities.

The regulations permit electing organizations to spend on lobbying, on a sliding scale, up to 20% of their first $500,000 in expenditures, $100,000 plus 15% of the excess of lobbying expenditures over $500,000 but less than $1 million, $175,000 plus 10% of lobbying expenses between $1 million but less than $1.5 million, $225,000 plus 5% of lobbying expenses between $1.5 million and less than $17 million, and $1 million maximum if $17 million or more.

Organizations can spend no more than a quarter of their lobbying expenses on grass-roots lobbying (communications to the general public that attempt to influence legislation through changing public opinion).

These regulations exclude certain expenditures from lobbying, including—

1. Communications to members of an organization that brief them on provisions of legislation, but do not urge that they take action to change those provisions.

2. Communications to legislators on issues that directly affect the organization's own existence, such as changes to tax-exempt status law, or lobbying law.

Of major importance to nonprofits, the organization would no longer be subject to the "death penalty" (i.e., the total revoking of their tax-exempt status) for violations. There is a system of sanctions replacing that.

All 501(c)(3)s must report the amount they spend on lobbying on their Form 990 annual federal tax returns.

IRS Regulations on Lobbying

The August 1990 regulations of the Treasury Department with respect to lobbying are quite complicated. An excellent 42-page publication, *Being a Player: A Guide to the IRS Lobbying Regulations for Advocacy Charities,* is available from The Alliance for Justice *(https://www.afj.org/; 202-822-6070).* The guide explains in clear and precise terms what is permitted under these regulations, and includes many sample forms and worksheets. The publication, last updated in 2011, can be downloaded free at: *https://bolderadvocacy.org/resource/being-a-player-a-guide-to-the-irs-lobbying-regulations-for-advocacy-charities/*

Contacts With Legislators

1. When visiting a legislator—

- Make an appointment, if at all possible.

- Arrive promptly, be warm and courteous, smile, and speak for five minutes or less on a single issue.

- Do not threaten or exaggerate your political influence. If you are really influential, the legislator will already know.

- Listen carefully to the legislator's response and take notes; be polite, but keep the legislator on the subject.

- Leave the legislator with something in writing on the issue, if possible.

- Request that the legislator do something to respond to the organization's position—vote in a specific way, take action on a problem, or send a letter to legislative leadership requesting action.

- Follow up the meeting with a thank-you note, taking advantage of this second opportunity to reinforce the organization's views and remind the legislator of the action requested.

- Do not feel slighted if referred to a staff member—legislators often have last-minute important meetings or unscheduled votes. Staff members are valued advisors who, in some cases, have as much or more influence than the legislator in the process and may have more time to help.

2. When writing to or emailing a legislator—

- Restrict letters/email to one issue; be brief and concise.

- Clearly indicate the issue of concern, the organization's position on it, and the bill number, if known.

- Write the letter/email in a manner that will require a written response and include a return address.

- Use facts to support positions, and explain how the issue affects the organization, its members, and the community.

- If a letter, use professional letterhead, if appropriate.

- Try not to indicate that the letter or email, as the case may be, may be a form letter/email sent to scores of other legislators.

- Make the letter/email positive—do not threaten the loss of votes or campaign contributions.

- Follow up after the vote on the issue to indicate to the legislator that the organization is following his or her actions with interest and that it appreciated or was disappointed by that vote.

3. When telephoning a legislator—

- Speak clearly and slowly.

- Make sure that callers identify themselves in a way that will permit the legislator to reach them or the organization by letter or telephone.

- Follow the guidelines listed above for writing and visiting that are equally appropriate for telephoning.

Online Resources to Explore:

Institute for Sustainable Communities
https://sustain.org/

Independent Sector
https://independentsector.org/

Indivisible
https://www.indivisible.org

Center for Effective Government (formerly OMB Watch)
https://www.foreffectivegov.org/npadv

NetAction's The Virtual Activist's Virtual Activist 2.0 Training Guide
https://www.netaction.org/training/

Tips:

- Those who expect to spend a substantial amount of time in legislators' offices should register as lobbyists, even if they feel the law may not require them to do so. The judge of whether a person doing advocacy is in compliance with lobbying laws will not be that advocate, but rather a regulator.

- Comply with all state and federal reporting requirements.

- If the nonprofit corporation is a human service provider, invite local legislators to tour the facility and observe the services being provided.

- If the organization has members, invite local legislators to speak to the membership.

- Encourage members to make individual contributions (but, of course, not to anyone specific). It is good advice not to get involved in partisan politics, particularly if the organization has 501(c)(3) status. Those who do choose to participate in partisan politics should be scrupulous about separating personal political activities from those of the organization and not using organizational resources for partisan political activities (see Chapter 20).

- Consider an email advocacy campaign. Many organization members are more comfortable sending an email to a legislator based on a sample provided on an organizational website than writing a conventional letter.

Chapter 20
Political Activity by Nonprofits

Synopsis: Charities are proscribed by law from engaging in electioneering. However, many political activities, such as candidate forums, questionnaires, awards, and compiling voting records, are not only permissible but are constructive activities for charities and other nonprofit organizations.

Just in the past few years, the extent to which tax-exempt nonprofit organizations may engage in political activities, already considered to be a murky area, has become even more uncharted. In recent years, this public policy discussion has become front-page news. The IRS has, in its attempt to address calls from the Congress and the public to reform its practices, made serious missteps in enforcing its rules, particularly with respect to 501(c)(4) organizations. In November 2013, the IRS issued a draft regulation that seeks to clarify its intent on what is permissible with respect to 501(c)(4)s, and was met with a firestorm of criticism from across the entire political spectrum, particularly for provisions that proposed to consider as proscribed political activities those that are currently considered to be benign, if not beneficial to society and consistent with the mission of many social welfare organizations. The proposal was subsequently withdrawn.

After perhaps a decade or so of increasing IRS interest in enforcing statutory limitations on political activity by nonprofits, particularly churches, the pendulum is starting to reverse its direction. Beginning with the 2004 election cycle, the IRS had established its Political Activities Compliance Initiative (PACI) to respond to allegations of violations. Despite these rules, the IRS apparently stopped enforcement of the law since 2009. And in May 2017, President Donald Trump signed an executive order giving the IRS authority not to enforce the statutory prohibition, known as the "Johnson Amendment," at the IRS's discretion. The Johnson Amendment was added to the tax code in 1954, and prohibits tax-exempt organizations from endorsing or opposing candidates for public office.

A publication of the IRS, *Tax Guide for Churches and Other Religious Organizations* (Pub. 1828, revised August 2015), provides guidance about acceptable and unacceptable political activities by religious congregations. It is available at: *https://www.irs.gov/pub/irs-pdf/p1828.pdf*. The Trump Administration did not enforce federal laws proscribing nonprofit political activities, including the Johnson Amendment, which was repealed in the House version of the tax reform legislation considered by the Congress in 2017.

Tax-Exempt Organizations and Political Activities—Background

Volunteer leaders and executives of nonprofit organizations are, generally, key opinion makers and play an important role, both in their organizations and in their personal lives, in shaping public policy. Many elected officials got their first taste of community service by serving as nonprofit board volunteers. Many elected officials continue to serve on nonprofit boards, and their expertise and political influence are often of great value.

Yet, there always has been a concern that nonprofits, particularly nonprofit charities, may be using taxpayer-financed subsidies to unduly influence the outcome of elections. This concern has been codified in federal and state law that, in general, prohibits 501(c)(3) organizations from helping candidates for public office and places severe restrictions on other tax-exempt organizations. Some state laws mimic federal law, prohibiting corporations and unincorporated associations, other than political action committees (PACs) and other organizations formed solely for political activity, from making contributions or expenditures in connection with the election of a candidate.

By federal law, a 501(c)(3) organization explicitly may "not participate in, or intervene in (including the publishing or distributing of statements), any political campaign on behalf of, or in opposition to, any candidate for public office." Moreover, any expenditures by a charity, for or against a candidate, can result in the loss of the organization's tax-exempt status, the assessment of a large excise tax, and potential fines against the charity's executives and volunteers. Charities may not endorse candidates or oppose candidates for public office. Generally, a person is considered to be a candidate for public office when he or she makes a public announcement to that effect, or files a statement with the elections commission of an intention to run.

Department of Treasury regulation §1.501(c)(4)-I(a)(2)(ii), as amended in 1990, expressly forbids 501(c)(4) organizations from engaging in direct or indirect participation in political campaigns on "behalf of, or in opposition to, any candidate for public office" as part of its definition of "social welfare." However, a subsequent IRS Ruling (Rev. Rul. 81-95, 1981-1 C. B. 332) has interpreted that this regulation does not impose a total ban on political activity by 501(c)(4)s. The level of political activity that is permitted by 501(c)(4)s without jeopardizing their tax exemptions is still unclear. What is clear is that the political activity by the organization must not be a substantial part of its activities, and the activity must be consistent with the organization's social welfare mission, according to the May 1992 *Harvard Law Review* (p. 1675), which provides substantial guidance and applicable case law on this complicated legal issue. Other classes of exempt organizations, including those that are exempt under Section 501(c)(5), (c)(6), (c)(7), and (c)(8), also are permitted to engage in political activity, provided it is secondary to their primary purpose.

Among the types of expenditures that may be considered political activity are candidate travel expenses, fundraising expenses, polls, surveys, candidate position papers, advertising and publicity, and money paid to the candidate for speeches or other services. Expenses relating to non-partisan voter registration drives are not considered political expenses.

Individuals who are associated with an exempt organization (or any other type of organization) may form an organization that is exempt under Section 527 of the Internal Revenue Code. Organizations exempt under this section are political action committees (PACs). These organizations have as their primary purpose engaging in political activity. They pay no federal tax on their operating income, but their investment income is subject to tax. Contributions made to them are not tax deductible. The excise tax that applies to political expenditures of social welfare organizations, exempt under Section 501(c)(4) of the Internal Revenue Code, does not apply to PACs.

These 527 organizations are coming under a lot of scrutiny. They are perceived as taking advantage of a loophole in the law that permits them to engage in "advocacy" activities that target the election or defeat of political candidates without any of the accountability and fundraising limits that apply to traditional political action committees. They are regulated by the IRS rather than the Federal Elections Commission (FEC).

Examples, such as the Leadership Forum, America Coming Together, and Move On, raised tens of millions of dollars to influence the outcome of the last few Presidential elections, all of it "soft money," without the traditional reporting requirements and contribution limits that applied to traditional political action committees under the McCain-Feingold campaign finance reform that went into effect in November 2002.

A 501(c)(3) organization cannot have its own PAC, but other exempt organizations are permitted to form one. Individuals associated with a 501(c)(3) may set up a "nonconnected political action committee," provided it receives no funds from the 501(c)(3), the individuals forming it do not imply any connection between the 501(c)(3) and the PAC, and the PAC is not controlled by the governing body of the 501(c)(3). For more details on this option, see FEC Advisory Opinion 1984-12.

Individual Political Activities

The *Federal Election Campaign Act of 1971,* as amended, prohibited all corporations, regardless of whether they are for-profit or nonprofit, from getting directly involved in federal political campaigns, with few exceptions. A 2002 law, known popularly as McCain-Feingold, prohibited the broadcast, cable or satellite transmission of "electioneering communications" paid for by corporations or

unions from their general funds in the 30 days before a presidential pri-
and in the 60 days before the general elections. However, a January 2010
Supreme Court decision in the case of *Citizens United v. Federal Elections
Commission* (No. 08-205) has determined that statutory restrictions on corporate and union funding of political campaigns are unconstitutional. In response,
Senator Charles Schumer (D-NY) and Rep. Chris Van Hollen (D-MD) introduced
the *Disclose Act* (S 3295/ HR 5175) to regulate campaign communications paid
for by corporations, labor organizations, and nonprofits exempt from taxation
under sections 501(c)(4), (c)(5) or (c)(6). The legislation was not approved before
the Congress adjourned in 2010, but it did pass the House with a controversial
amendment that was opposed by Independent Sector. This amendment would
have exempted organizations that have been 501(c)(4)s in each of the previous
ten calendar years that have at least 500,000 dues-paying members with at least
one member in each state, and that receive no more than 15 percent of their total
revenues from corporations or labor organizations.

Regardless of what the Congress decides to do about this issue, it is clear that
volunteers and staff of charities have the same First Amendment rights as anyone
else. There is no prohibition against such persons making political contributions,
volunteering to work on a campaign, signing letters of support (provided any reference to their charitable organization affiliation clearly indicates that the reference is for identification purposes only), and issuing statements on a candidate's
behalf. Moreover, the resources of the charity cannot be used for electioneering.
Charitable organization leadership and staff should not write letters on a charity's stationery in support of a candidate. They should not turn the offices into a
de facto campaign office for the candidate, using the telephone, copy machine,
computer, and other resources, even during non-business hours.

Penalties

Beyond the sanctions of loss of tax exemption authorized by the 1954 *Revenue Act*, the *Revenue Act of 1987* increased the sanctions available to the IRS
in enforcing the prohibition against political activities. It also provided the IRS
with the authority to seek an injunction to bring about an immediate cessation
of violations that are deemed to be "flagrant." Most political campaign expenditures by 501(c)(3)s and 501(c)(4)s are now subject to a 10% excise tax applied
to the organizations and a 2.5% excise tax (up to $5,000) applied to each of the
managers of the organization who knew that a political expenditure was being
made. This tax only applies if the expenditures were willful, flagrant, and not
due to reasonable cause. If the illegal expenditure is not corrected, an additional
100% tax is imposed on the organization and 50% (up to an additional $10,000)
on each manager who knew of the violation. Correcting the violation means that
the managers tried to recover the contribution and took steps necessary to stop
future violations.

While this area of law has a substantial gray area, there are several important general rules to be understood in guiding an organization's quasi-political activity. Each case decided by the IRS is fact-specific, and its rulings provide only general guidelines. The best advice for charitable organization leadership and staff is to provide a wide margin for error when contemplating involvement in political activities and not to engage in any activity that would even raise the specter of being improper, even if such an activity falls within the legal framework provided by current case law.

Quasi-Political Activities

Among the most common issues raised by charities are the following examples of borderline, quasi-political activities:

1. **Influencing Ballot Questions.** Federal law only prohibits organizations exempt under Section 501(c)(3) from engaging in political activity for or against a candidate for public office. Nothing in the law prevents efforts to influence ballot measures, such as constitutional changes, ballot initiatives, and referenda. These efforts, of course, must be insubstantial compared to the organization's activities in support of its primary purpose.

2. **Get Out the Vote Campaigns.** 501(c)(3) organizations may engage in non-partisan get out the vote campaigns, but may not demonstrate any bias for or against any candidate or political party.

3. **Voting Records.** There is nothing illegal about a charity annually publishing a compilation of voting records of the Congress or the General Assembly. Some guidelines to follow are that the compilation should not be released only before an election and should list the voting records of all of the public officials or those in a relevant region (rather than in selecting only those who are up for re-election or who are targeted by the organization because they consistently vote for or against the organization's public policy positions). It should also involve a wide range of subjects, not imply organizational approval or disapproval of the public officials, and should not be disseminated beyond the membership or mailing list of the organization (i.e., the general public).

4. **Questionnaires.** It is not only permissible but advisable for charities to communicate with candidates, informing them of the organization's positions on issues and requesting their views. When candidates run for office, it is a vulnerable time for the shaping of their public policy positions. Many regret the positions they have taken during the election in response to a seemingly innocuous questionnaire. However, the use of these responses by an organization can be troublesome.

The IRS has ruled (Rev. Ruling 78-248) that it is permissible for charities to send a questionnaire to candidates and publish the answers in a voter's guide. However, the charities should make an effort not to demonstrate obvious bias in the questions, or to favor one candidate over another by making editorial comment. Organizations with a narrow range of interest, such as a pro-life or pro-choice group, are more in jeopardy by publishing the results of a questionnaire than groups with a broader range of interests, such as the League of Women Voters. If viewed by the IRS as a back door method to influence how your constituency votes, then questionnaires could place an organization's exemption in jeopardy.

5. **Public Forums.** Many 501(c)(3) organizations have a Candidates' Night to permit their volunteers and staffs to meet the candidates and question them about issues. This is not illegal, and it is expressly permitted by the IRS, provided it ensures "fair and impartial" treatment of the candidates (Rev. Rul. 86-95). However, such programs should be conducted with common sense. The moderator should be someone who can be impartial. All bona fide candidates should be invited, although it is not a prerequisite that they all accept the invitation for the event to be scheduled. Organizational leaders should refrain from making editorial comments about the positions of the candidates. Any account of the event in the organization's newsletter or other publication should be unbiased and should refrain from making editorial comment in favor of, or in opposition to, a candidate's views.

6. **Mailing lists.** The mailing list of a charity may be a valuable asset in the hands of a candidate. Many organizations get substantial revenue from selling or renting their mailing lists. There is no prohibition against selling a mailing list to a candidate for public office. However, giving a mailing list to a candidate is tantamount to making a political contribution. Also, all candidates must be given the same opportunity to purchase or rent the mailing list; no favoritism is permitted. As noted elsewhere in this publication, the sale or rental income from organizational mailing lists is potentially subject to federal unrelated business income tax, despite court rulings that decided they are not.

7. **Awards.** Many charities give "Legislator of the Year" or "Public Citizen of the Year" awards or similar citations to elected officials. However, making such an award just prior to an election in which the awardee is a candidate may be considered improper electioneering. From a practical viewpoint, even if this is done without any intention to help that candidate, a charitable organization's volunteers or contributors who may not like that particular candidate could view it as a disguised attempt at electioneering. It is a good policy to avoid providing awards to candidates during election periods.

Note: The above analysis is not intended to serve as legal advice about any particular set of facts, but only as a review of currently available reference materials on this issue. Consult a lawyer for a definitive answer to any particular legal situation.

2013 Proposed IRS Rules Relating to 501(c)(4)s

As a result of the Supreme Court decision *Citizens United v. FCC* striking down political spending limits on corporations, applications to the IRS for 501(c)(4) status, the tax exemption reserved for social welfare organizations, doubled. 501(c)(4) organizations are not required to disclose the names of their donors, which many organizations forming for the purpose of funding political campaigns find attractive. Although 501(c)(4) organizations may engage in partisan political activities, organizations whose primary purpose is this activity are not permitted to qualify for 501(c)(4) status. Later that same year, the IRS began screening applications from organizations applying for 501(c)(4) status based solely on the name of the organization. The ostensible justification provided for doing so was that organizations with particular words in their name, such as "Tea Party" or "Patriots," were likely to have been formed principally to engage in political activities, and thus should not eligible for this status.

Congressional critics of the IRS charged that the agency was targeting conservative nonprofit groups for political reasons, not responding at all to many applications for months (and in some cases, three years), and requesting unnecessary information from applications. Defenders of the IRS responded that there was no evidence of White House involvement or political motivation, that the IRS also took similar actions against organizations with names suggesting support for liberal causes, and that the IRS was simply taking a shortcut to delay or deny exempt status to organizations that were most likely not to qualify. The issue became quite controversial, being the subject of at least four congressional committee investigations, one by the Justice Department, and one by the Inspector General of the Treasury Department. The Inspector General concluded that the IRS—

1) allowed inappropriate criteria to be developed and stay in place for more than 18 months, 2) resulted in substantial delays in processing certain applications, and 3) allowed unnecessary information requests to be issued.

This scandal was front-page news for months during 2013 through 2014, and resulted in the resignation, forced retirement, firing, or reassignment of several top IRS employees. Among them was Lois Lerner, director of the Tax Exempt and Government Entities Division at the IRS, who took the Fifth Amendment during two appearances before Congressional committees investigating the scandal. Ms. Lerner announced her retirement in September 2013, after being on paid leave for more than three months.

In 2013, the IRS cracked down on organizations that applied for 501(c)(4) status whose names suggested a mission of substantial political activity. The IRS apologized for inappropriately singling out organizations solely based on their names, but generally defended its actions as an effort to keep political organizations from qualifying as social welfare organizations. Proposed regulations published in 2013 tightening standards for receiving 501(c)(4) status were withdrawn after the agency received more than 150,000 public comments opposing the proposal. The Congress responded by adding language to the *Consolidated Appropriations Act* (P.L. 114-113), to require new organizations wishing to operate as a social welfare organization under Sec. 501(c)(4) after December 18, 2015, to notify the IRS within 60 days after the organization is established of its intent to operate as a Sec. 501(c)(4) organization. The IRS, however, announced that it would not enforce this new requirement until after final regulations were promulgated on this law.

Tips:

- If you as a nonprofit executive are a "political animal" who must get involved in partisan political activity, find another entity, such as a PAC or a political party committee, to channel those energies. Never use your organization's stationery for political purposes.

- Seek experienced and competent legal counsel before engaging in any political activity that falls into a gray area.

- Use permissible political activities to the advantage of the organization, such as candidate forums, candidate questionnaires, and awards to public officials.

- Encourage members to make individual political contributions. It is good advice not to get involved in partisan politics, particularly if the organization has 501(c)(3) status. Those who do choose to participate in partisan politics should be scrupulous about separating personal political activities from those of the organization and not using organizational resources for partisan political activities.

- Keep informed about developments related to the Supreme Court's decision in the case of *Citizens United v. FEC* and how this decision will affect the legality of political activities of tax-exempt organizations.

Chapter 21
Communications and
Public Relations

Synopsis: Organizations need to effectively communicate their objectives, activities, and accomplishments to attract funding, participation, and public support. Print and electronic publications, media contacts, and workshops are among the accepted methods used to do so.

A well-planned public relations/communications strategy is important for two reasons. First, the organizational leadership has made a major investment in forming a nonprofit corporation, and a solid public relations effort will promote the organization's purposes. Second, few newly formed nonprofits begin with a silver spoon in their mouths. The first few years are often a fight for financial survival. Sound intraorganizational communications and building a solid public image through a public relations strategy are instrumental in building and maintaining a donor base and attracting grants and contracts.

But there is often a "Catch-22" at work here. New organizations must accomplish something useful quickly to obtain the credibility necessary to attract financial assistance. Yet, the organizations often need this financial assistance to accomplish something useful.

Public relations serves an important function. It puts the organization in a positive light and generates the essential public support needed to perpetuate it. An organization may be quietly successful in changing public opinion, advancing a legislative agenda, or providing vital services to worthy clients and its members. But if the right people—the board, funders, and potential funders and leadership—are unaware of the organization's successes, then its continued existence may be at risk.

There are thousands of creative ways to get the name of an organization in front of the public in a positive context.

Menu of Nonprofit Communication Tools

Among the conventional techniques nonprofits use are—

1. Organizational Brochure

Each nonprofit organization, from the largest to the smallest, should have a brochure. The brochure should clearly include the organization's name, address, telephone number, email address, website and social networking addresses; its mission, its purposes and principal interests, its affiliations (if any); its federal tax-exempt status, and ways to make contributions; the names of its board members, advisory committee, and key staff people; and its major accomplishments. The organization's logo should appear on the brochure. If the organization is a membership organization, the brochure should provide information on dues and how to join.

The brochure should be distributed with all major fundraising solicitations. It should be a standard component of press packets, and should be distributed at speaking engagements made on behalf of the organization. All board members should have a supply of brochures to distribute to their friends and colleagues who may be interested in joining, contributing, volunteering, or assisting in other ways.

2. Print and Electronic Newsletter

No less than quarterly, the organization should publish a newsletter and distribute it free of charge to all board members, all dues-paying members, significant opinion leaders on the issue(s) of interest to the organization, political leadership (such as members of the state legislature, local members of Congress, and local elected officials), the media, current and potential funders, and colleagues in the field.

Among the items the newsletter may contain are—

- recent board decisions
- the organization's "wish list" of in-kind donations
- legislative action in Washington, the state capital, and municipal government of interest to the membership and clients
- planned giving information
- schedules of upcoming meetings, workshops, conferences, and training sessions
- messages from the executive director and/or board president
- articles contributed by experts on the board or the membership about issues of interest to the readership

- articles about organizational accomplishments, such as grants received, advocacy accomplished, coalitions joined, and letters of commendation received
- profiles of people involved in the organization
- general information about the status of issues of interest to the organization
- new features of the organization's website
- names of new donors
- a list of all board members and staff
- a form to join the organization, volunteer, or make a donation
- information on services and publications available from the organization.

The newsletter need not be fancy, but it should be as current as possible. It is advisable to select a creative and descriptive name for the publication and establish a master layout, so that subsequent issues will have the continuity of similar design.

The newsletter is often the only contact hundreds of influential people will have with an organization. As such, it is vitally important to present a professional, accurate, and eye-pleasing format. The newsletter should be carefully proofread and *all* typographical and grammatical errors eliminated. Make sure articles on one page continue correctly on subsequent pages.

Headlines should help busy readers find their way through the newsletter. Tricky headlines can be annoying. Double-check all headlines for appropriateness. Double check all names, telephone numbers, addresses, and website addresses.

3. News Releases

The media annually provide millions of dollars in free publicity to nonprofit organizations. The typical mode of communicating with the media is through the mailing, faxing, or emailing of a standard news release.

The news release is a pre-written "news" article that includes the name, organization, work telephone number, and email address of the key organizational contact person at the top. If the release is *really* important, include the home telephone number, as well. The release should be dated, along with "For Immediate Release" or "Embargoed Until (insert date/time)" as appropriate.

Examples of topics for news releases are—

- the initial formation of the organization
- an organization's official comment on a new law, legislative proposal, new regulation, or court decision affecting the organization's clients or members
- an accomplishment of the organization
- the release of a study or survey commissioned by the organization
- the hiring or promotion of a staff member, or change of leadership within the organization
- awards given by or to the organization.

News releases are distributed to those who are most likely to print or broadcast them. A news release to a TV or radio station should be no more than six or seven sentences, and no more than two double-spaced pages for the print media. Most news releases will be edited before final publication or broadcast, although many neighborhood newspapers will print news releases word-for-word.

The basic style of the body of a press release is—

- Precede the text with a catchy, descriptive headline.
- Put the most important sentence first.
- Place subsequent facts in descending order of importance.
- Include suitable quotes from organizational leadership when appropriate. The quotes should express a view/ opinion, rather than providing a fact that could appear in the release narrative.
- Make sure the text answers the basic questions of "who," "what," "where," "when," "why," and "how."

4. Press Conferences

Organizations with a story of major interest to the public may want to consider holding a press conference. To do so, a media advisory is distributed in the same manner as a news release, telling the press where and when the press conference will be held, the subject, and speakers. It may be helpful to make follow-up calls to the news desks of local newspapers and broadcast stations.

At the press conference, written materials (a press packet consisting of a copy of a written statement, the organization's brochure, and materials relating to the topic of the press conference) should be distributed.

Another good idea is to arrange for a high resolution photo to be taken of the organizational representative speaking at the press conference. The photograph may be accompanied by a picture caption and sent in a press packet to media outlets not covering the press conference.

Digital cameras have eliminated some of the frustration of having to wait for a picture to be developed commercially. The files of these pictures can be sent conveniently through the internet as email attachments to newspapers on deadline, or can be posted on the organization's website and social networking pages.

A banner with the organization's logo, draped in front of the podium, creates a photograph that is useful for future annual reports, newsletters, and related publicity.

5. Public Service Announcements

Many TV and radio broadcasters regularly broadcast public service announcements (PSAs) for nonprofit organizations without cost. PSAs are an excellent and cost-effective way to get an organization's message, and its name, across to thousands of viewers and listeners.

The last line of such an announcement can be: "This message is brought to you by (the name of the organization) and this station as a public service." The rest of the announcement can be a 30-second sound bite of information of interest to people—how to obtain a free service, how to avoid health and safety risks, or even how to join or volunteer for the organization while accomplishing some vital objective in the public interest.

Before preparing a PSA, check with a potential broadcaster for the technical specifications for the form and format of the announcement. Some stations may be willing to produce your announcement without charge, as well as broadcast it.

6. Conferences and Workshops

Well-planned conferences and workshops can serve a useful public relations function. A one-day conference can bring together interested volunteer leadership and professionals in a shared field of interest, introduce them to the organization, increase networking among the participants, and advance the organization's interests. The charge for the workshop can be set to cover all anticipated costs, or even generate net revenue—provided it is planned well in advance and the plan is executed properly.

There are scores of major decisions to make in planning a conference, such as choosing speakers who will generate attendance and excitement, preparing and distributing the conference brochure, selecting the site for the conference, and arranging for exhibit space and advertising. There are hundreds of minor decisions that need to be made as well, such as choosing the type of name tag to use, deciding who staffs the registration table, and choosing the luncheon menu. There are many sources of advice on how to run a successful conference, many of which can be borrowed from the local library.

7. Intraorganizational Communication

Board and key contacts need to know what is happening beyond what they read in the organization's newsletter. Periodically, it is useful to send out "Action Alerts" or "Background Briefings" by mail or email that describe the status of a problem and what they can do to participate in its resolution.

Some organizations have specially printed stationery for these messages. A sample letter may be included if the organization is encouraging its constituency to write advocacy letters. However, the organization should urge writers to use their own words rather than copy the sample exactly. The address or telephone number of the person they should contact should always be included.

Many organizations are sponsoring conference calls to update their stakeholders, using toll-free numbers. Or they are using services like Google Hangout, Skype, or Zoom for videoconferencing, although there are limitations to those who use the non-subscription accounts.

8. Annual Report

Among the typical publications produced by nonprofit organizations is the annual report. Many nonprofits use this opportunity to supplement the financial information provided to stakeholders with a report on the operations of the nonprofit during the fiscal year. Many organizations produce both a print and electronic version (typically PDF format) of their annual reports.

The annual report can be professionally designed with a fancy layout, fonts, charts, graphics, and color pictures, which imply progress and success in meeting organizational goals and objectives. It can also be a word-processed report photocopied on plain paper. In either case, the annual report offers the opportunity to communicate what the organization has been doing on behalf of its board and membership, clients, funders, and the public, as well as its goals and plans.

9. Other Publications

Many nonprofits publish small booklets about various issues of concern, which are disseminated to their constituents and other interested parties. This is one more way to get the name of the organization in front of additional people, and it is another effective way to communicate the organization's views to those whose opinions count. Subjects of such publications include—

- the latest developments on issues of interest
- how to contact government offices
- how to lobby on behalf of the organization's issues
- information about the state legislature, and who serves on committees of interest to the organization.

These publications can also be considered the written equivalent of the public service announcement. Many institutions, such as hospitals, community centers, nursing homes, day care providers, and libraries, will distribute these public relations booklets without charge to the organization's target audience.

10. Membership/Board Surveys

Membership and board surveys can be, but may not always be, a useful tool to obtain information and feedback. The target of the survey may feel a sense of connection to the organization, and the survey will provide useful input from the membership.

Member surveys can be tailored to suit the needs of the organization. For example, many advocacy nonprofits periodically survey their boards and/or membership to determine who among the board and membership has influence or personal relationships with key public policy decision-makers. Surveys can be used to gauge the effectiveness of organizational programs and activities.

Free or low-cost software is available to administer online surveys. There are also free and low-cost commercial services that provide high-quality surveys, but may include advertising. Among the services to check out (features change quickly in the dot-com environment) are Survey Monkey.com *(https://www.surveymonkey.com/),* Free Online Surveys *(https://freeonlinesurveys.com/),* and BraveNet Web Services *(https://www.bravenet.net/).*

11. Speakers' Bureaus

Many groups, such as men's and women's clubs, fraternal organizations, educational organizations, membership organizations, and places of worship, have speakers at their regular meetings. Organizational leaders may wish to proactively seek invitations to discuss the activities of their organizations with these groups.

Such meetings may be the source of volunteers, donations, ideas, or simply good will and public support. Local newspapers (do not forget the "Shopper" newspapers) list many of these club meetings and their leaders. Addresses can be found in the telephone book, if they are not listed in the newspaper announcement. Members of the board can be deputized to speak on behalf of the organization. Many of them have associations with other organizations and clubs that would be delighted to host a speaker.

12. Newspaper Op-Ed Articles

Virtually all newspapers print feature-length opinion articles on their Opinion/Editorial (Op-Ed) pages. Many will include a picture and a line of biographical material about the author. The Op-Ed page is usually the page most widely read by a newspaper's readership, along with the Letters to the Editor page. It is an excellent forum to share an organization's ideas on an issue and bring attention to the organization.

There are many cases in which a thoughtful Op-Ed article resulted in legislation being enacted by Congress or the state legislature to address the issue raised by the Op-Ed piece.

13. Letters to the Editor

Letters to the Editor are an effective way to "talk back" to a newspaper when the organization believes an article or editorial unfairly and erroneously shapes an issue. They can also be an effective medium for reinforcing a position and permitting the writer to expand on that position from the perspective of the organization.

The general guidelines for writing letters to the editor vary from paper to paper, but they usually provide for writing on a single issue, being concise (no more than three paragraphs), using non-threatening language, and providing information that might not be available to the readers from any other source.

Many, if not most, newspapers with online access provide for the ability for readers to post comments about each article. This provides a targeted opportunity to reach those individuals who have an interest in a particular topic covered by the newspaper.

14. Websites

Thousands of nonprofit organizations use their Web pages to communicate information about donations; volunteer opportunities; products, services, and publications; and general facts about the organization (see Chapter 22). These websites can be prepared and maintained for very little cost and permit the general public to access information by computer from the privacy of their own homes and offices. Podcasts, blogs, wikis, message boards, and chatrooms are some of the techniques nonprofit organizations are using to build online communities to generate support.

15. Coalitions

There is strength in numbers. Two heads are better than one. Whatever the cliché, many organizations find a benefit to pooling their resources to accomplish an objective. One strategy is to form a coalition with other organizations to address an issue of vital importance (See Chapter 24).

16. Social Networking Sites

Facebook, Twitter, Pinterest, and LinkedIn are among the social networking sites that thousands of nonprofit organizations are using to advantage. These free platforms are raising money, finding volunteers, coordinating advocacy, providing forums for interaction and relationship building, and serving as a quick and inexpensive means to communicate with stakeholders. Each of these sites, and there are hundreds of them, has its own personality and features. For more on this, see Chapter 22.

Online Resources to Explore:

Carter McNamara's Public and Media Relations
https://managementhelp.org/publicrelations/index.htm

Getting Attention
https://gettingattention.org/

Jayne Cravens's Community Relations With and Without Technology
http://www.coyotecom.com/tips2.html

Media Relations for Small Non-Profit Organizations
https://www.mnhs.org/sites/default/files/lhs/techtalk/techtalkmay1997.pdf

Minnesota Nonprofits Social Media 101
https://www.minnesotanonprofits.org/events/event-detail/2019/08/29/default-calendar/social-media-101

Tips:

- Use the power of the internet to reach a global audience to foster relationships between your organization and potential future stakeholders. Review Chapters 22 and 23 for more ideas.

- Do not hold a press conference unless you feel that the information being shared is truly newsworthy. Be prepared for every reasonable question (and perhaps unreasonable ones, as well) that may not have any direct relationship to the subject matter discussed.

Chapter 22
The Internet for Nonprofits

Synopsis: The COVID-19 pandemic of 2020 (and beyond) validated that nonprofits have a versatile resource in the internet. Once connected, organizations can share information inexpensively and quickly. Nonprofits can set up their own websites and utilize social media to have their messages go viral, generating donations and other revenue. E-Commerce applications offer additional opportunities to improve the bottom line, although security and privacy of data remain of concern.

In 2013, the ALS Association raised a total of $19.4 million for its programs to provide research and education about amyotrophic lateral sclerosis, also known as Lou Gehrig's disease. Amyotrophic lateral sclerosis (ALS) is a progressive neurodegenerative disease that affects nerve cells in the brain and the spinal cord of about 30,000 Americans at any one time, according to the home page of the organization *(https://www.als.org/)*. This is a much smaller number of people than those affected by "high profile" diseases such as heart disease, which is the cause of death of one in four Americans, or cancer, which kills almost 600,000 annually.

Almost three million new donors contributed to the organization in August 2014 alone, providing more than $100 million, compared to about $2.5 million the ALS Association raised during the same month the previous year. An online fundraising campaign called the "ice bucket challenge" went viral, perhaps fundamentally changing the way charities view the power of the internet. Interestingly enough, the campaign to pour a bucket of ice water over one's head or make a donation to the ALS Association came from a single individual from outside of the organization. The rest is history. Seventeen million individuals participated in the challenge, posted videos of their participation on Facebook and other social media sites, challenged their friends to do the same, and also made a donation to the ALS Association. Some chose to simply make donations, which eventually reached a worldwide total of $200 million for the cause by November 2020.

Among the participants were hundreds of celebrities. Many donors were young people who may never have contributed before to an established national charity. And even those who took the challenge and did so to avoid the peer pressure to make a financial contribution participated in encouraging others to participate in the campaign, a contribution in itself, which also served to raise awareness about ALS.

The recent explosion of useful resources for nonprofits on the internet is perhaps the most exciting positive development for this sector in years. Twenty-five years ago, many nonprofit leaders had barely heard of the internet. Now, particularly during the COVID-19 pandemic, it has become an essential part of our daily lives. Our children have grown up with it. And today, nonprofit organizations are not only connected, but have their own websites, pages on Facebook, podcasts, blogs, and wikis. They tweet the latest happenings on Twitter, hold virtual board meetings and conferences using Zoom and Skype, and create online communities to build organizational support.

Practical Applications of the Internet

Among the most popular services and applications of the internet for nonprofits are email, text messaging, electronic mailing lists, e-newsletters, videoconferencing, chat, blogs, social media, podcasts, and wikis.

Email: Nonprofit organizations typically use email as their prime method of communication with their stakeholders. Many organizations use it for direct fundraising appeals, although using email to communicate with those who have no previous relationship to the organization is frowned upon. Because email has become so important, nonprofit organizations should make every effort to obtain and update the email addresses of their stakeholders. Recipients should be given an opportunity to request that they be removed from the organization's mailings, often facilitated by an "unsubscribe" procedure at the bottom of each email.

Text Messaging: Texting is becoming the preferred mode of communication, particularly among the millennial generation. Text messages typically have more impact than email. However, they are annoying to many recipients (and even expensive) if/when they are paying for each message sent and received. Organizations can ask their supporters to enter a code into their cell phones with a text message, authorizing a small donation that appears on the donors' telephone bills. Utilizing this technique, the American Red Cross raised more than $43 million during a short period of time for relief efforts in Haiti following the January 2010 earthquake. A decade later, texting became the method of choice to raise funds quickly for causes, and proved its worth compared to email. Why? As explained by Daniel Souweine, who does political fundraising,"...five to ten percent of people will read an email, but 80 to 90 percent of people will read a text."

Electronic Mailing Lists: Mailing lists provide a way to have a discussion or distribute information to a group using email. Users who subscribe to a particular list may send a message on a topic of interest to that list. That message is automatically distributed as email to every subscriber on the list. Some mailing lists generate hundreds of messages a day. Others publish one or fewer each day. Subscriptions to almost all electronic mailing lists are free. To subscribe to a mailing list, the subscriber generally sends an email message to an administrative address, or simply clicks on a button on the website of the organization that offers subscriptions. See *https://www.arnova.org/page/arnoval* for instructions on how to join the mailing list of the Association for Research on Nonprofit Organizations and Voluntary Action (ARNOVA).

E-Newsletters. These are the electronic version of an organizational newsletter, going out on a regular schedule by email to stakeholders who subscribe to them. A nonprofit e-newsletter might include information about an upcoming conference, changes in staff, new features of the organization's website, full-text articles written by staff, links to articles of interest that can be found on the Web, and upcoming programs sponsored by the organization.

Videoconferencing/videochat: Using applications such as Facetime, Zoom, Skype, GoToMeeting, or Google Meet, nonprofits are engaging their stakeholders in virtual meetings in which the participants can see each other and share documents. Although there are free versions, some platforms offer more bells and whistles, such as the ability to host larger groups, for a fee. Some applications feature the ability to record the session for later use.

Chat: Using chat software, you can have a text-based, real-time conversation with an individual or a group. What you type and the response of the other participant(s) appears on your screen simultaneously. It is possible to have a nonprofit board meeting entirely by chat. Most commercial providers provide for privacy among those who participate. Many websites, including those of nonprofit groups, use software, often provided free by commercial providers, that permits visitors to participate in chats related to their mission. In return for the use of free chat rooms, the visitors often see advertising messages controlled by the software provider, not under the control of the organization that is sponsoring the individual chat room. For an example, see the chat site sponsored by the American Cancer Society's Cancer Survivor Network at: *https://csn.cancer.org/about*

Blogs: Short for "Web Log," a blog is a website that consists of a frequently updated journal or diary by an individual. The style of commentary is typically informal and personal—although in the years since the term "blog" was first used (in the late 1990s), these sites have become more sophisticated, with some of them resembling online magazines.

Blog entries are typically in reverse chronological order—the latest entry is placed on top. Each dated entry has its own Web address (called a "permalink"), making it easy for other blogs and search engines to link to any particular entry (rather than to the entire blog). Most allow comments, and many have an RSS (Really Simple Syndication) feed, a software application that lets viewers subscribe to blog updates by using an RSS reader or receiving the feed by email.

For the nonprofit community, blogs provide another mechanism to improve interaction with an organization's stakeholders, enhance the bond with donors, and create a dialogue with outsiders while giving them an inside look at what the organization is trying to accomplish. The technical tools are easily accessible. Blogs can be created free with Blogger, WordPress, and similar tools. Blogs serve many purposes for a nonprofit organization. If they are interesting or provocative, they draw readership—not only from the general public, but from the media and political leadership, as well. And these site visits often translate to new and more productive current donors, volunteers, advocates, and friends. Bloggers need to vigilantly monitor all comments, routinely deleting "comment spam" and inappropriate comments. You can find an example of a nonprofit blog at: *https://redcrosschat.org/#sthash.KRmu7qZH.dpbs* (American Red Cross).

Social Media: Today, with 2.6 billion accounts on Facebook alone, almost everyone with access to a computer either has one or more of these accounts, or has at least visited one or more social networking sites. Nonprofit organizations have recognized that online social networking can be an effective technique to drive traffic to their websites and blogs, raise awareness of their missions and programs, encourage people to take action (such as participating in advocacy efforts), find volunteers, market their services, increase donations, and enhance already-created relationships they have with their stakeholders.

Although initial results of using these sites to generate donations were disappointing, so was online fundraising in general when organizations first began using it. Technology that promotes micro donations has improved substantially since then, as the Obama for President campaign proved in 2008. We are in the midst of a major change in culture, and sites such as YouTube, Twitter, Pinterest, LinkedIn, Instagram, and Facebook are changing the landscape. Nonprofit organizations are often slow to respond to such culture shifts, but those that proactively take advantage of new technology can benefit.

The intent of these sites is to provide links that help connect individuals and groups to others that share some common interest or objective. And, by and large, they do this with unqualified success. Evidence of this is the fact that a search of jobs using the search term "social media" on the Idealist.com site I conducted in October 2020 identified more than 1,250 nonprofit organization job listings that included job duties involving social media management tasks. For some ideas on how to creatively use social media for fundraising, volunteer recruitment, and building cause awareness, download BluePrint Creative Group's white paper at: *https://www.blueprintcreativegroup.com/a-case-study-of-how-nonprofits-are-using-social-media-to-build-cause-awareness-and-fundraise*

Podcasts: Podcasting refers to the creation of audio files that can be uploaded to the internet and listened to at a later time by subscribers who are informed when the audio program is available. These files are typically in MP3 format and 5 to 60 minutes in duration, making them suitable for hearing on the subscriber's computer, smartphone, or tablet. Podcasting permits the organization's staff to be the producer of a radio show (or TV show) rather than a third party, and gives them the ability to reach their target audience when they are most perceptive to hearing what the organization wants to say about itself.

What makes podcasting an incredibly powerful means of communication is that anyone in the world with an internet connection can listen to podcasts at any time. This compares to traditional TV and radio shows, which are on at a specific time and require action on the part of the viewer/listener to first know that there is a program of interest and then take steps to either listen to it in real time or record it. Often, there is no advertising to listen to, although there is no law against a charity making a subtle plea for donations to support its mission. The broadcaster's costs for equipment typically reasonable, and the subscriber pays nothing for the service. For examples of a nonprofit organization podcast, see *https://player.fm/series/nonprofits-are-messy-lessons-in-leadership-fundraising-board-development-communications-1717493*

Wikis: A wiki is a feature of a website that facilitates collaboration and participatory contribution among its users, who can add, remove, or edit content quickly and easily. Perhaps the best known example is Wikipedia, which is supported by the nonprofit Wikipedia Foundation (*https://wikimediafoundation.org/*). Following Hurricane Katrina 15 years ago, a wiki was established permitting the public to create a master database of messages from those who were seeking information about missing friends and relatives, consolidating the message boards of dozens of those established by media outlets, disaster relief organizations, and others. Hundreds of volunteers, including me, participated in the project and were delighted by the convenient opportunity to respond to the tragedy in a more tangible way than by simply donating money. Wikis can be public or password-protected, and software supporting this feature can be accessed for free or at minimal cost. For more details, read the *Exploring the World of Wikis* article at *https://tavaana.org/sites/default/files/exploring_the_world_of_wikis_0.pdf*

Mobile Applications: Wireless phones are almost universal in this country, and nearly everyone has, or will soon have, a "smart" phone, such as an iPhone or Android, that can easily access the Web and customized applications ("apps"). At a minimum, nonprofits are finding it essential to develop mobile-friendly versions of their websites to facilitate access by those who depend on their smartphones. Many major nonprofits are recognizing that they can develop apps themselves that will assist them in their marketing efforts. Sophisticated, custom mobile apps currently cost $5,000-$500,000 to develop, according to Anastasiia Lastovetska of

MLSDev.com (Lastovetska, 2020), but this amount is spiraling downward quickly. Simple smartphone apps can now be created for a few hundred dollars using free templates. Looking for where to start? See a tutorial, last updated in May 2020 at: *https://learnappmaking.com/how-to-make-an-app/*

For example, the American Museum of Natural History has developed a free app to assist visitors exploring its collections. The Detroit Zoo's iPhone app, which sells for $1.99, tracks a visitor's location within the zoo and shares information about attractions nearby, can create a personalized schedule to make one's visit more efficient, and provides a photo gallery.

If you are ambitious, you might try creating your own mobile app. You can find some resources at: *https://www.zdnet.com/article/14-diy-mobile-app-development-resources-for-small-businesses/*

The Web

The sophistication of websites has evolved substantially in just the last few years. Organizations that started in the 1990s with static billboard-type web pages now have interactive, dynamic sites.

The number of websites grew from just a single one in 1991 to 1.74 billion in 2020. In 2008, Google engineers announced that they had achieved a milestone: access to more than one trillion unique Web pages (see: *https://googleblog.blogspot.com/2008/07/we-knew-web-was-big.html*), and this is only a fraction of those available.

Among the types of information that can be found on typical websites of nonprofits are:

> breaking news, blogs, newsletter, annual report, press releases, brochure, how to contribute or volunteer, financial data, action alerts, job openings, information about board and staff members, publications, upcoming conferences and seminars, product catalogs and order forms, a link to email the organization, links to connect to the organization via social media, and links to other organizations and government-based sites related to the mission and purpose of the organization.

Domain Names

A domain name is the part of the email address after the "@" sign or the part of a Web address after the "www." For example, the personal email address of the author of this book is: gary.grobman@gmail.com. Gmail is his email provider, and "com" indicates that it is a commercial provider. *Gmail.com* is the domain name. If you are just starting to develop a website for your organization, you will need to choose and register a domain name. Most organizations prefer to use "my organization.org" where "my organization" is the name of the organization. Go to a registrar's site (such as *https://www.register.com/* or *https://www.network-solutions.com/*) and follow the directions, which include steps to make sure the name you want is available.

Domain Extensions (also known as gTLDs)

You have registered yourorganization.org. Should you register domains with other generic top level domains (gTLDs—the letters to the right of the dot in the address), as well, such as yourorganization.com and yourorganization.info? One advantage of doing so is that anyone looking on the Web for "yourorganization" will be more likely to find you. Another is that it prevents someone else from setting up a website using your organization's name. Until recently, gTLDs were limited. In July 2014, scores of new top-level domain extensions became available. Many experts have suggested that this will cause more confusion, as for example, nonprofits may have to choose among several hundred possible extensions that have their name to the left of the dot. Registering for all of these is likely to be cost-prohibitive for most nonprofit organizations. For a list of top-level domains available now, see: *https://www.godaddy.com/domains/gtld-domain-names*

Developing Your Website

There are thousands of commercial services offering to design and administer websites for a fee. With a minimum of technical background, you can do it yourself. The days when you needed to learn the HTML language and hand-code your website are long gone. Open source content management systems, such as WordPress, are available free of charge and allow you to use templates to make your site look professional. Website builders such as SquareSpace *(https://www.squarespace.com/)* and Wix *(https://www.wix.com/)* are simple and low-cost.

Simply having a site is clearly not enough to bring your organization fame, friends, and fortune. The "build it and they will come" philosophy may work well for Hollywood baseball movies, but you need to take proactive steps to build a base of loyal visitors and keep them returning. See Chapter 23 for some ideas on how to do this.

Nonprofit E-Commerce

The term *e-commerce* refers to business that is conducted electronically. It includes the marketing of goods and services, using the internet to join an organization or subscribe to a publication, and automated customer service.

The business models and strategies used by for-profits can be adapted by nonprofits to generate revenue that will finance the expansion of nonprofit organizational programs and activities. At the very least, these techniques make it a bit easier to raise funds and thus reduce what must be one of the leading causes of stress and burnout among nonprofit executives and staff—the constant battle to raise dollars to balance organizational budgets.

For years, charities have generated income through a variety of programs and activities, such as selling newsletter subscriptions and other publications, collecting fees at conferences and workshops, operating thrift shops, conducting flea markets and running races, renting mailing lists, having auctions, scheduling fundraising dinners, and selling group outings to sporting events or theater performances.

The Web has made all of this easier, at least for many organizations, in two significant ways. First, it has provided organizations with a way to reach almost everyone, and to do this quickly and inexpensively. Using a combination of strategies, such as conventional mail, telephone, and media advertising, along with website and social media posts, mailing list postings, broadcast email, and Web advertising, an organization can reach its target market and expand its reach. Second, using sophisticated technology, organizations can take advantage of homebound volunteers (at one end of the scale) and pricey, professional "back end" providers (at the other end of the scale) to do much of the work.

As a result of email, the Web, electronic mailing lists, and social media, the velocity of business transactions has made a quantum leap. The internet has salient advantages over conventional sales marketing, such as—

- Overall marketing and order processing costs are lower using the Web.
- Organizations can reach a global, targeted market virtually instantaneously.
- A Web-based "store" is open 24 hours/day, seven days/week, and always has free parking.
- The playing field is leveled between small organizations and those with many more resources.
- Business transactions can be consummated electronically without the need for expensive labor or intermediaries, such as brokers.
- Internet search engines and directories bring potential customers to organizations without unreasonably expensive marketing efforts.
- Customer service can be almost completely automated.
- "Back office" for-profit organizations with substantial expertise, labor, and sophisticated software will do the necessary work and make it appear to customers that the nonprofit organization is performing the work.

Build, Buy, or Rent

An organization's website is the most visible ingredient of its e-commerce strategy. Organizations have three basic choices in deciding which direction to go. Making the choice depends on factors such as—

- the amount of financial investment they are prepared to make
- the amount of staff time they are willing to devote to building, maintaining, and troubleshooting
- whether they are comfortable with "off the rack" features or want a site that is state-of-the-art and custom-made
- their comfort level with outside vendors having access to their financial transactions
- whether they want to have complete control over their websites so, for example, they do not have to depend on private companies to update files when they have the time
- whether they are comfortable with paying an outside firm based on the amount of revenue that is transacted on their sites
- the importance to them of having all visitors stay on their sites rather than being routed to a private vendor who may subject the visitor to advertising that the nonprofit organization cannot control, or may be inconsistent with the organization's values.

Build: Almost all of the tools a nonprofit needs to build a credible e-commerce site can be found by searching Google using the terms "shopping cart" or "online store builder." Much of the software can be downloaded for free.

Buy: If an organization is as well-heeled as the Metropolitan Museum of Art *(https://www.metmuseum.org/)*, it can afford to buy the very best. From the appearance of this site, one can expect this organization's investment in hiring a private firm to custom-design a website will result in long-term financial dividends. This site was custom-designed by a locally-based outside firm, IconNicholson. Everything about this site is, pardon the pun, state of the art.

Rent: Application Service Providers (ASPs) and Software as a Service (SaaS) providers advertise in the nonprofit national media about the availability of their services. In this context, renting involves purchasing services from a firm that will, for a monthly or annual fee, provide nonprofit organizations a customized, "hosted" e-commerce (and donation processing) site based on a template. The pages usually reside on the server of the ASP.

Setting Up an Online Store

If your organization sells products and services, you can enhance these sales by adding a secure online store to your organization's website. Before opening your store, you should consider costs, how you will handle online transactions, customer service issues, receipts and invoices, tax issues, and shipping.

Handling Online Financial Transactions

Qualifying for merchant status to accept popular credit cards such as Visa, MasterCard, American Express, and Discover is often routine. An organization typically approaches its bank to set up a merchant account. One can find hundreds, if not thousands, of financial institutions willing to establish merchant accounts on the Web. One way to find them is to search under the terms "accepting credit cards" and "merchant accounts."

Startup fees, account maintenance fees, per transaction fees, and the bank's percentage of sales fee for processing each transaction varies by financial institution and may be negotiable.

An alternative to setting up a merchant account for credit card sales is to utilize the services of a third-party payment processor that will accept credit cards for you by using a secure, online platform. One such popular provider, PayPal *(https://www.paypal.com),* not only provides this service but also gives access to tools that you can use to build your online store, such as shopping carts, invoices, and shipping/tracking management services. From the home page, click on "Merchant Tools" for details about these services. There are no setup fees to establish an account as a merchant. PayPal charges nonprofits a basic fee of 2.9% (depending on sales volume) plus 30 cents per transaction. There are additional fees for foreign currency transactions. More than 346 million individuals worldwide have PayPal accounts, as of 2020. The company was purchased by eBay in 2002 and is quickly becoming the standard for making and receiving online payments, with $712 billion processed in 2019.

PayPal offers PayPal Payments Pro to accept credit cards and PayPal directly on your site. Charities with 501(c)(3) status are eligible for a discount on transaction fees.

Apple Pay, Google Pay, and Samsung Pay are relatively new alternatives to PayPal, with lots of features that make them attractive for electronic purchases. Purchasers can establish accounts for free. These applications are another step on the road to making shopping walletless, with customers having the ability to make convenient payments for goods and services using their wireless devices. Apple Pay is geared to iPhones, and Google Pay and Samsung Pay are geared to Android devices, although they can handle iPhone purchases with a handy app. The intent of these payment systems is to permit customers to make purchases in stores without using either cash or credit cards, and to complete a financial transaction using a mobile device quickly and securely. The applications are also able to conveniently process transactions completed online. It is only a matter of time until everyone with a smartphone will have one of these accounts.

For more information and a comparison of these competing systems, see: *https://www.creditcards.com/credit-card-news/samsung-pay-apple-pay-google-pay-set-up-security-rewards/*

Customer Service

Depending on what products and services are offered, many of the issues relating to customer service will be the same for a nonprofit as for a for-profit organization. Organizations will need to have policies for, and routines for, processing returns, exchanges, refunds, and shipping.

One obvious disadvantage of shopping over the internet is that shoppers cannot touch and feel the product, or try it on or try it out. People are more willing to make purchases over the internet when they feel that they can return the products if they are not completely satisfied. A refunds and returns policy should be posted on your site, and it should be a more liberal policy than one would expect to find at the local mall. This is good business practice; nonprofits certainly do not want to alienate a customer who is also a donor or potential donor. Among the issues that should be addressed are:

1. Will refunds be given in cash or credit for a future purchase?
2. What is the time limit for returns?
3. Can returns be made unconditionally, or only for defective products?
4. Is there a restocking fee?
5. Must the product be returned in salable condition in the original packaging?
6. Will shipping and handling also be refunded, or only the product purchase price?
7. Will the organization pay for shipping back returns?
8. Will certain products not be returnable (such as publications, electronics, or jewelry)?

Receipts and Invoices

Products should be shipped with a receipt if pre-paid, or an invoice if payment is due. If they were not prepaid, the invoice should state the terms of payment, such as when the bill is due, and the percentage added to the bill per month for any outstanding balance. The receipt should include the name of the purchaser; the name of the organization; the description of the product(s); the price of each purchase; and the amount of tax, shipping, and handling. Generic accounting software programs such as Quickbooks, Quicken, Zoho Books, or Sage (formerly Peachtree) provide forms for standard invoices and receipts.

Collecting Taxes

Only the states of Alaska, Delaware, Montana, New Hampshire, and Oregon do not have a state sales and use tax. The sales tax applies to sales made within a state to a purchaser from that same state. The use tax applies to sales of products bought in one state and taken into another. The use tax is intended to be paid by the purchaser and goes to the purchaser's state treasury, although this requirement is rarely, if ever, enforced. Generally, organizations are obligated to collect sales and use taxes on sales they make to customers within their own states.

There was once a general moratorium on internet sales taxes until December 31, 2015, and pending legislation such as *The Marketplace Fairness Act,* would establish a system whereby states could collect and remit sales taxes for remote sales from sellers with remote sales exceeding $1 million. However, this proposal has not been enacted into law. On June 21, 2018, the United States Supreme Court issued a ruling in the case *South Dakota v. Wayfair, Inc.* that set a major precedent for the collection of state sales tax by Internet-based retailers. The Court effectively provided that individual states can require online sellers to collect state sales tax on their sales. This ruling overturned the Court's 1992 decision in *Quill Corporation v. North Dakota* that prohibited states from requiring a business to collect sales tax unless the business had a physical presence in the state. In response to the court decision, a number of states have passed laws to take advantage of this new authority. See *https://www.salestaxinstitute.com/ resources/remote-seller-nexus-chart* for a directory detailing the status of state actions in response to this court decision.

Sales taxes still must be collected for intrastate purchases in states with sales taxes, although enforcement of this requirement is spotty. Even if an organization is tax exempt, most states, including Texas, still require nonprofit organizations to collect sales taxes on sales they make to customers within the state.

Typically, states require organizations to obtain a sales tax license and to transmit the collected taxes to the state using a provided form. It is advisable to check with a reputable local business organization, such as the Chamber of Commerce, to find out what the requirements are for collecting and transmitting state sales taxes in a particular state before engaging in the sale of goods and services there (see Chapter 27 for Texas requirements).

Shipping and Handling

Organizations need to decide how much they will charge for shipping and handling and display that information prominently on the site. Some shopping cart software provides for letting the customer decide how the product is to be shipped—automatically adjusting the amount for shipping and handling (such as by using a database provided by UPS or other shippers), based on how much the organization wants to add over the actual cost. They can charge a flat fee for shipping, charge by weight, charge by the number of products ordered, or provide for free shipping if the order exceeds a certain amount. Organizations should also consider policies with respect to out-of-country sales, which raise issues concerning payment, shipping, and customs duties.

Affiliate Marketing

Business models have emerged that permit nonprofit organizations to take advantage of technology and raise funds that would not have otherwise come their way. Even if your organization does not sell products or services of its own, you can generate revenue by marketing products and services of others through "affiliate" or "associate" programs.

The "affiliate" model was pioneered by Amazon.com. The Seattle-based company simply announced to the world that by placing coded links on your website, you can earn a commission on purchases of books, CDs, DVDs, videos, electronics, software, video games, toys, home improvement items, and many other products that are generated by those links.

Joining the Amazon Associates program involves visiting *https://affiliate-program.amazon.com,* electronically submitting a form provided on the site (after reading and agreeing to the operating agreement), and using tools provided on the site to set up your links to Amazon.com and promote products. Each link has your Associate ID code embedded in it, so when someone buys something from Amazon.com through a link on your site, your organization gets a commission.

An effective way to take advantage of this program is to have a book review section or recommended books section on your organization's website. For each book mentioned, include your Amazon Associate link to that book's page on Amazon.com.

Amazon Associates is perhaps the most popular affiliate marketing program for nonprofit organizations. For nonprofits and for-profits alike, this simple, yet revolutionary, business model is generating valuable revenue without the need for any investment or exposure to risk.

Similarly, affiliate programs exist for many other online retailers and online services. Your organization can become an affiliate of eBay, Buy.com, allPosters. com, or CareerBuilder.com, for example. Typically, if a site offers an affiliate program, there will be a link for it somewhere near the bottom of the page, leading to an explanation of how to join and how the program works.

When considering whether to join an affiliate marketing program, think about how the site with which you will be affiliating fits with your organization's mission, as well as how you will incorporate the affiliate program into your own site. For example, if you are joining an affiliate program of an online bookstore (such as Amazon.com), will you place reviews and links to carefully selected books that are in line with your mission? Or will you set up a complete store where your site's visitors can buy anything that is available in the affiliated store, encouraging your visitors to do all their shopping through your site, as a way of supporting your organization? Each of these approaches has its pros and cons.

Let's say your organization is an animal shelter. Using the first approach, you can create links to (and perhaps reviews of) books on animal care. This will keep the focus on your mission and promote products that will likely be of interest to your site's visitors. You can target these links to the visitor's interests, so a person who is reading an article about German shepherds will see a link on that page to a book on German shepherds. The conversion rate (from seeing the link to clicking on it to purchasing the item) on such links will be higher than that for random links that are unrelated to your site's content. You will need to monitor the links to make sure that they are up to date and the items are still available for purchase.

Using the second approach, you can build a store on your site using an automated data feed (if one is provided), and then encourage your visitors to support your organization by shopping there. If your visitors get in the habit of going through your site to make their purchases, you can do well with this method. They may buy animal care books, or they may buy office products, or both. Either way, you will earn the commission. However, keep in mind that you do not have complete control over the items that are shown through the data feed, and some items may not be consistent with the mission or character of your organization.

Advertising

Another way you can generate revenue from your organization's website is to allow advertisements to be placed on it. The quickest and easiest way to earn money through advertising is to join Google AdSense or a similar program. Once you join, you will be able to log in to Google's AdSense site and generate the code to put on your site. Then ads will begin to appear on your site that correspond with key words in your content. Google will send you a monthly automatic deposit for a portion of the advertising revenue from these ads.

One downside to this is that you do not have complete control over the content of the ads that appear on your site. You can filter the ads to a certain extent, but it will take some staff or volunteer time to monitor the ads to make sure they are appropriate.

Instead of or in addition to this approach, your organization may decide to sell classified and/or banner advertising directly on your site. You will need to develop a policy stating what types of ads you will accept, your advertising rates, and so forth. And you will need to develop a "media kit" telling advertisers the benefits of advertising on your site, the amount of traffic the site experiences, the procedure for placing an ad, technical specifications, and how to make payment. If your site is a popular one that is getting a significant amount of traffic in your niche, this can be an excellent way to use your site to generate revenue.

Security and Privacy

Even putting e-commerce transactions aside, nonprofit organizations have many reasons to protect the security and privacy of the computer files they generate and the communications they send over the internet. Human service organizations, for example, routinely use client files that, if disclosed in an unauthorized manner, could cause irreparable harm to their clients and result in lawsuits.

Email exchanges may involve sensitive personnel matters or contract negotiations with unions and other entities. Even if nothing sensitive is discussed in a file or email message, an organization still does not want any prying person, within the organization or outside of it, to be able to browse through its business.

SSL and Other Encryption Technology

Virtually every survey on internet security has demonstrated the pervasive fear of providing credit card numbers over the internet. The concern that unscrupulous merchants (or those who pretend to be merchants) will use the credit card information is mostly unfounded; even if this happened (and it does occasionally), there are limits on the amount of loss the consumer sustains (typically $50), and there is no exposure to loss if the problem is reported promptly.

The principal concern tends to be that hackers will tap into the transaction and steal the credit card data. Recent high-profile hacking incidents involving otherwise trusted for-profit retailers have made the front pages and have made many individuals wary of sharing valuable and personal data over the internet. Considerable effort has gone into making financial transactions over the internet safe by encrypting (that is, disguising) the data so that only the intended sender and receiver can read it.

Although there are several protocols for encryption, the industry standard for e-commerce has become Secure Sockets Layer, or SSL.

Certification/Authentication

Organizations that are serious about e-commerce should obtain an SSL certificate from a certifying authority to assure purchasers that they are who they say they are. A purchaser can see a lock icon or other indicator on his or her browser that authenticates encryption software if the organization has one of these certificates.

Many people will refuse to send their credit card information over the internet unless the organization has a valid certificate. Server certificates are available commercially from many different companies, and the cost varies. Some free certificates are available, but there may be problems using free versions on some browsers and these are best used for testing purposes only.

The most widely-used certificate authority in the United States is DigiCert (which acquired industry leader Symantec in 2017), *(https://www.digicert.com/)*. ComodoGroup *(https://www.comodo.com/)*, GoDaddy *(https://www.godaddy.com/)*, and GlobalSign *(https://www.globalsign.com)* are among its competitors. One recurring problem is that the certificates may not work on all browsers, so make sure to inquire about this information.

Protection of Customer Data

Organizations can have all of the sophisticated encryption systems in place, but it would not do any good if employees keep the printouts on their desks or put them in an accessible file on their computers. Employees should take reasonable precautions to keep all customer data protected.

Firewalls

A firewall is a type of internet security software that limits access to websites, allowing approved traffic in and out through a secure gateway. New computers typically have a firewall built into their operating systems (such as Windows 10 and Mac OS X). Firewalls can be downloaded for free (for example, find one at: *https://www.pfsense.org/*) or obtained for thousands of dollars.

Privacy Policies

Many commercial websites address privacy concerns by having a privacy policy posted online. The policy generally includes—

1. What information will be collected on the site.

2. What information will be shared with others, and under what circumstances. For example, many organizations sell or rent their mailing lists.

3. What information will not be shared with others. For example, obtaining a telephone number is helpful in the event of a problem with a customer's transaction. Although many business organizations will request the telephone number for that purpose, they will keep the customer's telephone number confidential.

4. What customers can do to keep their name, mailing address, and email address confidential. This may entail simply clicking a button on an electronic form.

TrustArc (formerly TRUSTe) is an organization established to set up privacy standards and to provide sanctions against participants who violate the standards. Websites that meet TRUSTArc's strict privacy standards in the areas of notice, choice, access, and security and submit to TRUSTArc's oversight program may display the organization's seal (still branded as "TRUSTe") for a fee. This has become the Web privacy equivalent of the "Good Housekeeping Seal of Approval."

Cookies

One feature of the internet that has contributed to fears about privacy violation is the cookie. Cookies are ASCII files (plain text) that can be created and accessed by a website visited by the browser. Cookies keep track of your movements within the website, assist you in resuming where you left off what you were doing when you left the site, and remember your preferences, and other aspects of your previous visits.

Cookies can be deleted, or the feature in the browser that creates them can be disabled. The benefit of the feature is that the cookie file lets the site being visited know something about the visitor and the visitor's interests by accessing it and permits the site to provide custom-designed information based on the cookie. Having a cookie can save a lot of time and keystrokes, because the site will "recognize" the visitor as a repeat visitor and "remember" what was done on previous visits. The downside is that the visitor may not wish to share this information.

Internet Tools for Nonprofit Organizations

Nonprofit organization leaders may feel overwhelmed by all of the complexity involved in making their online operations efficient and productive. Fortunately, there is healthy competition among major companies to develop creative software that makes it much easier for staff to coordinate and collaborate, utilizing the power of the internet. Google and Microsoft are among the companies offering innovative productivity suites with powerful features that have discounts available to nonprofit organizations and, in some cases, are available for free.

Google Workplace, formerly known as G Suite, is perhaps the most attractive, offering a free basic version to nonprofit organizations. The cloud-based suite of apps facilitates document sharing, scheduling, surveys, web building, email hosting, chat, video conferencing, file storage, domain name purchasing, custom app development, and many other useful applications. It includes standard office suite software, such as a word processing program, spreadsheet, and presentation slide creator that are compatible with the better-known Microsoft counterparts of Word, Excel, and PowerPoint. For more details, see: *https://workspace.google.com/*

Microsoft 365 *(https://www.office.com/)* competes head-to-head, but has a different approach. It is less cloud-based and a bit pricier. They each have their advantages and disadvantages. What they have in common is they have lots of functionality, and they both integrate seamlessly with all of their applications. A third competitor, Zoho Workplace *(https://www.zoho.com/workplace/)*, offers many of the same types of applications and has a slightly lower subscription price.

Charity Portals

Scores of for-profit and nonprofit companies have sites online that promise to take donations over the internet by credit card, and funnel the donation—sometimes after deducting an administrative fee—to the intended charity. For charities that receive an unsolicited check in the mail from one of these portal companies, this is a windfall. For the donor, using a charity portal can be convenient and often provides anonymity, if requested.

The donor can use the site search engine to find a suitable charity, and there is often other content on the portal site to influence donation decisions. The administrative fee pays the bills and provides a profit to the service provider who runs the portal. Some make money by selling advertising on their sites. Others charge charities to be listed.

Some of these portals may not be legitimate. Many others are, but it is difficult to tell simply by visiting the website.

For many charities, being listed on these portals is a way to publicize the existence of the organization and the importance of its mission, even if donations received through participation are minimal. For others, being associated with a firm that takes a commission on donations is unacceptable. According to a report that appeared in *The Chronicle of Philanthropy,* the World Wildlife Fund sent "cease and desist" letters threatening to take legal action if the sites did not remove its name from the list of organizations eligible to receive donations.

The Internal Revenue Service has raised questions about whether donations made through charity portals can be deductible for federal income tax purposes. Many are not likely to survive, since it takes a lot of marketing capital to draw people to the site to donate. In general, a site that requires charities to pay any kind of up-front fee is likely to be a scam.

As more and more charities use their own websites to routinely accept donations by secure credit card forms, donations made through portals are likely to be a small slice of the online donation pie.

Perhaps the leading charity portal is Network for Good *(https://www.networkforgood.com/),* founded by America Online, AOL-Time Warner Foundation, Cisco Systems, the Cisco Foundation, and other cooperating charities. Its website boasts that it has distributed more than $2.54 billion in donations so far to more than 300,000 charities, as of December 2020.

Charity Malls

For-profit dot-coms have established agreements with national retailers willing to offer enough discounts to allocate a percentage of a consumer purchase to a charity of the shopper's choice. These brokers will sign up charitable organizations for the purpose of driving traffic to the website of the retailers. A percentage of the discount is split between the charity and the broker. The charity encourages its stakeholders to shop at the mall by placing a link on its website. Examples are iGive.com and TheHungerSite.com.

Charity Auctions

The internet provides many advantages if an organization has goods and services to auction off, particularly those obtained from celebrities. Many people will be interested in what an organization has to offer, even if they have never heard of the organization or do not care about its mission, if the goods and services are attractive.

An almost infinite number of items can be offered, and the auction can be conducted 24 hours each day year-round with the participation of people down the street or on the other side of the world. Innovative software makes the process relatively easy, and there are websites that help organizations seeking to harness this strategy. To find links to these sites and application service providers that sell software to administer online auctions, Google "charity auctions."

Online Communities

An online community is any website or application that attracts people who have something in common, and allows them to contribute to content or discussions at the site. The types of services that are typically available are real time chat, blogs, forums, member directories, instant messaging, job/career information, shopping, and news and information. What members of the site have in common can be anything: their age, their social status, their profession, their religion, their politics, some health concern, or interest in a particular public policy issue.

What distinguishes online communities from other websites is that much of the content is contributed by visitors. This content may be moderated by the website manager, although in many cases, it is not.

Challenges of Online Communities

1. Creating and maintaining an online community requires substantial time and effort.

2. Some visitors post inappropriate content, such as putting slanderous or libelous messages on the message board, posting commercial messages, violating confidentiality, or infringing on a copyright.

3. Some words used in real-time posting may be offensive, requiring the use of filtering software. Organizations must choose which words to ban.

4. Online communities need an effective Code of Conduct.

Even when an online community is free, most require members to register and to select a username and password. Doing so ensures that the organization has at least minimal control and can deny access to those who consistently violate the site's Code of Conduct. There are also marketing reasons to have a password-protected site, such as having access to information about those who visit.

Online communities with powerful features can be created using third-party services such as those available at MightyNetworks (*https://mightynetworks.com*) and Discord *(https://discord.com/)*. But more and more, nonprofits are taking advantage of the opportunity to build free online communities through social media, such as LinkedIn, Facebook, Instagram, Twitter, and Pinterest. And, as evidenced by the number of jobs available for this type of work on the Idealist website (see page 290), many nonprofits are hiring specialists to manage their social media duties.

Legal Issues

Establishing an online community exposes an organization to legal liability in a number of areas that are unsettled, chiefly because many technology issues are new and have not been tested in the courts.

A Code of Conduct is a necessity, as is a privacy statement. The Code should include a declaration of what behaviors are not permitted by site users, such as flaming; obscene, sexist, anti-Semitic, or racist postings; the posting of copyrighted material without permission from the copyright owner; the uploading of files, such as software or other materials that are a violation of intellectual property laws; and engaging in fraudulent conduct or the harassment of other users.

Website Reviews

There are hundreds of websites that provide useful information to nonprofit organizations. The following are some of these that are of particular value, with a capsule summary of what can be found on their pages.

1. Idealist
https://www.idealist.org/

Since 1995, this searchable site has been connecting nonprofit organizations to individuals seeking jobs, internships, and volunteer assignments. As of December 2020, there were 319 jobs and 51,146 volunteer opportunities posted. (This compares to an excess of 7,000 jobs and 8,000 volunteer placements posted in pre-pandemic 2017.) More than 137,000 nonprofit organizations participate. And the site serves more than a million registered users.

2. Candid (formerly The Foundation Center and Guidestar)
https://candid.org/

Candid was formed in 2019 when GuideStar and Foundation Center joined forces. For decades, GuideStar gathered data on nonprofits to help funders obtain information and Foundation Center collected data on foundations to help nonprofits find funding. Candid is the largest information source on the social sector in the United States and, increasingly, around the world. The organization collects, organizes, analyzes, and distributes information about the work of the social sector in order to support excellence throughout the sector. In their own words, "Candid connects people who want to change the world to the resources they need to do it." Candid's Funding Information Network (FIN) program consists of more than 400 community-based organizations across the United States and around the world that house and provide—free of charge to the public—a suite of Candid trainings and tools, including one-on-one support to those with questions on the fundraising/proposal writing process, and access to Foundation Directory Online, Candid's web-based application of foundations and grantmaking organizations. Candid.org houses Candid's products, services, and websites.The Foundation Center's Ask the Online Librarian feature enables visitors to the site to ask questions about foundations, philanthropy, and fundraising research via e-mail (24 hours a day, 7 days a week) or live chat (9:30 a.m. to 8:00 p.m. EST, Monday through Wednesday; 9:30 a.m. to 4:30 p.m., Thursday and Friday). Online librarians will respond to requests for suggestions about books, periodicals, and Internet resources.

3. Nonprofit Managers' Library
https://managementhelp.org/

Much on this site is targeted to the needs of Minnesota nonprofits (such as local grant information). However, it is an excellent resource for all. It is a service of Carter McNamara the principal of Authenticity Consulting, who first developed the site in the 1990s. As many as a million visitors each month have viewed hundreds of pages of valuable content of interest to nonprofit leaders. The site boasts updated files on ethics, fundraising, communications skills, marketing, organizational change, risk management, strategic planning, and much more, sorted by 99 categories and indexed with almost 700 topics. There are numerous useful links to outside organizations that make this site an excellent resource for those interested in grants, foundations, government information, and general information useful to nonprofits. The site also hosts a free Nonprofit Organization and Management Development Program (a.k.a., Free Nonprofit Micro-eMBA) at: *https://managementhelp.org/freenonprofittraining/program-description.htm*

4. *Philanthropy Journal*
https://philanthropyjournal.org/

This online newspaper, based in North Carolina at the Institute for Nonprofits at North Carolina State University, was a service of *Philanthropy News Network,* a 501(c)(3). It ceased operations as of January 2020, but the site continues to maintain its archived articles.

5. *The Chronicle of Philanthropy*
https://www.philanthropy.com/

The site provides highlights from this print publication, which is the trade journal for America's charitable community. The tabloid-format monthly is the number one source for charity leaders, fundraisers, and grant makers, and the website provides more than just a taste of what its subscribers receive in snail mail. You can sign up for a free daily or weekly email update of news and new features of the site, plus breaking news when it occurs. Among the principal categories of this site are opinion, grants, and data and research. Also on the site are front-page news stories, a news summary, conferences, internet resources, products and services, and jobs. The "Jobs" link transports you to a searchable database of hundreds of positions available (800 when I last checked in December 2020). In some respects, this searchability makes the internet version of the *Chronicle* more useful than the conventional printed version, and there are many more articles to access. There is also a directory of "Products and Services." If you are a subscriber ($109.95/year), you will have access to a handy, searchable database of archived issues.

6. *The Nonprofit Times*
https://www.thenonprofittimes.com/

This is the online version of the monthly tabloid newspaper. It has full-text articles from the latest issue, as well as classified advertisements. The Resource Directory, accessible from the home page, links to a database of vendors, consultants, and other professionals who serve the nonprofit community. Click on "Articles & Reports" and then "grants" from the home page for free access to excellent articles about how to maximize your opportunities to find grants.

7. Independent Sector
https://independentsector.org/

Independent Sector is the leading advocacy coalition in Washington that serves the nonprofit sector. This site is the first place to go for definitive statistics of interest about the nonprofit sector (click on *Resources*). It also has files on ethics, advocacy, accountability, and leadership issues. There is current information about new laws and regulations affecting charities, as well as public policy advocacy updates. If you are interested in how various public policy proposals in Washington will affect the sector, this is the go-to site for analyses, testimony, and advocacy strategies.

8. USA.gov (formerly FirstGov.gov)

https://www.usa.gov/

Here you can access not only information about the billions of dollars in government grants, but also register to vote, apply for a passport, participate in government auctions, and access hundreds of other state and federal government services. This site's strength lies in its convenient and user-friendly links to federal departments and agencies—executive, legislative, and judicial—and an easy-to-use guide to access publications of importance to nonprofits, particularly those that are seeking government grants. Its search page can find information from more than a million government Web pages.

9. Volunteer Match

https://www.volunteermatch.org/

This searchable site provides a posting area for nonprofits to advertise volunteer opportunities that can be performed online, as well as general volunteering resources. Posting is free for organizations, and more than 13 million matches have been recorded since 1998. By December 2020, the site had more than 130,000 participating organizations with 2.9 million posted volunteer opportunities. Also available at this site are resources and blogs for volunteer recruiting, volunteer tracking and reporting, and many other applications of use to volunteer managers.

10. TechSoup (TechSoup Global)

https://www.techsoup.org/

TechSoup *(https://www.techsoup.org/)*, originally conceived by CompuMentor, a San Francisco-based nonprofit, has developed a reputation as being the place for nonprofits to visit for answers to questions about hardware and software, building websites, and taking advantage of all that technology can offer to help nonprofits achieve their vital missions. The content is all free and worthy of repeat visits. A service of TechSoup, DiscounTech receives major funding from The Bill & Melinda Gates Foundation, The Charles Stewart Mott Foundation, The Cisco Foundation, The Hearst Foundations, The Rockefeller Foundation, and The Surdna

Foundation. Since its founding in 1987, the organization has distributed donated Microsoft and other name-brand products. As one example from December 2020, eligible organizations were being offered Microsoft Office Standard 2019, a suite of six top-of-the-line office software packages, for just $39. Overall, this is one of the best sites on the internet for information about nonprofit technology issues, including hardware, software, connecting to the internet, and finding discounts on products and services offered to nonprofit organizations.

11. Network For Good
https://www.networkforgood.com/

Network for Good is a charity portal founded in November 2001 by AOL-Time Warner, Cisco Systems, and Yahoo!. Charities large and small can find extensive resources here to assist in their online fundraising efforts. Even more valuable is the service it provides to charities that register, enabling them to place customized fundraising software on their own Web pages (the basic fee is $200/month) to permit donors to make secure, online contributions without the charity needing its own merchant account. By December 2020, Network for Good delivered more than $2.54 billion to more than 300,000 charities. I applaud the sponsors for their vision in helping even the smallest charities build an infrastructure to accept real-time credit card donations.

12. Grants.Gov
https://www.grants.gov/

The objective of this site is to level the playing field, so that all eligible organizations, regardless of their size or grantsmanship sophistication, can have a fair opportunity to receive federal grants. The site directs grant seekers to funding programs offered by 26 grant-making federal agencies that aggregately award more than $500 billion annually from more than 1,000 different grant programs to state and local governments, academia, nonprofits, and other organizations. It not only makes it easier for organizations to find grants of interest; it streamlines the paperwork needed to apply for them and permits the entire process to be conducted online. All application forms, financial report data in support of organizational audit and performance measurement activities, grant management procedures, and information about grant programs have been standardized across these participating agencies. The site hosts everything an organization needs to find, apply, and manage a federal grant. Even grant notifications are made electronically. Site visitors download forms, work on them offline, and then submit completed applications electronically, saving hours of time and money. The site is divided into sections that help you engage in a six-step process, consisting of finding grant opportunities of interest, downloading the grant application package, registering with a Central Contract Registry, registering with a credentials provider, registering at the site to submit grant applications, and logging on. There is a toll-free number to use to request assistance. And there are resources to making your proposals better (click on "Grant Writing Tips" on the home page). This site is the first place to go if you have any interest in federal grant funds.

13. Texas Nonprofits
https://www.txnp.org/

The mission of this organization is as stated: TXNP strengthens Texas communities by providing up-to-date data and other resources and support via the Internet to help build stronger and bigger nonprofits that can perform and operate professionally, efficiently, and with greater accountability; TXNP also strives to facilitate and encourage connections between charitable causes and potential contributors. At the time of the review in February 2021, there were 21 Texas-based nonprofit jobs posted on the site. Here you can subscribe to a free e-newsletter that has articles of interest to the Texas nonprofit sector.

14. Secretary of State's Nonprofit Organization Business Filings page
https://www.sos.state.tx.us/corp/nonprofit_org.shtml

This site goes beyond having the forms and publications that are perfunctorily found on similar sites in other states. Here you can find valuable information and links to other Texas government sites that go far beyond what one might expect, including links here about how to qualify for Texas nonprofit tax exemptions.

15. Texas Community Building With Attorney Resources (Texas C-BAR)
https://www.trla.org/nonprofits

The mission of this organization, founded in 2000 with the support of the Texas Bar Foundation, is to improve the quality of life for low-income populations in Texas by providing pro bono business law resources to nonprofits and microentrepreneurs. There are lots of resources on this site of value to those in Texas who wish to startup and run a nonprofit organization, including a comprehensive, 20-page guide, Forming a Nonprofit Tax-Exempt Corporation in Texas, last updated in September 2018. Also of value is a 96-page booklet Forming a Nonprofit Tax-Exempt Corporation in Texas, also updated in 2018. Supplementing this publication is additional legal material, links to state and federal forms and publications, and lots of links to advice and other information. Perhaps the most valuable part of this site is access to C-Bar's Pro Bono Legal Referral Program. Eligible nonprofits are matched with qualified attorneys that will handle transactional and corporate legal matters on a pro bono basis. To apply, see: *https://www.trla.org/nonprofits*

16. Center for Nonprofit Studies (Austin Community College)
https://www.nonprofitaustin.org/resources/

This site, in addition to information about the institution's nonprofit leadership and management certificate programs, has a "nonprofit resources" page with links to scores of Web sites of interest in practitioners and academicians. From the menu, you can find a useful gateway to Texas and federal information about starting up a nonprofit, managing risk, and accessing a useful video/webinar library, along with the latest nonprofit news from national publications and back issues of the Center's own newsletter. Click on "downloadable resources" for access to publications on how to start up a charity in Texas, and links to other useful documents.

Tips:

- Subscribe to a general nonprofit electronic mailing list to keep current with what your colleagues in the field are thinking and discussing.

- Use popular search engines and search on your own organization's name. Take steps to ensure that what you find is accurate and up to date.

- Protect your domain names by paying your fees on time.

- Look at the websites of organizations similar to yours and see how they are harnessing the power of the internet.

- Make sure you are comfortable with the legal ramifications of e-commerce applications—such as privacy, security, copyright, and tax collection—before launching an e-commerce initiative.

Chapter 23
Fundraising on the Internet

by Gary Grobman and Gary Grant

Synopsis: The internet assists, but does not replace, traditional fundraising efforts. While not without its problems, there are many creative ways to mount a successful online fundraising campaign. The internet is a useful tool for development staff for use in prospect research, direct marketing, major gifts, corporate and foundation relations, and special events.

Editor's Note: This chapter is a summary of material that appeared in the book, Fundraising Online: How To Raise Serious Money for Your Nonprofit Organization *published by White Hat Communications in 2007. Some minor updates have been applied.*

On Tuesday evening, January 12, 2010, a magnitude 7.0 quake struck about 10 miles southwest of Haiti's capital, Port-au-Prince. Within minutes, Facebook and Twitter users viewed messages such as "Text 'HAITI' to 90999 to donate $10 to Red Cross relief efforts!" The American Red Cross raised $3.4 million just from text message donations in the first 36 hours following news of the disaster, an amount that increased to more than $31 million during the following four weeks. When another devastating natural disaster struck in Northern Japan on March 11, 2011, scores of charities competed to raise funds using the power of technology, harnessing social networking and other websites. The American Red Cross raised approximately $169.5 million during the first month of appeals, with text-message contributions accounting for more than $4 million of that total.

Of the $173 million raised by the International Red Cross within the first few weeks after the 2004 tsunami in the Indian Ocean, $73 million was donated via the organization's website, exceeding the total donated online after the September 11th terrorist attack. More than 45% of Catholic Relief Service's donations in response to the tragedy came online—almost $12 million. International relief organizations such as CARE, Save the Children, and Direct Relief International were all swamped with online donations. Doctors Without Borders/Médecins Sans Frontières (MSF), recipient of the 1999 Nobel Peace Prize, took what is believed to be an unprecedented step in January 2005 and raised almost $20 million for its tsunami relief efforts—and then decided that further fundraising would be counterproductive. According to a posting on the organization's website within about ten days after the disaster, the organization was inundated by donations, largely via its website's secure form. MSF noted that "at this time, MSF estimates that we have received sufficient funds for our currently foreseen emergency response in South Asia." MSF directed donors to donate either to the organization's general fund or to other international relief organizations.

In August 2005, hurricanes Katrina and Rita in the gulf coast of the U.S. resulted in 24-hour coverage by the news networks, followed by an almost constant appeal during commercial breaks to make cash contributions. More than a billion dollars appears to have been contributed online to the American Red Cross. In the first two weeks after Katrina, the Red Cross raised $439.5 million for relief efforts, and $227 million of that came in through the internet—according to the September 15, 2005 article about it in the *Chronicle of Philanthropy*. Impressive!

The spike in online giving has continued unabated since we first started writing about this topic in the late 1990s. According to South Carolina-based Blackbaud, a nonprofit technology consulting firm, cyber donations rose by 34.5 percent in 2010. Online donations accounted for 7.6 percent of all fundraising in 2010, which included data from nearly 2,000 nonprofits nationwide.

The Chronicle of Philanthropy's annual survey of online giving continues to show healthy growth, mirroring the results of the Blackbaud survey. Online giving expanding 34% in 2010 over the previous year for organizations in the Philanthropy 400—those charities that raise the largest amount of donations from private sources.

When we co-wrote the book *The Wilder Nonprofit Field Guide to Fundraising on the Internet* in 1999, our enthusiastic endorsement of using the internet for fundraising was met with some healthy skepticism from the nonprofit community. There were lingering questions about security of data, privacy, and the cost—in both time and money—of buying and maintaining the hardware and software necessary to take advantage of this new medium for attracting donations. There were also cultural barriers to overcome—such as the level of comfort donors would have to share their credit card information online and the virulent reaction most of us have to unsolicited email solicitations, often considered to be "spam." Adding to the confusion was a lack of clarity with respect to how state regulators viewed charitable contributions solicited via the internet.

Additionally, there were trust factors with which to grapple, such as whether to authorize third-party, for-profit providers to manage technology issues for nonprofit organizations. Doing so would permit leadership and staff of nonprofit organizations to focus on their primary missions. But it would also entail trusting outside organizations, which may or may not share the nonprofit's values, with both charitable contributions and sensitive data. A damaging scandal in 2003 involving PipeVine, one such third party provider—ironically a nonprofit itself—profoundly affected how we view relationships between charities and outside vendors with respect to being the steward for charitable donations. PipeVine, a donation processing application service provider, was forced to shut down operations in 2003 after it failed to deliver an estimated $19.1 million in contributions it collected, most of which were on behalf of California's Bay Area United Way. It could be years before nonprofit organizations recover from the fallout of the PipeVine scandal and again become comfortable working with outside organizations in managing online fundraising efforts.

Now, as we survey the landscape and chronicle the successes and failures of online fundraising, we have to report that many of these same issues—security, privacy, cultural adjustment, trust, and government regulation—have yet to be completely resolved to our satisfaction.

We continue to urge caution regarding these issues, but our earlier strong endorsement of using the internet for fundraising has proven warranted as it has clearly become a vital part of the operations of virtually every nonprofit organization. Today, the online donations generated by the Japan and Haiti earthquakes, the 2011 Mississippi River flooding and tornado outbreak, and the ALS ice bucket challenge experience have validated that the internet is quickly becoming the method of choice for donors who want to respond immediately to do something tangible to help those in need, whether they live next door or on the other side of the globe.

"The internet has gone from being one of several channels used by nonprofits for fundraising to being—in some cases—the primary vehicle being used to generate donations," says Dr. Harry Gruber, founder and CEO of Kintera. "Key reasons for this explosion in internet fundraising are efficiency for the organization and convenience for supporters. Donors are realizing that it's much easier to make a difference immediately with an online gift than by mailing a check."

Internet fundraising has become much more than simply having a "donate here" button linked to a page that can process credit card transactions. Online donations to charities made through third-party online charity portals, such as Network for Good and JustGive.org, have skyrocketed; both recorded a doubling of the number of people making gifts in this manner between 2002 and 2003. Network for Good boasts on its website (as of December 2020) that it has raised more than $2.54 billion for charities since 2001.

The direct appeal by charities to give money is only one strategy available via the internet. New models, assisted by sophisticated advances in technology, are providing innovative ways for charities to generate donor dollars.

According to The Hunger Site *(https://thehungersite.greatergood.com/click-togive/ths/home),* visitor clicks on a button embedded on the site's Web page resulted in almost four million pounds of food being donated for distribution to groups such as Mercy Corps and America's Second Harvest in 2013.

Much has changed in the ways charities use the internet to raise funds in the two decades since we first collaborated on a book about internet fundraising. One conclusion we have drawn from watching this online communications revolution is that online fundraising is not likely to replace its conventional, off-line counterparts any time soon. We certainly do not recommend that organizations drop their direct mail programs, telephone solicitation, charitable auctions, and face-to-face appeals because of the availability of raising funds via the internet. But we do see using the internet for fundraising as another tool in the fundraiser's toolbox, with its distinctive advantages and disadvantages, and as an attractive strategy to pursue.

With the advance of technology and creative business models advanced by third-party providers, even the smallest nonprofit can build and display a Web-based fundraising "public face" that will generate both funds and public support. The "playing field" has been leveled on the internet. Even the smallest nonprofit can create a sophisticated website with e-philanthropy and e-commerce functions that has the look and feel of the largest nonprofits with full-time Webmasters. The price of entry into building a highly attractive, professional website for the typical nonprofit is a few dollars a month for a host and some sweat equity. There are many Web hosting services that will even provide free Web space for nonprofits. Free and moderately priced content management software makes website design and content updating a breeze for the expert and novice alike.

If you are not taking advantage of the internet to raise funds for your organization, you are missing out on an opportunity to take your organization to the next level. It is not as hard to raise funds on the internet as you might think.

In putting together an online fundraising strategy, it is helpful to consider what makes online fundraising different from more conventional methods, such as direct mail, telephone solicitation, face-to-face meetings, and fundraising events. Doing so will permit you to take advantage of the strengths offered by online fundraising, and address how you will take into account its limitations.

Advantages of Internet Fundraising

Among the advantages are—

- The internet has a systemized culture that offers potential donors an invitation to find your organization.

  Traditionally, nonprofit organizations reach out to potential donors by purchasing targeted mailing lists, advertising in print publications, and culling newspaper articles for information about those with substantial wealth for future follow-up communication. Through the use of links from other websites, search engines, social networking sites, online and print directories, and even word of mouth, potential donors will find your organization even if you have not found a way to contact them directly. Your organization can enhance this possibility by publicizing its website through news releases and other organizational communications and publications. Read on for practical advice on attracting new visitors to your organization's website and keeping your visitors returning. The best such efforts lead donors to bookmark your site or link it to their personal home pages and blogs.

- There is almost universal access to the internet and increasing comfort with online transactions.

Even those without their own computers have access to the internet through their local schools and libraries, and free email accounts are available to everyone with the motivation to sign up for one. People who only a few years ago didn't have an email account eagerly participate in eBay auctions, purchase airline tickets and hotel rooms online, buy and sell securities, and examine PDF-format 990s online before they consider making a donation.

- Potential donors can make "contact" with your organization 24 hours a day, seven days a week from anywhere in the world for virtually no incremental cost on their part.

Donors can find your website's "donate here" button at any time of the day or night from any computer that has internet access. Free or inexpensive software makes it practical for online forms to capture and process identifying information, payment information, and acknowledge a gift in the blink of an eye, providing the donor the instant gratification that is unavailable through many conventional fundraising methods. Compare making an online donation to the hassles of writing a check, filling out a paper form, finding a stamp and envelope, and taking the envelope to the post office. Or waiting for the organization's office to open in the morning to call in a pledge. By that time, your donor may have gone back to sleep and forgotten that he or she even wanted to make a donation.

- In many cases, raising money online is cheaper and faster than traditional fundraising methods.

Compare making a change in a direct mail fundraising brochure to making the same change to the online brochure. Solicitation materials can be modified electronically at any time at virtually no cost, with no extra charges for color. Full-color, glossy, print brochures are often thrown away without having been read and are costly to update. Online fundraising messages can incorporate animations, scrolling messages, and flashing screens that make Web pages more dynamic than their print counterparts. These flashy bells and whistles can be added at no additional cost. Almost instantaneously, and at virtually no cost, your computer can transmit thousands of electronic newsletters, each containing information of interest to your organization's supporters, as well as a subtle request for funds to finance a new service or program. There are no long distance charges, such as are incurred by a broadcast fax. Your telephones are not tied up if you use a Web-based service for this task. Responses (in the form of online donations) can literally come in within seconds, compared to the weeks required just to lay out and publish a print version of an organization's newsletter or fundraising brochure.

- The internet is less intrusive and less annoying than many conventional methods of fundraising.

Direct mail and telephone solicitation appeals too often annoy and alienate. Both are getting less efficient: sending charitable bulk mail is getting more costly.

Telephone appeals are not as simple as in the past as a result of the popularity of "do-not-call" lists, caller ID, and other methods that potential donors use to screen calls from sources they do not know. To generate one donation from such a call, the organization must contact many individuals, most of whom will view your organization's contact as annoying.

Your fundraising message can be delivered by email and read at a time that is convenient for the reader, who actually has signed up to receive it (along with other communications). While you won't want to send "spam" messages to ask for funds, there are several techniques you can use (see pages 341-344) that ethically and appropriately rely on email to raise funds.

- Internet fundraising can easily be integrated with other marketing and promotional materials and programs.

Solicitations for donations can be coordinated with other features of an organization's website, such as being included in an electronic newsletter, posted on donor recognition Web pages, on links to an organization's sales of goods and services, and with testimonials about the organization that indirectly enhance opportunities for giving. Individuals will visit your website for many reasons other than to make a donation. A functional website can plant the seeds of future giving and make it convenient for those who make spur-of-the-moment gifts based on what they see on your site.

- There are decreased transaction costs for internet-based donation processing and donor outreach efforts.

New business models make it easy to partner with third parties to streamline the online donation process and reach donors who otherwise might never have heard of the organization. Computers using sophisticated software automate many processes, such as accounting, database management, donor acknowledgment, and contact management, which previously relied on time-consuming work by staff. Many of these useful software packages can be purchased off the shelf, obviating the need to rely on third party providers.

- There are increased opportunities to build positive relationships with the business community.

Many for-profit businesses are willing to sponsor the websites of charities, usually with no more than a "thank-you" or a link (typically in the form of the sponsor's logo) from your site to the sponsor's own website. Internet models such as "click-to-give," online shopping malls, and charity portals are innovatively harnessing the power of the internet to cement relationships between the business community and nonprofits that can carry over to relationships involving non-internet collaborations.

Disadvantages of Internet Fundraising

Using the internet for fundraising has its disadvantages, as well.

- The online medium can be impersonal compared to face-to-face fundraising.

Online fundraising, with rare exceptions—such as when using real-time conferencing—is not face-to-face. The personal, human contact, with the ability to read, interpret, and respond to body language and other non-text cues, is an important component of fundraising, particularly when soliciting large gifts. There are limitations in relying on only what can be viewed on a computer screen to communicate.

- Government regulation of online fundraising is unsettled.

There are unresolved legal and regulatory issues that have surfaced as a result of online fundraising. Among them are the degree to which the states regulate it, and what the roles are of third party for-profit dot-coms that agree to serve as intermediaries between donors and charities.

- There are vulnerabilities as a result of having to rely on for-profit third parties.

Many charities are unwilling or unable to build the infrastructure to seek and process online donations. For-profit providers are available to offer these services (see Chapter 22). Many of them have no track record for reliability, ethical conduct, or financial stability. In addition, new business models have been created that involve partnerships and affiliation agreements with for-profits. The need for clear agreements between charities and these third parties raises issues of the transaction costs of creating contracts, motivation, opportunities for outright fraud, privacy with respect to sensitive donor and charity data, and the potential inability of a charity to control a third party's use of that charity's logo. Abuse by third party providers in the name of a charity can stain a reputation that took years to build. The PipeVine scandal of 2003 placed a pall over relationships between charities and those who wish to help them raise funds. That said, there are scores of reputable for-profit application service providers (ASPs) that have exemplary relationships with their nonprofit clients.

Most charities are recognizing that, in almost every case, the advantages of using the internet to supplement traditional fundraising far outweigh the disadvantages. Almost every major charity in the United States has reported raising significant revenues utilizing the internet.

Most organizations do not dedicate staff solely to internet fundraising. Instead, most development teams are integrating internet approaches into their existing fundraising programs. So the question for these organizations is not necessarily, "How can I raise support online?" The more particular question may be, "How can the internet enhance our annual appeals, our major gift program, our fundraising events, and our capital campaigns?"

Direct Marketing

Organizations of all types utilize basic direct marketing to reach the broadest possible public for support. Through mailing campaigns, these organizations strive to gain vital revenue to maintain their operations. The goals of a direct marketing effort are to build a mailing list as large as possible, as engaged as possible, and abundant with the names and addresses of those who support loyally, often in unrestricted dollars.

The challenges posed by direct marketing are ideally addressed by Web-based efforts. First, the Web provides a cost-effective way to help the public know about the organization. For large national organizations, a Web presence is absolutely vital and most likely to result in people seeking and finding their way to the organization. But even on the local level, a Web presence will lead to results.

The Community Food Bank (CFB) in Tucson, Arizona *(https://www.communityfoodbank.org/Locations/Tucson)* set up its website hoping that the local community would learn about what it was trying to do and support its efforts. In only six months, the organization began seeing donations coming in every day through its website. A year later, donations of up to $1,000 were given regularly online.

Attract new donors

Direct marketing online may also attract a different kind of donor. The Community Food Bank was used to receiving support primarily from those over 50 giving through traditional direct marketing efforts. A survey of the organization's new online constituency demonstrated a dramatic increase in donors who were in their 30s and 40s. This younger contributor was being engaged for the first time thanks simply to an internet marketing approach.

Build the giving "habit"

Websites as a form of direct marketing are also credited for larger and repeated giving. Consider that most donors who respond to annual solicitations or direct marketing appeals give according to their income level. This contrasts with major donors, who give based on their assets. The size of an annual gift is based on disposable funds after meeting one's spending and saving needs at the time. When a gift is made only once each year, then the organization may only receive the contribution the person can afford in the particular month when the gift is made. Donors who give monthly will therefore tend to give larger gifts than those who give once in a year. Most donors do not save their disposable income each month to preserve their ability to give the largest contribution over the course of the year.

Promote monthly giving habits

For this reason, many organizations are seeing the value in promoting monthly giving habits. Donors who click to give often develop such habits. This is likely to be an especially effective mechanism for churches and temples to which contributions are often made in the form of monthly or weekly gifts. An online appeal may make it easier, especially for individuals who miss attending services in a given week. Any organization, however, that hopes to increase repeat giving will be served well by offering website giving options consistent with this approach.

Although monthly giving helps individuals maximize their philanthropy to organizations they care about, it is inconvenient to write a check that often. It requires time, stamps, and envelopes, and if any one of those is missing when the donor is ready to give, then the donor may not send the gift at all that month. Some organizations attempt to encourage frequent giving by mailing more often or soliciting pledges to be paid monthly and providing the materials to make the gift, but this is costly and may not appeal to all donors who are already inundated by mail.

Giving online addresses all of these concerns. It allows monthly giving habits to form without the inconveniences. Increasingly, people are getting used to paying their monthly bills online. Many donors are willing to support organizations in the same manner. Giving donors the option to automate giving or to give monthly shows that the organization is service oriented.

Cultivate a community of donors

Another aspect of Web-based direct marketing is the opportunity to cultivate a relationship with a large constituency. Direct marketers know that engagement is necessary to maintain their constituency's support over time. At a minimum, organizations need to communicate with donors and engage them in a participatory way. Personalization is important as organizations seek to build a real relationship with their donor public.

Conveying information can be a challenge if carried out primarily through direct marketing appeals. Letters and brochures convey only so much information. As a result, most are drafted to the needs of the largest segment of the donor public. A shotgun approach is necessary for effective fundraising. Thus, for example, if an environmental organization expects that the majority of its donors are more moved by hearing about its latest advocacy efforts than they are by learning about environmental impact research, then its appeals will likely focus on the former and neglect the latter. It's simply impractical to appeal to the smaller segments of the organization's constituency. A website, however, allows visitors to go to whatever topic interests (and moves) them, and these visitors can be invited to contribute while there.

Make giving easy

Several direct marketing fundraisers shared that online fundraising reduced barriers to giving. They advised us to make sure the option to give is pervasive on your site. The button to make a donation should exist on every page. Donors should not be required to leave what they are reading to navigate your site to find the place where a gift can be made. When possible, fundraisers can also relate the value of giving right at that point. How would $50 help advance the advocacy efforts of the organization? How would the same gift affect vital research supporting the cause?

Integrate and reinforce traditional direct appeals

Another helpful technique is to integrate mailings, phone appeals, and print ad forms of direct marketing with the organization's website. Repetition is often valuable in direct marketing. One message is easily missed. A letter can be tossed out because it is received at an inconvenient time. The website is a place where the same message can be viewed just because it's available when the donor wants to read it—even if that's at 3 a.m. Repetition helps to ensure that the message is seen.

Repetition may also strengthen the message. Seeing an image online that was previously seen in a magazine ad or reading a story that was heard in a phone call reinforces the message. The organization looks well organized and lively when something received in another medium is carried through online. This can demonstrate that the website is being maintained daily, consistently with other communications. Not everyone reads the "last updated" line to determine this.

One organization we spoke with tracks the relationship between its traditional media approaches and the website. A mailing, for example, will often refer the donor public to a particular place within the organization's website. The resulting traffic to that page can be tracked as another way to test the reaction to the mailing. From there, similar tracking can be done to determine if donors are then going to the donations page and making a gift. Over time, such research can be essential to perfecting a direct marketing approach to fundraising.

Engage donors in the organization

Communicating effectively with donors will help increase giving, but actively engaging donors can truly raise the bar on contributions. In an email newsletter, the Brookfield Zoo offered recipients the chance to name the latest zoo baby. This kind of participation encourages individuals to click from the email to the website and feel as if they are actively participating in the life of the organization.

The zoo's engagement, however, began earlier when individuals first opted to receive the email newsletter. Giving people the chance to opt in is a major tool for direct marketing fundraisers. By opting in, the subscriber gives an organization permission to write (and to solicit). This is familiar to many membership organizations, universities, and clubs. Such organizations have long benefited from the bond their constituency has agreed to accept from the start. Other organizations have been disadvantaged by inherently temporary, arms-length, one-sided relationships. If donors send checks in response to a direct mail appeal, they are not necessarily going to view themselves as a part of that organization in the long term. But if they ask to receive communications online, they may do so—especially if the organization takes the opportunity to create a personalized and welcoming environment.

Establish a bond with discussion forums

Donor discussion forums are another form of engagement. They can help a constituency establish a bond with the organization and a relationship for appeals that feel more individualized.

Dads and Daughters (*http://www.joekelly.org/dads-and-daughters*), for example, is an organization that has grown around an opt-in discussion forum. DADS seeks to help fathers be successful parents for their daughters and engages them in addressing cultural and commercial messages that may negatively affect girls or damage their self-esteem. From the first page, visitors are encouraged to sign up for the electronic mailing list. The email discussions are two-way. Participants can raise everyday parenting challenges and get input from other members. Email action alerts are sent to the list, as well as requests for support—from financial to in-kind needs. This works because each person has opted in and feels sufficiently engaged, so the requests for support are viewed as appropriate, even welcomed as convenient. (Author Note: this organization is no longer in operation.)

This approach is obviously more challenging for larger, well-established organizations, but any degree of engagement of one's donor public can enhance the level of giving, the frequency, and donor loyalty.

Even the simple act of registering at a site can create some level of engagement. Some organizations will encourage website visitors to register. Then when they return and "sign in," they get a degree of personalization from the site itself. Beginning with a "welcome back Mary" sign, the site can also be made to recognize various preferences or past activities. Online message boards, for example, may show what has been read and what has not.

Password protect the site

Having a password into a website encourages visitors to bookmark the site. By registering visitors, an organization can also request information. Visitors may voluntarily share a range of data on their interests, their contact information, including phone number, and even wealth information. Some organizations will retain credit card information with confidentiality. This can be done to make it even easier to give regularly. Donors don't even have to take their cards from their wallet or purse.

Prospect Research

Prospect research includes finding information not only on individuals, but also on corporate and private foundations and government agencies that will provide funds. It encompasses collecting and analyzing information to help fundraisers find out the ability and inclination of prospective donors to donate, and obtaining clues to the best strategy to assist donors in providing the largest gift that would feel comfortable to them. Good prospect research cannot guarantee successful "asks," but it can provide critical information about the background, needs, style, financial capacity, approachability, and interests of someone who can make or break your fundraising campaign. Before the internet revolution, prospect researchers used newspapers and magazines, real estate records, data and mailing lists purchased from private companies or other charities, annual reports from businesses, industry association directories, and biographical directories (such as Who's Who in America) to cull for juicy leads. Today, there is a plethora of electronic sources, many free, dwarfing those available a decade ago.

Treat $50 donors today as if they will be $5 million donors tomorrow

One cannot ever know when any particular $50 donor today may become a potential $5 million donor tomorrow, and thus it is important to treat every donor and potential donor as if his or her donation is the most important the organization will ever receive. Yet the mathematics are that a single $5 million donation has as much purchasing power as 100,000 donations of $50 each, and with a lot less transaction cost. No wonder charities are willing to make substantial investments in prospect research.

Find prospects using free online databases

When Gary Grobman speaks at conferences making his PowerPoint presentations on the subject of online fundraising, one prospect research technique never fails to leave his audience ooohing and aaahing. He points his Web browser to *https://www.melissa.com/v2/lookups/*. Then he clicks on "Campaign Contributors." Then he asks a fundraiser in the audience to provide him with a 5-digit ZIP Code of an upscale neighborhood in the area of his or her charity. When Gary submits that into the online form, it returns information about individuals who made contributions of at least $200 to a federal election campaign. Inevitably, the list is a "who's who" of philanthropists. It doesn't take much imagination to think about how such a database can be of use to fundraisers. Other sites that are favorites of professional prospect researchers include Edgar Online People *(https://www.dfinsolutions.com/products/edgar-online)*, DNB Hoover's Online *(https://www.dnb.com/products/marketing-sales/dnb-hoovers.html/)*, Forbes.com *(https://www.forbes.com/?sh=4d601c502254)*, and David Lamb's Prospect Research Page *(http://www.lambresearch.com/)*. Some of these sites are free; others require a subscription.

Identify interests, motivations, backgrounds, and financial capacity

In 2003, Jerold Panas wrote a riveting two-part column in *Contributions Magazine* about his harrowing, semi-successful experience in making a $50 million "ask" on behalf of a university fundraising campaign. Obviously, the preparation required for such an endeavor is more than, let's say, seeking a $50 donation, because the stakes are so much higher. Veteran fundraiser and *Washington Post* columnist Bob Levey often tells the story of a neophyte fundraiser who approached the legendary philanthropist and *Washington Post* owner Katherine Graham seeking a major gift for a worthy cause, only to be immediately shown the door after calling her "Katie."

Major gift officers and other high-level fundraising and executive staff want to know their prospects. They want to understand their potential so they can make realistic assessments for future solicitations. They want to understand their personalities so they can approach them in the right way. They want to learn their motivations so they can focus on what appeals to each particular individual and avoid pitfalls that might turn them off to the organization. They want ideas for making initial introductions.

The internet offers an efficient tool to access lots of publicly available information about individuals. Careful online research can answer many questions about potential donors.

Major Gifts

Major gift fundraisers work closely with a small set of an organization's top donors. Their donors contrast with annual supporters in making "stop and think" contributions ranging from once every few years to once in a lifetime. Major gifts tend to be given for special purposes—often restricted to projects with specific measurable outcomes. How do the internet and the organization's website and electronic communications assist the major gifts team?

Don't use the internet as a crutch

Fundraisers often view the internet with great hope for finding the key information and insight they feel they need. The reality is that the internet can be useful, but ought not be used as a crutch. For the most part, prospect research should be left to prospect researchers (if your organization has them), particularly for determining giving capacity. While many cannot help but "Google" a prospect before a visit or while planning an initial contact, fundraisers should be careful not to rely too heavily on cursory research or believe that they can truly understand the person from whatever they find. Major gift work still requires the traditional emphasis on face-to-face interactions for getting to know one's prospects and building a real relationship.

In addition to aiding in prospect research, the internet can be a valuable aid in all aspects of major gift fundraising, including identifying new donors, cultivating relationships, solicitation, and stewardship.

Find hidden potential donors using the internet

Identifying major gifts donors is one of a fundraiser's greatest challenges. Few donor prospects contact an organization requesting to have their relationships with the organization managed by a major gifts officer. Instead, they are often initially hidden. They may be hidden in the public at large, interested in the mission of your organization, but not yet connected. Or they may be hidden among the current annual donors. Some of the wealthiest individuals still give $25 or $50 gifts in response to direct mail appeals.

Sharing philanthropic news within your organization can also be an effective way to help encourage those who support far below their capacity to perhaps step forward and give more. Major gift stories provide a wonderful opportunity to communicate not only about the programs of the organization, but about the exciting support and endorsement a major gift demonstrates. To the extent possible, major gifts fundraisers want these stories to be shared broadly to set the highest possible bar on generous giving and to build a stronger culture of philanthropy throughout their donor constituency.

As you identify major donor prospects, the next step is to begin building a stronger affinity with the organization. This can mean several things, each of which may be enhanced through internet tools.

Educate major donors about the organization

Potential major donors need to get to know the organization and its mission over time. There is an education process that must happen. While the most important efforts will be face-to-face, you can enhance these interactions and develop a closer connection through email communications and referring donors to specific parts of your website. Email takes on a very different nature when the recipient knows the sender. If you are managing the fundraising for a political campaign, for example, and you tell a particular donor that the candidate will email directly with some information, this is quite different from getting a general letter from the candidate to a larger number of people.

In short, email can be a convenient form of communication but also extremely personal if it is combined with other one-on-one approaches. A fundraiser might send a note referencing a particular topic or article on your website for which they know the donor has interest. Fundraisers can facilitate communications with board members, leaders, and others as they help the donor understand how they operate and work to accomplish their goals. You might even have a program beneficiary write to a prospective donor to share information about the impact the organization has had.

If your organization has developed good case materials, you may want to adopt the common practice among successful fundraising programs of including case statements online in PDF format. You can see numerous samples of these simply by entering "case statement" into any popular search engine. In addition to educating donors about their organizations, fundraisers need to listen to major gift prospects and understand their needs, interests, and motivations. Again, the addition of internet communication into the traditional mix can help escalate input both ways.

Keep track of the relationship between donors and the organization

Similarly, major gift donors and prospects often need to develop a relationship with leadership and trust in their ability to guide the organization successfully. Enhancing face-to-face relationships through online communications can increase the leadership's ability to engage with prospects. Your organization's leader can interact with higher quality communications as well as with a greater quantity of donors. Major gifts fundraisers should actively recommend, draft, and track email conversations between leadership and top prospects.

Leadership should also remember to share valuable discussions with individuals who are supporting the organization. Remember to send a blind copy to relevant staff. Private conversations should be respected, but when appropriate, sharing information can avoid duplication of efforts or wasted time later.

Include contact information on the website

Although you may have given a donor prospect your card, it is common for anyone to misplace a number and seek you out through your website. websites that lack simple staff directories can create frustrations, and visitors may feel that you have failed to focus on helping them navigate your organization. With a staff directory, a donor will gain a more positive impression. Being able to "see" the staff they are trying to find will help make the communications seem more personal, warm, and friendly.

Ultimately, major gifts work leads to solicitations. Here your website can again support your efforts, beginning by detailing your organization's giving opportunities. Whether or not you have a case statement online, you should also detail major gift projects that can be funded. Because major donors tend to need specificity, it may be wise to give substantial details. Rather than just mentioning the organization's top giving levels, you can provide a description of how the organization can use gifts of $25,000 or $100,000 or $1 million. Your description can provide the impact, the visibility to the donor, and the reason why these opportunities are so high a priority.

Develop Web pages that encourage major gifts

While it may be unlikely that a donor will randomly visit your site and contact you interested in one of your top giving opportunities, the presence of these at the website can support gift discussions. Keeping these online reaffirms for donors that they authentically do represent the organization's top priorities. And you never know when your organization will receive a donation windfall as a result.

Planned Giving

In addition to presenting top gift opportunities online, you should also detail giving vehicles. Many organizations provide some information about planned giving options, estate gifts, and instructions for giving stock gifts or mutual funds. Such practical information can help donors as they consider making major contributions. Try to ensure that your site has all the details a donor would need and up-to-date contact information in case they have questions.

Here are some examples of planned giving pages:

American Red Cross *(https://www.redcrosslegacy.org/)*
Harvard Alumni *(https://alumni.harvard.edu/college/college-giving/gift-planning?utm_source=HCF_appeal&utm_medium=print&utm_campaign=phonathon12)*

In presenting both giving opportunities and giving vehicles, what can be particularly helpful are actual donor demonstrations. If donors are willing, you can share their stories as models for others. Major donors often are pleased to do this, because it ensures that their leadership gift is actually leading. Suppose you wish to show what a charitable gift annuity can do for a donor. While you probably don't want to share the exact financial details of any individual donor's gift annuity, you can still articulate and quote a donor to demonstrate why such gifts can be mutually advantageous.

The same can be done for giving options—adding a personal touch to your list of giving opportunities. In this way, you gain the endorsement of past donors to promote new major gift philanthropy. Donors might be asked to share what motivated them to make the gift. They can share their appreciation for the visibility or the chance a gift gave them to remember a loved one. They can articulate the impact they have seen their gift have and how that made them feel. All of this can make a significant difference to a new donor. It will also add value and interesting reading to the giving opportunities section, so you may have better reason to direct donors there.

Post donor recognition pages

Once you have secured a major gift, stewardship and recognition come into play. Here there are many options, and organizations may want to think through it carefully. There is no substantial research on the risks/benefits of recognizing gifts online. Some fundraisers are hesitant. Even if donors approve, they may worry about getting unwanted attention by being put online for their major gift. Organizations may worry that other organizations will fish for the recognition pages and immediately try to "steal away" their donors.

Others are more optimistic and see more value in the gains that publicizing a gift online can have. As we review these options, we leave it to the reader to weigh the pros and cons.

One method of recognizing gifts is to create an online donor board. Many organizations provide donor boards in their buildings, especially museums, universities, theaters, and other places that have high visitor traffic. Donors appreciate donor boards, because they provide visible recognition. Organizations enjoy the opportunity to encourage other gifts. Because websites often attract substantial visibility, an online board may be desirable. We may even see more of these in the future, in particular from organizations that do not have a suitable or sufficiently visible location for a traditional donor board.

Consider posting virtual donor plaques

If an organization is concerned that listing donor names on a donor board may lead to other competing organizations tapping into their donor constituency, it may consider using graphical donor "plaques" instead of a text list. A graphical plaque is even more attractive. It would mean that you put the donor's name on an image that appears like a real-life plaque. As an image, it cannot be found by regular search engine methods, provided that the donor's name is not used as the name of the image file.

A more detailed possibility for donor recognition is to build pages dedicated to donors. These can contain some combination of background on individuals and their families, and the programs they are funding. Such pages can be done in combination with a donor board, allowing individuals to click on the name for more information. Donor boards and donor pages offer the possibility for greater visibility and may make donors feel a greater sense of how they are creating a legacy for the organization.

A variation on this is the online press release. Oftentimes, donors hope for a press release in response to their gifts. Unfortunately, most newspapers and media outlets are not interested in pure philanthropic stories, short of the mega-gifts that happen from time to time. But a formal press release can be posted online and made visible to those visiting the website. While perhaps not as exciting as being in *The New York Times*, such visibility can at least be a practical compromise solution.

Again—be very careful to communicate with every donor as you do anything with his or her name online. Even seemingly harmless forms of recognition, such as attaching a name to a professorship or a program detailed online may upset a donor. Communicating in advance is necessary.

Special Events

A museum organizes an annual gala event. A health organization holds an annual bike-a-thon. A university seeks class gifts in preparation for its big re-union weekend. A political campaign organizes "meet up" events to raise money. A church group plans a concert to raise support.

Events, although all very different, are a mainstay in the fundraising menu of most every kind of nonprofit organization. But what does this have to do with the internet? How can the internet enhance such programs? How can it help them have a bigger impact? How can it help them grow over time? How can it help them attract larger numbers of people? How can it help increase their visibility?

Most special events fundraisers see their role as two-fold. First, they want to raise significant support for their organization while controlling costs. The second objective of special events is to create awareness and visibility for the organization. For this reason, gala events may be lavish affairs.

Increase visibility for your special event

Visibility as an objective serves multiple purposes. Walks, galas, and other high profile events, for example, have helped to educate and make the public more aware of devastating diseases, to move the government to support programs for the poor, and to build excitement about cultural events. Such events have direct mission benefits.

In addition, visibility can serve other fundraising goals. Fundraising events can help to identify new major gift donors or to recognize existing ones. They offer a special visible option for recognizing corporate philanthropy. They provide an opportunity to address a larger donor constituency and to build their knowledge of and commitment to the organization.

Attract corporate sponsorship with similar markets

Understanding the complex goals of a special event fundraiser, we can begin to look at how the internet might be helpful. Let's focus first on corporate event sponsorship. Highly visible special events provide an opportunity to link corporations to philanthropy in a context that is often particularly valued by the company. If a company has a market that is similar to your organization's beneficiary public, then it may be particularly attracted to event sponsorship.

Events covered by the media often acknowledge such philanthropy in a way they never would otherwise. Outright major gifts almost never get major publicity, unless they are extremely large, i.e., in excess of $25 million. But the news will often show a corporate check presentation as small as $10,000, if it is done in the context of a public event of interest.

Develop a page for your special event

As fundraisers look for and approach potential event sponsors, the more visibility they can offer them, the more appealing their proposal will be. Using the organization's website to show how the sponsor's name will be featured is one valuable part of that package, particularly for organizations with heavy traffic. This can be done on a special page dedicated to the event, but linked from the organization's home page. Doing the same in mass email communication to the organization's constituency about the event can be another aspect of this.

Is there value to a special page dedicated to an event like a gala? The short answer is "absolutely!" A page (or section) on a major event gives a fundraiser a chance to create an ongoing album for the event. It should contain photos of the most recent event, as well as substantive information about what the event is accomplishing. Over time, archived pages can be kept at the site, so visitors can look back to years past. A section of the website dedicated to a signature event can be a great point of pride for an organization and for its constituency as the program grows.

First time attendees will have a sense of the event if they visit the page. Individuals may encourage others to purchase seats or tables and may point friends to your site for this information. Previous attendees will enjoy seeing their own pictures there. Donors and sponsors may link to this part of your site.

Over the long run, an internet presence for a major gala event can enhance the program. It can create loyalty in those who have attended in the past and help to broaden the appeal of the event significantly. The gala page can celebrate the visibility achieved each year—linking to news coverage it received.

Put the gala program booklet online

Ultimately, this will all serve to help raise the fundraising for a gala style event. Donors can give through the gala site. Individuals who cannot attend the event might especially enjoy being part of the fundraising action in this way. Some organizations may wish to put their program booklet online and raise the price for a page by adding an internet version of the space in addition to the printed version. Auction items not purchased at the event can be auctioned off after the event, via the website.

In short, the internet gala page can bring a major event to life before and help keep the excitement going after the actual event itself. As participants feel a part of the site through the images and perhaps the words they add there, they will feel more closely bonded to your organization. These feelings of connection to the event and the organization may help plant the seeds for budding major donor relationships.

Create a life-long bond

It is not enough for an organization to have donors merely invest in their mission itself. Investments are made at arms length and may be impersonal. Organizations want donors to develop an emotional and life-long bond—to become part of their family. Similarly, organizations should want their galas to be more than just wonderful parties that people attend because they are fun and for a good cause. It is better if they become family celebrations and gatherings that represent keystone moments on a shared journey to accomplish a vital public interest objective.

Universities and many private high schools and other educational programs know this, as they have long focused on the life-long bond alumni relationships can create. These are celebrated and funds are raised around special class years during reunions. Reunion weekends have organically spawned tremendous innovation and creativity through their Web presence.

The reunion site

All the elements described for galas are regular features of many reunion websites. These sites are graphic intense with pictures of alumni, faculty, and students. These pages are also highly interactive, encouraging visitors to be involved through the site for a year or even more before the actual event. They serve, in this way, to build excitement. Any high school reunion today is likely to have some activity develop through commercial sites such as Classmates.com, Facebook, or similar resources. By the time the event happens, classmates have already connected and begun talking and sharing with one another.

A typical university reunion site will provide the schedule of events (why should anyone depend on the printed version, which is so easily lost?). It will include a listing of the reunion committee members with email addresses, so that everyone can provide input for the event early on. It will have a photo gallery, a full class list, and a variety of links to help graduates get caught up on information about the school today. It will have a section devoted to finding "lost" classmates who have moved away and for whom the event committee has no contact information.

Add a giving section

Of course, it will also have a giving section. These may describe special projects the class members have decided to join together to fund, or it could describe a variety of giving options. Reunion classes enjoy seeing how much they have raised, so a total to date is likely to be included. And just to further enhance the excitement of giving, there may be a friendly competition for the most dollars among different class years.

Many fundraisers feel that the purpose of special reunion fundraising efforts is to "bump up" giving over the alumni donor's lifetime. So while donors may give $25 each year their first few years out, perhaps by their 5th reunion, they will leap to $100 and may remain at about that level until their 10th or 25th, by which time they may leap to being $500 or $1,000 donors. In addition, reunions are events in which major gift giving becomes a special focus for fundraising. The reunion site is designed to help bolster these efforts. If their popularity is any sign, then they are succeeding.

Sometimes reunion sites are predominantly managed by volunteers. The organization might give over some control over the design so that volunteers rather than staff can develop the site. This can be a good idea for any school or organization that is concerned with the staff time it might take to manage a reunion site.

One of the conveniences of a reunion website is the ability for participants to register and pay for their participation in the event. Online registering, however, is turning out to be much more than just a convenience. It's turning out to be a boon for fundraising.

Special events that require registration

Today's walk-a-thon, bike-a-thon, and similar public fundraising events are benefiting hugely from organized online registration and fundraising. These kinds of fundraising events succeed when they are heavily attended. While a gala has limited seating and reunions are limited only to alumni graduates, walks can become enormous events in which hundreds or thousands participate. The sheer number of participants helps achieve the media coverage and visibility sought and the giving, because it's smaller on average, benefits by larger and larger attendance totals.

In years past, a family that was dealing with a devastating illness might join in a walk-a-thon to raise money for that cause. In the weeks before the event, they would take gifts and pledges through their personal solicitation of friends and family. They would call, write, or visit the individuals they were asking. It takes a significant commitment of time to do this.

Organize teams online

Today, most major walks organize their teams online. Commercial resources make this relatively simple to do. Typically, a person connected to the organization signs up online to be a team captain. The event's site will automatically allow a high degree of personalization. The volunteer can add personal pictures, personalize the message, and set his or her personal goals.

The sites then automate much of the fundraising (see *Personal Fundraising Pages* in this chapter). The volunteer just adds the names and addresses of those he or she knows (they can transcribe them all right from their email address book) and decide if they want the pre-written solicitation or if they would like to make it their own. Their friends and family can click right from the email message they get, give the gift by credit card (secured communications, of course), and then appear soon after on a scrolling banner of donors.

The volunteer's donors can return as needed to check on the progress toward the fundraising goal. They may even see the progress in a traditional fundraiser's "thermometer" and might decide to give a bit more to put the team over the top. The volunteer can get regular reports on progress. It's almost like giving them their own fundraising staff.

Generate financial support from nonparticipants

Many elements contribute to making this approach successful. It saves volunteers a lot of time, effort, and money, so they can be more active solicitors. Volunteer fundraisers can reach out to friends and family globally, yet personally. Because it is easier, it engages fundraising from those who may not be quite as focused or dedicated to the organization at this point. In the past, walk teams were comprised mostly of the diehard loyal donors and volunteers. Online fundraising broadens the participation. Many participants may not even attend the walk at all—but are happy to have helped raise the level of philanthropic support for something they do indeed care about.

In addition, donors report that fundraising in this way is simply fun. For many, asking for annual support from friends and family is an excuse to contact them. They may personalize their message for each one to catch up. How many of us need that excuse to contact Uncle Jack or our best friend from high school? The beneficiaries of this are the nonprofit organizations who are gaining greater support and more awareness and visibility for themselves and their missions.

Use automation and volunteers

In essence, this online fundraising technique is creating a mini-gala model, letting volunteers take over everything—providing a place for the event, food, invitations, and so on. All that the organization needs to do is to receive the check and use it wisely. Of course, to be very successful, the organization needs to support these efforts, providing the volunteers with good materials, both videos and printed, to make the event worthwhile for the participants. The most successful house party efforts may involve a phone-in period during which the candidate addresses multiple events simultaneously.

Innovative new and cutting-edge efforts such as these are in their early stages, but there are good signs that they represent how the internet is creating a more diverse set of fundraising practices under the broad net of special events. They appeal particularly to a younger new generation of fundraising volunteer—individuals comfortable with utilizing technology to build grassroots efforts.

Many of these first generation efforts still have a rough feel to them. In the future, we will see them become more elegant and much more common, perhaps in other fundraising venues. How long will it be before we see a neighborhood food pantry or a church group using the internet to support its fundraising in some of these ways and with some of these tools?

Make online fundraising event administration routine

We will also continue to see the internet change special event fundraising in more dramatic ways. Organizations are already exploring the idea of using the internet to actually be "at" a live event. Through video broadcasts over the internet, it is now possible for individuals to attend seminars and hear speeches online. The internet has become a common venue for certain fundraising events.

To sum up, the internet's benefit for special events includes a number of very basic ideas, such as using a website to publicize and draw in more participants and even gifts before and after the event. It includes some important broader concepts, as well, such as employing the internet to help build a different kind of connection to the organization, one that is more participatory and intimate while also more convenient.

Capital Campaigns

The capital campaign has become a way of life for many organizations, especially universities, public radio and television stations, and religious institutions. Not long ago, capital campaigns were held only occasionally and usually for a special need. Today, the planning for the next often begins as soon as the previous one ends. Capital campaigns build public excitement around fundraising. They serve to identify a set of needs and priorities, and in so doing make an organization's strategic plans a little more accessible to the organization's donor constituency. Capital campaigns also help make larger solicitations easier, creating urgency and the motivation of achieving a goal.

As capital campaigns have become more popular, they have given birth to the campaign website. As suggested above, the primary goals of a campaign website are to present the fundraising priorities and to generate excitement around giving.

Typical campaign sites include many or all of the following features:

- *A goal stated on the first page.* This can take the form of a graph or "thermometer" showing progress toward the goal. It will also include stories of key leadership gifts in the campaign.

- *Messages from the campaign chair or others about the effort.* Often these are presented in video or audio clips, as well as text, especially if high profile individuals or celebrities are helping to lead the campaign.

- *A case statement in PDF format.* The traditional case statement provides donors with a well-designed printed piece that explains the needs and attempts to motivate philanthropy toward them.

- *Detailed information about the institution.* Even institutions with complete websites will often reorganize and re-present their factual data, organizational structure, and history. Many campaign websites have a completely separate look from the main website of the organization. The purposes of doing this are to deliberately contrast with what the donors are used to on the site and thus grab their attention, or to create a more polished and prestigious look to appeal to high-scale donors. An organization with an extremely well branded look may simply want to draw greater attention by adopting a new campaign logo with different color schemes and page designs. The University of Chicago did this with its campaign website at *https://alumniandfriends.uchicago.edu/s/communities-giving-societies.* Here even the URL is unique. You can see the logo and color scheme versus the university's home page at: *http://www.uchicago.edu.* If the capital campaign is sufficiently large, then sub-branding or branding differently may be a good strategy. It may not be worth doing for smaller campaigns.

- *A list of needs and complete detail on them, as well as recognition levels.* These may be replicated in the case statement, but don't count on everyone printing out that document.

- *Pictures.* Appropriate pictures here are of people, program beneficiaries, and model construction planned. Some will include video feeds, allowing visitors to monitor 24 hours/day building projects under construction.

- *Current news.* News stories may help ensure that the site looks lively and up-to-date. The campaign website can be viewed as a secondary portal into the organization.

Market to donors rather than to the public

In essence, capital campaign websites recast the organization's online presence and market the organization very specifically to donors rather than the public at large. While the main gateway to the organization typically is focused on its mission, with philanthropy carefully and appropriately woven in, the campaign website can be unabashed in its drive for dollars. In a role reversal, fundraising becomes the highest priority on these pages, and the mission is woven in to show how essential fundraising is to meeting the organization's objectives.

Capital campaigns also often take place at large complex institutions and can serve an ancillary role of unifying multiple fundraising efforts. In a university, they bring together all of the college, graduate, and professional schools toward a common goal. They may connect geographically separate campuses, or organizations with separate chapters. The new Web portal can be a place to reflect that unity and to demonstrate the interconnectedness of an organization with multiple parts.

Online Fundraising Strategies

Email

Email is still considered the "killer application" of the internet, and with good reason. For charities that abuse it, it may well, indeed, earn its name. A charity that purchases a disk with 20 million email names on it and then indiscriminately emails a fundraising solicitation to the list is likely to make a name for itself. That name will be spelled "M-U-D." There is a consensus that using such a strategy is about as injudicious as one can get in using email for fundraising. Our culture accepts the "cost" of wading through junk snail mail, most of it from tax-exempt organizations seeking contributions. Perhaps there is a feeling that the sender at least made some effort to weed out duplicates and, at least, is trying to target the mailing because even the charitable bulk mail postage rate is getting fairly steep these days. Printing fundraising letters, return envelopes, and the "free gift inside" of personalized mailing labels, calendars, or greeting cards must cost something, let alone the cost of designing and sending out the mailing.

Avoiding spamming

We do not (and should not!) as yet feel the same way about unsolicited email. Pornographers, scam artists, crooks "phishing" for personal financial information, and purveyors of illegal drugs send a high percentage of the "spam" mail we all receive. Sending "spam" mail may associate an organization with these types of unsavory operations. No organization should want that.

The culture of participation in the internet community is still evolving. What is not totally clear is what types of email solicitation are acceptable, and what types are the most effective. Communicating organizational needs by email to stakeholders who already have some relationship with the organization, such as donors, board members, and those served by the organization, is usually appropriate. Sending out online newsletters to an organization's stakeholders who have opted in to receive them is even better.

Using email to interact with stakeholders

One legitimate use of direct email is to simply interact with your stakeholders and provide them with information and services that bring them closer to your organization. Email is a cost-effective means for increasing direct communication between your organization's actual and potential donors. Because of the convenience of the "reply" button available within all email programs, it also provides a convenient way for getting feedback. Sharing timely and informative news about what your organization is doing, and plans to do in the future, can keep your organization on the minds of your donors and maintain your visibility. Among information that can be shared with broadcast emails are the following—

- new features added to the organization's website
- requests for volunteers to help the organization with a program or service
- calls to action, such as to send letters or emails to public officials concerning an important, emerging public policy issue
- directions on how to participate in an online or offline survey
- information about an upcoming fundraiser
- details about an upcoming meeting or program (with driving directions).

Of course, even those who have expressed interest in your organization in the past may no longer maintain that enthusiasm. We recommend that you place instructions at the bottom of any mass-distributed email on how to be deleted from the list for future emails.

Collecting email addresses

Almost universally, online fundraising advocates agree that seeking a donor's email address is a positive strategy, even if there are no current plans to communicate with those donors online. Plans can change. Email remains the fastest and cheapest way an organization can communicate, even if it may not be the most appropriate way in every circumstance. But simply having the capacity to contact every stakeholder quickly by email is considered to be a top objective by those of us who give advice about online fundraising.

There are obvious strategies that will increase the percentage of donors who will give your organization their email addresses. Organizations should routinely include "email address" as a field in their donation forms and other forms (such as those used to request additional information from the organization). The online newsletter subscription is also a good method used to harvest email addresses from donors and supporters. Some organizations require Web visitors to register with their email addresses and other identifying information if they want to have access to some features of the site, such as the online community.

Turn your website into a catcher's mitt

The organization's website offers lots of opportunities to obtain email addresses, such as through electronic newsletter subscriptions, online surveys, information requests, email feedback to the organization, and similar online transactions in which the email address is routinely needed to respond. As Mathew Emery, of the application service provider Kintera, explained at a 2004 workshop on e-philanthropy sponsored by the Pennsylvania Association of Nonprofit Organizations, "The website has been (typically) treated like it's a brochure, but it's really a catcher's mitt. You want something on every single page where you can find something about the visitor." According to Emery, even if a donor doesn't make an online donation, online communications have a positive effect on direct mail. His organization found that there was a 10% increase in donations made as a result of a direct mail fundraising piece when an email was sent to donors prior to sending out the direct mail.

"Email to a Friend" strategies

Another fundraising strategy that appears to be effective is the online version of getting organization supporters to write personal letters to those they know, including friends and neighbors, appealing for donations. In the offline version, a charity might make a call to a past donor. Rather than requesting a direct donation, the charity requests that the donor send a note to ten or twenty neighbors requesting a donation. If the donor agrees, the charity provides the names of those it desires to solicit, perhaps a sample letter, and if appropriate, other support.

In the online version of this technique, donors are asked to email their friends and relatives with a donor appeal. The solicitations are not considered spam, because they are coming from personal friends and relatives. Recipients of the solicitations see the communication coming from someone they know, rather than an organization, and are more likely to open the email and respond.

There is increasing evidence that this type of email solicitation is effective. One application service provider, Kintera, acquired by Blackbaud in 2008, developed software to facilitate such online volunteer fundraising, called "Friends Asking Friends®." Hundreds of millions of dollars have been raised using this technique. It is particularly effective for specific fundraising events, in which an organization's supporters email their online contacts about an upcoming charity auction, race/walk, or benefit concert. The Kintera software package has integrated links providing information and the ability to donate or register for the event, and tracks donations and responses (see *Personal Fundraising Pages* in this chapter).

In addition to the obvious "donate here" link on your organization's website, there are new business models that facilitate online fundraising. Among them are creating partnerships with businesses who will provide the charity with funds in exchange for marketing opportunities, holding online charitable auctions, soliciting tribute gifts, creating online shopping malls, and engaging in search engine marketing—which involves placing advertisements on search engine websites that will appear on the search engine query results of those searching on a term related to the organization's mission. For each of these, there are for-profit application service providers (ASPs) to whom organizations can outsource all of the work. Many charities that engage in these strategies do this work in-house.

"Donate Here" Buttons

One obvious way charities have raised funds is by placing a "donate here" link on their website's pages. Clicking on the button links the donor to a secure page (i.e., where the information sent by the donor is encrypted). The page will have an online form that permits the donor to make a contribution and pay by credit card or through PayPal. It will typically also have information about other methods for making donations, such as a form that can be mailed or faxed to the organization, a telephone number to call during business hours to make donations, and information about planned giving. It may also have an offer for a modest "thank you" gift for donors, such as a mug with the organization's logo, a calendar, or a t-shirt.

The page should provide the donor information you need to process the donation, such as payment information, address, telephone number, and email address. The page should also include information such as the organization's address and telephone number, which the donor needs to mail in a check or call in a donation. Even for those donors who do not choose to take advantage of making an online donation, it is useful to request those donors' email addresses on the donation form.

Even for those organizations without merchant accounts to process credit cards or an application service provider who will (see Chapter 22), a clearly visible "donate here" button can link to a page that can be printed out and mailed with a check.

Cause-Related Marketing (CRM)

In her 1999 book, *Cause Related Marketing—Who Cares Wins,* Sue Adkins defined cause-related marketing as "commercial activity by which a business with a product, service or image to market builds a relationship with a cause or a number of causes for mutual benefit." While the term is relatively new, cause-related marketing efforts are often traced back to the 1960s, when the Insurance Company of America offered to make a donation to CARE for every insurance policy it sold. It reached prominence, however, by virtue of a well-publicized effort of American Express begun in 1983, when it pledged to donate a penny to the Statue of Liberty restoration fund for each time its card was used to make a purchase. According to press reports, this strategy was successful in increasing card use by 28% in a single year while raising substantial funds for the Statue of Liberty restoration project.

Since then, scores of mainstream charities have partnered with for-profits to exploit their brand names and raise funds. CRM is not without controversy. A joke continues to circulate about this exploitation: Some see it as "tainted" money, while others see it as " 't ain't enough." Regardless, CRM collaborations are raising millions of dollars for charities, including the American Lung Association, the American Cancer Society, and our personal favorite—the recipients of the $.10 General Mills donates to our kids' schools when we buy their cereal with the "Box Tops for Education" coupons on the top. For more on this revenue-generating strategy, see Chapter 18.

Involve celebrities in cause marketing efforts

In some cases, cause-related marketing can involve three partners—the organization, the corporation, and a celebrity spokesperson. The fundraiser is looking for a good synergy that may influence everyone. A celebrity may want to help a good cause, but may also appreciate positive publicity and a boost to his or her public image. The corporation is seeking increased revenues, brand loyalty, and a positive corporate image. The charity is looking for revenues and increased awareness among the general public.

Relationships built around cause-related marketing can be long-term. A good internet strategy can help cement and maintain the relationship over time. Via email, Web pages, and electronic newsletters, charities can communicate with their stakeholders about these cause-related marketing opportunities.

Tribute Gifts

Tributes are memorial gifts given in the name of a loved one, usually shortly after they die. Tribute gifts encourage family and friends to join together, and sometimes hundreds participate. Most fundraising offices do not have staff dedicated solely to tributes. Instead, they are folded into the work of other fundraisers, either in major gifts, direct marketing, special events, or other specialist or generalist fundraisers.

We mention tributes here because they often provide a particular challenge. Managing tribute gifts can be highly labor intensive. Often, the size of the tribute is not proportional to the amount of work it requires. Gifts need to be meticulously tracked and recorded. Communications need to be sent to the donors and to the family, keeping them apprised of each contributor and the total.

Soliciting tribute gifts requires sensitivity

While tributes are always highly valued and appreciated, fundraisers can see them as difficult to manage and distracting to the more proactive fundraising they are charged with doing. Smoothly managing tribute funds often goes unpraised, while the slightest error draws unwelcome attention and consequences. What manager wants to hear a complaint from a family at this deeply emotional time of their lives?

Furthermore, fundraisers have long sensed the potential to increase fundraising around tributes, but struggle with how to sensitively make an approach. Many of the largest gifts honor a lost loved one, but tribute gifts happen when a family isn't focused on philanthropy. The timing for discussing what the family could do is the worst possible, usually taking place around the funeral of a loved one. And often the connection, if there was any, was with the deceased, making it hard to re-engage with family members after enough time has passed. So, too often, the family and the organization part ways after a tribute fund is established, despite the possibility of greater support.

One new approach by Our Lasting Tribute *(see: https://tributefunds.com/)* seems interesting to us and may represent a creative way to use the internet to increase giving through a culture shift in traditional philanthropy. Although this company utilizes written materials in its approach, as well as the internet, we will focus on the role of the internet here.

Imagine that a family wishing to establish a tribute did so through the creation of a mini-campaign online. Automated technology can allow a donor to set up a Web page connected to your organization's. At this website, the family can put pictures and details about their loved one and why they have designated your organization as their charity of choice. Others visiting could add their own thoughts, poems, prayers, and memories, and at the same time pledge their support to the fund.

Set up an online tribute page

An online tribute page can alleviate many of the managerial headaches of tribute funds while maximizing their potential and respecting the needs of the family at a difficult time. Visitors automatically know the exact fundraising total. Family members can be informed of gifts through email, and while some paper acknowledgment and receipt is still needed, email versions can help cut down significantly on problems, perceived or real, and in doing so, reduce the number of complaints. Because this internet approach encourages families to come back to the question of philanthropy later, after the most difficult and immediate emotionally absorbing event, it can help resolve some of the timing and appropriateness issues associated with fundraising for tributes.

In short, the internet may hold a key to helping to unlock the untapped potential in tribute funds. It can help to empower families to do more and to take greater satisfaction in the impact they are having in the name of a loved one. This may in turn lead to more substantial relationships with such families, and in some cases may even transform them into lifelong supporters or major donors.

Personal Fundraising Pages

Donors, be they casual or wealthy philanthropists, are more likely to give when asked by someone they know, or to whom they have some connection. Colleges and universities ask current students to volunteer to solicit alumni. Charities provide their supporters with donor materials, and ask that they mail solicitations to their neighbors with a personalized appeal. Organizations hold galas and other special events and encourage the well-heeled to invite their friends to attend, or to make a contribution if they cannot be there in person.

The technology revolution has added new wrinkles to many existing fundraising techniques, eliminating some labor-intensive aspects, and streamlining invitations, donor processing, acknowledgment and substantiation, and collections. Technology has also spurred the development of new, creative fundraising models. Among them are charity malls, online auctions, "click-to-give," and electronic tribute gifts. Some of these models take advantage of using "personal" appeals of individuals to their friends, neighbors, and relatives, despite the fact that these appeals are highly automated and involve minimal labor on the part of either the charity or the solicitor.

One such model, the personal fundraising page, is rapidly catching on as an effective fundraising technique for charities on the cutting edge. It was successful recently in generating a donation from one of us, Gary Grobman, to a charity that he had not previously supported, the Leukemia and Lymphoma Society. Here's how it occurred.

ASPs can manage personal fundraising pages

In January 2005, Gary Grobman received an email from a casual friend and neighbor, Shalom Staub of Harrisburg, PA. The message, not particularly long or detailed, said Shalom was participating in a 100-mile bike ride around Lake Tahoe in June to raise millions of dollars for this particular charity, and he was committed to raising $3,800 himself. He asked for Gary's participation by clicking on a link embedded in his email. The link was to Shalom's personal fundraising page on Active.com. Gary complied, making a small donation online. Within minutes, he received two emails, one from the local chapter of the charity thanking him for his gift, and a receipt from the application service provider, Active.com. Apparently, scores of others responded to the appeal. In July, Gary received another "custom" email from his cyclist friend saying that more than 1,900 bike riders raised $7 million, and that he more than met his fundraising goal. Attached to the email were pictures of the event.

Active.com is a site managed by Active Giving Solutions, one of many application service providers who have developed software applications for personal fundraising pages. "We chose Active Giving Solutions for its customized technology and ability to integrate with our internal systems," said Richard J. Geswell, executive vice president, marketing and revenue generation for the Leukemia & Lymphoma Society, in a June 2005 press release. "We needed an easy tool to encourage and expand online fundraising by our participants. With Active's history of managing online transactions for participatory sports and its ties to the active lifestyle community, we're also looking forward to the additional exposure we gain through the partnership."

Perhaps the leader in the personal fundraising page model is Justgiving.com, with more than a million online donations received for its 1,200 nonprofit organization clients in the United States and Great Britain in its first five years of operations. A March 2005 survey of more than 1,000 Justgiving users validated the company's claim that making donations via this method is convenient, secure, and provides many other advantages over conventional methods of solicitation. One satisfied customer, Nathaniel Tilton, was diagnosed with Multiple Sclerosis in 2002. Rather than being impeded by his debilitating disease, he set a goal of running the Boston Marathon. Setting up his personal fundraising page on Justgiving.com, he raised more than $10,000 for his charity and finished the race in a respectable 4:43 on a hot day and challenging course (and likely passed Gary Grobman somewhere after Heartbreak Hill).

To Shalom Staub, this automated service relieved much of the anxiety and time involved in fund-raising.

"Some people who were distant to me, or who only knew of me through a friend or family member, donated quite generously," he told Gary in an email. "Others who are closer friends of mine, failed to, which was frustrating. The point is, you just never know who might feel a personal connection to your cause and who might be willing to make a contribution—so don't be afraid to ask!"

The technology made his plea for support painless at every step. The cost to charities is reasonable, with typical transaction fees being 5% or less of donations made through the Justgiving platform. From the home page (*https://www.justgiving.com/*), you can find the personal fundraising pages of some of the top fundraisers who use the service, and the names and comments of their donors.

Also started in 1999, CharityFocus is a California-based 501(c)(3) that is run completely by volunteers. Its basic services, including setting up personal fundraising pages (see: *http://www.pledgepage.org/*), are free, although there may be charges for any third-party costs the organization incurs on your behalf.

Third party application service providers are becoming more sophisticated in meeting the customized needs of charities that want to encourage their donors to set up personal fundraising pages. Typically, these pages permit the participant to upload pictures, provide progress reports on the amount of donations received, and have colorful graphics that illustrate how close the participant is to meeting his or her fundraising goal. Anecdotal evidence is strong that charities, participants, and donors alike appreciate the convenience of this online giving option. And it is another effective strategy charities can use to add to their donor lists and publicize the important mission they have, even among those who may not be interested in making a donation.

Tips:

- Purchase keywords from major search engines to attract donors to your website. Some organizations even purchase common misspellings of keywords!

- Email communications have a different tone than conventional letters. As one Direct Marketing manager shared, websites are all about the organization. The tone is focused on "we." Mail appeals, however, tend to start with "you," the donor. They bring the donor into the heart of the organization and reinforce the idea that the recipient is being asked to support "their" mission through "their" organization. Communications by email, whether solicitations or not, should similarly focus on the donor.

- An element that may help in cultivating prospect relationships is to have a staff directory at your website, preferably including pictures. For one thing, just as major gift officers want to be able to read something about their donors and prospects, donors may want to investigate your leadership. Giving a bio online can help them do this.

- Make sure the option to give is pervasive in your site. The button to make a donation should exist on every page. Donors should not be required to leave what they are reading to navigate your site to find the place where a gift can be made.

Chapter 24
Forming and Running a Coalition

> **Synopsis:** Many nonprofit organizations form and participate in coalitions to accomplish objectives that would be difficult to achieve by themselves. There are significant advantages and considerations to forming a coalition, and the fact that they flourish is indicative of their value. This chapter discusses the advantages and disadvantages of creating and/or participating in coalitions.

The tapestry of advocacy efforts at the international, national, state, and local levels is replete with collaborative initiatives that bring together diverse interests to accomplish a common goal. As a nonprofit organization seeks to accomplish its mission, its leadership often finds the value of creating formal and informal partnerships among like-minded organizations. As in any endeavor, there are traps and pitfalls in creating and running a coalition.

Although it is often said that "two heads are better than one," it is equally rejoined that "too many cooks spoil the broth." Both of these clichés are often equally valid when applied to a coalition, and it is important for an organizational leader to be able to assess which one applies predominantly before embarking on coalition-forming.

The Coalition

A coalition is a group of diverse organizations that join together to accomplish a specific objective that is likely to be achieved more quickly and effectively than if the organizations acted independently. There are many types of coalitions, and the structure is often dictated by political as well as financial considerations. The prototypical coalition involving state government issues starts with a convener coalition partner who has identified an issue, usually of direct importance to the convener's organizational membership.

The convener then "rounds up the usual suspects" by soliciting membership in the coalition from constituencies that will participate in the coalition. He or she schedules periodic meetings of the coalition at which members share information about the issue and develop a strategy to accomplish a specific goal of the coalition that, as is often the case, is the passage of legislation to solve the problem. It is not unusual for the coalition to continue even after the legislation upon which it focused on is enacted into law.

Structures of Coalitions

- *Formal organization.* Some coalitions structure formally, creating a distinct nonprofit corporate structure, such as a 501(c)(3), which will permit the coalition to hire staff, seek tax-deductible contributions from the public, rent office space, and have a system of governance that parallels, in many respects, the constituent organizations that comprise the coalition. Obviously, one would not seek to create such a complex legal entity if the objective of the coalition was to be achieved in the short term. It is not atypical for a new 501(c)(3) coalition staff to spend much of its efforts raising funds to keep it in business rather than focusing on the actual mission of the coalition. Even if funding is stable, many formal coalitions spend an inordinate amount of time on intraorganizational issues, compared to achieving their stated purposes. An example of a formal coalition is the 501(c)(3) Alliance for Justice, founded in 1979, which represents more than 120 organizations "to represent groups committed to progressive values and the creation of an equitable, just, and free society."

- *Semi-formal coalition.* These coalitions consist of organizations that have some financial resources themselves and are able to fund the activities of the coalition. Although not incorporated as separate legal entities, these coalitions nevertheless may have office space and staff. The office space may be provided as an in-kind contribution from one of the coalition members, and the staff may or may not be employees of one of the member organizations. An example of such a coalition is the Public Education Coalition to Oppose Tuition Vouchers.

- *Informal coalition.* Most coalitions are informal, with a convener organizational leader, but with no dedicated organizational staff or budget, or separate bank account. The convener organization convenes the coalition, sends out meeting notices, holds the meeting in the convener's office, and staffs the coalition as a part of its routine organizational duties. Costs can be shared among coalition members, and the convener duty can be rotated among members. In general, member organizations are not bound by the positions taken by the coalition. An example of such a coalition in Pennsylvania was the Charities Build Communities Coalition, sponsored by the Pennsylvania Association of Nonprofit Organizations.

- *Group networks.* A group network is a type of informal coalition that has been formed to serve an information-sharing function with less emphasis on coordinated action. These networks have no staff, no budget, take no positions, and are useful in raising the consciousness of participants about a particular issue or set of issues. These networks also are valuable in bringing people together to "network," and to build trust among organizational leadership. Although efforts to coordinate action on an issue are often the result of a network-based coalition, the network itself often does not take a formal role in the coordination; rather, the discussions among the participants during and after the meeting result in the synergistic effects of the network. Among examples of these coalitions in Pennsylvania have been coalitions formed to ban corporal punishment, increase welfare grants, support minimum wage increases, and expand the school breakfast program.

Advantages of Forming a Coalition

- Coalitions focus attention among the media, opinion leaders, and those with advocacy resources on a specific issue. Any organization, no matter how large and powerful, has a limited ability to get its message across to the public, government officials, and the media. Building a coalition is an effective strategy to call attention to an issue, since messages not perceived to be important when heard from one organization may be considered important from another.

- Coalitions bring together experts on a particular issue. A convener of a coalition often has a burning desire to solve a particular public-policy problem and has well-developed organizational skills, but may lack the technical expertise to develop the solution. Creating a coalition is a strategy to bring together experts in the field who collegially can participate in developing a solution.

- Coalitions provide a forum to resolve turf issues and to limit destructive competition. Very few important public policy issues are so narrow that a single organization is the only one with a direct interest in their resolution. Virtually any public policy issue, particularly one that influences human services, affects a broad range of advocacy organizations, whether it impinges on children, schools, the environment, business, the disabled, or the aged. Trying to solve a problem without the "buying in" of key decision-makers is a recipe for disaster. Coalitions provide the framework for obtaining the cooperation of opinion makers who otherwise would be threatened by any effort to change public policy that violates their political turf.

- Coalitions provide credibility to an issue and to the convener organization. One obvious application of this principle is the effort, often unsuccessful, of various extremist organizations not accepted in society, such as the KKK, to try to form or participate in coalitions that have a goal consistent with a community consensus. Another principle is that organizational messages viewed as self-interest are looked at negatively. When coalitions include organizations that are considered to be acting in the public interest (such as those affiliated with the religious community or the League of Women Voters), it is more beneficial to have the organization's message delivered by a coalition.

- Coalitions permit resources to be shared. Coalitions benefit by the resources of their membership, including money, volunteers, staff, office equipment, and meeting space. It is more cost-effective for an organization to form a coalition to permit resources to be shared, rather than having to pay the entire bill itself.

- Coalitions provide a path to inform new constituencies about an emerging issue. For example, the religious-based advocacy community's constituency may not have access to detailed information about a specific state budget problem, other than seeing an occasional newspaper article. It is one thing for welfare recipients to write to their legislators requesting a grant increase, and another for middle-class taxpayers to write advocating for an increase based on economic justice, not self-interest. Coalitions provide a framework for expanding constituencies beyond those of the convener.

- Coalitions result in positive public relations for a convener coalition-builder. New organizations build respect by forming and running a successful coalition. Although the "credit" for a success achieved single-handedly can be savored, achieving that success is often much more difficult than with help from a coalition. By bringing other organizations together and working for a common goal, those organizations learn to work with the convener, to build trust, to get visibility for the new organization, and to make it more likely that the convening organization will be invited to participate in other coalitions.

Disadvantages of Coalitions

- It is often difficult for members of a coalition to focus on an issue that is usually not the priority issue for any member of the coalition other than the convener.

- Coalition members who are not the convener often have an agenda that differs from that of the convener. They may seek to exploit the coalition for their own goals in a manner that may be inconsistent with the purpose for which the coalition was formed.

- Coalitions usually reach agreement on issues by consensus, which is sometimes difficult to achieve. When it is achieved, the result is often the lowest common denominator and dilutes the aggressiveness that might have been necessary to solve a problem.

- Coalitions require considerably more time to make decisions than would be required by the convener acting alone. Many coalition members require major decisions to be discussed by their own boards. There is a lag time between when a decision is requested and when a decision can be made by a coalition, compared with an individual organization. Even scheduling a coalition meeting to discuss when a coalition consensus can be developed can be extremely difficult at times.

- Many important coalition partners have organizational difficulties that make them accustomed to working independently rather than in coalition with others.

- Coalitions can require substantial organizational work, such as preparing agendas, mailing materials, and coordinating meeting times.

To Form a Coalition or Not

There are many questions that should be answered, and an honest assessment made, in determining whether forming a coalition to solve a problem is constructive. Among them are:

- What is the outcome I wish to achieve with this coalition? Is it realistic to achieve it by myself? Are the chances for success improved with a coalition?

- Whose turf am I treading on by trying to solve this issue alone? Is there a more appropriate organization to form this coalition?

- Are there constituencies in my own organization that will react negatively if I form this coalition?

- How much will a coalition cost me in terms of money, time, and focus?

- Who should be invited to participate; who should not be invited?

- Will I have better access to outside experts if I form a coalition?

- Will my prospective coalition participants get along?

- How will the coalition dissolve after my goals are achieved?

- What kind of commitment do I need from participants, and is it realistic to expect to receive these commitments?

How to Form a Coalition

- Make sure that there are no major irreconcilable differences between coalition participants, either as a result of ideology or personal enmities.

- Identify all organizations that have a direct or indirect interest in the issue.

- Invite, if appropriate, organizations that would enhance the credibility of the coalition.

- Make sure that the effort is not perceived to be partisan.

- Invite outside experts to either serve on the coalition or speak to it.

- Consider business, labor, education, religious advocacy, good government citizen groups, health, local government, state government, federal government, beneficiaries of success of the coalition's objective, provider associations, lobbyists, experts on the issue, community leaders, foundation and other grantmaker representatives, charities, and religious leaders as coalition members.

Online Resources to Explore:

Tools of Change
*https://toolsofchange.com/en/programs/
community-based-social-marketing/*

Community How To Guide on Coalition Building
*https://one.nhtsa.gov/people/injury/alcohol/
community%20guides%20html/Book1_CoalitionBldg.html*

National Coalition Building Institute
https://ncbi.org/

University of Kansas Coalition Building Community Toolbox
*https://ctb.ku.edu/en/table-of-contents/assessment/promotion-strategies/
start-a-coaltion/main*

Institute for Sustainable Communities
   https://sustain.org/

Tips:

- Remember that if the objective of the coalition were the most central focus of all members of the coalition, they would have formed it first.

- Respect the fact that your coalition is perhaps one of many, and keep meetings short with the agenda focused. Encourage all in attendance to participate, but do not dominate the discussion yourself or let any other participant dominate. Reach consensus as quickly as possible, and then move on.

- Delegate the work of the coalition to participants (such as by forming committees when necessary to develop a consensus).

- Make the meeting pleasant by being hospitable (such as providing soft drinks or lunch).

Chapter 25
Miscellaneous Administrative Issues

Synopsis: The offices of nonprofit corporations require computers, filing systems, and office equipment that are sensitive to organizational needs. The Postal Service offers discounted postage rates to organizations that prepare bulk mailings in a manner consistent with its format and regulations.

Forming and running a nonprofit organization involves much more decision-making than simply focusing on some societal problem and then figuring out what needs to be done to advance that cause. There are often scores of mundane administrative issues that arise that cannot be ignored. Among them are how to deal with office space and its contents, staff, filing systems, stationery and logos, computers and software, and postal issues.

Office Equipment

Many small nonprofit corporations are headquartered in the residences of their incorporators. There are obvious limitations to that, particularly if the corporation needs to expand its "shoebox" existence. For those who rent or own office space, some basic equipment items to consider (and budget for) are—

- file cabinets (legal or letter size)
- postage meter, postage scales
- copy machine
- telephone system, including cell phone
- telephone voice mail service
- computers (PCs, laptops, netbooks, tablets), printer, monitor, and peripherals, such as wifi, scanner, mouse, external drives
- office furniture (including desks, bookcases, supply shelves, cabinets, chairs, lamps, end tables, coat racks, umbrella stand).

Staffing Patterns

Thousands of registered nonprofits operate effectively with no paid staff, while others, such as colleges and hospitals, may have staff in the thousands. Salaries are, by far, the largest budget expenditure for organizations with paid staff. A typical one person staff configuration has an executive director or director who performs all of the operations of the organization. There may be the need for some part-time assistance to do bookkeeping or help with a special project on occasion, but it is not impossible for one versatile person to run a highly successful organization. More typical is a two-person office—an executive/administrator and an administrative assistant/secretary/clerk who performs the routine office management functions.

Nonprofits that can afford additional staff may have an assistant director, who may be responsible for publications, membership, or development (a euphemism for fundraising). Other typical generic staff positions of nonprofits are government relations representative, program director, publications specialist/newsletter editor, administrative assistant, public relations/community relations specialist, librarian, office manager, Webmaster, social media manager, and data processor. Many nonprofits provide specific services that require staff with some particular educational credentials or training. Hospitals will hire doctors, nurses, social workers, and lab technicians. Colleges will hire professors and deans. The organization's mission may determine the types of specialists hired (see Chapters 11-12).

Many nonprofits choose to start small—hiring one staff member—and then expand with experience and fundraising, so there is a reasonable expectation that the budget can be supported in the long run. If a nonprofit is too ambitious at first, the staff may end up spending most of its time raising funds to support salaries, rather than accomplishing the mission of the organization.

Stationery/Logo

Every nonprofit corporation needs to have letterhead stationery to provide a professional first impression. This stationery need not be fancy or expensive, although it is generally a good practice to print stationery on bond paper with some cotton content, which is heavier than the 20-lb. stock used in the copy machine. Most corporate stationery has a graphic (also known as a "logo") that is uniquely descriptive of the corporation. This graphic can also be used on the masthead of a corporate newsletter, website; mailing labels, brochures, press packets, and other promotional literature. Paying an artist to draw a distinctive and creative logo is usually a good investment, although it is often possible to make one by using some of the popular "clip art" or graphics software programs. If you don't have a scanner, a computer store may be willing to scan logo art work, so it can be printed out in various sizes or "imported" into computer-generated publications as needed.

The letterhead should also include the organization's name, address, email address, website address, and telephone number. Most organizations also list their board members, officers, and key staff members, as well.

Filing Systems

The filing systems of nonprofit corporations usually evolve over several years and are as individual as each organization. Several factors should be considered in setting up a paper-based filing system.

Keep files of the corporation's internal operations separate from other files. For example, keep the files relating to tax-exempt status, corporation budget, office leases, insurance, taxes, Certificate of Formation, membership, mailing lists, lobbying, and charitable registration in a different place from files about general political and public policy issues. A corporation should have correspondence files—one for "outgoing" and another for "incoming." One nonprofit always makes three copies of all outgoing correspondence—one for the "outgoing" file, one for the "incoming file" stapled to the incoming letter that generated the outgoing letter, and one for the subject file that relates to the issue of the letter. "External" files can be subject matter relating to the mission of the corporation. However, "internal" files will be similar from nonprofit to nonprofit. Among typical internal files are:

allocations, annual report, Certificate of Formation, bank statements, board meeting agendas, board minutes, board meeting packets, bookkeeping, brochure, budget, bylaws, computer, dues structure, expenses, financial reports, grass-roots alerts, insurance, mailing lists, newsletters, office equipment, office leases, payroll, personnel, photographs, planning, postal service, press mailing list, press clippings, press releases, printing, grants, publications, speeches and testimony, social media, special projects, tax-exempt status, taxes, and website. Some of these files will have sub-categories (e.g., newsletter—previous, newsletter—current), and others will be categorized by year.

Computer

The computer is, with good reason, a fixture in the modern nonprofit office.

The good news is that in the hands of a knowledgeable operator, a computer can do a variety of tasks and save thousands of expensive staff hours. The bad news is that it can be expensive and complicated to learn, may be vulnerable to computer viruses and other cyberterrorism, and can "crash" at the most inopportune times. It is fortunate that most software packages automatically back up your work occasionally, and there are convenient ways to save your files to the "cloud" to avoid disaster when a computer is lost, damaged, or is unable to function.

This handbook provides only the most cursory review of basic computer buying decisions. It is geared to the small nonprofit interested in the advantages and disadvantages of purchasing a personal computer and the basic options.

Among many issues to consider when purchasing a computer system are—

- Who will be using the system, and will they be sufficiently trained?

- Is software available that is compatible with your hardware, and will this software be capable of providing the output you need?

- Are you paying for features or capacity you are unlikely to ever need?

- Is there sufficient follow-up support to answer questions, troubleshoot problems, and provide maintenance?

A basic hardware decision is whether to use an Apple-compatible ("Mac") or IBM-Compatible ("PC") system. In the old days, these two types of computers were as incompatible as Beta format and VHS for VCRs. What were once uncrossable boundaries between these two hardware systems are now being crossed and integrated. Basically, the Apple-based Macintosh ("Mac") computers are considered to be more "user-friendly." On the other hand, IBM and IBM "clones" are generally less expensive and have more programs that are compatible. IBM and its imitators have developed software that imitates the user-friendliness of the Mac. Increasingly, the Mac-based hardware is permitting the use of files created using IBM-compatible software. The state-of-the-art is advancing so swiftly that this decision may become moot in the near future.

Typical Software for Nonprofits

Thousands of programs are being used by nonprofits. In general, several families of programs exist that are useful in a typical computer-based nonprofit office. Among them are:

- *Word Processing*—Microsoft Word, LibreOffice Writer, Google Docs, Corel WordPerfect, and Apache OpenOffice Writer are among the most popular word processing programs. An advantage of word processing programs is that an entire document does not have to be retyped to make corrections or multiple copies. This is a major productivity enhancement if an organization desires to send a "personal" letter to 50,000 potential contributors.

- *Spreadsheet*—Microsoft Excel, Google Sheets, LibreOffice Calc, and Apache OpenOffice Calc are among the most popular spreadsheet programs. In simple terms, the objective of a spreadsheet is to perform operations and calculations on numbers and automatically adjust a total when one number in a sum is changed. Spreadsheets are indispensable for bookkeeping, budgeting, and similar documents. Many spreadsheets contain graphics capability that permits numerical data to be displayed in pleasing and informative formats.

- *Database*—Lotus Approach, MySQL, IBM DB2, LibreOffice Base, Brilliant Database, and Microsoft Access are among the most popular database programs. The objective of a database is to sort data into various fields, which can then be used to generate mailing lists, store information that can be sorted, and perform other similar tasks.

- *Desktop Publishing* (DTP)—Adobe InDesign, Corel Ventura, Microsoft Publisher, and Quark Xpress are among the most popular DTP or page layout programs. These programs import graphics and output from word processing programs and can manipulate the result on the screen in an eye-catching format. Text can be formatted in a variety of typefaces and sizes, giving documents the appearance of having been professionally designed and typeset.

- *Presentation Software*—Microsoft PowerPoint, Google Slides, Prezi Business, and OpenOffice Impress are among the most popular presentation software programs. These are used with LED screens to project speaker presentations of short bites of text and graphics for large audiences, and can be coordinated with music and video files.

- *Accounting Software*—Zero, Wave, and QuickBooks are among the most widely used accounting software packages by nonprofit organizations.

- *Email*—Microsoft Outlook, Gmail, Opera Email Client, DreamMail, and Mozilla Thunderbird are popular email programs.

- *Web Browsers*—Google Chrome, Microsoft Edge (replacement for Internet Explorer), Safari, and Mozilla Firefox are popular Web browsers.

There are software "suite" packages that provide the above types of programs all-in-one and are designed to allow the programs to work with each other. Some of the most popular are Microsoft Office, LibreOffice, Google Workspace, Zoho, Google G Suite, Apple IWork, Zoho Office Suite, and Apache OpenOffice (formerly known as "Star Office"). Before purchasing any software (which can be obtained for free or cost thousands of dollars), it is best to seek advice of those who are knowledgeable about the advantages and disadvantages of each program.

Nonprofits affiliated with a state or national association should check with the staff of that organization to ascertain what software packages are used. Often, these organizations share data among their affiliates in only one format. While software is available to make conversions between formats and hardware configurations, substantial time, energy, and money can be saved by having compatible computer systems.

Open Source Software

Open source software is quickly becoming the choice of thousands of charities for applications including operating systems (Linux), productivity office suite packages (LibreOffice), browsers (Mozilla Firefox), email (Mozilla Thunderbird), databases (MySQL), and website content management (Joomla). The term refers to software whose source code is public. Often, the software is licensed to users using a standardized form that sets rules for changing it and using it—but for the most part, there is no charge for using open source software. The open source software model is intended to encourage collaboration for the purpose of making a software product better for every user, rather than making money for the developer. There are several advantages—you don't have to pay for periodic updates, you can put the software on as many computers as you like, and there is a community of software developers who collaborate to improve the product and eliminate bugs. However, keep in mind that there may not be stable technical support, quality control may be "iffy," and the software may not run on all operating systems. Generally, open source software can be high quality, and it is worthy for charities to consider.

Credit Card Sales

Nonprofit organizations are businesses and have many aspects in common with for-profit businesses. They sell products and services, such as memberships, publications, counseling, and tickets to events. They also solicit donations from the public, and it is not unusual for many contributors to be comfortable making these donations by credit card, either through secure forms on the internet, using cashless methods linked to their smartphones (such as Google Pay and Apple Pay—particularly during a pandemic) or, more conventionally, through the mail. Inexorably, we are becoming a cashless society, and the public increasingly relies on credit cards for financial transactions. Nonprofit organizations should consider whether having "merchant status" is advantageous. For more information about how to obtain this status, see Chapter 22.

Postal Service Issues

Nonprofit corporations typically generate a large volume of mail in the course of sending out annual reports, newsletters, program brochures, fundraising solicitations, surveys, grass-roots action alerts, and meeting notices. As a result of U.S. Postal Service advances in technology, mass mailings have become more complicated. Because of recent reforms that substantially change the way both organizations that qualify for nonprofit mailing status and others must prepare bulk mail, the USPS has expanded its outreach by providing educational programs.

The Postal Service offers free training on how to process bulk mailings. Call your U.S. Postal Service's regional bulk mail center to get information on the next scheduled workshop.

General Postage Rates

The U.S. Postal Service publishes the *Postal Bulletin,* which details the latest rates, fees, and changes in regulations. Subscriptions to this bi-weekly publication are available for $163/year. You can download back issues for free at: *https:// about.usps.com/resources/postal-bulletin.htm*

A more comprehensive publication, *Domestic Mail Manual,* is published twice annually, and is available electronically at *https://pe.usps.com/text/dmm300/ dmm300_landing.htm*

Postage Meters

Postage meters permit organizations to affix exact postage to letters and packages without the inconvenience of purchasing stamps of varying denominations. The postage is printed by the meter, and the organization pays in advance for the postage used. Most new postage meter systems permit postage accounts to be replenished by telephone/modem. Postage machines are not sold but, in accordance with federal law, are rented by commercial companies. A license is required from the Postal Service, but the paperwork is handled by the vendor. Pitney-Bowes is the firm that developed the system and is the leader in the field. Competing companies can be found online or in the Yellow Pages under "Mailing Machines and Equipment." The monthly cost of renting a postage meter is $22.95 and up, including a postage scale, depending on the system's sophistication.

Stamps.com and other competitors allow for a similar service that is internet-based. Postage is provided by establishing an online account and printing out postage from your computer.

Bulk Mail Permit Procedures

The USPS has information about its bulk mail discounts, which you can find at: *https://pe.usps.com/BusinessMail101/Index?ViewName=Prices*

Organizations that desire to participate in the bulk mailing program must first obtain an imprint authorization from the Postal Service using Form 3615. As of January 2021, there is a $240 fee for first-class and $240 for marketing class mail, and the permits must be renewed annually. Organizations seeking nonprofit mailing status should file Form 3624. Forms are available online at: *https://about.usps.com/resources/forms.htm.* The Postal Service automatically forwards the correct form when it is time to renew the permits.

Having such an imprint entitles the organization to pay the postage in advance without having to affix postage to each individual piece of mail. The permit also provides a discount, provided there are at least 200 pieces or 50 pounds in the marketing mail bulk mailing and the mailing is sorted and processed in accordance with post office regulations. Each piece must have the correct ZIP Code or it will not be accepted.

Once in receipt of the imprint permit, the organization can affix the imprint to mail pieces using a rubber stamp, or they can print it directly on the piece.

The bulk mail discount can be large. The rate for a first-class letter as of January 2021 is 55 cents per ounce (20 cents for each additional ounce starting January 24, 2021). A comparable piece of mail sent Full Service Intelligent Mail option bulk rate can be sent for about a nickel/piece, depending on how it was prepared (see: *https://postalpro.usps.com/node/699*). There are substantial discounts to encourage barcoding of bulk mailings.

501(c)(3)s (or organizations that have the characteristics of such organizations) may qualify for the U.S. Postal Service's Nonprofit Standard Mail rates. Organizations that may apply for this discount rate are agricultural, educational, fraternal, labor, philanthropic, religious, scientific, and veterans' nonprofit organizations. Organizations that are not eligible are auto clubs, business leagues, chambers of commerce, citizens and civic improvement organizations, mutual insurance associations, most political organizations, service clubs (such as Lions clubs and Rotary clubs), social and hobby groups, and trade associations. To apply, you need to file a PS 3624 form, which is available from any post office. The application will require you to submit your Certificate of Formation, proof that your organization fits one of the eligible categories, a list of activities, a financial statement, and documents that show how your organization operates, such as brochures, newsletters, and board minutes. The Post Office reviewers pay close attention to any advertising you may have in your newsletter. For more details on this benefit to nonprofits, consult *Quick Service Guide 670* published by the U.S. Postal Service.

As of December 2020, the basic nonprofit marketing mail rate for letters under 3.3 ounces was as low as 10 cents. This rate increases depending on whether the mailing piece can be processed by automated equipment (such as by using bar-coding), the nature of the presort, and the destination of the letters. For all rates, publications, and rate calculators, visit: *https://pe.usps.com/*

Automation

Nonprofit marketing mail postage rates are substantially lower for mail that can be handled by automated equipment. Computer software is available at reasonable cost that will automatically place a U.S. Postal Service-compatible barcode on each label generated by your computer. Even if you do not have barcoding capability, providing enough space for the Postal Service's equipment to optically read the address on each label and place its own barcode, while not reducing your postage rate, will qualify you for time-saving reductions in bulk mail preparation. Consult the U.S.P.S. for more information about this "upgradeable mail."

The entire system for presorting to comply with Postal Service regulations is too complicated to be described here, but some useful information about it is included at: *https://pe.usps.com/text/qsg300/Q240c.htm#ep1030100*

Size of Standard-Class Letter Mail

The dimensions of letter-size bulk mail are limited to the following:

length: 5 inches - 11 1/2 inches
width: 3 1/2 inches - 6 1/8 inches
thickness: .007 inches - .25 inches (enough to send a 20-page newsletter on 20-lb. paper, folded once)

Marketing Mail Sorting

To obtain nonprofit marketing mail discount postage rates, mail must not only meet certain criteria to be considered "machinable" such as those relating to length, width, thickness, and aspect ratio, but must be delivered to the Post Office's business mail entry unit in trays sorted by ZIP Code. Note that trays are provided free by the USPS Business Mail Entry Unit. Only certain designated post offices are equipped to accept marketing mail mailings.

Tray Requirements

Trays should be at least 85% full. If not, skip the step that created that tray. The U.S.P.S. wants you to provide them with full trays. "Full" is defined as at least 85% full, so choose either a one-foot tray or two-foot tray to comply with this requirement.

Trays must be enclosed by a tray sleeve and bound with polyethylene strapping. Strapping material can be purchased from a commercial office supply house. The trays must be labeled appropriately to reach the correct destination. The Postal Service can provide correct tray labeling information.

The applicable postage must be deposited in the organization's postage account if the current balance is not enough to cover the postage for the mailing. A mailing statement provided by the Postal Service that identifies the organization, its nonprofit marketing mail account, and the number of pieces being mailed for each standard-class category, must accompany each mailing.

The marketing mail operation is performed successfully by hundreds of for-profits and nonprofits alike every day. It can save thousands of dollars in postage compared with mailing every piece first-class. It also saves the bother of affixing individual postage stamps. While it may appear intimidating at first, it becomes routine with practice.

In general, the Postal Service attempts to deliver marketing class mail within ten days of receipt. Often, this mail is delivered just as expeditiously as first-class mail, although a four- or five-day time period for processing is not unusual. As a general rule, nonprofits should think twice before mailing anything marketing class that absolutely must be received within 12 days after the organization delivers the mailing to the Business Mail Entry Unit.

There are commercial services that specialize in processing bulk mailings. Some volunteer organizations will offer to help nonprofit organizations do these, as well.

Tips:

- When creating a mailing list, it is useful to have the list in ZIP Code order or to be capable of sorting it in ZIP Code order. Otherwise, letters must be sorted by hand to take advantage of the nonprofit marketing mail discounts.

- Most of the popular word processing programs will perform a ZIP Code sort operation and create mailing labels, and all of the database programs do. Many are capable of automatically inserting a barcode, which further reduces postage rates if printed in accordance with U.S. Postal Service regulations.

- Contact the U.S. Postal Service for help with marketing mail preparation or rates. A useful telephone number is: 1-800-238-3150—National Customer Support Center (USPS website: *https://www.usps.com/*)

Chapter 26
Nonprofits and Small Business Competition

> Synopsis: Some small business advocates have charged that nonprofits have unfair advantages when they compete in the sale of goods and services. Legislation and regulations to remove these advantages are a clear threat to the ability of the nonprofit sector to function effectively.

An issue has emerged on the agenda of small business advocates that could jeopardize the ability of many nonprofits to perform their vital missions. Tracing its beginning to the early 1980s, the issue of alleged unfair competition between nonprofits and small business earned its first stamp of legitimacy when the U.S. Small Business Administration issued a report in late 1983 entitled *Unfair Competition by Nonprofit Organizations with Small Business: An Issue for the 1980's.*

Small businesses had, until then, complained with muted voices that nonprofit corporations possessed advantages in the marketplace that hindered the ability of small businesses to compete. Among these advantages were said to be—

- *Tax exemptions*—the most tangible benefit of nonprofits
- Reduced postage rates
- *Tax deductions*—for those who contribute goods and services to nonprofit organizations
- *Use of venture capital*—the ability to use contributions and non-taxable surpluses for expansion, state-of-the-art equipment, and seed money for new activities that may compete with private enterprise
- *"Captured referrals"*—"sweetheart deal" arrangements between affiliated nonprofits that eliminate competition from non-affiliated businesses
- *Use of plant, staff, supplies, and equipment*—these are resources donated or funded by grants to spur unrelated business enterprises that may compete with small business
- *The "halo effect"*—referring to the willingness of the public to do business with a nonprofit because of the perception that the organization is serving the public good rather than being operated for a private profit motive.

During the 1970s, nonprofit corporations were becoming increasingly sophisticated in their efforts to generate revenue. These efforts accelerated during the 1980s, when many social service nonprofits were hit by the loss of government funding during the retrenchment of domestic spending under the Reagan Administration. Nonprofit hospitals were a particular target of small business owners, who resented the establishment of laundry and pharmaceutical services that competed with them. Small business advocates continue to complain that state government has no effective mechanism to track funds that may be channeled between a nonprofit organization and its for-profit affiliates.

Also targeted nationally were YMCAs and their Jewish counterpart JCCs. Some of the YMCAs and JCCs began marketing their lucrative health club services to an "upscale" market segment to generate revenues to cross-subsidize services provided to their needier clients. Such facilities were caught in a "Catch 22." If they charged less than the market rates, they were accused of undercutting small business by taking advantage of their tax exemptions and other advantages. If they charged the same or more than the private health clubs, they were accused of operating just as any other business and thus, not deserving of any tax exemption. Private health clubs across the nation, through the guidance of their associations, participated in legal actions against several YMCAs and instigated reviews by local taxing authorities designed to challenge the historical tax-exempt status of these facilities. An effort by nine private health clubs in the Pittsburgh area to challenge the tax exemption of the Golden Triangle YMCA in Pittsburgh was partially successful.

Colleges and universities garnered the wrath of small business owners who objected to college bookstores selling television sets and refrigerators, marketing surplus computer time, operating testing services, establishing travel agencies, or otherwise entering markets in direct competition with small business.

These small business owners found a voice in the Small Business Administration. On July 27, 1983, the Small Business Administration's Office of Advocacy held a one-day symposium on this issue, and followed up the conference with a November report entitled *Unfair Competition by Nonprofit Organizations With Small Business: An Issue for the 1980's.* This report charged that "traditional 'donative' nonprofits, such as the Red Cross and the Salvation Army, which rely primarily on gifts and contributions for their operating revenue, are being replaced by 'commercial nonprofits'... which derive all or nearly all of their income from the sales of goods or services they produce." The report charged some of the nonprofit sector with creating an oversupply of goods, and charging significantly less than the prevailing market rates as a result of exemptions from laws and regulations. The report concluded—

It is the responsibility of the Congress and the Executive Branch to make a systematic inquiry into whether these exemptions are still justified in light of the emergence of the commercial nonprofit sector.

Among other recommendations, the report called for—

- levying a higher tax on, or outright prohibiting, unrelated business activities by nonprofits

- defining "substantially related" more clearly and narrowly for purposes of what constitutes an unrelated business

- establishing a threshold above which a nonprofit engaging in unrelated business activities would lose its tax exemption

- eliminating the "convenience" exception for the payment of unrelated business income taxes.

Soon after the report was released, approximately 20 national business associations, many of which participated in drafting the 1983 SBA report, formed the "Coalition for Fair Business Competition" to lobby on behalf of business interests on this issue.

The issue of nonprofit competition with small business was among the most compelling of the issues reported by small business owners at the 1986 White House Conference on Small Business. Conference delegates designated it the number three issue on a list of 40 major concerns culled from a list of 2,232 proposed by small business owners nationwide. Legislation was introduced in several states in response to this conference.

Federal Unrelated Business Income Tax (UBIT)

Federal law stipulates that nonprofit corporations pay federal taxes on unrelated business income. Corporations with at least $1,000 of such income are required to file a 990-T annually. Income is defined as "unrelated" if it is derived from a trade or business, is regularly carried on, and is substantially unrelated to the exempt purpose of the corporation. Income clearly exempt from UBIT includes that generated from activities performed by volunteers; from selling merchandise received as gifts or contributions; and dividends, interest, royalties, and capital gains. Also exempt is income from business operations conducted for the "convenience" of an organization's members, students, patients, and staff, such as a hospital cafeteria or college bookstore.

In 2020, the Internal Revenue Service reported that $1.195 billion in UBIT was collected from nonprofit organizations for the FY 2019 tax year.

Both the Congress and the Internal Revenue Service have been skeptical about whether charities should have a broad exemption from paying taxes on business income. The House Ways and Means Committee's Oversight Committee held a series of hearings in June 1987 on the issue of changing federal policy on unrelated business income taxes. The subcommittee followed up on its hearings by issuing a press release on March 31, 1988, describing policy options on changes to UBIT, many of which caused concern in the nonprofit sector. The options included suggestions to narrow the "substantially related" test for exempting organizations from UBIT, repeal the "convenience" exception (which, for example, permits college bookstores and cafeterias to be tax exempt), apply UBIT to fitness/health clubs unless the program is "available to a reasonable cross section of the general public such as by scholarship or by fees based on community affordability," and apply UBIT to advertising income and allow deductions from UBIT only on direct advertising costs (a major concern to exempt nonprofits whose publications accept commercial advertising to defray expenses of the parent organization).

In March 1990, a revised report leaked from the subcommittee entitled *Summary of Main Issues in Possible Modification of Oversight Committee UBIT Options*. The draft proposal eliminated many of the controversial proposals that caused so much concern to nonprofits. While the "substantially related" test was retained in the proposal, the "convenience" exception was repealed. Most indirect and overhead expenses relating to advertising income would be deductible, but such expenses could not reduce net income by more than 80%. The subcommittee membership was unable to reach a consensus on UBIT proposals.

The Internal Revenue Service has aggressively audited some charities focusing on UBIT issues, and has taken charities to court to promote its policy of restricting UBIT exemptions. During the 1990s, the Internal Revenue Service expanded its attention to enforcement of UBIT and developed policies with respect to some of the borderline areas that were problematic to charities. Some cases involving the interpretation of what constitutes unrelated income were litigated. Several decisions on generic UBIT issues have been decided in favor of charities. Three examples have been cases involving mailing list rental income, affinity credit card income, and income from bingo games.

A case decided in August 1996 in U.S. District Court involving the American Academy of Family Physicians determined that the organization's income from a group insurance plan offered to its members underwritten by a private insurance carrier was not subject to UBIT. Again, the facts of this case may not be typical of conventional agreements between an insurance carrier and an exempt organization, but the opinion of the court on the issue was a favorable development.

Differences Between Nonprofits and For-Profits

There are clear and fundamental differences between the operations and motivations of nonprofits and for-profits. The buildings of some types of nonprofit charities and their for-profit counterparts may, in some cases, be similar. For-profit and nonprofit hospitals, nursing homes, day care centers, and recreational/youth service facilities may have the same equipment and physical plants, and they may provide some of the same services. Yet, these similarities often are exaggerated in an effort by some overzealous small business advocates to discredit the tax exemptions of those they perceive as competitors. The YMCAs in a growing number of communities particularly have endured vicious attacks from some private health club owners. In specific cases around the nation, these attacks have been given a credibility unsupported by the facts and have resulted in the loss of tax-exempt status.

Among the differences between nonprofit charitable organizations and for-profits are—

- A nonprofit charity is driven by its service mission philosophy rather than by the profit motive.

- A nonprofit charity serves those who cannot afford to pay full costs.

- Any excess revenue over expenditures is funneled back into the institution to further its exempt purpose.

- The charitable institution likely will remain in the community even if it suffers financial losses.

- The nonprofit charity is more accountable to its board for public service.

- The nonprofit charity often will proactively look for ways to respond to community needs without regard to any profit motive.

- A nonprofit charity may not compensate its employees higher than "reasonable" rates, as is evident from the successful prosecution of several television religious broadcasters who were paid exorbitant salaries and benefits.

- A nonprofit charity's board of directors is typically comprised of unpaid community leaders motivated by public service and serving the unmet needs of the community rather than making a profit.

- A nonprofit charity, because of its legal mission to serve rather than to make profits, often attracts thousands of hours of volunteer time and philanthropic contributions that further its purposes.

Tips:

- Don't publicly advertise products and services in a manner that underscores price competition with the for-profit sector.

- Refrain from entering markets that are not substantially related to the mission of your organization, and be prepared to pay unrelated business income taxes (UBIT) on income derived from activities not "directly" related.

- Review all activities that could be construed as commercial, and identify all those that require the filing of a 990-T and payment of Unrelated Business Income Tax (UBIT).

- In exploring options for generating new revenue, be sensitive to meeting needs that are unmet by the for-profit sector, rather than relying on undercutting the price of goods and services already being offered in the marketplace.

- Support efforts to improve disclosure and accountability of the voluntary sector. Cooperate with expanded enforcement of laws governing this sector, so that the few nonprofits that are abusing the law do not stain the reputation of the entire sector.

- Periodically review the organization's bylaws and tax-exempt status purposes, and update these documents to reflect changing conditions.

Chapter 27
State and Local Tax Exemptions

Synopsis: Texas imposes a 6.5% general sales and use tax, and provides some exemptions to organizations exempt under Section 501(c)(3), (4), (8), (10) and (19) of the Internal Revenue Code, but they must collect the tax on goods and services they sell. Many nonprofit organizations qualify for exemption from local property taxes, as well. There are reasons why it is important to maintain tax exemptions for nonprofit organizations.

It is a myth that once a nonprofit organization is incorporated, it is automatically exempt from paying all taxes on the goods and services they buy and the goods and services they sell. Most states, including Texas, do provide exemptions from having to pay local and state taxes upon application. These exemptions, particularly local real estate tax exemptions, have been under political attack in recent decades. Included in this chapter is a justification for why these exemptions should continue.

Sales and Use Tax Exemptions

All but five states (Alaska, Delaware, Montana, New Hampshire, and Oregon) levy a sales and use tax or equivalent on purchases of goods and/or services made by the public.

The state sales tax rate in Texas is 6.25%. Counties, cities and some other government jurisdictions may add an additional local sales tax on top of the state sales tax, although the aggregate rate may not exceed 8.25%. All medicine and groceries are exempt from all sales taxes, and automobile and boat sales are only subject to state sales tax (not local or municipal sales taxes). Lodging and hotels are taxed at a special state rate of 6%, although local governments can add to this amount. Organizations that sell goods and services that would be otherwise taxable and that are exempt from paying sales taxes still must collect and remit this tax. However, organizations must submit an application to the Texas Comptroller of Public Accounts to qualify for exemption on sales tax, hotel occupancy tax, and, if incorporated, the Texas Franchise tax.

Organizations need not have federal tax-exempt status to qualify for exemption. Texas tax law explicitly provides an exemption from sales taxes on goods and services purchased for use by organizations exempt under Section 501(c)(3), (4), (8), (10) or (19). However, this automatic exemption does not apply to the hotel occupancy tax.

Procedure for Application for Exemption

There are four forms for various types of nonprofit organizations to apply for these tax exemptions:

Form AP-205: For charitable organizations
Form AP-206: For homeowners associations
Form AP-207: For educational organizations
Form AP-209: For religious organizations

The completed form with documentation is sent to:

Comptroller of Public Accounts
Exempt Organizations Section
P.O. Box 13528
Austin, TX 78711-3528

Documentation required for the charitable exemption includes—

- The organization's actual or proposed two-year budget
- A detailed description of all of the organization's activities
- Any amount of charges for services, how the charges are determined, and the criteria the recipients must meet to receive the services
- A written statement or brochures, pamphlets or Web site addresses that describe the activities of the organization is also required
- A copy of any application used to determine eligibility for the organization's services
- A copy of the IRS determination letter, if the organization is exempt under a qualifying section of the Internal Revenue Code (IRC) or if the organization is affiliated with a parent entity that has a federal group exemption under one of the qualifying IRC sections. (Attach a letter of verification from the parent entity that confirms the organization is a recognized subordinate under its federal group exemption).
- If the parent organization has not yet obtained exemption from the Texas franchise tax and/or sales tax, the organization should provide a copy of the parent organization's entire IRS group exemption ruling letter along with the letter of affiliation.

Local Property Tax Exemptions

Section 11.18 of the Tax Code authorizes the exemption of property owned by qualified charitable organizations, depending on how the property is used. Real and personal property owned by organizations engaged primarily in performing charitable functions are exempt. Before applying for an exemption with the appraisal district, an organization must obtain from the Comptroller's office a determination letter stating the organization is engaged primarily in performing charitable functions. The chief appraiser determines if the organization uses its property for its charitable purposes.

The 4-page form is available at: *https://comptroller.texas.gov/forms/50-299. pdf.* It is filed with the appropriate office in the county in which the property is located rather than the Comptroller's office. You must file the completed application with all required documentation (including the organization's governing documents) beginning Jan. 1 and no later than April 30 of the year for which you are requesting an exemption. If the organization acquired the property after Jan. 1 and seeks to qualify for the exemption for the current year, it must apply before the first anniversary of the date it acquired the property, or before the first anniversary of the date any property was acquired after Jan. 1.

An organization is required to obtain a new Comptroller's office determination letter every five years.

Streamlined Sales and Use Tax Agreement

The purpose of the Streamlined Sales and Use Tax Agreement is to "to simplify sales and use tax collection and administration by retailers and states. The Agreement minimizes costs and administrative burdens on retailers that collect sales tax, particularly retailers operating in multiple states. It encourages 'remote sellers' selling over the internet and by mail order to collect tax on sales to customers living in the Streamlined states." It was created by a partnership between the National Governor's Association (NGA) and the National Conference of State Legislatures (NCSL) in the fall of 1999 to simplify sales tax collection, and respond to a court case that made it more difficult for states to collect sales taxes on Interstate sales. The Agreement consists of uniform definitions and forms relating to the sales and use tax. It defines sixty-nine different administrative terms and products and services that businesses in participating states can apply to the collection of sales tax.

States must enact conforming laws for the Agreement to take effect in their state. As of January 2021, 24 of 44 participating states have done so: Arkansas, Georgia, Indiana, Iowa, Kansas, Kentucky, Michigan, Minnesota, Nebraska, Nevada, New Jersey, North Carolina, North Dakota, Ohio, Oklahoma, Rhode Island, South Dakota, Tennessee, Utah, Vermont, Washington, West Virginia, Wisconsin and Wyoming. According to the Streamline Sales Tax Governing Board, Inc.'s website FAQ at *https://www.streamlinedsalestax.org/Shared-Pages/faqs/faqs-*

--*about-streamlined,* a business making sales into a Streamlined state only needs to know whether the product or service they sell is taxable or exempt.

Nonprofit charities are exempt in many states from paying sales taxes on their purchases, and state governments issue sales tax exemption certificates upon application (see above for Texas's exemption requirements). Most states require nonprofit charities to collect sales tax on their own sales, unless the purchaser is exempt. In participating states, a uniform exemption certificate (available at: *https://www.streamlinedsalestax.org/docs/default-source/issue-papers/certificate-of-exemption-form.pdf?sfvrsn=6606c0bb_6)* is accepted by businesses in states that participate in the agreement.

Why User Charges Are Not the Answer

As I write this, many Texas cities are distressed as a result of the COVID-19 pandemic, and have been stressed by economic downturns for decades.

No reasonable ways exist to measure the public services that are directly utilized by charitable nonprofits.

Property taxes, by themselves or disguised as "user charges," neglect the factors by which these institutions have earned their tax exemptions in the first place. In accordance with state law, these institutions have been founded, maintained, and endowed by public and private charity. They are, for the most part, created to provide benefits to the community. The tax exemption provided to these organizations is a benefit that is returned to the communities many times over.

The amount of financial support accruing to municipalities by taxing charities is generally not believed to be substantial. At least one study done in Wisconsin showed that 67% of the state's tax-exempt property belonged to government, and that an additional 10% was owned by religious organizations. All of this property would continue to be exempt under legislative proposals to authorize municipalities to impose user charges on tax-exempt property. While the reduction in local property taxes that would result if such legislation were enacted would be negligible, the impact on the charities themselves would be real and would threaten their continued viability. By state law, all incremental revenue over expenses of these charities is returned to the operations of the organization. There is no profit that is distributed into private pockets. Thus, the payment of taxes would result in a limited set of options for charitable nonprofits, all of which are injurious.

The first option is that charities can decide that they are unable to continue operations, since the property tax payment required could be substantial in comparison to their total budgets. A second available option is to reduce services. A third option is to increase the cost of their services, but doing so often makes the service inaccessible to those who most need them.

In any one of these cases, the cost of reducing the activities of these charities is eventually borne by the community. That is why these organizations have been granted tax-exempt status in the first place—to assure that their total resources are dedicated to meeting community needs.

Even with tax-exempt status, times are tough for these institutions. Government support for many nonprofit charitable activities has substantially declined since 1981. Demographic trends—including the aging of our population, the increase in homelessness, drug abuse, single-parent families, domestic violence, children living in poverty, and the increasing economic necessity of two parents in the family working in order to make ends meet—have resulted in the demand for more free and subsidized services. Private enterprise has, in recent years, invaded the traditional turf of nonprofit human service agencies. In virtually every case, the for-profit business has marketed its services to garner the most lucrative market segment, siphoning away clients who generated incremental revenue that was used by the nonprofit charities to cross-subsidize services for the needy. By skimming off this market share, private enterprise has placed an additional burden on the charitable nonprofit sector.

Finally, economic instability in Texas has had an impact on not only an increase in service demand, but also a decrease in the revenue depended upon by charities, including fees for service and charitable contributions.

Justification for the Charitable Tax Exemption

It is imperative that charities continue to reinforce the public policy reasons why this exemption deserves to be protected and continued.

Some of the reasons are:

1. Charitable nonprofits augment and, in some cases, replace the role of government in responding to and preventing society's problems. Tax-exempt status is an acknowledgment that these organizations have been deputized to act in the public interest and to improve societal conditions, rather than to serve any private interest. As a result, such tax-exempt organizations have a special responsibility to ensure that their programs and activities are consistent with these principles and that the level of accountability is on par with the government's.

2. Nonprofit charities have many advantages in responding to societal problems that are not available to government. Among them are:

- Nonprofit charities can be galvanized to attack a problem much more quickly than can government. Those who disagree with this need only consider how long it took for government to respond to problems such as AIDS, homelessness, and drug abuse compared with individual nonprofit charities. Clearly, nonprofits can respond to problems before a political consensus is developed by either the public at large or a legislative body. Charitable nonprofits can, in many cases, direct resources toward solving the problem without the typical government bureaucracy and lag time between the identification of a problem and the approval of a statute, budget, regulation, request-for-proposal (RFP), and the actual expenditure of funds to solve the problem.

- Nonprofits can effectively and efficiently respond to and solve problems that are localized in nature. This is a politically difficult task to accomplish under our present governmental system. Our political system often requires that a problem be universal in nature before resources are allocated to it. Also, politics make it more likely that government will be unable to target resources to solve a problem because there is often a cost to obtaining the necessary votes to pass a law.

- Nonprofits attract volunteers. Volunteers, both on boards and doing the actual work of the agency, include many who would not be attracted to government service and the constraints of government-affiliated organizations.

- Nonprofits can provide services when government programs, because of a limit on tax revenues, cannot expand. Charitable nonprofits often fill the void between what government provides to those who are destitute and what the for-profit sector provides to those who can afford the market rate for services. These charities provide services to those caught in the middle, who are not "poor enough" for government entitlement programs, but yet would be denied services by the for-profit sector. By charging fees for services on a sliding scale, these nonprofits are able to serve many who would otherwise not be served. This permits government to concentrate on serving only the neediest, while private business serves those who can afford to pay market rates.

The entire public benefits from the improvement of society resulting from the activities of these organizations. The tax exemption provided to charities is a cost to the entire public, but is only a small fraction of the public benefit accruing from these activities. Beyond the monetary benefit of this exemption, which permits these charities to commit all of their resources to the mission of the organizations, there is a principle involved. The tax exemption is an acknowledgment that the public values this type of altruistic activity and has foregone the collecting of taxes. It makes a statement that these organizations play an important role in strengthening the safety net that the government alone cannot offer.

It is in the public interest to promote the health of these charitable organizations, because government could not perform their missions as creatively, efficiently, or as cost-effectively.

Tips:

- To protect tax-exempt status, serve clients who cannot afford to pay the full cost of services and make services accessible to some clients who cannot afford to pay at all.

- Periodically quantify the dollar amount of free and subsidized services provided to the organization's clients and to the public at large and communicate that to the public.

- If state and local tax-exempt status is desired, develop a careful and honest outline of how the organization complies with state and local criteria. If staff members feel that compliance with these criteria is problematic, then consider changing operations to reasonably meet them.

Chapter 28
Mergers and Consolidations

Synopsis: Mergers involving nonprofit organizations are increasingly common and require planning. There are steps that should be taken when planning for a merger between nonprofit organizations to meet legal requirements and promote a successful transition.

It wasn't too long ago that many nonprofit boards considered liquidation to be a preferable alternative to mergers. Considering the loss of identity was just too painful, and the term "merger" conjured up a vision of a corporate shark gobbling up weaker entities. Since then, mergers and consolidations among nonprofit organizations have become increasingly common, spurred in part by cost-containment pressures that have been affecting the delivery of social services for several decades now, particularly in the healthcare industry. The lingering pandemic-induced recession that began in March 2020 and just never seems to go away has also motivated many nonprofits to consider merging.

Managed care, cuts in Medicare and Medicaid, DRG payments, and increased competition have been among the factors that have induced hundreds of nonprofit mergers among hospitals. There are increasing incentives for all nonprofit organizations to improve their efficiency and effectiveness. With the entry of for-profit organizations into providing services historically provided by nonprofits, competition for service dollars has increased. To create new sources of revenue, even staid nonprofits have become entrepreneurial and are offering services that may only be indirectly related to their core mission. Unwittingly, they may be siphoning off revenue from colleague organizations.

Factors That Trigger Merger Consideration

Among the events that trigger consideration of nonprofit mergers are—

- Organizations that deliver similar services recognize that economies of scale can be achieved.

- Organizations that are struggling financially seek a partner to stave off bankruptcy and liquidation.

- National organizations may place restrictions on local affiliates, such as having a minimum asset level, technology capability, and service menu, which cannot be met without combining with another local affiliate.

- Two nearby agencies find themselves engaging in destructive competition.

- Changes in leadership capability, both of staff and within the board, may trigger a strategic plan that recognizes an organization's inability to continue with the status quo.

- Scandal or other ethical challenges might surface in which merger or consolidation is seen as an alternative to liquidation.

- Changes in the outside regulatory environment or economic environment (e.g., managed care) may make it more attractive to increase economic power to maintain a viable market niche.

- A loss of membership may make it difficult or unfeasible to continue.

- The organization's mission has been accomplished successfully.

Generally, the reasons for suggesting a merger can be divided into three categories:

Economic reasons: A merger will help the organization become more efficient, take advantage of economies of scale, increase its access to members and/or clients, help it raise more donations and grants, and contain costs. The nonrenewal of a major grant that provided overhead expenses to the organization can threaten its continued existence. There is no longer the cash flow necessary to continue the operation.

Programmatic reasons: Organizations recognize that a strong synergy can be created by combining each organization's expertise to create new programs or offer a streamlined menu of existing services to a common population, permitting clients to avoid having to negotiate two or more organizational systems and venues to access services.

Strategic reasons: Strategic reasons include—

- An organization may be in a precarious state either economically or programmatically.
- Competition from for-profits or other nonprofits is becoming destructive, and funders are complaining.
- The board might be losing interest.
- A long-term CEO may be retiring, and there is no one to take his or her place with the vision necessary to lead the organization.
- The staff is demoralized because of an ineffective CEO who cannot be removed for political reasons.

- The public or funders have lost confidence in the organization as a result of ethical lapses or a reputation for poor quality.
- An organization in the outside environment is identified that, if a merger occurred, would create a strong collaboration.

How to Begin

At a 1997 workshop session on nonprofit mergers sponsored by the Pennsylvania Association of Nonprofit Organizations, William Morgan of Performance Industries and Paul Mattaini of Barley, Snyder, Senft & Cohen distributed a list of areas to consider when contemplating a merger.

Among the issues they raised were—

- the importance of infusing key leadership with the view that merging is a viable option

- whether the CEO will find a way to sabotage the merger because of ego

- whether the merger will fit into the organization's mission

- finding the right candidate to merge with, and finding the right staff (such as an attorney, accountant, and consultant)

- bringing together the two organizational cultures

- handling the public relations and community relations aspects.

Four Steps to a Merger

1. Each participating board should adopt a resolution in favor of the general principle of merging.

2. Each board should appoint a merger committee of board members and staff.

3. An outside, experienced merger consultant should be jointly hired to structure negotiations, with the cost shared by the participating organizations.

4. Meetings should be scheduled among the parties to discuss the goals of the merger; determine whether merging is feasible and makes sense for all parties; and negotiate, over time, the details, such as the change in

the mission and values, new name, staffing, logo, merger budget, board selection, bylaws, personnel policies, location, and what happens to staff who are no longer needed.

Budgeting

Mergers cost money. There are likely to be legal fees, consultant fees, audit fees, personnel costs relating to layoffs, moving costs, costs relating to covering the liabilities of the non-surviving corporation (which may be substantial, and responsible for triggering the merger idea in the first place), and even providing new building signs, printing new stationery and business cards, and designing a new logo.

As David La Piana writes in *Nonprofit Mergers: The Board's Responsibility to Consider the Unthinkable*—

> *Although it is unlikely that the financial position of two merging organizations will immediately improve as a result of a merger, well-conceived and -implemented mergers can raise staff morale, better focus the organization's activities, and increase overall energy levels—that will help the new group tackle difficult problems. Thus, a successful merger can offer relief and renewed hope for nonprofit boards, staff, and donors, and, most importantly, benefit clients because of the greater energy, increased funding, and better management possible with a more stable organization. In contrast, poorly conceived mergers may simply bring together two weak organizations that compound each other's problems.*

Obstacles to Merger

Virtually every article about the difficulty of merging two or more organizations refers to the two scourges that often scuttle the best laid plans: "turf" and "ego." Many, if not most, mergers of nonprofit organizations involve a financially strong organization merging with an organization that is merging to stave off bankruptcy or liquidation. The surviving organization will have one chief executive, and it is often a traumatic and, at times, potentially humiliating experience for the chief executive of the non-surviving organization to hand over the reins of decision-making. It is not unusual for an otherwise "routine" merger to be derailed by petty squabbling over the name of the combined organization, the logo, or the office space that will be provided to the staff of the non-surviving organization.

Legal Requirements

The legal procedures for mergers and consolidations that involve nonprofit corporations can be found in Texas law (Chapter 22.251 et seq.). Obviously, experienced, professional legal advice is necessary to carry out a successful merger.

Consolidations

Technically, a consolidation is different from a merger because the organizations merging form an entirely new organization. The new organization is often referred to as the "successor" organization. Some states do not differentiate between mergers and consolidations. For all practical purposes, they have most of the same issues to resolve as a merger. A blog article on nonprofit consolidations, which also applies to mergers in many respects, can be accessed at: *https://blog.concannonmiller.com/4thought/nonprofit-consolidation-the-pros-and-cons-and-how-to-do-it*

Tips:

- Merging organizations is not a "do it yourself" task. Always consult qualified professionals.

- If you are unable to assure employees that their jobs will not be in jeopardy as a result of a merger, plan to offer outplacement services.

- Don't take advantage of a merger situation by humiliating a party to a merger by flexing your power. The Golden Rule makes perfect sense in this situation.

Chapter 29
Quality Issues

Synopsis: Quality is as important to nonprofit organizations as it is to for-profit businesses, if not more so. Nonprofits need quality programs to compete for donations, clients, board members, workers, and political support.

Those who govern and manage nonprofit organizations are increasingly finding them subject to many of the same economic pressures as their for-profit counterparts. Their operations often resemble their for-profit competitors in both organizational structure and corporate culture. They are increasingly led by those trained in business rather than the social sciences, and their mentality and administrative style often reflect this. Stereotypically, managers trained in business school often make the "bottom line" paramount above the needs of clients.

In many cases, the products and services once provided solely by nonprofit, charitable organizations are now being provided by for-profits. One can often find health clubs, hospitals, online schools and universities, nursing homes, and day care centers—both for-profit and nonprofit—competing for clients on an equal basis within communities. When there is this direct competition, particularly in the delivery of human and educational services, cost is just one factor in a customer's decision. Quality of service is often even more important, and nonprofits that offer high-quality products and services obviously have a competitive edge. Those that cannot offer quality may find themselves out of business.

Many thousands of other nonprofit organizations do not have direct economic competition from others providing the same service. There is only one United Way affiliate in each community, one Arts Council, one Arthritis Foundation, one AARP affiliate, and one Special Olympics affiliate. Except under unusual circumstances, it is unlikely that another organization will sprout up to directly challenge one of these. It would be easy to jump to the conclusion that having a monopoly of this nature would mean that quality and performance are not as important as they are to those with direct, head-to-head competition for providing a particular product or service. That conclusion would be flawed.

Why Quality is Important to Nonprofit Organizations

Quality is important to all nonprofit organizations. None is immune from the consequences of neglecting it. Charities rely on loyal "customer" support, particularly at a time when there is an increasing reliance on fee-for-service revenues (see Chapter 26). Even if a nonprofit is not involved in direct economic competition, there is substantial competition for things that indirectly affect the viability of organizations. Among them are:

1. **Competition for government and foundation grants.** Most charitable nonprofits depend on grants to supplement any client fees they receive. Foundations are acutely aware of organizations that have poor reputations with respect to skimping on service quality. No one wants to be associated with such an organization. It is no wonder that first-class organizations often have little trouble attracting funding, because everyone wants to be associated with them.

2. **Competition for private donations**. Would you make a donation to a charity that had a reputation of treating its clients like animals? Unless that organization is the Society for Prevention of Cruelty to Animals (SPCA), you are more likely to look elsewhere for a charity worthy of your donation.

3. **Competition for board members.** Why would anyone want to serve on the board of a second-class nonprofit and risk being condemned or otherwise embarrassed by the media, the political hierarchy, and clients? There are only so many skilled, committed civic leaders in each community who are willing to donate their time and expertise to serve on nonprofit boards, and it is clearly not attractive to serve on the board of a charity with a reputation for poor quality.

4. **Competition for volunteers.** What can be said for board members goes double for service delivery and other volunteers. No one wants to be associated with an organization with a reputation for poor quality. Many volunteers see their volunteer work as a springboard for a career, and volunteering for a pariah in the community does not serve their interests.

5. **Competition for media.** The media play an important role in helping a nonprofit charity promote its fundraising, encourage clients to utilize its services, and improve employee morale. Poor quality can result in the media ignoring an organization or, worse, highlighting its shortcomings for the entire world to see.

6. **Competition for legislative and other political support.** Nonprofit charities have benefited from the support of political leaders—directly through the provision of government grants, and indirectly through the provision of favors such as cutting

government red tape and legislation to help solve the problems of the organization and those of its clients. Political leaders are certainly not going to be responsive to an organization if they receive letters of complaint about the organization's poor quality.

7. **Competition for qualified employees.** Quality nonprofits have less employee turnover and find it easier to attract employees to fill vacancies and for expansion. Considering the high transaction costs of recruiting, training and retaining workers, this continues to be an important consideration.

The consequences of poor quality, or the reputation (public perception) of having it, can result in the board of directors throwing up its hands and deciding to liquidate the organization. Or, in extreme cases, a state government agency might step in and liquidate the organization. Imagine the aftermath of a day care agency that failed to perform a quality background check on an employee who later was found to be a child abuser, or the hospital that failed to adequately verify whether a staff member it hired was adequately board-certified.

As pointed out by Dr. John McNutt, most, if not all, states look at the community benefit provided by a nonprofit organization in considering whether it is eligible for nonprofit status in the first place. Quality and community benefit are inextricably linked.

In 1998, an investigation by *The Chicago Tribune* uncovered that some international relief nonprofit organizations were asking donors to sponsor specific children, and failed to inform their donors that their sponsored child had died (see: *https://www.christianitytoday.com/ct/2001/december3/5.50.html*). Who knows how many millions of dollars will not be contributed because one official from one such organization did not feel it was important to inform donor sponsors that their sponsored child had died several years earlier?

The Cost of Poor Quality

An *Associated Press* article on January 8, 2002 reported that the American Red Cross disposed of 49,000 pints of blood collected after the September 11th disaster because of a lack of storage space. Many still think twice before responding to an urgent future call from that organization for blood donations, despite the obvious need to continually replenish the nation's blood reserves.

The cost to organizations with poor quality standards can be substantial. Just read the newspapers and you can find many more examples. Owners of assisted-living residences have failed to see the value of installing sprinkler systems and, as a result, have seen the loss of life and of their properties. Doctors have mistakenly removed the wrong kidney from a patient. Hospital maternity ward staff have given the wrong newborn to the wrong parents. The consequences of such lapses far exceed the financial loss and loss of prestige to the organization—human suffering for the clients and potentially huge, successful lawsuits against the nonprofit organization.

Quality in the Nonprofit Organizational Context

For the typical nonprofit that does not deliver client services, quality should mean much more than the ability to answer the telephone on the first ring. It means having a newsletter without typographical errors. It means having an attractive, periodically updated website. It means spelling the names of donors correctly in letters acknowledging donor gifts. It means delivering on promises made to legislators for follow-up materials. It means having conferences at which participants feel they get their money's worth. It means ensuring that each board member has all of the necessary and appropriate information to make governing decisions. It means that volunteers know in advance what is expected of them.

For those who deliver direct human services, it means, among other things:

- treating each client with the dignity he or she deserves
- respecting confidentiality
- providing on-time services
- providing timely resolution to legitimate complaints
- providing services in a safe and secure setting
- providing services in a facility that is accessible, clean, and functional
- delivering services provided by competent, trained personnel
- ensuring that services meet high standards and respond to the clients' needs
- obtaining informed consent from clients before services are provided
- seeking constant feedback from clients to improve the delivery of services
- using advances in technology to improve communication between the organization and its clients.

Online Resources to Explore:

National Institute of Standards and Technology's Baldrige National Quality Program
    https://www.nist.gov/baldrige

University of Wisconsin's Center for Quality and Productivity Improvement
    https://cqpi.wisc.edu/

American Society for Quality
https://asq.org/

The W. Edwards Deming Institute
https://deming.org/

Tips:

- Consider providing all organizational staff with training that focuses on improving quality.

- Make it organizational policy to promote "continuous quality improvement" of every program, activity, and work process.

- Continually seek feedback from the organization's funders, clients, and staff to identify problems before they evolve into serious quality deficits.

Chapter 30
Change Management

Synopsis: Change management strategies, such as Total Quality Management, Business Process Reengineering, Benchmarking, Outcome-Based Management, Large Group Intervention, Six Sigma, and Lean are potential ways to improve nonprofit organizational quality and performance.

In the context of this chapter, "change management" does not refer to a prescription for getting rid of the people who run the organization. Rather, it is a menu of strategies to change the philosophy of management to accomplish an objective or set of objectives such as, for example, improving efficiency and competitiveness, motivating employees and increasing their job satisfaction, or reducing absenteeism. In this sense, "change" is used as an adjective rather than a verb.

There is general agreement among scholars, practitioners, and management experts that organizations must adapt to changing conditions to survive. Technology advances; markets change; the requirements and expectations of customers evolve; and the needs of workers are altered as a result of demographics, economic conditions, and changes in culture, among other things.

Businesses, both for-profit and nonprofit, go out of existence every day. This is attributable to many causes. There may be an organizational scandal that causes the public to lose confidence or the government to take action. There may be quality lapses. The services provided by an organization may no longer be needed, or a competitor skims off a lucrative market share. The organization's operations may be too economically inefficient to support it. Government funding priorities or regulatory requirements may shift, leaving an organization in the lurch. The list of possible causes goes on.

For years, the for-profit business community has utilized formal change management strategies to improve operations and keep organizations competitive and vibrant, improve efficiency, generate loyalty, and maintain or expand support from customers. One time-tested change management strategy, strategic planning, is described in more detail in Chapter 6. It has only been recently that the nonprofit community, with health care institutions leading the way, started implementing some of these newer, more unconventional strategies.

Among the most popular change management strategies being considered by nonprofit organizations are Total Quality Management (TQM), Business Process Reengineering (BPR), Benchmarking, Outcome-Based Management (OBM), Large Group Intervention (LGI), Six Sigma, and Lean.

Total Quality Management (TQM)

TQM is an innovative, humanistic, general approach to management that seeks to improve quality, reduce costs, and increase customer satisfaction by restructuring traditional management practices. It requires a continuous and systematic approach to gathering, evaluating, and acting on data about what is occurring in an organization. The TQM management philosophy includes the following nine principles:

1. It asserts that the primary objective of an organization is to meet the needs of its "customers" by providing quality goods and services, and to continually improve them. In the nonprofit organizational context, customers include not only the direct recipients of services, such as clients, but the organization's board, elected and appointed government officials, the media, and the general public.

2. It instills in all of the organization's members an *esprit de corps,* assuring them that having quality as the number one goal is an important tenet. Every organizational member is responsible for quality, even if it is related to an issue beyond the scope of his or her job. Eliminating the "It's not my job" mentality becomes an achievable organizational objective.

3. It continuously searches for ways to improve every activity, program, and process. It does so by constantly seeking feedback from the organization's customers and promoting suggestions from all sources, both external and internal, on how to improve.

4. It rewards quality, not only internally, but from its suppliers. It recognizes that poor quality from an organization's collaborators, be they suppliers or other organizations, affects its own quality.

5. It recognizes that all staff members must receive continuous training to improve their work performance.

6. It encourages all components of the organization to work as a team to solve problems and meet customer needs rather than compete against each other.

7. It empowers workers at every level. It permits them to be actively engaged in decisions that affect the organization and to constantly look for ways to improve it.

8. It permits employees the opportunity to have pride in what they produce for the organization and to see the fruits of their labor measured in the quality of the service they provide, rather than just receiving a paycheck.

9. It promotes a planning process geared toward continuously improving quality in everything the organization does.

In 1992, the United Way of America developed the *Excellence in Service Quality Award* (ESQA) for nonprofit human service agencies. The purpose was to recognize that quality improvement is just as important, if not more so, in charities as in private business. 501(c)(3) charities were eligible for four levels of recognition. Judging and criteria were patterned after the Baldrige Award, which is given to for-profit corporations. The United Way of America discontinued this program in 1999. In 2004, the Congress enacted legislation authorizing nonprofit organizations to apply for the Baldrige Award beginning in 2007, with a one-year pilot program commencing in 2006. Two nonprofit organizations were among the five awardees in 2007, one nonprofit was among the three awardees in 2008, and two nonprofits were among the five awardees in 2009. Nonprofits dominated the six winners for 2019, who were Adventist Health White Memorial, Los Angeles, CA (health care); Center for Organ Recovery & Education (CORE), Pittsburgh, PA, (nonprofit); City of Germantown, Germantown, TN (nonprofit); Howard Community College, Columbia, Maryland (education); Illinois Municipal Retirement Fund, Oak Brook, Il (nonprofit); and the Mary Greeley Medical Center, Ames, IA (health care).

TQM principles are finding their way into nonprofit settings other than health care, such as community centers, arts organizations, and human services agencies. Focusing on the needs of the "customer" rather than on the "bottom line" is a value with which the nonprofit sector should feel comfortable compared with its for-profit counterpart. When a nonprofit organization's leadership becomes excited about TQM, the excitement can become contagious, provided that the behaviors of the leaders are consistent with their words. When it "happens," those in a TQM environment notice the difference, whether they work there or benefit from the organization's services. Workers feel empowered. Clients notice a positive difference in staff attitudes. Everyone associated with the organization feels good about it.

Business Process Reengineering (BPR)

If your heart stops beating and you keel over breathlessly, a professionally trained medical professional often can revive you by administering CPR. But if it's your *organization's* heart that fails, BPR, administered by professionally trained consultants or by those within an organization, is increasingly becoming the TLA ("three-letter acronym") of choice for cutting-edge managers. BPR is a successor to TQM as the latest management bromide for reviving comatose organizations.

Business Process Reengineering is defined by Michael Hammer (1948-2008), BPR's leading guru, as "the fundamental rethinking and radical redesign of business processes to achieve dramatic improvements in critical measures of performance (cost, quality, capital, service and speed)."

Fanatical interest in Total Quality Management peaked in the 1980s, but its once-pervasive influence seems to have waned in recent years. One of the reasons often given for TQM's apparent decline in the United States is that the philosophy of slow, incremental, and continuous improvement is generally inconsistent with American culture. Perhaps this is so; American organizational leaders are perceived as more impatient to see the tangible results of their business management interventions compared with their Asian, African, and European counterparts. They want to see quantum leaps of measurable improvement rather than the tortoise-paced improvement promised by TQM advocates. The tenure of many organizational leaders is short; several CEOs may come and go before TQM had had the time to be fully implemented to show results.

A major strategy involved with BPR efforts is to look at a business process involving many tasks that have been performed by several specialists. Then, the specialists are replaced with generalists (or the specialists are retrained to become generalists) who can handle all of the tasks of the process and have access to all of the information they need to do so.

BPR requires a new way of thinking. Unlike TQM, which requires the involvement of everyone in the organization, BPR is necessarily implemented from the top. It is the zero-based budgeting of business processes, contending that, at least theoretically, the past should have no bearing on what is planned for the future. It makes the assumption that organizations have evolved incrementally, reflecting a history of culture, tradition, technology, and customer needs that may not be particularly relevant today. BPR suggests that managers step out of the constraints of their current physical plant, work processes, organizational charts, and procedures and rules, and look at how the work would be performed if they were starting from scratch.

BPR requires an organizational leader to step back and answer the question: If I were building this organization today from scratch, knew what I know now, had the technology and human resources that I have now, and knew the customer needs that I have now, would I still be doing things the same way? More often than not, the answer is a resounding "no"! In the nonprofit environment, this might mean redesigning data collection and reporting, client intake, billing, purchasing, and every other process.

In many cases, new and more efficient technology is available. For example, a human service agency may receive a telephone call from a client requesting even a minimal change in service as a result of some change in circumstances. The person answering the telephone may have to put the person on hold and call the client's caseworker, who has the client's case file. The caseworker may have to put the person on hold and check with the supervisor for a decision on whether to waive a rule, and the supervisor may have to meet with the caseworker to make the decision.

Following BPR, the person answering the telephone may be able to pull up the case file on a computer screen and be preauthorized to approve a change in services within a constraint programmed into the computer. Or the person answering the telephone may be able to give the caller technical advice on how to solve a problem by searching a "frequently asked questions" file on a computer screen, instead of transferring him or her to a technical specialist.

Another way of looking at this is that everyone in the organization is conventionally functioning solely as his or her part of a process rather than on the actual mission of the organization. The receptionist answers the telephone. The case manager holds the file for a particular set of clients. The supervisor makes decisions authorizing variances from the organization's rules. BPR permits a work process to change so that the true objective of the process—responding to the client's needs—does not require the intervention of several people in the organization. The revolutionary advances in information technology permit this.

With the use of networked computers and an educated labor force, it is possible for a single person to process and troubleshoot an entire client request that previously may have required being passed serially from person to person in the organization, taking many days to complete. And the less hands involved in a process, the lower probability of an error.

Seven major principles of BPR are:

1. Use modern technology to redesign work processes rather than work tasks, concentrating on permitting a single person to achieve a desired outcome/objective.

2. Let the worker who uses the output of a process also perform the process. For example, instead of having a purchasing department make purchases of pencils and paper clips for the accounting

department and other departments, the accounting department orders its own pencils and paper clips and other "inexpensive and nonstrategic" purchases.

3. Let those in the organization who collect information be the ones who process it. For example, when the public relations department wants to send out its newsletter to a mailing list, it should be able to generate the mailing labels itself rather than having to make a request to a data processing department.

4. Treat decentralized organizational resources as centralized, utilizing information technology to bring them together. A college with several satellite campuses, for example, could link its bursars so that a student making a payment at either the main office or a satellite campus would have the payment show up in the records of the registrars of all of the campuses.

5. Electronically link disparate parts of an organization to promote coordination.

6. Let those who perform the work make the decisions, thereby flattening the pyramidal management layers and eliminating the bureaucracy and delay that slow down a decision-making process.

7. Use relational databases and other technology to collect and store information only once, eliminating both redundancy and error.

Generally, BPR often enables a single person to perform all of the steps in a process by using information technology. One advantage of BPR is that the need for many employees may be eliminated. This saves a lot of money for organizations. One downside is that implementing BPR, in some cases, has been known to terrorize a work force.

Benchmarking

Benchmarking refers to the process by which organizations study how organizations similar to theirs perform the same business processes and learn how to adapt those that are most efficient, innovative, and successful. Obviously, no two organizations are alike, and there is no guarantee that copying something from another organization will automatically work well in another. But certainly there is value in exploring how various organizations perform some of the same tasks and discussing what efficiencies they may have found that would improve business operations of similar organizations. For-profit organizations have been doing this in a formalized way for many years. Nonprofit organizations are only recently recognizing the value of benchmarking.

There are two types of benchmarking that nonprofit organizations might wish to consider. The first, internal benchmarking, looks at an organization and projects future goals, including a process by which employees are encouraged to meet performance targets. External benchmarking, on the other hand, tries to determine the "best practices" of similar organizations. Rather than reinventing the wheel, external benchmarking permits the allocation of minimal resources to finding how others have solved a problem, or have exponentially increased productivity with respect to some process, rather than having to discover that by themselves.

Many nonprofit organizations are not only willing to share this information, but are quite proud to do so. The fact that competition among nonprofit organizations is almost always either friendly or nonexistent promotes benchmarking in a manner that avoids some of the troublesome potential conflicts and ethical dilemmas in the for-profit context.

Jason Saul, writing in *Benchmarking for Nonprofits: How to Measure and Improve Performance*, says that nonprofits should typically consider benchmarking in three general categories: A *process* (such as screening job applicants or organizing inventory in a food bank), a *policy* (such as a salary structure or incentive plan), or a *program* (such as welfare-to-work or educational incentives).

Three approaches taken to benchmarking include:

1. *technical approach*—using computer models, statistics, spreadsheets, and other quantitative methods

2. *committee approach*—bringing in a team of experts from outside the organization to gather data and make judgments about which changes would be beneficial

3. *survey approach*—combining the above two models by creating a team of individuals from within the organization to identify which processes should be benchmarked, define the measures and organizational performance, obtain the "best practices" information, and implement these practices.

Saul, who is the co-founder of The Center for What Works, a Chicago-based clearinghouse for those studying solutions to social problems, recommends a seven-step process for benchmarking. It includes self-assessment, measuring performance, assembling the team, data collection, evaluating practices, translating best practices, and continuously repeating the process.

Outcome-Based Management (OBM)

To improve quality in a larger organization, simply adopting a progressive management philosophy such as TQM or BPR is not going to suffice in today's modern competitive business climate. As an organization grows, there are more pressures for accountability, not only internally from a board of directors, but externally from elected officials, government funders, foundation funders, individual donors and volunteers, and the public. Leaders of large organizations generally do not have the ability to visualize every aspect of their organization's operations and assess what is going on just by looking out their office windows or by engaging in informal conversations with their staff and clients. The proverbial "one-minute manager" is an ideal construct that is not particularly well suited to crystallizing the information a CEO needs to make judgments on how to allocate precious resources.

To accomplish the important task of determining what is really going on, most large organizations have a Management Information System (MIS). An MIS permits the aggregation of data in a form that can be analyzed by a manager, enabling him or her to see trouble spots and make adjustments in operations and to generate reports required by the government, funders, auditors, and the board of directors.

For many larger nonprofits, particularly those that depend on government and foundation grants rather than private donations, the objective of "meeting clients' needs" has become a more formalized process. Times have changed within just the last decade or so. Traditionally, measures of organizational performance for human service organizations were based on a model more appropriate for industrial processes, where raw materials were turned into finished products. In the language of industrial systems analysis, inputs (the raw material) were processed into outputs (the finished product).

In adopting an analogous frame of reference to industry, the conventional thinking was that human service agencies took in unserved clients (input), provided services (process), and changed them into served clients (output). In this way of thinking, organizations improved their output by increasing the number of clients served.

An exciting new way of looking at the output of an organization is called outcome-based management (OBM) or "results-oriented accountability" (ROA). Most recently, results-oriented management and accountability (ROMA) has become the buzzword describing this general tool. OBM focuses on program outcomes rather than by simply quantifying services delivered. Program outcomes can be defined as "benefits or changes for participants during or after their involvement with a program" (from *Measuring Program Outcomes: A Practical Approach, United Way of America*).

For example, an organization that deals with reducing drug abuse may have a stellar record of attracting clients through a flashy outreach program. It may be exemplary in convincing doctors in the community to donate thousands of hours of free services to the program, thereby reducing unit costs per client. It may have few complaints from the clients, who feel the staff are competent and treat them with dignity. An analysis of conventional data might indicate that there is little room for improvement. But, perhaps, no data were collected on whether those treated for drug abuse by the organization are successfully able to become independent, avoid future interactions with the criminal justice system, and abstain from drug use for an extended period of time—all measurable outcomes for a successful substance abuse program. If most of these clients are back on the street and abusing drugs, is that organization providing successful treatment, even if drug abuse services are being provided? Are funders and taxpayers getting a fair return on their investment?

In the outcome-based management model, the number of clients served is an input. The outcome is considered to be a measurement of the change in the condition of the clients after receiving the services. For example, if thousands of clients are served, but the condition of the clients has not improved, then the outcome is zero, even if the services were provided 100% on time, every client received a satisfactory number of hours of services, and there were no client complaints. It is no longer indicative of the effectiveness and value of an organization to only collect data on how many clients sought services, how many of these were accepted into the client stream rather than being referred or turned down, how many hours of service were provided, and how much each service cost and was reimbursed. Outcome data, together with the above process data, are needed to measure the effectiveness and value of an organization.

In addition to a significant change in attitude about the accountability of the private nonprofit sector, the passage in 1993 of the *Government Performance and Results Act*, PL 103-62, changed the way federal agencies plan, budget, evaluate, and account for federal spending. The intent of the act is to improve public confidence in federal agency performance by holding agencies accountable for program results and improving Congressional decision-making. The act seeks to accomplish this by clarifying and stating program performance goals, measures, and costs "up front." These changes were implemented beginning in September 1997.

For some organizations, the shift to outcome-based management will have modest cost implications. It may mean more data being collected from clients during intake. It may mean follow-up surveys to see what happens to clients after they have availed themselves of the organization's services. When this information is available, it is of extraordinary value to those who design, administer, and deliver those services.

What makes outcome-based management attractive to the human services sector is that it is common sense. What is the point of investing thousands, if not millions, of dollars of an organization's resources if the end result is not accomplishing what is intended by the investment—improving the lives of the organization's clients?

Our human service organizations have been established to make our lives better. When our organizations change their focus to concentrate on doing what it takes to do this, as opposed to simply providing human services, it is much more likely that this worthy goal can be accomplished successfully. Outcome-based management is compatible with the values of most in the sector, who often make financial sacrifices to make a difference in the lives of those who need human services.

In cases in which the data show that an organization is successfully providing services, but those services are not having the intended effect on the clients, the leadership should be the first to recognize that it is wasteful to continue business as usual. Outcome-based management is a powerful tool that allows organizations to allocate their precious resources to do the most good. If successfully implemented, it also can provide the ammunition to fight the increasing public cynicism about what is often perceived to be a poor return on investment of tax dollars and a competitive edge to organizations that adopt it.

Large Group Intervention (LGI)

Large Group Intervention (LGI) is the generic term given to a family of formal change management strategies that involve placing large parts of an organization, or even the entire organization, in simultaneous contact with one another to plan how the organization is going to change.

Proponents and users of LGIs believe these methods are particularly well suited to organizations seeking to establish a shared vision of their future and to build a road to get there. Some LGI models are designed specifically for organizations that seek to change the way their work is done (e.g., through reengineering or business process redesign).

Although many different LGI models have been developed and are in current use, they generally have common origins and are rooted in similar principles. Among these principles are getting the "whole system" into interactive discussion, using a carefully designed mixture of communication elements and processes designed to make effective use of participants' emotions as well as thoughts, and facilitating effective dialogue while validating differing perspectives.

Strategies such as TQM and BPR, as well as strategic planning itself, demand that each member of the organization thinks about the needs of the entire organization rather than his or her piece of it. "Democratic," participatory efforts by organizations may facilitate their members to see beyond the borders of their individual organizational niche and develop the spirit required to make TQM not simply a "program" but a working philosophy.

The general philosophy inherent in planning change is recognizing that there is resistance to change within organizations. Change is more likely to be successfully implemented when people affected can participate in the process, influence the process, and prepare for its consequences.

Much more than a device for overcoming psychological resistance, LGI is an effective approach to substantially improve the probability that a planned change will achieve its objectives, and have more desirable results for the organization. One dimension of additional benefits is more effective communication about the planned changes. Plans become far less distorted when everyone affected is hearing the same message at the same time, rather than having it communicated through the grapevine, through regular hierarchical channels, or not at all.

Another advantage of LGI is that those affected by the changes can provide invaluable input. It is rare that a few layers of management (or a subset of the full breadth of functions) within an organization can have an adequately detailed grasp of the whole. In most change management strategies, those at the bottom of the hierarchy—usually the most aware of the "nuts and bolts" of current reality—are often frozen out of the planning process. Most LGI models bring in a broad base of stakeholders to brainstorm together and weed out problems and unintended consequences that typically are invisible to the unrepresentative group of employees on the planning staff.

A third advantage of LGI is that it builds a diverse and broad base of support for planned changes. Useful in all cases, this advantage becomes particularly powerful when circumstances alter, planned changes need to be modified, and time is of the essence. Circumstances that otherwise could be expected to derail well-laid plans can be addressed by a robust and already engaged subset of the organization. Plans are far more open to effective alteration midstream when developed via an LGI approach.

LGIs tend to bring together people from various hierarchical levels within the organization, who otherwise may have minimal direct interaction. Many organizational development experts believe that this pays an additional dividend of creating positive social linkages among organizational members that otherwise would not have been created. Large Group Interventions create a new and different organizational bonding, which increases networks of informal communication within an organization and provides for more flexible and adaptive capabilities.

All of this can occur in a three-day period, significantly curtailing the process time of conventional change management planning.

Permitting workers affected by planning to participate in the planning process is one strategy to erode resistance to organizational change. LGIs also generate fresh ideas from people who have expertise as a result of doing their jobs every day. They may have shied away from making valid, responsible suggestions, not only because "no one ever asked us," but because they may feel that their views are not important, or that management does not have an interest in listening to them.

Large Group Interventions are usually staged in a setting away from the workplace, where participants can focus on the objective at hand without the distractions of the normal work environment. Artificial boundaries within organizations, such as functional departments, are routinely and intentionally fractured to facilitate communication and participation. These boundaries often get in the way of addressing important needs of organizations.

Among the most popular models for LGIs are the Search Conference, Future Search Conference, and Real-Time Strategic Change.

Six Sigma

Six Sigma (a.k.a. "6 Sigma"), a registered trademark of the Motorola Corporation, refers to a statistically-based technique to reduce variability in business processes. Its intent is to reduce waste and rework, and streamline these business processes, eliminating unnecessary steps that may add to defects, and improve processes to further the intended goal of producing "virtually perfect" outcomes—thus increasing profits and increasing customer satisfaction.

It gets its name from the Greek letter (σ) used in the statistical term representing standard deviation. Its goal is to reduce the number of events in which a product falls outside of intended acceptable limits to .0034%, equivalent to six standard deviations from the mean. In practical terms, this means that the goal is to reduce defects to 3.4 per million events.

Six Sigma conjures up a new way of thinking about business processes—"how to work smart" rather than "how to work hard." It has much in common with the earlier versions of quality improvement management strategies, such as TQM and BPR. Like TQM, it involves the participation of every member of the organization and infuses employees with a spirit of improving the quality of the organization's product or service delivery in every possible way it can. Like BPR, it is a "top down" management tool, and it systematically seeks to redesign any business process that is either unnecessary or contributes to defects. And by doing so, it has the potential to promote the elimination of jobs and parts of jobs that are not adding to the organization's value.

All nonprofits, as business organizations, have some work processes in common that are ripe for Six Sigma interventions. Invoicing, accounts payable and receivable, personnel recruitment, and customer scheduling are examples. Eliminating waste from fundraising procedures and volunteer management are some that are unique to the sector.

As a formal change management strategy, Six Sigma may not be attractive to the small soup kitchen, day care center, or symphony orchestra, partly because the cost of implementing it—for consultants, specialized computer software, compensation packages, and training—might well exceed the entire budget of the small nonprofit. Despite that limitation, it can be constructive to learn about Six Sigma concepts, if only to think about what imperfections exist in the way work processes are being carried out that contribute to mistakes being made.

Nonprofits have limited resources, and wasteful spending often means that worthy clients cannot be served. Staff resources, almost always limited, can be better devoted to expanding services rather than dealing with the consequences of defects in the provision of services. It is often much more efficient and less costly to change a system that creates defects than to correct those mistakes after they occur.

In larger nonprofits, particularly in the healthcare and higher education sectors, Six Sigma programs are potentially cost-effective, and in some cases, in a transformational way. One additional advantage is that many of these organizations already have TQM programs in place, reducing any disruption as a result of piggybacking Six Sigma efforts and making existing TQM outcomes more successful. Integrating Six Sigma into a current TQM program can enhance the outcomes.

One can make a strong case that it is a good outcome to reduce defects in television sets to a standard of 3.4 per million events (99.9997%) from three standard deviations, 66,800 per one million events (93.3%). It is frustrating to a customer and costly to a manufacturer to respond to customer complaints about a defective newly-purchased television. Now, compare that to the value to society taking into consideration the consequences of a surgical team taking out the wrong kidney or a child protective services worker placing a vulnerable child with abusive foster parents.

Mistakes are going to be made by workers, regardless of circumstances. That is one aspect of the human condition. Yet, every organization, in achieving some mission or program goal, has procedures that contribute, through their design, to increasing or decreasing the probability that a mistake will be made. The philosophy of Six Sigma is that using statistical techniques and collecting sufficient data, it is possible to see where current procedures relating to work processes are contributing to mistakes, and then to analyze what steps can be implemented to redesign these processes to reduce the probability that the mistakes will reoccur.

A 2008 study commissioned by the Society of Actuaries calculated that the cost of medical errors in the United States was $19.5 billion, causing 2,500 deaths and 10 million lost work days annually as a result of 1.5 million errors. A subsequent study that factored in additional economic factors, such as the costs of lost workdays and the value of the lives that were cut short, estimated that the cost approached $1 trillion. Even if Six Sigma could reduce this unnecessary cost by only 1%, that is certainly substantial, even putting aside the immeasurable cost to society of needless suffering.

For making any particular manufacturing process effective, Six Sigma uses the DMAIC method:

- Define
- Measure
- Analyze
- Improve
- Control

"Define" involves identifying the process that is to be targeted for improvement.

"Measure" relates to assessing which parts of a particular business process affects customer satisfaction and which can be improved in a way that reduces defects.

"Analyze" pertains to the phase in which the business process is studied to determine all potential sources that result in variability, and thus contribute to a defect.

"Improve" is the phase in which the process is redesigned and implemented, and a cost-benefit analysis is conducted.

"Control" is the final phase, in which what has been achieved is documented and monitored, and results are verified using statistical control processes,

Lean

Lean is a management technique related to Six Sigma that focuses primarily on looking at business processes in the context of what is really of value to the end customer. Thus, if any particular business process or part of one doesn't really add anything that is of value to the customer, measured as something that the customer would be willing to pay more for, then it is eliminated—unless, of course, it is required by law or regulation or would otherwise provide some competitive advantage. So, Lean analyzes business processes to eliminate waste and reduce the time it takes to complete each business process. Lean Six Sigma combines these two compatible change management strategies into one.

Eight categories of waste in the context of Lean Six Sigma are:

1. Defects—This involves choices among scrapping, reworking, returns from the customer, and all other problems emanating from the production of a product/service that does not meet customer specifications.

2. Overproduction—Creating more capacity of the product or service than the market is willing to buy means no revenue is ever generated from the work that went into creating that product or service.

3. Waiting—This encompasses not only waiting for raw materials and partially completed products to be received by the next business process, but also obtaining approvals and quality checks before the next process can be implemented. For example, an entire team of professionals may be kept waiting because of a delay in the intake process of another team.

4. Personnel inefficiencies—Unnecessary meetings and conference calls are among the examples of how the time of large numbers of people can be "wasted."

5. Transportation—This involves the costs and time delays of moving materials around during the production process.

6. Inventory—There are consequences of having too much or too little inventory. Too much ties up capital and limits storage space, and it requires more management to keep track of it. Too little means that important components might not be available when they are needed, adding to wait time.

7. Motion—This refers to keeping resources (including people, but including tools and materials) farther away the less important they are, and arranging personnel and materials efficiently to reduce the time it takes to coordinate all business processes.

8. Extra Processing—This refers to eliminating processes that cost money but do not add to the value of the finished product, such as overheating or air conditioning, or using machines to deliver parts when simple gravity could replace them.

Online Resources to Explore:

Top 15 Change Management Blogs & Websites To Follow
https://blog.feedspot.com/change_management_blogs/

Change Activation
https://changeactivation.com/

15 Change Management Tools To Effectively Manage Organizational Change
https://academy.whatfix.com/change-management-tools/

The Deming Institute
https://deming.org/

American Society for Quality (ASQ) Resources page
https://asq.org/quality-resources

Tips:

1. Do not fall into the "goal displacement" trap by concentrating more on the paperwork involved in making a TQM program run than on the actual change in culture and staff attitudes that make TQM an attractive change management strategy.

2. Consider the steps that might be necessary to undo a change management strategy in the event that it simply does not work for one reason or another.

3. Make sure your change management strategy does not bring about the undesirable outcome of making your organization more streamlined, efficient, and effective, but with employees who cannot stand to be there anymore.

4. Incorporate useful concepts in this chapter, such as benchmarking and outcome-based management, into your strategic planning process in the event your organization engages in such planning.

Chapter 31
Organization and Program Evaluation

Synopsis: A formal program evaluation process is often a requirement of funders, but is otherwise an important exercise to determine whether nonprofit organizations and programs are effective. There are two major types of evaluations—formative and summative. Evaluations may be performed by in-house staff or outside consultants, and each has its advantages and disadvantages. Regardless of who performs an evaluation, organizations should engage in a thorough planning process.

In the opening to his seminal book *Utilization Focused Evaluation,* the required textbook in the graduate school course on program evaluation that I took at Penn State, Michael Quinn Patton relates the following parable:

> *In the beginning, God created the heaven and the earth.*
> *And God saw everything that He made. "Behold," God said, "it is very good." And the evening and the morning were the sixth day.*
> *And on the seventh day God rested from all His work. His archangel came then unto Him asking, "God, how do you know that what you have created is 'very good'? What are your criteria? On what data do you base your judgment? Just exactly what results were you expecting to attain? And aren't you a little close to the situation to make a fair and unbiased evaluation?"*
> *God thought about these questions all that day and His rest was greatly disturbed. On the eighth day God said, "Lucifer, go to hell."*
> *Thus was evaluation born in a blaze of glory...*

I love this story for many reasons, but I think it crystallizes in my mind some of the dilemmas of program evaluation in a humorous way. To those who run programs, an evaluation is often perceived as a way outsiders find fault with how they operate their programs and make decisions. To the evaluators, they often find that staff are not forthcoming because of a fear that blame for any shortcomings will fall on them. Yet, it clearly makes no sense for those who run and fund programs not to step back occasionally and determine whether what they are doing is really working as they expect, and how their programs could be improved.

Evaluation is a general term that describes determining whether an existing organization or a particular program of an organization is fulfilling its purposes, goals, and objectives, and if it is achieving results from its efforts and allocation of resources. The term is also used in the context of determining how well an organization's employees are functioning.

Organizations are increasingly being asked to engage in formal evaluation exercises by stakeholders, including the organization's own board, government grantors, private foundations, and donors. Many subsectors within the nonprofit sector, such as hospitals, universities, and nursing homes, are required to have periodic formal evaluations by the private agencies that have been formed to provide accreditation. Virtually every government or foundation grant includes a requirement for an evaluation of the program being funded at the end of the grant period. And, as described in Chapter 30, the scope of evaluations has ratcheted upward with a movement to focus on program outcomes, evaluating not simply whether an organization is doing the work that it says it is doing—such as providing so many hours of counseling—but determining whether those who are receiving the organization's services are actually having their lives and the community in which they live changed for the better as a result of having received those services.

According to the Government Accountability Office, the *Government Performance and Results Act of 1993* was enacted "to shift the focus of government decision-making and accountability away from a preoccupation with the activities that are undertaken—such as grants dispensed or inspections made—to a focus on the results of those activities, such as real gains in employability, safety, responsiveness, or program quality." The United Way of America displayed leadership in adopting an outcome-based approach and advocating for its implementation by nonprofit organizations funded by its affiliate umbrella fundraising charities.

Program evaluation has in recent years become a routine requirement, as nonprofit organizations are increasingly being asked to be accountable for the dollars being spent to further their missions. And this is a good thing, generally. It certainly doesn't make much sense to spend government tax dollars and funds gratuitously donated by foundations, corporations, and the public on programs that are not accomplishing much. Even the fact that there will be an evaluation of a program can serve as motivation to continue to improve its operation, so as to avoid the consequences of a poor evaluation. Evaluations often uncover flaws in program management that might not otherwise be discovered, thus improving the delivery of services to those who need them and making programs both more efficient and effective. For the leadership of nonprofit organizations, this is valuable information.

One downside is that those involved in programs being evaluated often view evaluations as something that is being done to them rather than with them, and there can be a real fear that a poor evaluation, regardless of whether this is performed by an outside consultant or in-house staff, could result in a program being terminated, putting their jobs at risk. Evaluations cost money and other scarce resources, and they often require staff to put aside their work of providing services to participate in the data collection process.

The intent of formal program evaluations is to provide objective assessments of what is going on in an organization and/or its programs. Ideally, the evaluation should be carried out by someone experienced in the tools and techniques of program evaluation, and who has no bias with respect to judging the program and its staff. This is easier said than done. It is quite clear that it is much more subjective and a clear conflict of interest for the staff of an organization's programs to be the ones who evaluate their own organization or program. Yet, evaluations performed by outside consultants can be expensive, and such consultants often do not have the background and know the staff well enough to reach conclusions about what might improve a program.

Regardless of who carries out the evaluation, the more "objective" the evaluator can be, the more likely the evaluation will address program shortcomings in a fair way. Evaluations should be focused on making programs better in the future rather than pointing the finger of blame, and crafted in language that provides a clear roadmap for implementing constructive changes.

What Is Program Evaluation?

Program evaluation is a form of research. It involves data collection and analysis of that data. Program evaluation is a process that involves the systematic collection of information about an organization to determine how well the organization or its individual programs are working, and what might be done to improve performance. Information that is collected might include the program's activities; program outputs; program outcomes; program work processes and policies; data about program quality; how stakeholders, including clients, perceive the program; and judgments about ways the organization's program could improve to reach its stated goals.

There are two general forms of a program evaluation. A summative evaluation is one that focuses primarily on the effectiveness of a particular program. Typically, a summative evaluation is conducted after a program is completed, and its purpose is to determine whether the program is effective enough to continue. This is the type of evaluation most requested by funders, who need to determine whether to continue funding the program for future years. A formative evaluation is one that is used to determine how a program might be improved. Formative evaluations look at a program's strengths and weaknesses, problems that exist with implementation and how they might be addressed, changes in the program that are being suggested by stakeholders, unintended consequences of program implementation, and new ideas that might be tested to improve performance. Stakeholders are staff and board of the organization, its funders, those who directly benefit from its services (clients, patients, and consumers are among the terms used by organizations to describe recipients of their services, and each one has a connotation that can be viewed as positive or negative, depending on the organization's culture), community leaders, government leaders, and the public at large.

The distinction between the two is that summative implies a final judgment about the program; formative does not. As related in Patton's book, Bob Stake, an evaluation theorist at the University of Illinois, came up with an apt metaphor to describe the difference:

> *When the cook tastes the soup, that is formative; when the guests taste the soup, that's summative!*

Why Program Evaluation Is Performed

The most common reason why program evaluation is performed is somewhat obvious—it is required by an organization's stakeholder with power to require it (such as an accreditation body), or a grantor (such as the government or a foundation). Yet there are clear benefits for an organization's board or CEO to insist that a program or the entire organization be periodically evaluated.

Benefits include—

- Evaluations uncover flaws in a program, which can lead to corrective action, improving service delivery, outcomes of clients, and more efficient use of scarce organizational resources.

- They can help determine whether a program is really doing what it was designed to do.

- They validate that a "good" program is really a "good" program by having this determined by an objective third party, rather than the organization itself.

- They help program staff step back and reflect on what they can do to improve efficiency and effectiveness of a program. Staff can brainstorm and communicate ideas to someone trained in looking for patterns, and who may have experience in working with other organizations that have responded to the same type of problems. Program staff may otherwise be too engrossed in providing the services and have little time to consider how the delivery of these services could be improved, or communicate about program policies that they feel are barriers to overcoming problems.

Who Performs a Program Evaluation

There are generally three options in deciding who will perform a program evaluation: using an outside consultant, using staff from the organization itself, or using a combination of the two. For example, an outside consultant may design and direct the evaluation with organization staff performing a major role in collecting and analyzing the data. Outside evaluators are often found in research think tanks and educational institutions. There are also many private consultants who offer this service.

Each option has its own advantages and disadvantages.

Outside Consultants

Advantages

- Outside consultants typically have special training in how to perform formal program evaluations.
- They can be more objective than an in-house staff evaluator, as they have no direct stake in the findings of the evaluation.
- They have experience working with other organizations and can provide a perspective that in-house evaluators do not have.
- They can do much of the work of an evaluation, freeing the organization's staff from tasks that would otherwise disrupt their routines.

Disadvantages

- Outside consultants are expensive compared to in-house evaluators.
- They are likely to not have too much background about the organization.
- They are likely to not have as much background about the program's recipients.
- They may be unable to get close enough to the program to understand what is really going on.
- They may be willing to provide an organization with a more "positive" evaluation than warranted by the facts, knowing that this may enhance their potential for obtaining future evaluation contracts from the organization.

In-House Staff

Advantages

- In-house staff are likely to be less expensive than outside consultants.
- They are more likely to understand the program's objectives.
- They are more likely to understand the programs themselves, their target populations, and their other stakeholders.
- They are more likely to understand and be sensitive to the internal politics of the organization and already know the staff, organization structure, and culture.

Disadvantages

- In-house staff are more likely to be perceived as being less objective than an outside consultant.
- They are less likely to know how other, similar organizations are dealing with work processes.
- They may be too busy doing their other tasks for the organization to do a good job evaluating.

Combination of the Two Models

Some organizations use an evaluation method that combines these two models. An outside consultant can direct the evaluation, develop the methodology, and analyze the data, while staff can do the leg work and collect the appropriate data. Or a staff member can direct the evaluation and a consultant can make sure the data collection and analysis are both appropriate and valid. This assures that there is some outside technical expertise that can be accessed, but that staff feel more buy-in to the results if they have a major role in participating in the evaluation.

Obviously, whatever model is chosen must be consistent with the practices and standards of the stakeholder requiring the evaluation.

Planning for Program Evaluation

The planning for program evaluation begins at the point at which a program is conceived, often at a point before funding is obtained to implement it. First, each program needs to be associated with a concrete, measurable set of goals and objectives. What must be measured are aspects of the program that relate to how well the organization is providing its services. This is typically done by compiling a set of outputs and outcomes that are hoped to be achieved before a program is started. A list of these benchmarks is typically provided to a funding organization in advance of funding as part of the grant application. Although it seems to be common sense, organizations don't always design their management information systems to capture this data, even though doing so saves a lot of time and effort when it is time to perform an evaluation.

For example, let's consider a program to assist homeless people in a community in not engaging in using illegal substances and alcohol. In applying for grant funds for such a program, an organization would likely provide data on how many people in the community are homeless and how many of them use illegal drugs and/or alcohol. The organization would carefully document the lack of other programs that sufficiently provide these services, to demonstrate that this new program would not be duplicative and would fill a need. The organization that received a grant to provide such a program would have intake of homeless clients with a drug or alcohol problem, provide treatment, and then attempt to keep track of these clients over time and measure whether they still use illegal drugs and alcohol after completing the program. Of course, this is not so simple; homeless people tend to be transient. It may not be possible to know whether someone is using drugs and alcohol (although it may be possible to know that clients are being admitted to other programs in the area for treatment, or are entering the criminal justice system for drug- and alcohol-related crimes—data that could serve as a surrogate for other data that would be much harder to collect). But the point is that data should be routinely collected that will help evaluators determine whether a program is being effective, and it makes sense to have a system in place that has this data collected before it is required for an evaluation rather than after.

An excellent model for planning an evaluation can be found at: *https://managementhelp.org/evaluation/program-evaluation-guide.htm#anchor4294569952*

Another useful document is provided by the Office of Planning, Research & Evaluation of the Department of Health and Human Services' Administration for Children and Families (OPRE). In Chapter 6 of this free, online, evaluation guide, the Office recommends that organizations consider scores of issues when designing their program evaluation. Among them are four recommendations:

1. *Designate the evaluation framework.* This includes the program objectives; evaluation questions; evaluation time frame; and a discussion of the context for the evaluation, particularly the aspects of the organization, program staff, and participants that may affect the evaluation.

2. *Consider procedures and methods.* These include those that will be used to obtain the evaluation data and answer the evaluation questions. Organizations need to decide where the data will come from (e.g., client records, staff interviews, observations by evaluators of clients receiving services, data already collected by the MIS system), whether the data will consist of samples or comprise the entire population being studied, what types of survey instruments will be used (such as email questionnaires, telephone interview questions, focus groups), how to keep the information collected confidential and secure while respecting the privacy of respondents, how to design consent forms permitting the release of data from individuals, who will administer the instruments or otherwise collect the data, and the methods that will be used to analyze the data.

3. *Select your evaluation design.* The design should allow you to assess whether participation in the program is really responsible for making a difference seen in the recipients or is perhaps caused by some other factor(s). This gets to the issue of causality. For example, let's assume that you run a drug treatment center that provides services to individuals. Your data show that those who received services used illegal drugs less after one year in the program. One interpretation is that the program was effective in reducing drug use. But there are other possible explanations: Perhaps the price of drugs increased beyond the ability of these individuals to afford them. Or, perhaps new laws and increased drug law enforcement put drug pushers in jail, so that users no longer had easy access to drugs. Or perhaps these individuals simply "grew up" and no longer felt the need to use illegal drugs.

Evaluators often use scientific procedures to eliminate threats to validity, as they are called, that call the explanation of results of a study into question.

For example, there are a lot of threats to validity when evaluators rely on a simple pre-test/post-test design of an evaluation. That is, the evaluator measures some variable that is considered important (e.g., drug use) before services are delivered, and measures the same variable in the individuals after the services are delivered.

Many threats to validity are eliminated by using a control group. The evaluator may randomly assign two groups of individuals, one group receiving the treatment and the other not receiving any treatment, and then do pre-test/post test to determine if there are any differences between the two groups. There are problems with this procedure, as well, as it may be unethical for an organization to deny services to those who need them simply because of an evaluation experimental design. But putting ethical considerations aside, using a control group with random assignment is much preferable to a simple pre-test/post-test research design in determining whether the program itself is the cause of improvement in program recipients. Many nonprofit organizations can ethically use control groups in their evaluations, because the demand is so great for their services that there is often a large waiting list of unserved clients.

But the bottom line remains. As the OPRE document summarizes, evaluations are designed to answer basic questions such as:

- Did program participants demonstrate changes in knowledge, attitudes, behaviors, or awareness?
- Were the changes the result of the program's interventions?

Those who are trained in administering evaluations have a lot of research and statistical tools, including effective experimental designs, at their disposal to get valid answers to these questions.

4. *Manage and monitor the evaluation.* This involves how staff will be trained and monitored with respect to working on the evaluation, making sure the survey instruments are culturally appropriate and clear, making sure staff are informed about what is going on and their responsibilities to cooperate with the evaluation, and validating that the evaluation will answer the right questions.

The full text of the OPRE document, *The Program Manager's Guide to Evaluation, Second Edition,* can be accessed at:

https://www.acf.hhs.gov/opre/resource/the-program-managers-guide-to-evaluation-second-edition

Conclusion

Many nonprofit executives have a fear of program evaluation, but in most cases, this fear is unfounded. For those who are committed in the sector to serving the needs of the most vulnerable in our society, program evaluation is one of the most useful tools available to improve the management of nonprofit organizations. A nonprofit organization's board and staff leadership have a stake in identifying what is working and not working in their programs. They have an obligation to document to funders and the public that their dollars are being used wisely, and that the organization is accountable for the trust placed in it to provide services that are appropriate and high quality. In many cases, an evaluation provides the evidence that the organization is meeting its obligations and worthy of being funded. As more and more evaluations of organizations occur, the knowledge base of what works and what doesn't is expanding, and society is the main beneficiary of this effort.

Tips:

- Design organization programs before implementation begins so that evaluations can be performed easily if and when they are required.

- If you are performing the evaluation in-house, determine what the interests are of stakeholders, such as funders.

- Take advantage of the data collected and analysis of that program to improve your organization's performance, rather than simply considering it to be an exercise.

Appendix A

Sample Texas Certificate of Formation for organizations seeking 501(c)(3) federal tax-exempt status (Use Form 202)
(review by an attorney before submission is highly recommended)

Article 1 – Entity Name and Type

The filing entity being formed is a nonprofit corporation. The name of the entity is: (insert name)

Article 2 – Registered Agent and Registered Office

A. The initial registered agent is (insert name)

C. The business address of the registered agent and the registered office address is: (insert business address)

Article 3 – Management

The management of the affairs of the corporation is vested in the board of directors. The number of directors constituting the initial board of directors and the names and addresses of the persons who are to serve as directors until the first annual meeting of members or until their successors are elected and qualified are as follows: (A minimum of three directors is required.)

Director 1_____
First Name M.I. Last Name Suffix, Street or Mailing Address, City,, State Zip Code Country

Director 2_____
First Name M.I. Last Name Suffix, Street or Mailing Address, City,, State Zip Code Country

Director 3_____
First Name M.I. Last Name Suffix, Street or Mailing Address, City,, State Zip Code Country

Article 4 – Membership
The nonprofit corporation will have no members.

Article 5 – Purpose
The nonprofit corporation is organized for the following purpose or purposes:

This corporation is organized exclusively for one or more purposes as specified in Section 501(c)(3) of the Internal Revenue Code or the corresponding section of any future federal tax code, including, for such purposes, the making of distributions to organizations that qualify as exempt organizations under Section 501(c)(3) of the Internal Revenue Code, or the corresponding section of any future tax code.

Supplemental Provisions/Information

No part of the net earnings of the corporation shall inure to the benefit of, or be distributable to its members, trustees, officers, or other private persons, except that the corporation shall be authorized and empowered to pay reasonable compensation for services rendered and to make payments and distributions in furtherance of the purposes set forth in Article Third hereof. No substantial part of the activities of the corporation shall be the carrying on of propaganda, or otherwise attempting to influence legislation, and the corporation shall not participate in, or intervene in (including the publishing or distribution of statements) any political campaign on behalf of or in opposition to any candidate for public office. Notwithstanding any other provision of these articles, the corporation shall not carry on any other activities not permitted to be carried on (a) by a corporation exempt from federal income tax under section 501(c)(3) of the Internal Revenue Code, or the corresponding section of any future federal tax code, or (b) by a corporation, contributions to which are deductible under section 170(c)(2) of the Internal Revenue Code, or the corresponding section of any future federal tax code

Upon the dissolution of the organization, assets shall be distributed for one or more exempt purposes within the meaning of Section 501(c)(3) of the Internal Revenue Code, or corresponding section of any future federal tax code, or shall be distributed to the federal government, or to a state or local government, for a public purpose.

Organizer

The name, street or mailing address of the organizer: _____

_____

Effectiveness of Filing

This document becomes effective when the document is filed by the secretary of state.

Execution

The undersigned affirms that the person designated as registered agent has consented to the appointment. The undersigned signs this document subject to the penalties imposed by law for the submission of a materially false or fraudulent strument and certifies under penalty of perjury that the undersigned is authorized to execute the filing instrument.

Date: _____

_____
signature of organizer

_____
printed or typed name of organizer

Appendix B
Sample Bylaws

Note Bylaws are an important legal document, and should be examined, if not drafted, by an experienced attorney. The intent of this sample is to provide a list of traditional provisions of bylaws of nonprofit organizations. I recommend that bylaws be custom-designed to serve the needs of the organization.

Note 2: These sample bylaws are for organizations that choose to be governed by a board of directors, rather than its members. For a different set of sample bylaws for organizations in Texas, see:

https://www.austintexas.gov/sites/default/files/files/EDD/Sample%20Non-profit%20Bylaws.pdf

Bylaws of the _____

INTRODUCTION and PURPOSE

1. These bylaws constitute the code of rules adopted by the _____, a non-profit organization, for the regulation and management of its affairs. The purposes of the corporation are to _____ and, further, to engage in any other lawful business purpose to be conducted on a not-for-profit basis. In carrying out such purposes, the corporation shall not exercise any powers not permitted to be exercised by an organization exempt under Section 501(c)(3) of the United States Internal Revenue Code of 1954.

MEMBERSHIP

2. The Corporation shall have no "members."

DIRECTORS

3. Definition of Board of Directors: The Board of Directors is that group of persons vested with the management of the business and affairs of this Corporation subject to the law, the Certificate of Formation, and these bylaws.

4. Qualifications: Directorships shall not be denied to any person on the basis of race, creed, sex, religion, sexual orientation, or national origin.

5. Number of Directors: The Board of Directors shall consist of _____ or more natural persons. The number of directors shall be determined from time to time by Resolution of the Board of Directors.

6. Terms and Election of Directors: The Directors shall serve a maximum of _____ terms beginning at the January board meeting, and ending at the January board meeting approximately one year thereafter, until they resign or are removed in accordance with the provisions of these bylaws.

7. Procedure at Board Meetings: The rules contained in the Handbook on Parliamentary Procedure ("Robert's Rules of Order") shall govern the meetings of the board of directors.

8. Resignations: Any Director can resign at any time by delivering a written resignation to the President of the board or to the Secretary of the Corporation. Resignations of directors shall become effective immediately or on the date specified therein and vacancies will be deemed to exist as of such effective date.

9. Removal: Any director may be removed at any time (with or without cause) by a vote of 4/5ths of the total number of incumbent directors (not counting vacancies or the director subject to the removal action) at a meeting of the board of directors properly called in accordance with the terms of these bylaws. Directors may be removed by a majority vote of the board of directors at a properly called meeting with a quorum attendance when he or she misses three consecutive regular meetings.

10. Vacancies: Vacancies can be created by resignations, removals, or an increase in the size of the board of directors. Vacancies on the Board of Directors can only be filled by a majority vote of the remaining Directors, though less than a quorum.

11. Place of Director's Meetings: Meetings of the board of directors, regular or special, will be held at the primary place of business for this Corporation or at any other place within or without the _____ metropolitan area as provided or such place or places as the board of directors may designate by resolution duly adopted.

12. Meetings: Board meetings shall be held at least four times each year. Special meetings of the Board of Directors may be called by:

    A. at least two-thirds of the Board of Directors
    B. the President
    C. the Secretary upon the written request of at least two-thirds of directors.

13. Notice of Board Meetings: Notice of all board meetings shall be given to each board member no less than five (5) days prior to the meeting.

14. Waiver of Notice: Attendance by a Director at any meeting of the Board of Directors will constitute a waiver of notice of such meeting except where such Director attends the meeting for the express purpose of objecting, at the beginning of the meeting, to the transaction of business because the meeting is not lawfully called or convened.

15. Quorum: A third of the incumbent directors (not counting vacancies or directors under the age of 18) shall constitute a Quorum for the conduct of business. At Board meetings where a quorum is present, a majority vote of the Directors attending shall constitute an act of the Board unless a greater number is required by the Certificate of Formation or any provision of these bylaws. Attendance by telephone conference call or video conference call whereby all members physically present at a board meeting can hear any participant not physically present and vice-versa shall constitute being present for purposes of determining whether a quorum is present.

16. Self Dealing: No director shall use confidential information gained by reason of being a member of the board of directors for personal gain to the detriment of the corporation.

OFFICERS

17. Roster of Officers: The Corporation shall have a President, Vice President, Secretary, and Treasurer.

18. Selection and Removal of Officers: All officers shall serve _____ year terms. Officers shall be elected by the Board of Directors at the board's first meeting of the calendar year or as soon as practical thereafter. Officers shall remain in office until their successor has been selected. The Board of Directors may elect a single person to any two or more offices simultaneously, except that the offices of President, Vice President, Treasurer, and Secretary must be held by separate individuals.

19. President: The President will perform all duties incident to such office and such other duties as may be provided in these bylaws or as may be prescribed from time to time by the Board of Directors. The President shall preside at all board meetings and shall exercise parliamentary control in accordance with Roberts Rules of Order.

20. Vice-President: The Vice-President shall perform the duties of the President in the absence or unavailability of the President, or when the office of President is vacant.

21. Secretary: The Secretary will keep minutes of all meetings of the Board of Directors, will be the custodian of the corporate records, will give all notices as are required by law or these bylaws, and generally, will perform all duties incident to the office of Secretary and such other duties as may be required by law, by the Certificate of Formation, or by these bylaws.

22. Treasurer: The Treasurer will have charge and custody of all funds of this Corporation, will oversee and supervise the financial business of the corporation, will render reports and accountings to the Directors as required by the Board of Directors, and will perform in general all duties incident to the office of Treasurer and such other duties as may be required by law, by the Certificate of Formation, or by these bylaws or which may be assigned from time to time by the Board of Directors.

23. Removal of Officers: Any officer elected or appointed to office may be removed by the Board of Directors whenever in their judgment the best interests of this Corporation will be served. Such removal, however, will be without prejudice to any contract rights of the Officer so removed.

INFORMAL ACTION

24. Waiver of Notice: Whenever any notice whatever is required to be given under the provisions of the law, the Certificate of Formation, or these bylaws, a waiver of such notice in writing signed by the person or persons entitled to notice, whether before or after the time stated in such waiver, will be deemed equivalent to the giving of such notice. Such waiver must, in the case of a special meeting of members, specify the general nature of the business to be transacted.

25. Action by Consent: Any action required by law or under the Certificate of Formation or by these bylaws, or any action which otherwise may be taken at a meeting of either the members or board of directors may be taken without a meeting if a consent in writing, setting forth the action so taken, is signed by all of the persons entitled to vote with respect to the subject matter of such consent, or all directors in office, and filed with the secretary of the Corporation.

COMMITTEES

26. Appointment of Committees: The Board of Directors may from time to time designate and appoint one or more standing committees as it sees fit. Such committees shall have and exercise such prescribed authority as is designated by the Board of Directors.

27. Executive Committee: The officers of the Corporation designated in these by-laws shall constitute the executive committee. The board of directors may, if it so chooses, appoint other persons to serve on the Executive Committee. The President shall act as chairperson of the executive committee. The Executive Committee shall have such authority as may be given to it from time to time by Resolution of the Board of Directors.

OPERATIONS

28. Fiscal Year: The fiscal year for this Corporation will be the calendar year, unless the Board otherwise so designates by majority vote.

29. Inspection of Books and Records: All books and records of this Corporation may be inspected by any Director for any purpose at any reasonable time on written demand.

30. Loans to Management: This Corporation will make no loans to any of its Directors or Officers.

31. Execution of Documents: Except as otherwise provided by law, checks, drafts, and orders for the payment of money of this Corporation shall be signed by at least two persons who have previously been designated by a Resolution of the board of directors, unless the Board by majority vote approves authorizing one person for this purpose in cases of payments for amounts of less than $500 in the aggregate for any single purpose. Contracts, promissory notes, leases, or other instruments executed in the name of and on behalf of the Corporation shall be signed by one or more persons who have been authorized and directed to do so by the board of directors. No contract shall be valid unless it is authorized or ratified by a properly adopted Resolution of the board of directors.

32. Conflict of Interest and Whistleblower Policies. This Corporation shall have a conflict of interest policy consistent with the Sample Conflict of Interest policy of the Internal Revenue Service and a whistleblower policy.

33. Dissolution. Upon the dissolution of the corporation, assets shall be distributed for one or more exempt purposes within the meaning of section 501(c)(3) of the Internal Revenue Code, or the corresponding section of any future federal tax code, or shall be distributed to the federal government, or to a state or local government, for a public purpose. Any such assets not so disposed of shall be disposed of by a Court of Competent Jurisdiction of the county in which the principal office of the corporation is then located, exclusively for such purposes or to such organization or organizations, as said Court shall determine, which are organized and operated exclusively for such purposes.

AMENDMENTS

34. Amendments. The Board of Directors may alter, amend, suspend or repeal these Bylaws at any regular or special meeting called for that purpose, except as restricted by state or federal law.

PUBLIC STATEMENTS

35. Authority to make Statements. No person, except for the President or staff authorized by the Board to do so are authorized to make any public statements, whether written or oral, purporting to represent the official policy, position, or opinion of this Corporation, without first having obtained the approval of the Board of Directors.

36. Limitation on Statements. Any person who is authorized to make any public statement, whether written or oral, purporting to represent the official policy, position, recommendation or opinion of the Corporation, shall first make it clear that he or she is representing the Corporation. Thereafter, throughout the entire presentation, he or she shall confine his/her presentation only to those matters which have been properly approved by the Corporation. He or she shall not at the same time present any statement purporting to represent any other firm, group, or organization or purporting to represent his or her own personal views.

37. Electronic Meetings. Subject to the provisions of applicable law and these bylaws regarding notice of meetings, Members may, unless otherwise restricted by statute, by the Certificate of Formation or by these bylaws, participate in and hold any meeting of the members by using conference telephone or similar communications equipment, or another suitable electronic communications system, including videoconferencing technology or the internet, or any combination, if the telephone or other equipment system permits each person participating in the meeting to communicate with all other persons participating in the meeting. If voting is to take place at the meeting, reasonable measures must be implemented to verify that every person voting at the meeting by means of remote communications is sufficiently identified and a record must be kept of any vote or other action taken. Participation in a meeting pursuant to this section shall constitute presence in person at such meeting, except when a person participates in the meeting for the express purpose of objecting to the transaction of any business on the ground that the meeting was not lawfully called or convened.

INDEMNIFICATION

38. Indemnification of Directors, Officers, Employees and Agents. The Corporation may indemnify any person who was or is a party or is threatened to be made

a party to any threatened, pending, or completed claim, action, suit, or proceeding, whether civil, criminal, administrative, or investigative (other than an action by or in the right of the Corporation) by reason of the fact that he or she is or was a director, officer, employee, or agent of the Corporation, or is or was serving at the request of the Corporation as a director, partner, officer, employee, or agent of another corporation, partnership, joint venture, trust, or other enterprise, against expenses (including attorneys' fees inclusive of any appeal), judgments, fines, and amounts paid in settlement actually and reasonably incurred by him in connection with such claim, action, suit, or proceeding if he or she acted in good faith and in a manner he or she reasonably believed to be in or not opposed to the best interests of the Corporation, and with respect to any criminal action or proceeding, had no reasonable cause to believe his or her conduct unlawful. The termination of any claim, action, suit, or proceeding by judgment, order, settlement, conviction, or upon a plea of nolo contendere or its equivalent, shall not, of itself, create a presumption that the person did not act in good faith and in a manner which he or she reasonably believed to be in or not opposed to the best interests of the Corporation, and, with respect to any criminal action or proceeding, had reasonable cause to believe that his or her conduct was unlawful. The Corporation may indemnify any person who was or is a party or is threatened to be made a party to any threatened, pending, or completed claim, action, or suit by or in the right of the Corporation to procure a judgment in its favor by reason of the fact that he or she is or was a director, officer, employee, or agent of the Corporation, or is or was serving at the request of the Corporation as a director, partner, officer, employee, or agent of another corporation, partnership, joint venture, trust, or other enterprise against expenses (including attorneys' fees inclusive of any appeal) actually and reasonably incurred by him or her in connection with the defense or settlement of such claim, action, or suit if he or she acted in good faith and in a manner he or she reasonably believed to be in or not opposed to the best interests of the Corporation and except that no indemnification shall be made in respect of any claim, issue, or matter as to which such person shall have been adjudged to be liable for negligence or misconduct in the performance of his duty to the Corporation unless and only to the extent that a court of competent jurisdiction (the Court") in which such claim, action, or suit was brought shall determine upon application that, despite the adjudication of liability but in view of all the circumstances of the case, such person is fairly and reasonably entitled to indemnity for such expenses which the Court shall deem proper. To the extent that a director, officer, employee, or agent of the Corporation has been successful on the merits or otherwise in defense of any claim, action, suit, or proceeding referred to in Section, or in defense of any claims, issue, or matter therein, he or she shall be indemnified against expenses (including attorneys' fees inclusive of any appeal) actually and reasonably incurred by him or her in connection therewith, notwithstanding that he or she has not been successful (on the merits or otherwise) on any other claim, issue, or matter in any such claim, action, suit, or proceeding. Any indemnification this provision (unless ordered by the Court) shall be made by the Corporation only as authorized in the specific case upon a determination that indemnification of the director, officer, employee, or agent is proper in the circumstances because he or she has met the applicable standard of conduct set forth in this provision. Such determination shall be made (a) by the Board of Directors by a majority vote of a quorum consisting of directors who were not parties to such action, suit, or proceeding, or (b) if such a quorum is not obtainable, or, even if obtainable, a quorum of disinterested directors so directs, or by independent legal counsel in a written opinion. Expenses incurred in defending a civil or criminal action, suit, or proceeding may be paid by the Corporation in advance of the final disposition of such action, suit, or proceeding as authorized by the Board of Directors in the specific case upon receipt of an undertaking by or on behalf of the director, officer, employee, or agent to repay such amount unless it shall ultimately be determined that he or she is entitled to be indemnified by the Corporation as authorized in this Article. The indemnification provided by this provision shall not be deemed exclusive of any other rights to which those indemnified may be entitled under any statute, rule of law, provision of the Certificatge of Formation, Bylaws, agreement, vote of disinterested directors, or otherwise, both as to action in his or her official capacity and as to action in another capacity, while holding such office, and shall continue as to a person who has ceased to be a director, officer, employee, or agent and shall inure to the benefit of the heirs, executors, and administrators of such a person. Where such other provision provides broader rights of indemnification than these Bylaws, said other provision shall control. The Corporation shall have power to purchase and maintain insurance on behalf of any person who is or was a director, officer, employee, or agent of the Corporation, or is or was serving at the request of the Corporation as a director, partner, officer, employee, or agent of another corporation, partnership, joint venture, trust, or other enterprise against any liability asserted against him or her and incurred by him or her in any such capacity, or arising out of his status as such, whether or not the Corporation would have the power to indemnify him or her against such liability under the provisions of this Article.

CERTIFICATION

I hereby certify that these bylaws were adopted by the Board of Directors of the_____at their meeting held on _____.

_____
Secretary

Appendix C
Addresses of IRS Taxpayer Assistance Centers in Texas

Abilene
500 Chestnut Street
Suite 109
Abilene, TX 79602
(325) 676-5709

Amarillo
7201 W. Interstate 40
Ste. 105
Amarillo, TX 79106
(806) 359-2160

Austin
825 E. Rundberg Ln.
Austin, TX 78753
(512) 499-5127

Corpus Christi
Suite 1614
Corpus Christi, Texas 78401
(361) 903-1919

Dallas
1100 Commerce St.,
Rm. 121
Dallas, TX 75242
(214) 413-6010

El Paso
700 E. San Antonio
El Paso, TX 79901
(915) 834-6508

Farmers Branch
4050 Alpha Rd.,
Rm. 170
Farmers Branch, TX 75244
(214) 413-6010

Ft. Worth
819 Taylor St.,
Rm. 6A14
Ft. Worth, TX 76102
(682) 707-0177

Harlingen
1810 Hale Ave.
Harlingen, TX 78550
(956) 365-5185

Houston (Downtown)
1919 Smith St.
Houston, TX 77002
(281) 721-7021

Houston (NW)
12941 I45 N
Houston, TX 77060
(281) 721-7021

Houston (SE)
8876 Gulf Freeway
Houston, TX 77017
(281) 721-7021

Houston (SW)
8701 S. Gessner
Houston, TX 77074
(281) 721-7021

Longview
913 NW Loop 281,
Ste. 212
Longview, TX 75604
(903) 297-3142

Lubbock
1205 Texas Ave.,
Rm. 606
Lubbock, TX 79401
(806) 401-8891

Midland
1004 N. Big Spring
Midland, TX 79701
(432) 686-9977

San Angelo
33 E. Twohig
San Angelo, TX 76903
(325) 653-0082

San Antonio
8122 Datapoint Drive
San Antonio, TX 78229
(210) 841-2090

Texarkana
500 N. Stateline St.
Texarkana, TX 75501
(903) 794-8214

Tyler
909 ESE Loop 323,
Rm. 300
Tyler, TX 75701
(903) 561-2732

Waco
6801 Sanger Ave.,
Ste. 1000
Waco, TX 76710
(254) 741-2312

Wichita Falls
4309 Jacksboro Hwy.
Wichita Falls, TX 76302
(940) 766-6317

Appendix D
Foundation Center Funding Information Network Partners

Amarillo
Amarillo Area Foundation
Grants Center
801 S. Fillmore, Ste. 700
Amarillo, TX 79101
Phone: (806) 376-4521

Arlington
Arlington Public Library
George W. Hawkes Central Library
101 W. Abram St.
Arlington, TX 76010
Phone: (817) 459-6900

Austin
Texas Grants Resource Center
505 East Huntland Drive
Suite 270
Austin, TX 78752
Phone: (512) 475-7373

Beaumont
R. C. Miller Memorial Library
Beaumont Public Library System
1605 Dowlen Rd.
Beaumont, TX 77706
Phone: (409) 866-9487

Burleson
Burleson Public Library
248 SW Johnson Avenue
Burleson, TX 76028
Phone: (817) 426-9210

Dallas
Dallas Public Library
Urban Information
1515 Young St.
Dallas, TX 75201
Phone: (214) 670-1400

Denton
University of North Texas
Eagle Commons Library
307 Avenue B
Sycamore Hall
Denton, TX 76203
Phone: (940) 369-7815

El Paso
University of Texas at El Paso
Center for Civic Engagement
500 W. University
Benedict Hall 103
El Paso, TX 79968
Phone: (915) 747-7969

Houston
United Way of Greater Houston
50 Waugh Dr.
PO Box 3247
Houston, TX 77007
Phone: (713) 685-2312

Houston Public Library
500 McKinney St.
Houston, TX 77002
Phone: (832) 393-1313

Kingsville
Texas A&M University - Kingsville
James C. Jernigan Library
700 University Blvd., MSC 197
Kingsville, TX 78363
Phone: (361) 593-3416

Longview
Longview Public Library
222 W. Cotton St.
Longview, TX 75601
Phone: (903) 237-1350

San Angelo
Tom Green County
Public Library
33 W. Beauregard Ave.
San Angelo, TX 76903
Phone: (325) 655-7321

San Antonio
San Antonio Area Foundation
303 Pearl Pkwy., Ste. 114
San Antonio, TX 78212
Phone: (210) 225-2243

Sherman
Austin College
Abell Library
900 N. Grand Ave.
Sherman, TX 75090
Phone: (903) 813-2236

Temple
Temple Public Library
100 W. Adams Ave.
Temple, TX 76501
Phone: (254) 298-5702

Tyler
United Way of Tyler/Smith County
East Texas Center for Nonprofits
4000 Southpark Dr.
Tyler, TX 75703
Phone: (903) 581-6376 Ext. 107

Appendix E
New Year's Resolutions for Nonprofit Executives

by Gary M. Grobman
(reprinted with permission from *Pennsylvania Nonprofit Report*)

It's December, and another year has slipped by. Replacing calendars on the wall is often an excuse for introspection. I've made some New Year's resolutions of my own, and it's not too late for you to do so if you haven't. Let me make a few suggestions.

1. Become an exemplary, ethical individual, every minute, every day. Don't use organizational resources for personal use and don't tolerate others in your organization who do. Consider whether you are creating conflicts of interest with your decisions. Don't cheat on your expense account. Register your organization with the state agency that regulates charitable organizations if you are required to do so. Consider registering with that agency and disclosing information even if you are not required to do so because your fundraising is under the threshold requirements. Be honest with your board and staff (most boards are much more tolerant of mistakes made than they are of lying about it, anyway!). Your standard of ethics reflects not only upon you and your organization, but also upon our sector as a whole. The shock waves surrounding the New Era debacle and the United Way fiasco in the 1990s are still being felt. The public is becoming more cynical about how charities operate. Don't be someone who adds to this sense of cynicism. It's also easier to sleep at night when you know you didn't do something dishonest or questionable during the day.

2. Make sure you have a healthy, vibrant personal life. It is so easy running an organization to become consumed by the pressures, challenges, and demands that accompany leadership and neglect your health, family, hobbies, and vacation needs. If you are one of those who find it impossible to leave the office to take vacation, remember that even the President plays golf and takes vacations, and he's a really busy executive! If your organization is such that it can't survive with you away for a few days, then that is a sign that something is unhealthy with either you or the organization. Fix it. And then go take a hike (on the Appalachian Trail). If you are getting too many evening calls from your board chair or (God forbid!) unnecessary calls in the middle of the night, politely inform him or her that you are no longer willing to take these calls, and that there are 900 numbers available for late night companionship needs.

3. If your organization can afford it, consider making a voluntary contribution to a local government or a foundation established to support local governments. There is some legitimacy to the view of local governments that charities use their services and do not pay for it, and this places a strain on their ability to function. There is also legitimacy to our sector's view that as charities, we should be exempt from taxes or involuntary monetary payments. Yet many in our sector recognize that we have a partnership with local governments to make society better. One way to do so is to help our local governments, on a voluntary basis, when we can do so. If your organization cannot or will not provide money, then offer services.

4. Be sensitive to the legitimate concerns of small business. Small business people are not the enemies of charities. They serve on our boards. They provide us with valuable products and services. They purchase our products and services. How would you feel if you invested not only your entire life savings but your entire emotional capital in a business, and a local charity used its profits as venture capital to establish a commercial business (i.e., designed not to serve any charitable mission but to generate net revenue) to compete head-to-head with yours, and had the advantage of not paying taxes, paying cheaper postage rates, had volunteers, access to capital, and the public relations value that comes from being a "charity"? There is clearly a role for charities to generate revenue to fund services for the community. But there is a right way and a wrong way of doing this. The Jewish Community Center or YMCA that places advertisements in general circulation newspapers seeking corporate memberships touting that its fees are slightly lower than the private health club a mile away is probably not violating any laws. But they are violating the spirit of why the JCC health club and YMCA are eligible for tax-exempt status. The hospital that markets its laundry service to the general public may be paying unrelated business income taxes on its revenue, but this style of marketing creates tensions within the small business community, and for good reason. Should my public library be offering best-sellers and videos for fees that undercut existing small businesses? A gray area, and we could argue that one for a long time. But my point stands: Before establishing or expanding a commercial business under the aegis of charitable tax-exempt status, even if it is not violative of any unfair business competition provisions of your state law, think twice. There are ways to generate income by providing services and products that don't step on toes.

5. Join and support a state advocacy association. The non-profit charitable community faces problems and challenges that are too big for any individual to face alone. There are associations based in most state capitals and Washington whose job is to identify these problems and challenges, devise a strategy to meet them head on, and coordinate advocacy. Many of these organizations are starved for membership and resources because it is easy for a charity to avoid its responsibilities and let the burden fall on the "other guy." There is strength in numbers, and if you run an agency that thinks it can save a few dollars by not making an investment in its future, you're being short-sighted. And while you are at it, join a professional organization, as well.

6. Get some continuing education to improve your ability to manage your organization. Whether it is in the grants writing, computer, management, strategic planning, time management, or board/staff relations areas, virtually every nonprofit organization manager can benefit by some outside training. Taking a course also offers a break from the office routine and brings you in contact with peers from other disciplines. It's good for networking, good socially, good for your brain, and, best of all, many organizations will pay all of the costs!

7. Take advantage of the internet, and set up social networking pages and use mobile apps that hawk your products and services. The communications revolution shouldn't leave you and your organization behind. Each day, thousands of "newbies" access these sites, which have become the access points of choice for information about volunteering, charitable giving, news and views, demographic data, and contacts within your field. A modest home page; active presence on Twitter, Facebook, and LinkedIn; blog; and online store can be established and maintained for surprisingly low cost and effort. And, believe it or not, it's lots of fun.

8. Invite your local legislators to visit your agency and/or meet with your board. Whether at the City Council/County Commissioner, state legislature, or Congressional level, the decisions made by our elected officials affect our organizations, our clients, our volunteers, our board members, and us. There are many benefits in establishing a relationship with these officials before you need something from them. This is especially important if your agency is the recipient of government funding, or hopes to be in the future.

Appendix F
Sample Financial Reports: Association for Research on Nonprofit Organizations and Voluntary Action (ARNOVA)

ASSOCIATION FOR RESEARCH ON NONPROFIT ORGANIZATIONS AND VOLUNTARY ACTION
STATEMENTS OF FINANCIAL POSITION
DECEMBER 31, 2019 AND 2018

ASSETS

	2019	2018
Cash	$ 241,604	$ 413,447
Cash held by others (Note 10)	31,917	21,119
Total cash	273,521	434,566
Investments	1,027,725	847,593
Accounts receivable	39,921	10,907
Grants receivable	460,000	995,500
Prepaid expenses	7,478	8,055
Equipment and software, net	3,814	4,112
Total assets	$ 1,812,459	$ 2,300,733

LIABILITIES AND NET ASSETS

LIABILITIES

	2019	2018
Accounts payable	$ 153,694	$ 207,452
Accrued payroll and benefits	58,002	47,028
Deferred revenue	21,439	5,430
Funds held on behalf of others (Note 5)	49,975	-
Total liabilities	283,110	259,910

COMMITMENTS (NOTE 11)

NET ASSETS

	2019	2018
Without donor restrictions		
Undesignated	572,979	531,978
Board designated (Note 6)	286,148	289,838
Total net assets without donor restrictions	859,127	821,816
With donor restrictions	670,222	1,219,007
Total net assets	1,529,349	2,040,823
Total liabilities and net assets	$ 1,812,459	$ 2,300,733

See accompanying notes to financial statements.

3

ASSOCIATION FOR RESEARCH ON NONPROFIT ORGANIZATIONS AND VOLUNTARY ACTION
STATEMENT OF ACTIVITIES
FOR THE YEAR ENDED DECEMBER 31, 2019
WITH COMPARATIVE SUMMARIZED INFORMATION FOR THE YEAR ENDED DECEMBER 31, 2018

	WITHOUT DONOR RESTRICTION	WITH DONOR RESTRICTION	2019 TOTAL	2018 TOTAL
REVENUE AND SUPPORT				
Grants	$ 61,392	$ 65,500	$ 126,892	$ 893,000
Membership dues	144,020	-	144,020	161,395
Conference revenue and sponsorships	207,838	184,392	392,230	315,160
Publications and royalties	184,681	20,000	204,681	176,966
Contributions	11,565	-	11,565	1,140
In-kind contributions (Note 1)	-	263,700	263,700	263,700
Investment income (loss), net (Note 4)	180,424	-	180,424	(64,060)
Other	2,850	-	2,850	3,749
Net assets released from restrictions	1,082,377	(1,082,377)	-	-
Total revenue and support	1,875,147	(548,785)	1,326,362	1,751,050
EXPENSES				
Program				
Events	668,892	-	668,892	585,236
Publications	327,081	-	327,081	331,474
Membership services	183,182	-	183,182	162,658
Other programs	423,903	-	423,903	474,089
Total program expenses	1,603,058	-	1,603,058	1,553,457
Management and general	192,954	-	192,954	173,576
Fundraising	41,824	-	41,824	60,004
Total expenses	1,837,836	-	1,837,836	1,787,037
INCREASE (DECREASE) IN NET ASSETS	37,311	(548,785)	(511,474)	(35,987)
NET ASSETS, BEGINNING OF YEAR	821,816	1,219,007	2,040,823	2,076,810
NET ASSETS, END OF YEAR	$ 859,127	$ 670,222	$ 1,529,349	$ 2,040,823

ASSOCIATION FOR RESEARCH ON NONPROFIT ORGANIZATIONS AND VOLUNTARY ACTION
STATEMENT OF ACTIVITIES
FOR THE YEAR ENDED DECEMBER 31, 2018

	WITHOUT DONOR RESTRICTION	WITH DONOR RESTRICTION	TOTAL
REVENUE AND SUPPORT			
Grants	$ 5,000	$ 888,000	$ 893,000
Membership dues	161,395	-	161,395
Conference revenue and sponsorships	206,360	108,800	315,160
Publications and royalties	151,966	25,000	176,966
Contributions	1,140	-	1,140
In-kind contributions (Note 1)	-	263,700	263,700
Investment loss, net (Note 4)	(64,060)	-	(64,060)
Other	3,749	-	3,749
Net assets released from restrictions	1,074,139	(1,074,139)	-
Total revenue and support	1,539,689	211,361	1,751,050
EXPENSES			
Program			
Events	585,236	-	585,236
Publications	331,474	-	331,474
Membership services	162,658	-	162,658
Other programs	474,089	-	474,089
Total program expenses	1,553,457	-	1,553,457
Management and general	173,576	-	173,576
Fundraising	60,004	-	60,004
Total expenses	1,787,037	-	1,787,037
INCREASE (DECREASE) IN NET ASSETS	(247,348)	211,361	(35,987)
NET ASSETS, BEGINNING OF YEAR	1,069,164	1,007,646	2,076,810
NET ASSETS, END OF YEAR	$ 821,816	$ 1,219,007	$ 2,040,823

ASSOCIATION FOR RESEARCH ON NONPROFIT ORGANIZATIONS AND VOLUNTARY ACTION
STATEMENTS OF CASH FLOWS
FOR YEARS ENDED DECEMBER 31, 2019 AND 2018

DECREASE IN CASH

	2019	2018
CASH FLOWS FROM OPERATING ACTIVITIES		
Cash received from members and others	$ 1,404,733	$ 775,188
Cash paid to employees and suppliers	(1,564,037)	(1,325,150)
Interest and dividends received, net of fees	19,830	18,824
Net cash used in operating activities	(139,474)	(531,138)
CASH FLOWS FROM INVESTING ACTIVITIES		
Capital expenditures	(2,033)	(3,030)
Purchases of investments	(19,538)	(18,387)
Net cash used in investing activities	(21,571)	(21,417)
DECREASE IN CASH	(161,045)	(552,555)
CASH, BEGINNING OF YEAR	434,566	987,121
CASH, END OF YEAR	$ 273,521	$ 434,566

See accompanying notes to financial statements.   8

ASSOCIATION FOR RESEARCH ON NONPROFIT ORGANIZATIONS AND VOLUNTARY ACTION
STATEMENTS OF CASH FLOWS, CONTINUED
FOR YEARS ENDED DECEMBER 31, 2019 AND 2018   Page 2 of 2

RECONCILIATION OF CHANGE IN NET ASSETS TO NET CASH
USED IN OPERATING ACTIVITIES

	2019	2018
CHANGE IN NET ASSETS	$ (511,474)	$ (35,987)
ADJUSTMENTS TO RECONCILE CHANGE IN NET ASSETS TO NET CASH USED IN OPERATING ACTIVITIES		
Depreciation and amortization expense	2,331	2,724
Unrealized and realized (gain) loss on investments	(160,594)	82,884
(Increase) decrease in operating assets		
Accounts receivable	(29,014)	29,445
Grants receivable	535,500	(793,000)
Prepaid expenses	577	27,366
Increase (decrease) in operating liabilities		
Accounts payable	(53,758)	164,181
Accrued payroll and benefits	10,974	3,916
Deferred revenue	16,009	(12,667)
Funds held on behalf of others	49,975	–
Total adjustments	372,000	(495,151)
NET CASH USED IN OPERATING ACTIVITIES	$ (139,474)	$ (531,138)

See accompanying notes to financial statements.   9

Appendix G
National and Texas Organizations/Publications of Interest

National Organizations

American Society of Association Executives and the Center for Association Leadership
1575 I Street, NW
Washington, D.C. 20005-1103
Phone: (202) 371-0940, Fax: (202) 371.8315
Email: asaeservice@asaecenter.org
Website: *https://www.asaecenter.org/*

Association for Research on Nonprofit Organizations and Voluntary Action
441 W. Michigan St.
Indianapolis, IN 46202
Phone: (317) 684-2120; Fax: (317) 684-2128
Contact form: *https://www.arnova.org/* general/?type=CONTACT
Website: *https://www.arnova.org/default.aspx*

Candid (The Foundation Center)
32 Old Slip, 24th Floor
New York, NY 10005-3500
Phone: (212) 620-4230; Fax: (212) 807-3677
Contact form: *https://support.candid.org/case. html?type=all&mode=popup*
Website: *https://candid.org/*

Independent Sector
1602 L Street
Suite 900
Washington, D.C. 20036
Phone: (202) 467-6161; Fax: (202) 467-6101
Contact form: *https://independentsector.org/contact/*
Website: *https://independentsector.org/*

National Council of Nonprofits
1001 G Street, NW, Suite 700 East
Washington, DC 20001
Phone: (202) 962-0322; Fax: (202) 962-0321
Contact form: *https://www.councilofnonprofits. org/contact-us*
Website: *https://www.councilofnonprofits.org/*

BoardSource
750 9th Street, NW
Suite 650
Washington, D.C. 20001-4793
Phone: (202) 349-2544
Email:members@boardsource.org
Website: *https://boardsource.org/*

Association of Fundraising Executives
4300 Wilson Boulevard
Suite 300
Arlington, VA 22203
Phone: (703) 684-0410; Fax: (703) 684-1950
Email: afp@afpglobal.org
Website: *https://afpglobal.org/*

National Publications

Nonprofit Issues (monthly)
PO Box 482
Dresher, PA 19025-0482
Phone: (215) 542-7547; Fax: (215) 542-7548
Contact form: *https://www.nonprofitissues.com/web-form/contact-us*
Website: https://www.nonprofitissues.com/

Nonprofit Times (monthly)
Circulation Department
201 Littleton Road
Second Floor
Morris Plains, NJ 07050
Phone: (973) 401-0202; Fax: (973) 401-0404
Email: info@nptimes.com
Website: *https://www.thenonprofittimes.com/*

Chronicle of Philanthropy (monthly)
1255 23rd Street, NW
Washington, DC 20037
Phone: (202) 466-1200; Fax: (202) 446-2078
Email: subscriptions@philanthropy.com
Website: *https://www.philanthropy.com/*

Nonprofit and Voluntary Sector Quarterly
SAGE Publications
2455 Teller Road
Thousand Oaks, CA 91320
Phone: (800) 818-7243, Fax: (800) 583-2665
Email: journals@sagepub.com
Website: *https://journals.sagepub.com/home/nvs*

Contributions Magazine
15 Brook Street, #6
Medfield, MA 02052
phone: (508) 359-0019; fax: (508) 359-2703
Contact form: *https://www.emersonandchurch.com/ pages/contact-us*
Website: *https://www.emersonandchurch.com/pages/ contact-us*

Texas Organizations

Center for Nonprofit Studies
Austin Community College
5930 Middle Fiskville Rd, #414
Austin, TX 78752
Phone: (512) 223-7076
Email: lisa.bussett@austincc.edu
Website: https://www.nonprofitaustin.org/

Center for Philanthropy and Nonprofit Leadership
Rice University
6100 Main
Houston, TX 77005-1827
Phone: (713) 348-6009
Email: cpnl@rice.edu
Website: https://glasscock.rice.edu/departments/
center-philanthropy-nonprofit-leadership

CNM Connect (Center For Nonprofit Management)
6688 N. Central Expressway
Suite 1025
Dallas, TX 75206
Phone: (214) 826-3470
Email: expert@CNMConnect.org
Website: https://thecnm.org/

Executive Service Corps of Houston
7575 San Felipe St.
Suite 235
Houston, TX 77063
Phone: (713) 780-2208
Website: https://execservicecorpchouston.org/

Mission Capital
8303 N. MoPac Expwy
Suite A201
Austin TX 78759
Phone: (512) 477-5955; Fax: (512) 477-5911
Website: https://missioncapital.org/

Nonprofit Connection
United Way of Greater Houston
50 Waugh Drive
Houston, Texas 77007
Phone: (713) 685-2300
Website: https://www.unitedwayhouston.org/non-
profit-connection/

Nonprofit Development Center
c/o United Way of Smith County
911 S. Broadway
Tyler, Texas 75711
Phone: (903) 581-6376
Website: https://uwsmithcounty.org/

Nonprofit Management Alliance of Texas
OneStar Foundation
9011 Mountain Ridge Drive
Suite 100
Austin, Texas 78759
Phone: (512) 287-2000
Website: *http://onestarfoundation.org/initia-*
tives-volunteerism/nmat/

Nonprofit Management Center of the Permian Basin
3500 North A Street
Suite 2300
Midland, Texas 79705
Phone: (432) 570.7971
Email: info@nmc-pb.org
Website: *https://www.nmc-pb.org/*

Center for Nonprofit Management & Leadership at MSU Texas
3410 Taft Blvd. DCOBA Room 147
Wichita Falls, TX 76308
Phone: (940) 397-4962
Email: marla.malone@msutexas.edu
Website: *https://thecentermsu.org*

RGK Center for Philanthropy and Community Service
LBJ School of Public Affairs
University of Texas at Austin
2315 Red River Street
Austin, Texas 78712
Phone: (512) 232-7062
Website: *https://rgkcenter.org/*

Southeast Texas Nonprofit Development Center
700 North St.
Suite O
Beaumont, Texas 77701
Phone: (409) 832-6565
Email: ddrago@setxnonprofit.org
Website: *https://setxnonprofit.org/*

Appendix H
About the Author

Gary M. Grobman (B.S., Drexel University; M.P.A., Harvard University, Kennedy School of Government; PhD, Penn State University) is special projects director for White Hat Communications, a Harrisburg-based publishing and nonprofit consulting organization formed in 1993. The title of Dr. Grobman's doctoral dissertation is *An Analysis of Codes of Ethics of Nonprofit, Tax-Exempt Membership Associations: Does Principal Constituency Make a Difference?* He has taught nonprofit management classes as an adjunct faculty member at Bay Path University, Indiana University of Pennsylvania, Marylhurst University, and Gratz College.

He served as the executive director of the Pennsylvania Jewish Coalition from 1983-1996. Prior to that, he was a senior legislative assistant in Washington, DC, for two members of Congress, a news reporter, and a political humor columnist for *Roll Call.* He also served as a lobbyist for public transit agencies. In 1987, he founded the Non-Profit Advocacy Network (NPAN), which consisted of more than 50 statewide associations that represented Pennsylvania charities.

He has served on the board of directors as an officer of the Greater Harrisburg Concert Band, the Harrisburg Area Road Runners Club, and the Citizens Service Project—the statewide 501(c)(3) that was established to promote citizen service in Pennsylvania. He is the author of *The Holocaust—A Guide for Pennsylvania Teachers, The Nonprofit Handbook, Improving Quality and Performance in Your Non-Profit Organization, The Nonprofit Management Casebook, Ethics in Nonprofit Organizations, Just Don't Do It! A Fractured and Irreverent Look at the Ph.D. Culture,* and other books published by White Hat Communications and Wilder Publications (now Fieldstone).

Dr. Grobman may be contacted at: White Hat Communications, P.O. Box 5390, Harrisburg, PA 17110-0390. Telephone: (717) 238-3787; Fax: (717) 803-3008; Email: gary.grobman@gmail.com

Appendix I
Texas Nonprofit Handbook—2nd Edition
Reader Survey

Return Survey To:
White Hat Communications
PO Box 5390
Harrisburg, PA 17110-0390

My name and address (please print legibly):

1. I would like to suggest the following corrections:

2. I would like to suggest the following topics for inclusion in a future edition:

3. I have the following comments, suggestions, or criticisms:

For Further Reading

General

Chisholm, A. (2019). *Start a 501c3 Nonprofit that doesn't ruin your life: How to legally structure your nonprofit to avoid I.R.S. trouble, lawsuits, financial scandals & more!* (Self-published).

Hopkins, B. (2017). *Starting and managing a nonprofit organization: A legal guide.* (7th ed.). Wiley & Sons.

Hopkins, B. (2019). *The law of tax-exempt organizations* (12th ed.). Wiley & Sons.

Hyman, D. & Brenner, L. (2019). *Nonprofit Management 101: A Complete and Practical Guide for Leaders and Professionals* (2nd ed.). Wiley & Sons.

Levy, J. (2017). *Nonprofit: How to start your nonprofit the right way so it will survive and thrive; Practical step-by- step guide to forming a 501(C) nonprofit corporation.* CreateSpace

Mancuso, A. (2017). *How to form a nonprofit organization* (13th ed.). Nolo Press.

Pakroo, P. (2017). *Starting & building a nonprofit: A practical guide.* (7th ed.). Nolo Press.

Sand, M. (2005). *How to manage an effective nonprofit organization.* Career Press.

Chapter 1/Chapter 2/Chapter 3

American Bar Association (2014). *Guidebook for directors of nonprofit corporations.* Author.

Hopkins, B. (2019). *The law of nonprofit organizations* (12th ed.).Wiley & Sons.

Hutton, S. (2017). *Nonprofit kit for dummies.* (5th ed.). For Dummies (Wiley & Sons).

Levy, J. (2017). *Nonprofit: How to start your nonprofit the right way so it will survive and thrive; Practical step-by- step guide to forming a 501(C) nonprofit corporation.* CreateSpace

Chapter 4

Board Source. (2012). *Nonprofit board answer book* (3rd ed.). Author.

Carver, J. (2006). *Boards that make a difference. A new design for leadership in nonprofit and public organizations.* Jossey-Bass.

Hopkins, B. (2015). *The law of nonprofit organizations* (11th ed.). Wiley & Sons.

Hopkins, B. (2017). *Starting and managing a nonprofit organization: A legal guide.* (7th ed.).Wiley & Sons.

Hutton, S. (2017). *Nonprofit kit for dummies.* (5th ed.). Wiley.

Ingram, R. (2015). *Ten basic responsibilities of nonprofit boards* (3rd ed.). Board Source.

Leblanc, R. (2020). *The handbook of board governance: A comprehensive guide for public, private, and not-for-profit board members.* Wiley & Sons.

Pakroo, P. (2017). *Starting & building a nonprofit: A practical guide.* (7th ed.). Nolo Press.

Chapter 5

Angelica, E. (2013). *The Wilder nonprofit field guide to crafting effective mission and vision statements.* Fieldstone Alliance.

Arams, L. (2013). *How to create memorable, practical mission, value, vision and business philosophy statements for non-profits* (Kindle Edition). Amazon Digital Services.

Briggs, B. (2007). *Mission expert: Creating effective mission and vision statements.* Kinetic Wisdom.

Schreim, S. (2020). *Vision, mission, values, aspirations, Do they matter?: A business professionals' guide to drafting vision/mission statements and their purpose.* Business Model Hackers.

Talbot, T. (2003). *Make your mission statement work.* (2nd ed.). How to Books.

Taylor, R. (2014). *The mission statement: A framework for developing an effective organizational mission statement in 100 words or less.* (Kindle Edition). Amazon Digital Services.

Villareal, M. (2017). Mission, vision & values resource tool kit (Kindle Edition). Amazon Digital Services.

Chapter 6

Allison, M., & Kaye, J. (2015). *Strategic planning for nonprofit organizations: A practical guide for dynamic times.* John Wiley & Sons.

Bryson, J. & Alston, F. (2015). *Creating and implementing your strategic plan: A workbook for public and nonprofit organizations.* (3rd ed.). San Francisco, CA: Jossey-Bass.

McNamara, C. (2018). *Field guide to nonprofit strategic planning and facilitation* (4th ed.). Authenticity Consulting.

Mintzburg, H. (1994). *The rise and fall of strategic planning.* MacMillan.

Chapter 7

Ethics Resource Center. (2007). *Ethics Resource Center's national nonprofit ethics survey: An inside view of nonprofit sector ethics.* Author.

Grobman, G. (2018). *A practical guide to ethics in your nonprofit organization* White Hat Communications.

Grobman, G. (2018). *Ethics in nonprofit organizations: Theory and practice (3rd ed.).* White Hat Communications.

Guttman, D. (2006). *Ethics in social work: A context of caring.* Haworth.

Independent Sector. (2015). *Principles for good governance and ethical practice, 2015 Edition.* Author.

Johnson, C. (2017). *Meeting the ethical challenges of leadership* (6th ed.). Sage.

Pettey, J. (2008). *Ethical fundraising: A guide for nonprofit boards and fundraisers.* Wiley.

Reamer, F. (2006). *Social work values and ethics.* (3rd ed.). Columbia University Press.

Smith, D. H. (in press). *Misconduct and deviance in nonprofit organizations.* Chapter in *Global encyclopedia of public administration, public policy, and governance,* by Farazmand, A. (Ed.). Springer.

Svara, J. (2014). *The ethics primer for public administrators in government and nonprofit organizations* (2nd ed.). Jones & Bartlett Learning.

Chapter 8

Deja, S. (2020, July). *Real help with your own 501(c)(3) application. Sandra Deja.* http://www.501c3book.com/about.html

Fishman, J. & Schwarz, S. (2015). *Taxation of nonprofit organizations, cases and materials* (4th ed.). (University Casebook Series). Foundation Press.

Hopkins, B. (2017). *Starting and managing a nonprofit organization: A legal guide.* (7th ed.). Wiley & Sons.

Hopkins, B. (2019). *The law of tax-exempt organizations* (12th ed.). Wiley & Sons.

Hutton, S. (2017). *Nonprofit kit for dummies.* (5th ed.). For Dummies (Wiley & Sons).

Levy, J. (2017). *Nonprofit: How to start your nonprofit the right way so it will survive and thrive; Practical step-by- step guide to forming a 501(C) nonprofit corporation.* CreateSpace.

Mancuso, A. (2017). *How to form a nonprofit organization* (13th ed.). Nolo Press.

Pakroo, P. (2019). *Starting & building a nonprofit: A practical guide.* (8th ed.). Nolo Press.

Chapter 9

Goanos, L. (2019). D&O 101: *A holistic approach: Understanding directors & officers liability insurance.* Wells Media Group.

Herman, M., Head, G., Fogarty, T. & Jackson, P. (2004). *Managing risk in nonprofit organizations: A comprehensive guide.* Wiley.

Herman, M. (2003). *Ready in Defense: A liability, litigation and legal guide for nonprofits.* Nonprofit Risk Management Center.

Herman, M. (2009). *Ready...or not: A risk management guide for nonprofit executives.* Nonprofit Risk Management Center.

Jackson, P. (2006). *Nonprofit risk management & contingency planning: Done in a day strategies.* Wiley.

Marks, N. & Herman, M. (2017). *World-class risk management for nonprofits.* Nonprofit Risk Management Center.

Mathias, Jr., J., Kroeger, D., Neumeier, M. & Burgdoerfer, J. (2017). *Directors and officers liability: prevention, insurance and indemnification.* Law Journal Press.

O'Leary, M.; Blancett, J.; Davisson, M.; Guirgis, R., Scheiner, E.; & Smerdon, E. (2019). *Directors & officers liability insurance deskbook.* (4th ed.). American Bar Association.

Patterson, J. & Oliver, B. (2002). *The season of hope: A risk management guide for youth-serving nonprofits.* Nonprofit Risk Management Center.

Tenconi, D. & Medrano, J. (2017). *Non-profit guidance: For the non-profit board member.* CreateSpace.

Chapter 10

Coe, C. (2011). *Nonprofit financial management: A practical guide.* Wiley.

Dropkin, M., Halpin, J. & La Tiouche, B. (2021). *The budget-building book for nonprofits: A step-by-step guide for managers and board (4th ed.).* Jossey-Bass.

Ittelson, T. (2017). *Nonprofit accounting & financial statements: Overview for board, management, and staff (2nd ed.).* Mercury Group.

McKinney, J. (2015). *Effective financial management in public and nonprofit agencies (4th ed.).* Praeger Publishing.

McLaughlin, T. (2018). *Streetsmart financial basics for nonprofit Managers.* (4th ed.). Wiley.

Weikart, L., Chen, G., & Sermier, E. (2012). *Budgeting and financial management for nonprofit organizations: Using money to drive mission success.* CQ Press.

Zietlow, J., et at. (2018). *Financial management for nonprofit organizations: Policies and practices.* Wiley.

Chapter 11

Barbeito, C. (2006). *Human resource policies and procedures for nonprofit organizations.* Wiley.

Denhardt, R., Denhardt, J.,& Aristiguesta, M. (2021). *Managing human behavior in public and nonprofit organizations.* (5th ed.). Sage.

Dresang, D. (2017). *Personnel management in government agencies and nonprofit organizations (6th ed.).* Routledge.

Drucker, P. F. (2006). *Managing the nonprofit organization.* HarperBusiness.

Gilbert, J. (2020). *Human Resource management essentials you always wanted to know.* Vibrant.

Word, J., and Sowa, J. (2017). *The nonprofit human resource management handbook.* Routledge.

Chapter 12

Bagley, B. (1996, April). *Necessary v. nosey—Guidelines and strategies for hiring.* PA Society of Association Executives Society News, 20.

Brown, J. (2011). *The complete guide to recruitment: A step-by-step approach to selecting, assessing and hiring the right people.* Kogan Page.

Muller, M. (2013). *The manager's guide to hr: Hiring, firing, performance evaluations, documentation, benefits, and everything else you need to know (2nd ed.).* Amacom.

Chapter 13

Atlantic Publishing Group. (2017). *365 Ideas for recruiting, retaining, motivating and rewarding your volunteers: A complete guide for non-profit organizations (2nd ed.).* Author.

Conners, T. (2011). *The volunteer management handbook: Leadership strategies for success.* Wiley.

Ellis, S. (2005). *The volunteer recruitment (and membership development) book.* Energize.

Fletcher, K. B. (1987). *The 9 keys to successful volunteer programs.* Taft Group.

Friedman, J. (2010). *Boomer volunteer engagement.* AuthorHouse.

Lipp, J. (2010). *The complete idiot's guide to recruiting and managing volunteers.* Alpha.

Masaoka, J. (2011). *The nonprofit's guide to human resources: Managing your employees & volunteers.* Nolo.

McCurley, S. & Lynch, R. (2011). *Volunteer management.* (3rd ed.). Interpub Group.

Yeager, B. (2017). *Volunteer management for non-profit organizations: The art of people management.* CreateSpace.

Chapter 14 (For Further Reading)

Bach, M. (2020). *Birds of all feathers: Doing diversity and inclusion right.* Page 2.

Catlin, K. & McGraw, S. (2019). *Better allies: Everyday actions to create inclusive, engaging workplaces.* Karen Catlin Consulting.

Diez, M. (2020). *The 5 dualities of diversity and inclusion.* Networlding Publishing.

Thiedman, S. (2019). *The diversity and inclusion handbook.* Walk the Talk.

Unerman, S., Kathryn Jacob, et al. (2020). *Belonging: The key to transforming and maintaining diversity, inclusion and equality at work.* Bloomsbury Business

Chapter 14 (References)

Berghoef, K. (updated June 21, 2019). Implicit bias: What it means and how it affects behavior. https://www.thoughtco.com/understanding-implicit-bias-4165634

Biography. (2020). Treyvon Martin. https://www.biography.com/crime-figure/trayvon-martin

BoardSource. (2017). Leading with intent: 2017 national index of nonprofit board practices. Author.

Bridges, J. (2020). 5 diversity, equity, and inclusion trends we can expect in 2020. https://everfi.com/blog/workplace-training/5-diversity-equity-and-inclusion-trends/

Brooksbank, T. (2020, April 12). Health care workers fear losing their jobs during coronavirus pandemic. https://abcnews.go.com/Health/health-care-workers-fear-losing-jobs-coronavirus-pandemic/story?id=70087102

Building Movement Project. (2019). Race to lead revisited: Obstacles and opportunities in addressing the nonprofit racial leadership gap. https://racetolead.org/race-to-lead-revisited/

Burns, C. (2012, March). The costly business of discrimination. Center for American Progress. https://www.scribd.com/document/81214767/The-Costly-Business-of-Discrimination

Carey, K. (2020, May 26). Risky strategy by many private colleges leaves them exposed. *New York Times*. https://www.nytimes.com/2020/05/26/upshot/virus-colleges-risky-strategy.html

Center for Effective Philanthropy. (2018, July). Nonprofit diversity efforts current practices and the role of foundations. https://cep.org/portfolio/nonprofit-diversity-efforts-current-practices-and-the-role-of-foundations/

Centers for Disease Control and Prevention. (2020, June 19). Coronavirus disease 2019 case surveillance — United States, January 22–May 30, 2020. https://www.cdc.gov/mmwr/volumes/69/wr/mm6924e2.htm?s_cid=mm6924e2_w

Colby, S. L. & Ortman, J. M. (2015, March). Projections of the size and composition of the U.S. population: 2014 to 2060, current population reports, P25-1143, U.S. Census Bureau. https://www.census.gov/content/dam/Census/library/publications/2015/demo/p25-1143.pdf

Ellison, A. (2020, June 3). 29 hospital bankruptcies in 2020. https://www.beckershospitalreview.com/finance/29-hospital-bankruptcies-in-2020.html

Fernandez, I. & Brown, A. (2015, May 12). The state of diversity in the nonprofit sector. https://communitywealth.com/the-state-of-diversity-in-the-nonprofit-sector/

Fernandes, D. (Updated 2020, May 8). Amid coronavirus pandemic, a growing list of colleges in financial peril. https://www.bostonglobe.com/2020/05/08/metro/amid-pandemic-growing-list-colleges-financial-peril/

Fuerte, S. (2020, June 11). American Cancer Society eliminates 1,000 jobs amid COVID-19 pandemic. https://abcnews.go.com/US/american-ancer-society-eliminates-1000-jobs-amid-covid/story?id=71211646

Future State. (2017, September 9). 7 everyday benefits of increasing diversity in the workplace. https://bthechange.com/7-everyday-benefits-of-increasing-organizational-diversity-400e9066e307

Gaille, L. (2018, December 13). 22 advantages and disadvantages of diversity in the workplace. https://vittana.org/22-advantages-and-disadvantages-of-diversity-in-the-workplace

Galewitz, P. (2015, April 14). Why urban hospitals are leaving cities for fancy suburbs. Kaiser Health News. https://www.governing.com/topics/health-human-services/why-urban-hospitals-are-leaving-cities-for-fancy-suburbs.html

Gamboa, J. (2008, April 2). Foundation leadership on diversity is missing. *Houston Chronicle.* https://www.chron.com/opinion/article/Foundation-leadership-on-diversity-is-missing-3221616.php

Gwartney, J., and C.Haworth. (1974). Employer costs and discrimination: The case of baseball. *Journal of Political Economy* 82(4): 873–881.

Harris, R.and Stiffman, E. (2020, June 20). How to tackle race at your organization. *The Chronicle of Philanthropy.* https://tinyurl.com/y522smn6

Haseltine, W. (2020). A new CDC report shows COVID-19 disproportionately affects those with underlying disease and disadvantaged minorities. https://tinyurl.com/y3tr88fu

Hewlett, S., Marshall, M., & Sherbin, L. (2013, December). How diversity can drive innovation. *Harvard Business Review,* https://hbr.org/2013/12/how-diversity-can-drive-innovation

The Indiana University Lilly Family School of Philanthropy Project Team. (2018, February). The impact of diversity: Understanding how nonprofit board diversity affects philanthropy, leadership, and board engagement. https://scholarworks.iupui.edu/bitstream/handle/1805/15239/board-diversity180220.pdf?sequence=1&isAllowed=y

Independent Sector. (2016). Diversity, equity, & inclusion. https://dev-sandbox-is-web.pantheonsite.io/focus-areas/diversity/

Koenig, R. (2016, August 11). Why and how to build a diverse nonprofit board. *The Chronicle of Philanthropy*. https://www.philanthropy.com/article/WhyHow-to-Build-a-Diverse/237433

Lexico.(2020). Tokenism. https://www.lexico.com/en/definition/tokenism

López, C. (2019, Dec 11). Merriam-Webster named 'they' word of the year because of the rise in people openly identifying as non-binary. https://www.insider.com/merriam-webster-they-word-of-year-nonbinary-gender-lgbtq-transgender-2019-12

Merriam-Webster. (2020). Affirmative action. https://www.merriam-webster.com/dictionary/affirmative%20action

Miller, J. J. (2020). Beyond inclusion initiatives, toward expansive frameworks. https://www.socialworker.com/feature-articles/practice/beyond-inclusion-initiatives-toward-expansive-frameworks/

Kapila, M., Hines, E., & Searby, M. (2016, October 6). Why diversity, equity, and inclusion matter. https://independentsector.org/resource/why-diversity-equity-and-inclusion-matter/

Patz, E. (2018, March 8). Where are all the women in nonprofit leadership? https://topnonprofits.com/women-nonprofit-leadership/

PolicyLink.org. (n.d.) Home page. https://www.policylink.org/

Price, R. (2019, July 13). United Way to make more diversity on nonprofit boards part of funding process. https://www.dispatch.com/news/20190713/united-way-to-make-more-diversity-on-nonprofit-boards-part-of-funding-process

Reich, R. (2018). Just giving: Why philanthropy is failing democracy and how it can do better. Princeton University Press.

Sandoval, T. (2017, July 25. How to overcome implicit bias in the hiring process. *The Chronicle of Philanthropy.* https://www.philanthropy.com/article/how-to-overcome-implicit-bias-in-the-hiring-process/

Wing, S. (2010, November 17). Microaggressions: More than just race. https://www.psychologytoday.com/us/blog/microaggressions-in-everyday-life/201011/microaggressions-more-just-race

Thys, F. (2020, May 8). One third of private 4-year colleges are at high risk financially, model predicts. https://www.wbur.org/edify/2020/05/08/higher-education-financial-crisis

Tomkin, A. R. (2020, May 26). How white people conquered the nonprofit industry. https://nonprofitquarterly.org/how-white-people-conquered-the-nonprofit-industry/

U.S. Supreme Court. (2020, June 15). Bostock v. Clayton County. https://www.supremecourt.gov/opinions/19pdf/17-1618_hfci.pdf

Wallace, N. (2017, March 7). Tackling diversity in a new way. *The Chronicle of Philanthropy.* https://www.philanthropy.com/article/tackling-diversity-in-a-new-way/

Wessler, S. (2015, April 6). Your college professor could be on public assistance. NBC News. https://www.nbcnews.com/feature/in-plain-sight/poverty-u-many-adjunct-professors-food-stamps-n336596

Williams, J. (2019, July 10). Code red: The grim state of urban hospitals. https://www.usnews.com/news/healthiest-communities/articles/2019-07-10/poor-minorities-bear-the-brunt-as-urban-hospitals-close

Wyllie, J. (2018, December 5). Here's why nonprofits still have problems with diversity and how to fix it. *The Chronicle of Philanthropy.* https://www.philanthropy.com/article/heres-why-nonprofits-still-have-problems-with-diversity-and-how-to-fix-it/

Yancey-Bragg, N. (2020, June 15). What is systemic racism? Here's what it means and how you can help dismantle it. USA Today. https://www.usatoday.com/story/news/nation/2020/06/15/systemic-racism-what-does-mean/5343549002/

Chapter 15

Blazek, J. (2020). *Tax planning and compliance for tax-exempt organizations: Rules, checklists, procedures (Wiley Nonprofit Authority)* (6th ed.) Wiley.

Chapter 16

Bray, I. (2019). *Effective fundraising for nonprofits: Real-world strategies that work (6th ed.).* Nolo.

Cannon, C. (2011). *An executive's guide to fundraising operations: Principles, tools & trends.* Wiley.

Davis, M. (2013). *The fundraising rules.* (Self-Published): CreateSpace.

Eisenstein, A. (2017). *50 asks in 50 weeks: A guide to better fundraising for your small development shop* (2nd ed.). CharityChannel Press.

Grobman, G. & Grant, G. (2006). *Fundraising online: Using the internet to raise serious money for your nonprofit organization.* White Hat Communications.

McCrea, J., Walker, J., & Weber, K. (2013). *The generosity network: New transformational tools for successful fund-raising.* Deepak Chopra.

Mutz, J.& Murray, K. (2010). *Fundraising for dummies.* Wiley and Sons.

Seltzer, M. (2002). *Securing your organization's future: A complete guide to fundraising strategies.* The Foundation Center.

Stallings, B., & McMillion, D. (1999). *How to produce fabulous fundraising events: Reap remarkable returns with minimal effort.* Building Better Skills.

Warwick, M. (2013). *How to write successful fundraising appeals.* Jossey-Bass.

Weinstein, S. (2017). *The complete guide to fundraising management (4th ed.).* (The AFP/Wiley Fund Development Series). Wiley.

Worth, M. (2015). *Fundraising: Principles and practice.* Sage.

Chapter 17

Brown, L. G., & Brown, M. (2001). *Demystifying grant seeking: What you really need to do to get grants.* Jossey-Bass.

Browning, B. A. (2008). *Perfect phrases for writing grant proposals.* McGraw Hill.

Browning, B. A. (2016). *Grant writing for dummies.* (6th ed.). Wiley & Sons.

Carlson, M. & O'Neal-McElrath, T. (2013). *Winning grants step by step* (4th ed.). Jossey-Bass.

Geever, J. C. (2012). *The foundation center's guide to proposal writing.* (6th ed.). The Foundation Center.

Harris, D. (2008). *The complete guide to writing effective & award-winning grants: Step-by-step instructions with companion CD.* Atlantic Publishing Company.

Karsh, E. & Fox, A. S. (2019). *The only grant-writing book you'll ever need: Top grant writers and grant givers share their secrets.* (5th ed.). Basic Books.

Omnigraphics. (2017). *Government assistance almanac 2017: The guide to federal domestic financial and other programs.* (24th ed.). Author.

O'Neal-McElrath, T. et al. (2019). *Winning grants step by step: The complete workbook for planning, developing, and writing successful proposals.* Jossey-Bass.

Schladweiler, K. (2004). *Foundation fundamentals: A guide for grantseekers.* (7th ed). Foundation Center.

Smith, N. (2012). *The complete book of grantwriting.*(2nd ed.). Sourcebooks.

Chapter 18

Durham, S. (2020). *The nonprofit communications engine: A leader's guide to managing mission-driven marketing and communications.* Big Duck Studio.

Grau, S. (2014). *Marketing for Nonprofit Organizations.* Lyceum Books.

Manktelow, J. & Carlson, A. (n.d.). *The marketing mix and 4 Ps: Understanding how to position your market offering.* https://www.mindtools.com/pages/article/newSTR_94.htm

Miltenburg, A. (2018). *Brand the change: The branding guide for social entrepreneurs, disruptors, not-for-profits and corporate troublemakers.* BIS Publishers.

Chapter 19

Arons, D. & Berry, J. (2005). *A voice for nonprofits.* Brookings Institution Press.

Avner, M., Wise, J., Narabrook, J. & Fox, J. (2013). *Lobbying and advocacy handbook for nonprofit organizations: Shaping public policy at the state and local level.* (2nd ed.). Fieldstone Alliance.

Clerk of the House. (2017). *Lobbying Disclosure Act guidance. https://lobbying-disclosure.house.gov/amended_lda_guide.html*

Clerk of the House. (2019, March 19). Guidance Memo. *https://lobbyingdisclosure.house.gov/Notice_re_JACK_Act.pdf*

deKieffer, D. (2007). *The citizen's guide to lobbying Congress.* Chicago Review Press.

Gelek, D. (2008). *Lobbying and advocacy: Winning strategies, resources, recommendations, ethics and ongoing compliance for lobbyists and Washington advocates.* TheCapitol.Net, Inc.

Guyer, R. L., & Guyer, L. K. (2013). *Guide to state legislative lobbying.* (3rd ed.). Engineering the Law.

Jansson, B. (2017). *Becoming an effective policy advocate (8th ed.).* Brooks Cole.

Libby, P. (2021). *The lobbying strategy handbook* (2nd ed.). Sage.

Maskell, J. (2009). *Lobbyist registration and compliance handbook: The Honest Leadership and Open Government Act of 2007 (HLOGA) and the Lobbying Disclosure Act Guide.* TheCapitol.Net, Inc.

Pekkanen, R., Smith, S. & Tsujinaka, Y. (2014). *Nonprofits and advocacy: Engaging community and government in an era of retrenchment.* Johns Hopkins Univ. Press.

Smucker, B. (1999). *The nonprofit lobbying guide: Advocating your cause—and getting results.* (2nd ed.). Jossey-Bass.

Arons, D. & Berry, J. (2005). *A voice for nonprofits.* Brookings Institution Press.

Chapter 20

Guo, C. & Saxton, G. (2020). *The quest for attention: Nonprofit advocacy in a social media age,* Stanford Business Books

Walzer, M. & Wiener, J. (2019). *Political action: A practical guide to movement politics.* NYRB Classics.

Chapter 21

Bonk, T., Tynes, E. Griggs, H. & Sparks, P. (2008). *Strategic communications for nonprofits: A step-by-step guide to working with the media* (2nd ed.). Jossey-Bass.

Durham, S. (2010). *Brandraising: How nonprofits raise visibility and money through smart communications.* Jossey-Bass.

Dunham, S. (2020). *The nonprofit communications engine: A leader's guide to managing mission-driven marketing and communications.* Big Duck Studio.

Patterson, S. & Radtke, J. (2009). *Strategic communications for nonprofit organizations: Seven steps to creating a successful plan.* Wiley.

Salzman, J. (2003). *Making the news: A guide for nonprofits and activists.* (Revised & Updated Edition). Westview Press.

Taylor, C. (2009). *Publishing the nonprofit annual report: Tips, traps, and tricks of the trade.* Jossey-Bass

Williams, E. (2012). *The essential non-profit public relations guide: Tips on great public relations for non-profits.* CreateSpace.

Chapter 22

Bennett, R., Kerrigan, F., & O'Reilly, D. (2017). *New horizons in arts, heritage, nonprofit and social marketing (Key issues in marketing management).* Routledge.

Campbell, J. (2017). *Storytelling in the digital age: A guide for nonprofits.* CharityChannel Press.

Campbell, J. (2020). *How to build and mobilize a social media community for your nonprofit in 90 days*. Bold and Bright Media.

Hart, T., Greenfield, J., MacLaughlin, S. & Geier, Jr., P. (2010). *Internet management for nonprofits: Strategies, tools and trade secrets*. Wiley.

Kanter, B. & Fine, A. (2010). *The networked nonprofit: Connecting with social media to drive change*. Jossey-Bass.

Saunders, M. (2020). *The digital charity: Becoming a digital leader in the non-profit sector*. Michael Terrence Publishing.

Windpassinger, J. (2018). *Digitize or die: Transform your organization. Embrace the digital evolution. Rise above the competition*. IoT Hub.

Chapter 23

Grobman, G. and Grant, G. (2007). *Fundraising on the internet*. White Hat Communications.

Hart, T., Greenfield, J. & Haji, S. (2008). *People to people fundraising: Social networking and web 2.0 for charities*. Wiley.

Hart, T., Greenfield, J., MacLaughlin, S. & Geier, Jr., P. (2010). *Internet management for nonprofits: Strategies, tools and trade secrets*. Wiley.

Marwick, T. & Allen, N. (Eds.). (2009). *Fundraising on the internet: The ePhilanthropyFoundation.org's guide to success online* (2nd ed.). Jossey-Bass.

Warner, B. (2020). From the Ground Up: Digital Fundraising For Nonprofits Tangram Editions.

Chapter 24

Brown, C. R. (1984). *The art of coalition building— A guide for community leaders*. American Jewish Committee.

Kahn, S. (1991). *Organizing: A guide for grassroots leaders*. NASW Press.

Leavitt, M. & McKeown, R. (2013). *Finding allies, building alliances: 8 elements that bring—and keep—people together.* Jossey-Bass.

Roberts, J. (2005). *Alliances, coalitions and partnerships: Building collaborative organizations.* British New Society Publishers.

Smutny, M. (2019). *Thrive: The facilitator's guide to radically inclusive meetings.* Civic Reinventions.

Van Dyke, N. & McCammon, H. (2010). *Strategic alliances: Coalition building and social movements.* University of Minnesota Press.

Wolff, T. (1997). *From the ground up! A workbook on coalition building & community development.* AHEC/Community Partners.

Chapter 25

Dabel, G. (1998). *Saving money in nonprofit organizations: More than 100 money-saving ideas, tips, and strategies for reducing expenses without cutting your budget.* Jossey-Bass.

Mancuso, A. (2017). *How to form a nonprofit organization* (13th ed.). Nolo Press.

McIlroy, J. (2018). *The New Executive Assistant: Exceptional executive office management.* Executive Assistant Network.

Chapter 26

Gallaway, J. (1982). *The unrelated business income tax.* Wiley.

Government Accountability Office. (2019). *Tax-Exempt Organizations and the Unrelated Business Income Tax Kindle Edition.* Author.

Grobman, G. (1994). *The issue of competition between non-profit and for-profit Corporations.* Pennsylvania Jewish Coalition.

Wellford, H. & Gallagher, J. (1985). *The myth of unfair competition by nonprofit organizations.* Family Service Association of America.

Chapter 27

Bookman, M. (1992). *Protecting your organization's tax-exempt status.* Jossey Bass.

Grobman, G. (1994). *The issue of tax-exempt status for Pennsylvania non-profit charities.* Pennsylvania Jewish Coalition.

National Council of Nonprofit Associations. (Summer 1994). *State tax trends.* Volume 2, No. 4.

Chapter 28

Dickmeyer, L. (2009). *No risk no reward: Mergers of membership associations and nonprofits.* Expert Publishing, Inc.

Guth, D. (2013). *Strategic unions: A marriage guide to healthy not-for-profit mergers* (Kindle Edition). National Council for Behavior Health.

Harrington, R. & La Piana, D. (2013). *Nonprofit mergers workbook Part I: The leaders guide to considering, negotiating, and executing a merger (2nd ed.).* Fieldstone Alliance Books.

McCormick, D. & McCormick, K. (2015). *Nonprofit mergers: The power of successful partnerships.* Amazon Digital Services.

McLaughlin, T. (2010). *Nonprofit mergers and alliances.* Wiley.

Sanders, M. (2017). *Joint ventures involving tax-exempt organizations: 2016 Cumulative supplement.* Wiley.

Chapter 29

Creech, B. (1994). *The five pillars of TQM: How to make total quality management work for you.* Penguin Books.

Crosby, P. B. (1979). *Quality is free.* McGraw Hill.

Garvin, D. A. (1988). *Management quality: The strategic and competitive edge.* Free Press.

Goetsch, D. & Davis, S. (2015). *Quality management for organizational excellence: Introduction to total quality.* (8th ed.). Pearson.

Grobman, G. (1999). *Improving quality and performance in your non-profit organization: Change management strategies for the 21st century.* White Hat Communications.

Just Visualize It. (2018). *Quality management: Notes, ideas, actions, checklists.* Author.

Kemp, S. (2013). *Quality Management demystified.* McGraw-Hill.

Martin, L. (1993). *TQM in human service organizations.* Jossey-Bass.

Webber, L. & Wallace, M. (2007). *Quality control for dummies.* For Dummies.

Chapter 30

Brothers, J. & Sherman, A. (2011). *Building nonprofit capacity: A guide to managing change through organizational lifecycles.* Jossey-Bass.

Bunker, B. and Alban, B. (1997). *Large group interventions: Engaging the whole system for rapid change.* Jossey-Bass.

Bunker, B. & Alban, B. (1992). What makes large group interventions effective? *Journal of Applied Behavioral Science* 28(4).

Cameron, E. & Green, M. (2015). *Making sense of change management: A complete guide to the models, tools and techniques of organizational change.* (4th ed.). Kogan Page.

Carter, R. (1983). *The accountable agency.* Sage Publications.

Creech, B. (1994). *The five pillars of TQM: How to make total quality management work for you.* Penguin Books.

Deming, W. E. (1975). On some statistical aids toward economic production. *Interfaces,* v5, n4. Aug. 1975. The Operations Research Society of America and the Institute of Management Sciences.

Friedman, M. (1997). *A guide to developing and using performance measures in results-based budgeting.* The Finance Project.

Goetsch, D. & Davis, S. (2015). *Quality management for organizational excellence: Introduction to total quality.* (8th ed.). Pearson.

Hammer, M. (1990). Reengineering work: Don't automate: obliterate. *Harvard Business Review,* July-Aug. 1990, pp. 104-112.

Hammer, M. & Champy, J. (1993). *Reengineering the corporation: A manifesto for business.* HarperBusiness. 1993.

Hammer, M. & Stanton, S. (1994). *The reengineering revolution: A handbook.* HarperBusiness.

Nelson, K. & Aaron, S. (2013). *The change management pocket guide (2nd ed.).* Change Guides, LLC.

Osborne, S. & Brown, K. (2005). Managing innovation and change in public service organizations. Routledge. See: *http://library.smaratungga.web.id/repository/[Kerry_Brown]_Managing_Change_and_Innovation_in_Pu(BookFi.org).pdf*

Revere, L. (2003). Integrating Six Sigma with total quality management: A case example for measuring medication errors. *Journal of Healthcare Management.* November/December 2003 48(6), pp. 377-391.

Richmond, F., & Hunnemann, E. (1996). What every board member needs to know about outcomes. Management and Technical Assistance Publication Series No. 2, Positive Outcomes.

Rouda, R., & Kusy, Jr., M. (1995). Organization development—The management of change. *Tappi Journal* 78(8), 253.

Watson, G. H. (1992). *The benchmarking workbook: Adapting best practices for performance improvement.* Productivity Press.

Chapter 31

Festen, M. & Philbin, M. (2006). *Level best: How small and grassroots nonprofits can tackle evaluation and talk results.* Jossey Bass.

Giancola, S. (2020). *Program evaluation: Embedding evaluation into program design and development.* Sage.

Gray, Sandra T. (1997). *Evaluation with power: A new approach to organizational effectiveness, empowerment, and excellence.* Jossey-Bass.

McNamara, C. (2017). *Field guide to nonprofit program design, marketing and evaluation (5th ed,).* Authenticity Consulting, LLC.

Newcomer, K.& Hatry, H. (2015). *Handbook of practical program evaluation (6th ed.).* Jossey-Bass.

Ridge, J. (2020). *Program evaluation: How to stop putting lipstick on the pig.* (Independently published).

Index

The Texas Nonprofit Handbook, 2nd Edition

by Gary M. Grobman

The Texas Nonprofit Handbook, 2nd Edition is the most up-to-date and useful publication for those starting a nonprofit or for those already operating one. This 480-page, 31-chapter Handbook is based on the *Pennsylvania Nonprofit Handbook,* originally published in 1992 with the help of more than two-dozen nonprofit executives and attorneys, and now in a 12th edition. Each easy-to-read chapter includes a synopsis, useful tips, and resources to obtain more information. This essential reference tool includes:

- Information about current laws, court decisions, and regulations that apply to nonprofits in Texas
- Practical advice on running a nonprofit, including chapters on grant-writing, communications, fundraising, quality management, insurance, lobbying, personnel, fiscal management, nonprofit ethics, and 22 other chapters
- Information on applying for federal and state tax-exempt status
- How to write effective grant applications
- How to hire and fire
- Internet resources for nonprofits
- How to develop a strategic plan
- How to plan for a program evaluation

We know you will find ***The Texas Nonprofit Handbook*** to be an essential resource for every library's reference collection.

ISBN13: 978-1-929109-94-4
8½ x 11 softcover
480 pages including index
$39.95 U.S.

Table of Contents

Nonprofit management titles published by White Hat Communications

The Nonprofit Handbook
The Pennsylvania Nonprofit Handbook
The Texas Nonprofit Handbook
The Florida Nonprofit Handbook
The Nonprofit Management Casebook
Ethics in Nonprofit Organizations
A Practical Guide to Ethics in Your Nonprofit Organization
Improving Quality and Performance in Your Non-Profit Organization

Social work titles published by White Hat Communications

Days in the Lives of Social Workers, 5th Ed.
More Days in the Lives of Social Workers
Days in the Lives of Gerontological Social Workers
The Field Placement Survival Guide
Is it Ethical?
Beginnings, Middles, and Ends
Riding the Mutual Aid Bus and Other Adventures in Group Work

Visit Our Websites/Social Networking Sites:

http://www.whitehatcommunications.com
http://www.socialworker.com
http://www.socialworkjobbank.com
http://www.facebook.com/newsocialworker
http://www.twitter.com/newsocialworker

Online Store
http://shop.whitehatcommunications.com